Yamaha YBR125ED, YBR125 Custom, XT125R and XT125X
Service and Repair Manual

by Matthew Coombs

With information on 2010 models onwards by Phil Mather

(4797 - 2AS3 - 240)

Models covered

YBR125ED. 2005 to 2016
YBR125 Custom. 2008 to 2016
XT125R. 2005 to 2009
XT125X. 2005 to 2009

Printed in India

J H Haynes & Co. Ltd.
Sparkford, Yeovil, Somerset BA22 7JJ, England

Haynes North America, Inc
859 Lawrence Drive, Newbury Park, California 91320, USA

Disclaimer

There are risks associated with automotive repairs. The ability to make repairs depends on the individual's skill, experience and proper tools. Individuals should act with due care and acknowledge and assume the risk of performing automotive repairs.

The purpose of this manual is to provide comprehensive, useful and accessible automotive repair information, to help you get the best value from your vehicle. However, this manual is not a substitute for a professional certified technician or mechanic.

This repair manual is produced by a third party and is not associated with an individual vehicle manufacturer. If there is any doubt or discrepancy between this manual and the owner's manual or the factory service manual, please refer to the factory service manual or seek assistance from a professional certified technician or mechanic.

Even though we have prepared this manual with extreme care and every attempt is made to ensure that the information in this manual is correct, neither the publisher nor the author can accept responsibility for loss, damage or injury caused by any errors in, or omissions from, the information given.

Contents

LIVING WITH YOUR YAMAHA YBR

Introduction

Pre-ride checks

MAINTENANCE

Routine maintenance and servicing

Contents

The XT125R

Yamaha haven't had a 125 road bike in their range since the long-running SR125 was discontinued in 2003. In 2005 they launched two new models which shared the same engine, yet were built at two totally different sites. The YBR125ED road bike was built in Japan, whereas the enduro-styled XT125 was built by Malaguti in Italy. Unlike other manufacturers who'd produced high tech 125cc bikes with fuel-injection and water-cooling, Yamaha's 123.7 cc sohc four-stroke was air-cooled and had fuel supplied through a Mikuni carburettor, making it economic, simple and reliable. Power output for UK models was 12.5 hp, well below the 14.6 hp limit.

Similarity between the YBR and XT models was solely mechanical, both have very different cycle parts. Whereas the YBR had functional simplicity with its rear disc brake and understated styling, the XT's styling was in keeping with larger capacity enduro/adventure models in the range. Of the two XT models on offer from Yamaha, the enduro styled XT125R's styling was pretty much borrowed from the larger engined XT660R. The XT125X on the other hand had supermotard styling, with 17 inch wheels, smooth tyres and sharper steering geometry.

A later introduction to the range was the YBR125 Custom, introduced in 2008. The machine's 'big-bike' looks were obtained through bodywork and styling changes to the existing YBR. It had a teardrop fuel tank, mock air intakes, 9-spoke wheels with a 16 inch rear, and lots of chrome. Mechanically the same as the other models, but with fuel injection which had already appeared on the standard YBR the previous year.

Acknowledgements

Our thanks are due to Taylors Motorcycles of Crewkerne, Fowlers Motorcycles of Bristol, Morse's Motorcycles of Weston-super-Mare and Bransons Motorcycles of Yeovil who supplied the machines featured in the illustrations throughout this manual.

We would also like to thank NGK Spark Plugs (UK) Ltd for supplying the colour spark plug condition photographs, the Avon Rubber Company for supplying information on tyre fitting, Draper Tools Ltd for some of the workshop tools shown and Yamaha Motor (UK) Ltd for supplying model photographs.

About this Manual

The aim of this manual is to help you get the best value from your motorcycle. It can do so in several ways. It can help you decide what work must be done, even if you choose to have it done by a dealer; it provides information and procedures for routine maintenance and servicing; and it offers diagnostic and repair procedures to follow when trouble occurs.

We hope you use the manual to tackle the work yourself. For many simpler jobs, doing it yourself may be quicker than arranging an appointment to get the motorcycle into a dealer and making the trips to leave it and pick it up. More importantly, a lot of money can be saved by avoiding the expense the shop must pass on to you to cover its labour and overhead costs. An added benefit is the sense of satisfaction and accomplishment that you feel after doing the job yourself.

References to the left or right side of the motorcycle assume you are sitting on the seat, facing forward.

We take great pride in the accuracy of information given in this manual, but motorcycle manufacturers make alterations and design changes during the production run of a particular motorcycle of which they do not inform us. No liability can be accepted by the authors or publishers for loss, damage or injury caused by any errors in, or omissions from, the information given.

Illegal Copying

The YBR125 Custom

YBR125ED and Custom

The YBR125ED was launched in 2005. It has a single cylinder air-cooled engine. Drive to the single overhead camshaft which actuates the two valves via a pair of rocker arms is by chain from the left-hand end of the crankshaft. A balancer shaft driven directly off the crankshaft keeps things smooth. The clutch is a conventional wet multi-plate unit and the gearbox is 5-speed constant mesh. Drive to the rear wheel is by chain and sprockets. The engine has both a kick-starter and electric starter motor.

On 2005 and 2006 models a single Mikuni slide carburettor supplies fuel and air to the engine. 2007-on models are fuel injected via a single Mikuni throttle body. An electronic ignition system ignites the mixture via a single spark plug. A catalyst is incorporated in the exhaust system.

The steel frame uses the engine as a stressed member. Front suspension is by oil-damped 30 mm forks. Rear suspension is by twin shock absorbers via a steel tube swingarm that pivots through the frame.

Wheels are cast alloy.

The front brake system is hydraulic and has a single piston sliding caliper acting on a conventional disc. The rear brake is a mechanically actuated drum.

In 2010 the YBR125ED underwent a number of changes. The kickstart is no longer fitted and a closing cable has been added to the throttle body. The speedometer, tachometer and warning lights are enclosed in a single instrument cluster, a newly designed tail light unit is fitted and the conventional headlight bulb has been replaced by a halogen bulb.

Cosmetic changes have made to the exhaust system with the addition of an end cap and restyled heat shield, and side covers have been added to the fuel tank. The seat, seat cowling and luggage rack are redesigned and the luggage strap brackets are no longer fitted.

Since these modifications, the YBR125ED remained unchanged until 2014 when a new headlight unit was introduced together with a small front fairing and windshield. The assembly was mounted on a modified version of the earlier headlight bracket.

In 2008 a Custom version was launched. It retains the engine frame and running gear of the standard bike, but has different seat, handlebars, fuel tank, silencer, side panels, mudguards, tail light and rack.

XT125R

The XT125R Enduro was launched in 2005. It has a single cylinder air-cooled engine. Drive to the single overhead camshaft which actuates the two valves via a pair of rocker arms is by chain from the left-hand end of the crankshaft. A balancer shaft driven directly off the crankshaft keeps things smooth. The clutch is a conventional wet multi-plate unit and the gearbox is 5-speed constant mesh. Drive to the rear wheel is by chain and sprockets. The engine has both a kick-starter and electric starter motor.

A single Mikuni slide carburettor supplies fuel and air to the engine. An electronic ignition system ignites the mixture via a single spark plug. A catalyst is incorporated in the exhaust system.

The steel frame uses the engine as a stressed member. Front suspension is by oil-damped 36 mm telescopic forks. Rear suspension is by a single shock absorber via a box-section steel swingarm that pivots through the frame.

Wheels are steel rimmed with wire spokes.

The front and rear brake systems are hydraulic and each have an opposed-piston caliper acting on a conventional disc.

XT125X

The XT125X Supermoto was launched in 2005. It has a single cylinder air-cooled engine. Drive to the single overhead camshaft which actuates the two valves via a pair of rocker arms is by chain from the left-hand end of the crankshaft. A balancer shaft driven directly off the crankshaft keeps things smooth. The clutch is a conventional wet multi-plate unit and the gearbox is 5-speed constant mesh. Drive to the rear wheel is by chain and sprockets. The engine has both a kick-starter and electric starter motor.

A single Mikuni slide carburettor supplies fuel and air to the engine. An electronic ignition system ignites the mixture via a single spark plug. A catalyst is incorporated in the exhaust system.

The steel frame uses the engine as a stressed member. Front suspension is by oil-damped 36 mm telescopic forks. Rear suspension is by a single shock absorber via a box-section steel swingarm that pivots through the frame.

Wheels are steel rimmed with wire spokes.

The front brake system is hydraulic and has a twin-piston sliding caliper acting on a conventional disc. The rear brake system is hydraulic and has an opposed-piston caliper acting on a conventional disc.

Bike spec

Engine

Type	Four-stroke, single cylinder
Capacity	123.7 cc
Bore	54.0 mm
Stroke	54.0 mm
Compression ratio	10.0 to 1
Cooling system	Air-cooled
Camshaft	SOHC, chain-driven
Fuel system	
2005 and 2006 YBR models	Mikuni slide carburettor
2007-on YBR models	Mikuni throttle body with single injector
XT models	Mikuni slide carburettor
Ignition system	CDI with electronic advance
Clutch	Wet multi-plate
Transmission	Five-speed constant mesh
Final drive	Chain and sprockets

Chassis – YBR125ED

Frame type	Steel
Rake and Trail	
2005 to 2009	26.33°, 90 mm
2010-on	26.33°, 92 mm
Fuel tank	
Capacity (including reserve)	
2005 and 2006 models	12.0 litres
2007-on models	13.0 litres
Reserve volume	
2005 to 2009 models	approx. 3.0 litres
2010-on models	3.4 litres
Front suspension	
Type	30 mm oil-damped telescopic forks
Wheel travel	
2005 to 2009 models	105 mm
2010-on models	120 mm
Rear suspension	
Type	Twin shock absorber, tubular steel swingarm
Adjustment	Spring pre-load
Wheel travel	105 mm
Wheels	18 inch alloys
Tyres	
Front	2.75-18 42P – 2005 and 2006 tubed, 2007-on tubeless
Rear	90/90-18 57P – 2005 and 2006 tubed, 2007-on tubeless
Front brake	Single 245 mm disc with single piston sliding caliper
Rear brake	Drum

Chassis – YBR125 Custom

Frame type	Steel
Rake and Trail	27.42°, 102 mm
Fuel tank	
Capacity (including reserve)	12.0 litres
Reserve volume	approx. 3.0 litres
Front suspension	
Type	30 mm oil-damped telescopic forks
Wheel travel	105 mm
Rear suspension	
Type	Twin shock absorber, tube steel swingarm
Adjustment	Spring pre-load
Wheel travel	105 mm
Wheels	18 inch alloys
Tyres	
Front	3.00-18 47P tubeless
Rear	3.50-16 58P tubeless
Front brake	Single 245 mm disc with single piston sliding caliper
Rear brake	Drum

Chassis – XT125R models

Frame type	Steel
Rake and Trail	28°, 114.4 mm
Fuel tank	
Capacity (including reserve)	10.0 litres
Reserve volume (when fuel warning light comes on)	approx. 2.0 litres
Front suspension	
Type	36 mm oil-damped telescopic forks
Wheel travel	170 mm
Rear suspension	
Type	Single shock absorber, box-section steel swingarm
Wheel travel	170 mm
Wheels	
Front	21 inch steel spoke
Rear	18 inch steel spoke
Tyres	
Front	90/90-21 54S tubed
Rear	120/80-18 62S tubed
Front brake	Single 245 mm disc with opposed piston caliper
Rear brake	Single 218 mm disc with opposed piston caliper

Chassis – XT125X

Frame type	Steel
Rake and Trail	26.74°, 78.33 mm
Fuel tank	
Capacity (including reserve)	10.0 litres
Reserve volume (when fuel warning light comes on)	approx. 2.0 litres
Front suspension	
Type	36 mm oil-damped telescopic forks
Wheel travel	170 mm
Rear suspension	
Type	Single shock absorber, box-section steel swingarm
Wheel travel	170 mm
Wheels	17 inch steel spoke
Tyres	
Front	100/80-17 52S tubed
Rear	130/70-17 62S tubed
Front brake	Single 260 mm disc with twin piston sliding caliper
Rear brake	Single 218 mm disc with opposed piston caliper

Dimensions and weights

YBR125ED

Overall length
  2005 to 2009 . . . . 1980 mm
  2010-on . . . . 1985 mm
Overall width . . . . 745 mm
Overall height . . . . 1080 mm
Wheelbase . . . . 1290 mm
Seat height . . . . 780 mm
Ground clearance
  2005 to 2009 . . . . 175 mm
  2010-on . . . . 160 mm
Weight (wet)
  2005 and 2006 models . . . . 120 kg
  2007 to 2009 models . . . . 124 kg
  2010 to 2013 models . . . . 125 kg
  2014-on models . . . . 126 kg
Maximum weight (carrying) capacity
  2005 and 2006 models . . . . 200 kg
  2007 to 2009 models . . . . 196 kg
  2010-on models . . . . 153 kg

YBR125 Custom

Overall length . . . . 2055 mm
Overall width . . . . 845 mm
Overall height . . . . 1125 mm
Wheelbase . . . . 1290 mm
Seat height . . . . 760 mm
Ground clearance . . . . 140 mm
Weight (wet) . . . . 130 kg
Maximum weight (carrying) capacity . 190 kg

XT125R

Overall length . . . . 2110 mm
Overall width . . . . 860 mm
Overall height . . . . 1130 mm
Wheelbase . . . . 1340 mm
Seat height . . . . 860 mm
Ground clearance . . . . 300 mm
Weight (wet) . . . . 120 kg

XT125X

Overall length . . . . 2040 mm
Overall width . . . . 860 mm
Overall height . . . . 1090 mm
Wheelbase . . . . 1340 mm
Seat height . . . . 830 mm
Ground clearance . . . . 271 mm
Weight (wet) . . . . 120 kg

Frame and engine numbers

The frame serial number is stamped into the right-hand side of the steering head. The engine number is stamped into the top of the crankcase on the right-hand side. Both of these numbers should be recorded and kept in a safe place so they can be given to law enforcement officials in the event of a theft. There is also a model code label, on the left-hand side of the frame just behind the battery on YBR models, and on the top of the rear mudguard on XT models. The carburettor or throttle body (according to model) has an ID number stamped into its body.

The frame serial number, engine serial number, and colour code should also be kept in a handy place (such as with your driver's licence) so they are always available when purchasing or ordering parts for your machine.

The procedures in this manual identify models by their model code (e.g. YBR or XT), and for sub-divisions of each model by their model type (e.g. YBR-ED or YBR Custom, or XT-R or XT-X), and where necessary the year of production (e.g. 2005 and 2006 YBR models). The model code or production year is printed on the model code label which is stuck to the frame left-hand side on YBR models (remove the side panel for access) and to the underseat compartment on XT models.

Buying spare parts

Once you have found all the identification numbers, record them for reference when buying parts. Since the manufacturers change specifications, parts and vendors (companies that manufacture various components on the machine), providing the ID numbers is the only way to be reasonably sure that you are buying the correct parts.

Whenever possible, take the worn part to the dealer so direct comparison with the new component can be made. Along the trail from the manufacturer to the parts shelf, there are numerous places that the part can end up with the wrong number or be listed incorrectly.

The two places to purchase new parts for your motorcycle – the franchised or main dealer and the parts/accessories store – differ in the type of parts they carry. While dealers can obtain every single genuine part for your motorcycle, the accessory store is usually limited to normal high wear items such as chains and sprockets, brake pads, spark plugs and cables. Rarely will an accessory outlet have major suspension components, camshafts, transmission gears, or engine cases.

Used parts can be obtained from breakers yards for roughly half the price of new ones, but you can't always be sure of what you're getting. Once again, take your worn part to the breaker for direct comparison, or when ordering by mail order make sure that you can return it if you are not happy.

Whether buying new, used or rebuilt parts, the best course is to deal directly with someone who specialises in your particular make.

The frame number is stamped into the right-hand side of the steering head

The engine number is stamped into the right-hand side of the crankcase

Professional mechanics are trained in safe working procedures. However enthusiastic you may be about getting on with the job at hand, take the time to ensure that your safety is not put at risk. A moment's lack of attention can result in an accident, as can failure to observe simple precautions.

There will always be new ways of having accidents, and the following is not a comprehensive list of all dangers; it is intended rather to make you aware of the risks and to encourage a safe approach to all work you carry out on your bike.

Asbestos

● Certain friction, insulating, sealing and other products - such as brake pads, clutch linings, gaskets, etc. - contain asbestos. Extreme care must be taken to avoid inhalation of dust from such products since it is hazardous to health. If in doubt, assume that they do contain asbestos.

Fire

● Remember at all times that petrol is highly flammable. Never smoke or have any kind of naked flame around, when working on the vehicle. But the risk does not end there - a spark caused by an electrical short-circuit, by two metal surfaces contacting each other, by careless use of tools, or even by static electricity built up in your body under certain conditions, can ignite petrol vapour, which in a confined space is highly explosive. Never use petrol as a cleaning solvent. Use an approved safety solvent.

● Always disconnect the battery earth terminal before working on any part of the fuel or electrical system, and never risk spilling fuel on to a hot engine or exhaust.

● It is recommended that a fire extinguisher of a type suitable for fuel and electrical fires is kept handy in the garage or workplace at all times. Never try to extinguish a fuel or electrical fire with water.

Fumes

● Certain fumes are highly toxic and can quickly cause unconsciousness and even death if inhaled to any extent. Petrol vapour comes into this category, as do the vapours from certain solvents such as trichloroethylene. Any draining or pouring of such volatile fluids should be done in a well ventilated area.

● When using cleaning fluids and solvents, read the instructions carefully. Never use materials from unmarked containers - they may give off poisonous vapours.

● Never run the engine of a motor vehicle in an enclosed space such as a garage. Exhaust fumes contain carbon monoxide which is extremely poisonous; if you need to run the engine, always do so in the open air or at least have the rear of the vehicle outside the workplace.

The battery

● Never cause a spark, or allow a naked light near the vehicle's battery. It will normally be giving off a certain amount of hydrogen gas, which is highly explosive.

● Always disconnect the battery ground (earth) terminal before working on the fuel or electrical systems (except where noted).

● If possible, loosen the filler plugs or cover when charging the battery from an external source. Do not charge at an excessive rate or the battery may burst.

● Take care when topping up, cleaning or carrying the battery. The acid electrolyte, evenwhen diluted, is very corrosive and should not be allowed to contact the eyes or skin. Always wear rubber gloves and goggles or a face shield. If you ever need to prepare electrolyte yourself, always add the acid slowly to the water; never add the water to the acid.

Electricity

● When using an electric power tool, inspection light etc., always ensure that the appliance is correctly connected to its plug and that, where necessary, it is properly grounded (earthed). Do not use such appliances in damp conditions and, again, beware of creating a spark or applying excessive heat in the vicinity of fuel or fuel vapour. Also ensure that the appliances meet national safety standards.

● A severe electric shock can result from touching certain parts of the electrical system, such as the spark plug wires (HT leads), when the engine is running or being cranked, particularly if components are damp or the insulation is defective. Where an electronic ignition system is used, the secondary (HT) voltage is much higher and could prove fatal.

Remember...

✗ **Don't** start the engine without first ascertaining that the transmission is in neutral.

✗ **Don't** suddenly remove the pressure cap from a hot cooling system - cover it with a cloth and release the pressure gradually first, or you may get scalded by escaping coolant.

✗ **Don't** attempt to drain oil until you are sure it has cooled sufficiently to avoid scalding you.

✗ **Don't** grasp any part of the engine or exhaust system without first ascertaining that it is cool enough not to burn you.

✗ **Don't** allow brake fluid or antifreeze to contact the machine's paintwork or plastic components.

✗ **Don't** siphon toxic liquids such as fuel, hydraulic fluid or antifreeze by mouth, or allow them to remain on your skin.

✗ **Don't** inhale dust - it may be injurious to health (see Asbestos heading).

✗ **Don't** allow any spilled oil or grease to remain on the floor - wipe it up right away, before someone slips on it.

✗ **Don't** use ill-fitting spanners or other tools which may slip and cause injury.

✗ **Don't** lift a heavy component which may be beyond your capability - get assistance.

✗ **Don't** rush to finish a job or take unverified short cuts.

✗ **Don't** allow children or animals in or around an unattended vehicle.

✗ **Don't** inflate a tyre above the recommended pressure. Apart from overstressing the carcass, in extreme cases the tyre may blow off forcibly.

✔ **Do** ensure that the machine is supported securely at all times. This is especially important when the machine is blocked up to aid wheel or fork removal.

✔ **Do** take care when attempting to loosen a stubborn nut or bolt. It is generally better to pull on a spanner, rather than push, so that if you slip, you fall away from the machine rather than onto it.

✔ **Do** wear eye protection when using power tools such as drill, sander, bench grinder etc.

✔ **Do** use a barrier cream on your hands prior to undertaking dirty jobs - it will protect your skin from infection as well as making the dirt easier to remove afterwards; but make sure your hands aren't left slippery. Note that long-term contact with used engine oil can be a health hazard.

✔ **Do** keep loose clothing (cuffs, ties etc. and long hair) well out of the way of moving mechanical parts.

✔ **Do** remove rings, wristwatch etc., before working on the vehicle - especially the electrical system.

✔ **Do** keep your work area tidy - it is only too easy to fall over articles left lying around.

✔ **Do** exercise caution when compressing springs for removal or installation. Ensure that the tension is applied and released in a controlled manner, using suitable tools which preclude the possibility of the spring escaping violently.

✔ **Do** ensure that any lifting tackle used has a safe working load rating adequate for the job.

✔ **Do** get someone to check periodically that all is well, when working alone on the vehicle.

✔ **Do** carry out work in a logical sequence and check that everything is correctly assembled and tightened afterwards.

✔ **Do** remember that your vehicle's safety affects that of yourself and others. If in doubt on any point, get professional advice.

● If in spite of following these precautions, you are unfortunate enough to injure yourself, seek medical attention as soon as possible.

Engine oil level

Before you start:

✔ Start the engine and let it idle for 3 to 5 minutes.
Caution: Do not run the engine in an enclosed space such as a garage or workshop.
✔ Stop the engine and support the motorcycle upright on level ground. Allow it to stand for a few minutes for the oil level to stabilise.

The correct oil:

● Modern, high-revving engines place great demands on their oil. It is very important that the correct oil for your bike is used.
● Always top up with a good quality motorcycle oil of the specified type and viscosity and do not overfill the engine. Do not use engine oil designed for car use.

Oil type	API grade SG or SH, JASO MA standard
Oil viscosity	SAE 10W30, 10W40, 10W50, 15W40, 20W40 or 20W50

Bike care:

● If you have to add oil frequently, check the engine joints, oil seals and gaskets for oil leakage. If not, the engine could be burning oil, in which case there will be white smoke coming out of the exhaust (see *Fault Finding*).

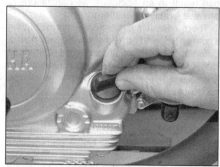

1 The oil level dipstick is incorporated with the oil filler cap, which is on the right-hand side of the engine.

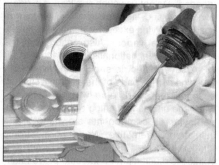

2 Unscrew the cap and wipe the dipstick clean.

3 Insert the dipstick so that the cap contacts the engine, but do not screw it in.

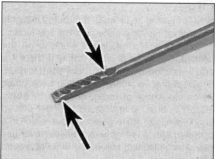

4 Remove the dipstick and check the oil mark – it should lie between the upper and lower level lines (arrowed).

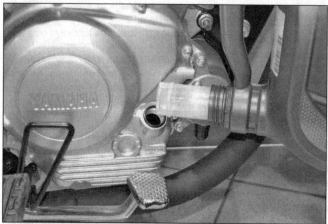

5 If the level is on or below the lower line, top up the engine with the recommended grade and type of oil to bring the level almost up to the upper line. Do not overfill.

6 On completion, make sure the O-ring (arrowed) on the underside of the cap is in good condition and properly seated. Fit a new one if necessary. Wipe it clean and smear new oil onto it. Fit the cap, making sure it is secure in the cover.

Tyres

The correct pressures:

● The tyres must be checked when **cold**, not immediately after riding. Note that incorrect tyre pressures will cause abnormal tread wear and unsafe handling. Low tyre pressures may cause the tyre to slip on the rim or come off.

● Use an accurate pressure gauge. Many forecourt gauges are wildly inaccurate. If you buy your own, spend as much as you can justify on a quality gauge.

● Proper air pressure will increase tyre life and provide maximum stability and ride comfort.

YBR125	Front	Rear
Rider only	25 psi (1.75 Bar)	29 psi (2.0 Bar)
Rider and pillion	25 psi (1.75 Bar)	41 psi (2.8 Bar)

XT125	Front	Rear
Rider only	26 psi (1.8 Bar)	27.5 psi (1.9 Bar)
Rider and pillion	29 psi (2.0 Bar)	30.5 psi (2.1 Bar)

Tyre care:

● Check the tyres carefully for cuts, tears, embedded nails or other sharp objects, and excessive wear. Riding a motorcycle with excessively worn tyres is extremely hazardous, as traction and handling are directly affected.

● Check the condition of the tyre valve and ensure the dust cap is in place.

● Pick out any stones or nails which may have become embedded in the tyre tread. If left, they will eventually penetrate through the casing and cause a puncture.

● If tyre damage is apparent, or unexplained loss of pressure is experienced, seek the advice of a tyre fitting specialist without delay.

Tyre tread depth:

● At the time of writing UK law requires that tread depth must be at least 1 mm over 3/4 of the tread breadth all the way around the tyre, with no bald patches. Many riders, however, consider 2 mm tread depth minimum to be a safer limit. Yamaha recommend a minimum of 1.6 mm. Refer to the tyre tread legislation in your country.

● Many tyres now incorporate wear indicators in the tread. Identify the location marking on the tyre sidewall to locate the indicator bar and replace the tyre if the tread has worn down to the bar.

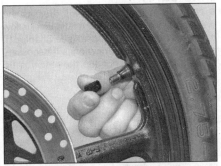

1 Remove the dust cap from the valve and do not forget to fit it after checking the pressure.

2 Check the tyre pressures when the tyres are cold.

3 Measure tread depth at the centre of the tyre using a depth gauge.

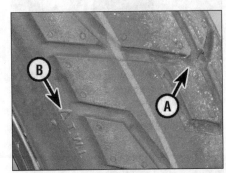

4 Tyre tread wear indicator (A) and its location marking (B) on the edge or sidewall (according to manufacturer).

Brake fluid level

⚠ *Warning: Brake hydraulic fluid can harm your eyes and damage painted surfaces, so use extreme caution when handling and pouring it and cover surrounding surfaces with rag. Do not use fluid that has been standing open for some time, as it is hygroscopic (absorbs moisture from the air) which can cause a dangerous loss of braking effectiveness.*

Before you start:

✔ The front brake fluid reservoir is on the right-hand handlebar.
✔ On XT models the rear brake fluid reservoir is between the seat and the swingarm on the right-hand side.
✔ Make sure you have a supply of DOT 4 brake fluid.
✔ Wrap a rag around the reservoir to ensure that any spillage does not come into contact with painted surfaces.

Bike care:

● The fluid in the reservoir will drop as the brake pads wear down. If the fluid level is low check the brake pads for wear (see Chapter 1), and replace them with new ones if necessary (see Chapter 6). Do not top the reservoir up until the new pads have been fitted, and then check to see if topping up is still necessary – when the caliper pistons are pushed back to accommodate the extra thickness of the pads some fluid will be displaced back into the reservoir.
● If either fluid reservoir requires repeated topping-up there is a leak somewhere in the system, which must be investigated immediately.
● Check for signs of fluid leakage from the hydraulic hoses and/or brake system components – if found, rectify immediately (see Chapter 6).
● Check the operation of both brakes before taking the machine on the road; if there is evidence of air in the system (spongy feel to lever or pedal), it must be bled (see Chapter 6).

FRONT

1 Set the handlebars so the reservoir is level and check the fluid level through the window in the reservoir body – it must be above the LOWER level line (arrowed).

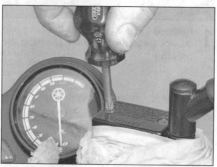

2 If the level is on or below the LOWER line, undo the two reservoir cover screws and remove the cover, diaphragm plate (where fitted), and diaphragm.

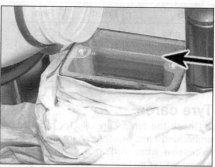

3 Top up with new clean DOT 4 hydraulic fluid, until the level is up to the UPPER line (arrowed) on the inside of the reservoir. Do not overfill and take care to avoid spills (see **Warning** above).

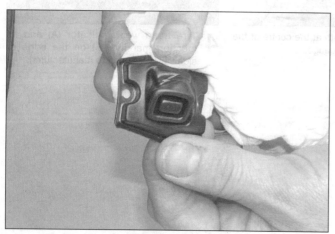

4 Wipe any moisture off the diaphragm with a tissue.

5 Ensure that the diaphragm is correctly seated before fitting the plate and cover. Secure the cover with its screws.

REAR (XT models only)

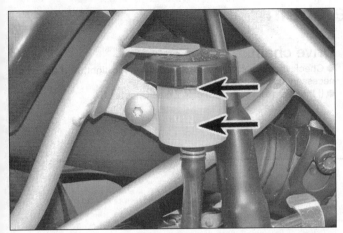

1 The rear brake fluid level is visible through the reservoir body – it must be between the MAX and MIN level lines (arrowed).

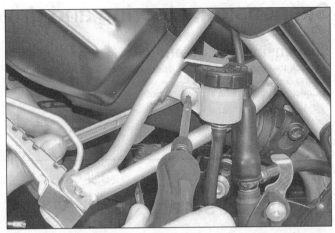

2 If the level is on or below the MIN line undo the reservoir screw, counter-holding the nut on the back and noting there is a washer, and displace the reservoir.

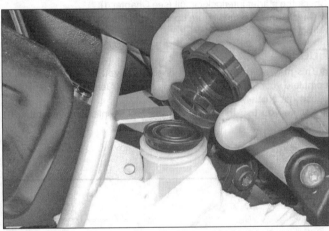

3 Undo the cap and remove the diaphragm plate and diaphragm.

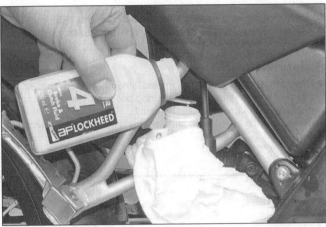

4 Top up with new clean DOT 4 hydraulic fluid, until the level is up to the UPPER line. Do not overfill and take care to avoid spills (see **Warning**).

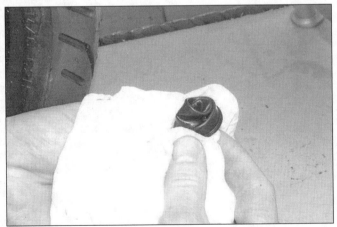

5 Wipe any moisture off the diaphragm with a tissue.

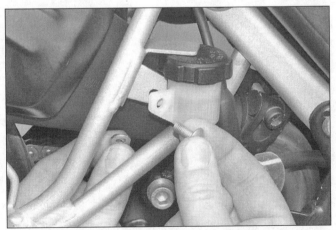

6 Ensure that the diaphragm is correctly seated before fitting the plate and cap. Fit the reservoir back onto its bracket.

Suspension, steering and drive chain

Suspension and Steering:
● Check that the front and rear suspension operates smoothly without binding (see Chapter 1).
● Check that the steering moves smoothly from lock-to-lock.

Drive chain:
● Check that the chain isn't too loose or too tight, and adjust it if necessary (see Chapter 1).
● If the chain looks dry, lubricate it (see Chapter 1).

Legal and safety

Lighting and signalling:
● Take a minute to check that the headlight, tail light, brake light, licence plate light (XT only), instrument lights and turn signals all work correctly.
● Check that the horn sounds when the button is pressed.
● A working speedometer, graduated in mph, is a statutory requirement in the UK.

Safety:
● Check that the throttle grip rotates smoothly when opened and snaps shut when released, in all steering positions. Also check for the correct amount of freeplay (see Chapter 1).
● Check that the brake lever and pedal, clutch lever and gearchange lever operate smoothly. Lubricate them at the specified intervals or when necessary (see Chapter 1).
● Check that the engine shuts off when the kill switch is operated. Check the starter interlock circuit (see Chapter 1).
● Check that sidestand return springs hold the stand up securely when retracted.

Fuel:
● This may seem obvious, but check that you have enough fuel to complete your journey. If you notice signs of fuel leakage – rectify the cause immediately.
● Ensure you use the correct grade fuel – unleaded, minimum 91 RON.

Chapter 1
Routine maintenance and servicing

Contents

Degrees of difficulty

Easy, suitable for novice with little experience 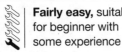	**Fairly easy,** suitable for beginner with some experience	**Fairly difficult,** suitable for competent DIY mechanic	**Difficult,** suitable for experienced DIY mechanic	**Very difficult,** suitable for expert DIY or professional

Specifications

Engine

Spark plug type
 YBR models . . . . NGK CR6HSA
 XT models . . . . NGK CR7HSA or Denso U22FSR-U
Spark plug electrode gap
 YBR models . . . . 0.6 to 0.7 mm
 XT models . . . . 0.6 mm
Idle speed
 2005 and 2006 YBR models . . . . 1400 to 1500 rpm
 2007-on YBR models . . . . 1300 to 1500 rpm
 XT models . . . . 1650 to 1850 rpm
Valve clearances (COLD engine)
 Intake valves . . . . 0.10 mm (0.08 to 0.12 mm)
 Exhaust valves . . . . 0.12 mm (0.10 to 0.14 mm)
CO density – carburettor engined models
 YBR models . . . . 3 to 5% with AIS hose disconnected
 XT models 4.5%

Chassis

Brake pad friction material minimum thickness	1.0 mm
Clutch cable freeplay	10 to 15 mm
Drive chain slack	
YBR models	20 to 30 mm
XT models	25 to 40 mm
Drive chain stretch limit (see text)	
YBR models	191.5 mm
XT models	119.7 mm
Throttle cable freeplay	
YBR models	3 to 7 mm
XT models	3 to 5 mm
Front brake lever freeplay	
YBR models	0 to 7 mm
XT models	2 to 5 mm
Rear brake pedal freeplay (YBR models)	20 to 30 mm
Rear brake pedal height (XT models)	12 to 15 mm
Tyre pressures	see *Pre-ride checks*

Lubricants and fluids

Engine oil	see *Pre-ride checks*
Engine oil capacity	
Oil change	1.0 litres
Following engine overhaul	1.2 litres
Brake fluid	DOT 4
Drive chain	Aerosol chain lubricant suitable for O-ring chains, or engine oil
Steering head bearings	Lithium based multi-purpose grease
Bearing seal lips	Lithium based multi-purpose grease
Gearchange lever/rear brake pedal/footrest pivots	Lithium based multi-purpose grease
Clutch lever pivot	Lithium based multi-purpose grease
Sidestand pivot	Lithium based multi-purpose grease
Throttle twistgrip	Lithium based multi-purpose grease
Front brake lever pivot and piston tip	Silicone grease
Cables	Aerosol cable lubricant

Torque settings

Brake torque arm nut (YBR models)	19 Nm
Camshaft sprocket cover bolts	10 Nm
Engine oil drain plug	20 Nm
Fork clamp bolts (top yoke)	
YBR models	23 Nm
XT models	20 Nm
Rear axle nut	
2005 and 2006 YBR models	91 Nm
2007-on YBR models	80 Nm
XT models	85 Nm
Spark plug	
YBR models	13 Nm
XT models	12.5 Nm
Steering head bearing adjuster nut – YBR models	
Initial setting	33 Nm
Final setting	22 Nm
Steering stem nut	
YBR models	110 Nm
XT models	30 Nm
Valve clearance adjuster access caps	18 Nm

YBR125ED 2005 to 2009, YBR125 Custom, all XT models

Note: *The Pre-ride checks outlined in the owner's manual cover those items which should be inspected before every ride. Also perform the pre-ride inspection at every maintenance interval (in addition to the procedures listed). The intervals listed below are the intervals recommended by the manufacturer for the models covered in this manual.*

Pre-ride

☐ See *'Pre-ride checks'* at the beginning of this manual.

After the initial 600 miles (1000 km)

Note: *This check is usually performed by a Yamaha dealer after the first 600 miles (1000 km) from new. Thereafter, maintenance is carried out according to the following intervals of the schedule.*

Every 600 miles (1000 km) – YBR models, every 300 miles (500 km) – XT models

☐ Check, adjust, clean and lubricate the drive chain (Section 1)

Every 3750 miles (6000 km)

☐ Check the spark plug (Section 2)
☐ Clean the air filter element and check the crankcase breather system (Section 3)
☐ Check and adjust the valve clearances (Section 4)
☐ Check and adjust the engine idle speed (Section 5)
☐ Check the fuel system and hoses (Section 6)
☐ Check and adjust the throttle cable, and on XT models the choke cable (Section 7)
☐ Check the brake pads/shoes for wear (Section 8)
☐ Check the brake system and brake light switch operation (Section 8)
☐ Check and adjust the clutch cable freeplay (Section 9)
☐ Check the sidestand, centrestand where fitted, and starter interlock circuit (Section 10)
☐ Check the front and rear suspension (Section 11)
☐ Check the condition of the wheels, wheel bearings and tyres (Section 12)
☐ Lubricate the clutch and brake levers, brake pedal, centrestand pivot (where fitted), sidestand pivot, and the throttle and choke cables (Section 13)
☐ Change the engine oil (Section 14)
☐ Check the tightness of all nuts, bolts and fasteners (Section 15)
☐ Check and adjust the steering head bearings (Section 16)
☐ Check the air induction system (YBR models) (Section 17)
☐ Check the battery (Section 18)

Every 7500 miles (12,000 km) or 12 months

Carry out all the items under the 3750 mile (6000 km) check, plus the following:
☐ Fit a new spark plug (Section 2)
☐ Fit a new air filter element (Section 3)
☐ Check the fuel tap filter (2005 and 2006 YBR models) (Section 6)
☐ Re-grease the steering head bearings (XT models) (Section 16)

Every 15,000 miles (24,000 km)

☐ Re-grease the steering head bearings (YBR models) (Section 16)
☐ Re-grease the swingarm bushes (2005 and 2006 YBR models and all XT models) (Section 11)

Every 30,000 miles (50,000 km)

☐ Re-grease the swingarm bushes (2007 to 2009 YBR models) (Section 11)

Every two years

☐ Change the brake fluid (Section 8)

Every four years

☐ Fit new brake hoses (Section 8)

Non-scheduled maintenance

☐ Fit new brake master cylinder and caliper seals (Section 8)
☐ Fit new fuel system hoses (Section 6)
☐ Change the front fork oil (Section 11)

YBR125 2010-on models

Note: The Pre-ride checks outlined in the owner's manual cover those items which should be inspected before every ride. Also perform the pre-ride inspection at every maintenance interval (in addition to the procedures listed). The intervals listed below are the intervals recommended by the manufacturer for the models covered in this manual.

Pre-ride
☐ See *'Pre-ride checks'* at the beginning of this manual.

After the initial 600 miles (1000 km)
Note: This check is usually performed by a Yamaha dealer after the first 600 miles (1000 km) from new. Thereafter, maintenance is carried out according to the following intervals of the schedule.

Every 600 miles (1000 km)
☐ Check, adjust, clean and lubricate the drive chain (Section 1)

Every 3750 miles (6000 km)
☐ Check the spark plug (Section 2)
☐ Clean the air filter element and check the crankcase breather system (Section 3)
☐ Check and adjust the valve clearances (Section 4)
☐ Check and adjust the engine idle speed (Section 5)
☐ Check the fuel system and hoses (Section 6)
☐ Check and adjust the throttle cable (Section 7)
☐ Check the brake pads/shoes for wear (Section 8)
☐ Check the brake system and brake light switch operation (Section 8)
☐ Check and adjust the clutch cable freeplay (Section 9)
☐ Check the sidestand, centrestand where fitted, and starter interlock circuit (Section 10)
☐ Check the front and rear suspension (Section 11)
☐ Check the condition of the wheels, wheel bearings and tyres (Section 12)
☐ Lubricate the clutch and brake levers, brake pedal, centrestand pivot (where fitted), sidestand pivot, and the throttle cables (Section 13)
☐ Change the engine oil (Section 14)
☐ Check the tightness of all nuts, bolts and fasteners (Section 15)
☐ Check and adjust the steering head bearings (Section 16)
☐ Check the air induction system (Section 17)
☐ Check the battery (Section 18)

Every 6000 miles (10,000 km)
☐ Re-grease the swingarm bushes (Section 11)

Every 7500 miles (12,000 km) or 12 months
Carry out all the items under the 3750 mile (6000 km) check, plus the following:
☐ Fit a new spark plug (Section 2)
☐ Fit a new air filter element (Section 3)

Every 14,000 miles (22,500 km)
☐ Re-grease the steering head bearings (Section 16)

Every two years
☐ Change the brake fluid (Section 8)
☐ Fit new brake master cylinder and caliper seals (Section 8)

Every four years
☐ Fit new brake hoses (Section 8)

Non-scheduled maintenance
☐ Fit new brake master cylinder and caliper seals (Section 8)
☐ Fit new fuel system hoses (Section 6)
☐ Change the front fork oil (Section 11)

1 This Chapter is designed to help the home mechanic maintain his/her motorcycle for safety, economy, long life and peak performance.

2 Deciding where to start or plug into the routine maintenance schedule depends on several factors. If your motorcycle has been maintained according to the warranty standards and has just come out of warranty, start routine maintenance as it coincides with the next mileage or calendar interval. If you have owned the machine for some time but have never performed any maintenance on it, start at the nearest interval and include some additional procedures to ensure that nothing important is overlooked. If you have just had a major engine overhaul, then start the maintenance routine from the beginning. If you have a used machine and have no knowledge of its history or maintenance record, combine all the checks into one large service initially and then settle into the specified maintenance schedule.

3 Before beginning any maintenance or repair, the machine should be cleaned thoroughly, especially around the oil drain plug, valve cover, body panels, drive chain, suspension, wheels, etc. Cleaning will help ensure that dirt does not contaminate the engine and will allow you to detect wear and damage that could otherwise easily go unnoticed.

4 Certain maintenance information is sometimes printed on labels attached to the motorcycle. If the information on the labels differs from that included here, use the information on the label.

Maintenance procedures

1 Drive chain and sprockets

Check chain slack

1 As the chain stretches with wear, adjustment will be necessary. A neglected drive chain won't last long and will quickly damage the sprockets. Routine chain adjustment and lubrication isn't difficult and will ensure maximum chain and sprocket life.

2 To check the chain, on YBR models place the bike on its centrestand so the rear wheel is off the ground; on XT models place the bike on its sidestand. Make sure the transmission is in neutral. Make sure the ignition switch is OFF.

3 Push up on the bottom run of the chain and measure the slack midway between the two sprockets, then compare your measurement to that listed in this Chapter's Specifications (see illustration). Since the chain will rarely wear evenly, turn the rear wheel or roll the bike forward (according to model) so that another section of chain can be checked; do this several times to check the entire length of chain, and mark the tightest spot.

Caution: Riding the bike with excess slack in the chain could lead to damage.

4 In some cases where lubrication has been neglected, corrosion and dirt may cause the links to bind and kink, which effectively shortens the chain's length and makes it tight (see illustration). Thoroughly clean and work free any such links, then highlight them with a marker pen or paint. Take the bike for a ride.

5 After the bike has been ridden, repeat the measurement for slack in the highlighted area. If the chain has kinked again and is still tight, replace it with a new one (see Chapter 6). A rusty, kinked or worn chain will damage the sprockets and can damage transmission bearings. If in any doubt as to the condition of a chain, it is far better to install a new one than risk damage to other components and possibly yourself.

6 Check the entire length of the chain for damaged rollers, loose links and pins, and missing O-rings and replace it with a new one if necessary. Note: Never fit a new chain onto old sprockets, and never use the old chain if you fit new sprockets – replace the chain and sprockets as a set.

7 Inspect the drive chain slider on the front of the swingarm for excessive wear and damage and replace it with a new one if necessary.

Adjust chain slack

8 Set the tightest spot of the chain at the centre of its bottom run.

9 On YBR models turn the rear brake freeplay adjuster nut anti-clockwise a few turns (see illustration). Slacken the nut on the brake

1.3 Push up on the chain and measure the slack

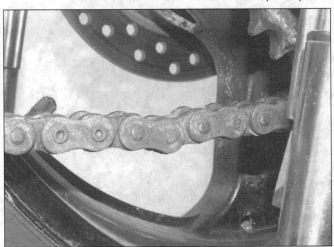

1.4 Neglect has caused the links in this chain to kink

1.9a Turn the nut (arrowed) a few turns anti-clockwise

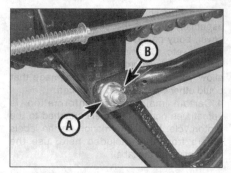

1.9b Slacken the nut (A), removing the split pin (B) if required

1.9c Slacken the axle nut (arrowed)

1.9d Slacken the locknut (arrowed) on each side . . .

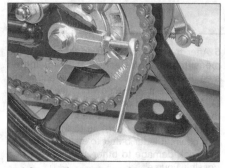

1.9e . . . then turn each adjuster by an equal amount

1.10a Slacken the axle nut (arrowed)

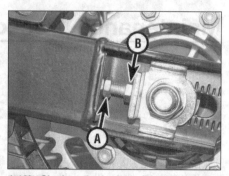

1.10b Slacken the locknut (A) on each side then turn each adjuster (B) by an equal amount

torque arm bolt – there should be enough thread exposed between it and the split pin, but remove the pin if required, or if its ends are in the way (see illustration). Slacken the rear axle nut (see illustration). Slacken the locknut on the adjuster on each side of the swingarm (see illustration). To reduce chain slack turn the adjuster on each side evenly clockwise until the amount of freeplay specified at the beginning of the Chapter is obtained at the centre of the bottom run of the chain (see illustration).

10 On XT models slacken the rear axle nut (see illustration). Slacken the locknut on the adjuster on each side of the swingarm (see illustration). To reduce chain slack turn the adjuster on each side evenly anti-clockwise until the amount of freeplay specified at the beginning of the Chapter is obtained at the centre of the bottom run of the chain.

11 Following adjustment, check that the index line on the chain adjustment marker on YBR models or the back edge of the chain adjustment marker on XT models aligns with the same index line on each side of the swingarm (see illustrations). It is important the alignment is the same on each side otherwise the rear wheel will be out of alignment with

the front. Also make sure that the wheel is pushed fully forwards in the swingarm. If there is a difference in the positions, adjust one of them so that its position is exactly the same as the other. Check the chain freeplay again and readjust if necessary.

12 To increase chain slack turn the adjuster on each side of the swingarm anti-clockwise on YBR models and clockwise on XT models, then push the wheel forwards in the swingarm. Apply the same principles given in Step 11 for checking alignment.

13 From time to time check the amount of chain stretch (Steps 18 to 20).

1.11a Chain adjuster alignment marks – YBR models

1.11b Chain adjuster alignment marks – XT models

1.16 Using a chain cleaning brush

1.17 Apply the lubricant to the overlapping sections of the sideplates

14 When adjustment is complete, counter-hold the adjusters to prevent them turning and tighten the locknuts **(see illustration 1.9d or 1.10b)**. Tighten the axle nut to the torque setting specified at the beginning of the Chapter. Recheck the adjustment as above, then make sure the wheel turns freely.

15 On YBR models reset the rear brake adjuster (see Section 8, Step 6). Tighten the brake torque arm nut to the specified torque, then if removed fit a new split pin through the hole in the end of the bolt and bend its ends round **(see illustration 1.9b)**.

Clean and lubricate the chain

16 If required, wash the chain using a dedicated aerosol cleaner, or in paraffin (kerosene) or a suitable non-flammable or high flash-point solvent that will not damage the O-rings, using a soft brush to work any dirt out if necessary – specially shaped chain cleaning brushes are available from good suppliers **(see illustration)**. Wipe the cleaner off the chain and allow it to dry. If the chain is excessively dirty remove it from the machine and allow it to soak in the paraffin or solvent (see Chapter 6).

Caution: Don't use petrol (gasoline), an unsuitable solvent or other cleaning fluids which might damage the internal sealing properties of the chain. Don't use high-pressure water to clean the chain. The entire process shouldn't take longer than ten minutes, otherwise the O-rings could be damaged.

17 The best time to lubricate the chain is after the motorcycle has been ridden. When the chain is warm, the lubricant will penetrate the joints between the side plates better than when cold. **Note:** Yamaha specifies engine oil or an aerosol chain lube that it is suitable for O-ring (sealed) chains; do not use any other chain lubricants – the solvents could damage the chain's sealing rings. Apply the lubricant to the area where the sideplates overlap – not the middle of the rollers **(see illustration)**.

> **HAYNES HiNT**
>
> *Apply the lubricant to the top of the lower chain run, so centrifugal force will work the oil into the chain when the bike is moving. After applying the lubricant, let it soak in a few minutes before wiping off any excess.*

> ⚠ *Warning: Take care not to get any lubricant on the rear tyre or brake system components. If any of the lubricant inadvertently contacts them, clean it off thoroughly using a suitable solvent or dedicated brake cleaner before riding the machine.*

Check drive chain stretch

18 Measure the amount of chain stretch as follows:

19 Adjust the chain as described in Steps 9

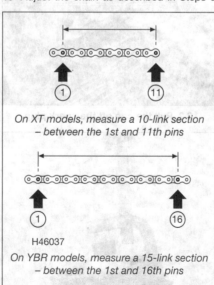

On XT models, measure a 10-link section – between the 1st and 11th pins

H46037

On YBR models, measure a 15-link section – between the 1st and 16th pins

1.19 Chain stretch measurement

to 11 until all slack is taken up, but not so much that the chain is taut. Measure along the bottom run of the chain, a 15 link section on YBR models, and a 10 link section on XT models **(see illustration)**. Rotate the rear wheel so that several sections of the chain can be measured, then calculate the average and compare it to the stretch limit specified at the beginning of the Chapter. If the chain stretch measurement exceeds the service limit it must be replaced with a new one (see Chapter 6).

20 If the chain is good, reset the adjusters so that there is the correct amount of freeplay (see Steps 12, 14 and 15).

Caution: Never fit a new chain onto old sprockets, and never use the old chain if you fit new sprockets – replace the chain and sprockets as a set.

Check sprocket wear

21 Remove the front sprocket cover (see Chapter 6). Check the teeth on the front sprocket and the rear sprocket for wear **(see illustration)**. If the sprocket teeth are worn excessively, replace the chain and both sprockets with a new set. Check that the sprocket fasteners are tight (refer to Chapter 6 Specifications for torque settings).

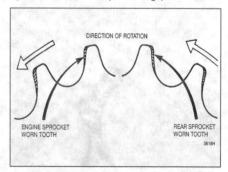

1.21 Check the sprockets in the areas indicated

2.1a On YBR models remove the side cover to access the toolkit (arrowed)

2.1b On XT models undo the screw (arrowed) and remove the cover to access the toolkit

2 Spark plug

Check and adjustment

1 Make sure your spark plug socket is the correct size (16 mm) before attempting to remove the plug – a suitable one is supplied in the motorcycle's tool kit, which on YBR models is stored above the battery and is accessed by removing the left-hand side cover (see Chapter 7), and on XT models is stored in a compartment in the left-hand side of the front deflector panel, and is accessed by removing the compartment cover **(see illustrations)**.

2 Pull the cap off the spark plug **(see illustration)**.

3 Clean the area around the base of the spark plug to prevent any dirt falling into the engine.

4 Unscrew and remove the plug from the cylinder head **(see illustration)**.

5 Check the condition of the electrodes, referring to the spark plug reading chart on the inside rear cover of this manual if signs of contamination are evident.

6 Clean the plug with a wire brush. Examine the tips of the electrodes; if a tip has rounded off, the plug is worn. Measure the gap between the two electrodes using a feeler gauge or a wire type gauge **(see illustration)**. The gap should be as given in the Specifications at the beginning of this chapter; if necessary adjust the gap by bending the side electrode **(see illustration)**.

7 Check the threads, the washer and the ceramic insulator body for cracks and other damage.

8 If the plug is worn or damaged, or if any deposits cannot be cleaned off, replace the plug with a new one. If in any doubt as to the condition of the plug replace it with a new one – the expense is minimal.

9 Thread the plug into the cylinder head until the washer seats **(see illustration)**. Since the cylinder head is made of aluminium, which is soft and easily damaged, thread the plug as far as possible by hand. Once the plug is finger-tight, the job can be finished with a spanner on the tool supplied or a socket drive **(see illustration 2.4)**. If a new plug is being installed, tighten it by 1/2 a turn after the washer has seated. If the old plug is being reused, tighten it by 1/4 turn after the washer has seated, or if a torque wrench can be applied, tighten the spark plug to the torque setting specified at the beginning of the Chapter. Otherwise tighten it according to the instructions on the box. Do not over-tighten it.

2.2 Pull the cap off the spark plug

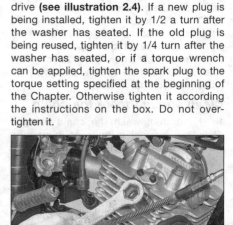

2.4 Unscrew and remove the plug

2.6a Using a wire type gauge to measure the spark plug electrode gap

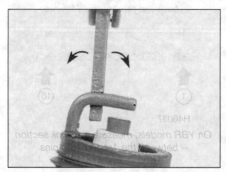

2.6b Adjusting the gap using the fitting provided on the tool

2.9 Thread the plug into the head by hand to prevent cross-threading

10 Fit the spark plug cap, making sure it locates correctly onto the plug **(see illustration 2.2)**.

HAYNES HiNT *A stripped plug thread in the cylinder head can be repaired with a Heli-Coil insert – see 'Tools and Workshop Tips' in the Reference section.*

Renewal

11 At the prescribed interval, whatever the condition of the existing spark plug, remove the plug as described above and install a new one.

3 Air filter and crankcase breather

Air filter

Caution: If the machine is continually ridden in wet or dusty conditions, the filter should be cleaned more frequently.

YBR models

1 Remove the right-hand side cover (see Chapter 7).
2 Undo the five screws securing the air filter cover **(see illustration)**. Remove the cover.

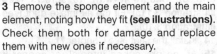

3.2 Undo the screws (arrowed) and remove the cover

3 Remove the sponge element and the main element, noting how they fit **(see illustrations)**. Check them both for damage and replace them with new ones if necessary.
4 Tap the main element on a hard surface to dislodge any dirt, then use compressed air to blow through it, directing the air in the opposite way to normal flow, i.e. from the inner side to the outer **(see illustration)**.
5 Soak the sponge element in solvent, then squeeze it dry – do not wring it out as it will be damaged **(see illustration)**. Allow the sponge to dry.
6 Make sure the cover seal is properly seated **(see illustration)**. Fit the main element into the housing, then fit the sponge element **(see illustrations 3.3b and a)**. Fit the cover

3.3a Remove the sponge element . . .

and secure it with its screws **(see illustration)**.
7 Install the side cover (see Chapter 7).
8 At the prescribed interval, or sooner if the bike is constantly ridden in dusty or wet conditions, remove the main element and replace it with a new one whatever its apparent condition.

⚠ *Warning: Only using a cleaning solvent to clean the sponge element. DO NOT use petrol.*

XT models

9 Remove the seat (see Chapter 7).
10 Remove the air intake duct from the top of the filter housing **(see illustration)**.
11 Undo the screws and withdraw the filter from the housing, noting how it fits **(see**

3.3b . . . and the main filter element

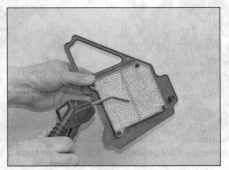

3.4 Direct the air in the opposite direction of normal flow

3.5 Clean the sponge element as described

3.6a Make sure the seal is in its groove

3.6b Fit the cover onto the housing

3.10 Remove the intake duct . . .

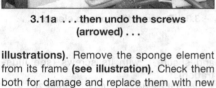

3.11a . . . then undo the screws (arrowed) . . .

3.11b . . . withdraw the filter . . .

3.11c . . . and draw the element off its frame

illustrations). Remove the sponge element from its frame **(see illustration)**. Check them both for damage and replace them with new ones if necessary.

12 Soak the sponge element in kerosene (paraffin), then squeeze it dry – do not wring it as it will be damaged. Apply engine oil to the entire surface of the element, then squeeze out any excess – the element should be coated with oil but not dripping.

13 Fit the sponge element over the frame, then fit the filter into the housing, making sure it is properly seated **(see illustrations 3.11c**

and b). Secure it with its screws **(see illustration 3.11a)**. Fit the air intake duct **(see illustration 3.10)**.

14 Install the seat (see Chapter 7).

15 At the prescribed interval, or sooner if the bike is constantly ridden in dusty or wet conditions, remove the filter element and replace it with a new one whatever its apparent condition.

Crankcase breather

Caution: If the machine is continually ridden in wet conditions or at full throttle,

the crankcase breather should be drained more frequently.

16 Locate the crankcase breather drain on the underside of the air filter housing **(see illustrations)**. Place some rag under the drain, then release the clamp and remove the collector. Allow any residue to drain from the housing, and clean out the collector.

17 Check the crankcase breather hose between the engine and the air filter housing for signs of cracks, hardening and deformation, and replace it with a new one if necessary **(see illustration)**.

3.16a Crankcase breather drain collector (arrowed) – YBR models

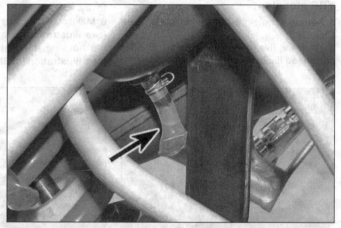

3.16b Crankcase breather drain collector (arrowed) – XT models

3.17a Crankcase breather hose (arrowed) – YBR models

3.17b Crankcase breather hose (arrowed) – XT models

4.3a Unscrew the bolts (arrowed) and remove the sprocket cover

4.3b Unscrew the adjuster access caps (arrowed)

4.4 Remove the crankshaft end cap (A) and the timing inspection cap (B)

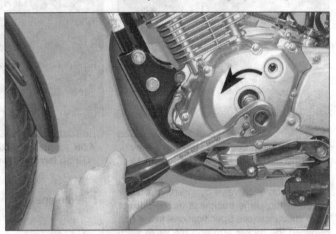

4.6a Turn the engine anti-clockwise using the nut . . .

4 Valve clearances

Special tool: *A set of feeler gauges is necessary for this job (see illustration 4.7).*
1 The engine must be completely cool for this maintenance procedure, so let the bike stand overnight before beginning.
2 Remove the spark plug (see Section 2).
3 Unscrew the camshaft sprocket cover bolts and remove the cover **(see illustration)**. Unscrew the valve clearance adjuster access caps from the front and back of the cylinder head **(see illustration)**. Discard the O-rings – new ones must be used.
4 Unscrew the timing inspection cap and the crankshaft end cap from the alternator cover on the right-hand side of the engine **(see illustration)**. Check the condition of the cap O-rings and replace them with new ones if necessary.
5 To check the valve clearances the engine must be turned to position the piston at top dead centre (TDC) on its compression stroke so that the valves are closed.
6 Turn the engine anti-clockwise using a

suitable socket on the alternator rotor nut until the index line on the rotor (which on YBR models comes just before the ignition timing H mark – do not get them mixed up) aligns with the pointer inside the inspection hole, and the index line on the camshaft sprocket is above the centre of the sprocket and aligned with the pointer on the top of the cylinder head **(see illustrations)**. There should now be

some freeplay in each rocker arm (i.e. they are not contacting the valve stem). If the index line on the sprocket is below the centre, rotate the engine anti-clockwise one full turn (360°) until the index line on the rotor again aligns with the pointer inside the inspection hole – the index line on the sprocket will now be above the centre.
7 With the engine in this position, check the

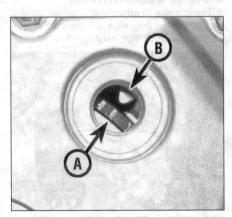

4.6b . . . until the line (A) on the rotor aligns with the pointer (B) . . .

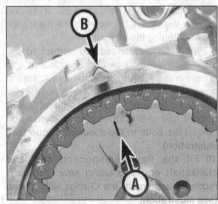

4.6c . . . and the line (A) on the camshaft sprocket aligns with the pointer (B)

4.7 Insert the feeler gauge between the base of the adjuster on the arm and the top of the valve stem as shown

4.8a Locknut (A) and adjuster (B) . . .

4.8b . . . turn the adjuster with the gauge in place until the gap is correct, then hold the adjuster while tightening the locknut

4.9a Fit each access cap using a new O-ring (arrowed) smeared with grease

4.9b Fit the sprocket cover using a new O-ring (arrowed) smeared with grease

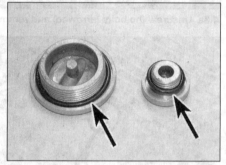

4.10 Fit the caps using new O-rings (arrowed) if required and smear them with grease

clearance on each valve by inserting a feeler gauge of the same thickness as the correct valve clearance (see Specifications) in the gap between the rocker arm and the valve stem **(see illustration)**. The intake valve is on the back of the cylinder head and the exhaust valve is on the front. The gauge should be a firm sliding fit – you should feel a slight drag when you pull the gauge out.

8 If the gap (clearance) is either too wide or too narrow, slacken the locknut on the adjuster in the rocker arm **(see illustration)**. Turn the adjuster as required using a very small spanner (Yamaha can supply a special tool, part No. 90890-01311), or a pair of pliers, until the gap is as specified and the feeler gauge is a sliding fit **(see illustration)**. Hold the adjuster still and tighten the locknut. Recheck the clearance after tightening the locknut.

9 When the clearances are correct fit the access caps using new O-rings smeared with grease and tighten them to the torque setting specified at the beginning of the Chapter **(see illustration)**. Fit the sprocket cover using a new O-ring smeared with grease and tighten the bolts to the specified torque **(see illustration)**.

10 Fit the timing inspection cap and crankshaft end cap using new O-rings if required, and smear the O-rings with grease **(see illustration)**.

11 Install the spark plug (Section 2). Check and adjust the idle speed (see Section 5).

5 Idle speed

Engine idle speed

1 The idle speed should be checked at the specified interval. It should also be checked and if necessary adjusted after the valve clearances have been adjusted. Make sure the air filter is clean (Section 3).

2 The engine should be at normal operating temperature, which is usually reached after 10 to 15 minutes of stop-and-go riding. Make sure the transmission is in neutral.

3 The idle speed adjuster is a screw located on the right-hand side of the carburettor or throttle body on YBR models and on

5.3a Idle speed adjuster (arrowed) – fuel injected YBR model

the left-hand side of the carburettor on XT models **(see illustrations)**. With the engine running, turn the screw until the engine idles at the speed specified at the beginning of the Chapter. Turn the screw clockwise to increase idle speed, and anti-clockwise to decrease it.

4 Snap the throttle open and shut a few times, then recheck the idle speed. If necessary, repeat the adjustment procedure. On completion check and adjust throttle cable freeplay (Section 7).

5 If a smooth, steady idle can't be achieved, and if not already done, check the spark plug, air filter element and valve clearances (Sections 2, 3 and 4). Additionally on fuel injected models, if there is a problem with cold starting or fast running when warm, check the fast idle solenoid (FID) – see Chapter 3B.

5.3b Idle speed adjuster (arrowed) – XT models

Exhaust gas CO content

6 Yamaha specify that on carburettor-engined models the exhaust gas CO content is measured. This will need to be done by a dealer equipped with the appropriate exhaust gas analyser. If found to be outside of the figure given in the Specifications at the beginning of this Chapter, adjustment can be made via the pilot air screw. Contributing problems could be an air leak in the intake duct between the carburettor and the cylinder head, or a problem within the carburettor itself – refer to Fault Finding at the end of the book, and to Chapter 3A.

6 Fuel system

Warning: Petrol (gasoline) is extremely flammable, so take extra precautions when you work on any part of the fuel system. Don't smoke or allow open flames or bare light bulbs near the work area, and don't work in a garage where a natural gas-type appliance is present. If you spill any fuel on your skin, rinse it off immediately with soap and water. When you perform any kind of work on the fuel system, wear safety glasses and have a fire extinguisher suitable for a Class B type fire (flammable liquids) on hand.

1 Remove the fuel tank (see Chapter 3A or 3B). Check all the hoses from the fuel tank, the carburettor or throttle body and the air filter housing, and on YBR models the air induction system (see Section 17), for signs of cracks, leaks, deterioration or damage. In particular check that there are no leaks from the fuel hose or hose unions. Make sure each hose is secure on its union at each end and retained by a clamp. Replace any hose that is cracked or deteriorated with a new one – refer to Chapter 3A or 3B if required.

2 Check the fuel tank for signs of fuel leakage. If the joint between the fuel tap (2005 and 2006 YBR models) or valve (XT models) or the fuel pump (2007-on YBR models) and the tank is leaking, ensure the fasteners are tight; if the leak persists remove the tap, valve or pump and fit a new seal (see Chapter 3A or 3B).

3 On 2005 and 2006 YBR models and XT models inspect the carburettor, particularly around the float chamber on the bottom, for signs of leakage. If there are any leaks, remove the carburettor and fit new seals (see Chapter 3A).

4 On 2007-on YBR models inspect the throttle body and injector for signs of leakage. Remove the injector and fit new seals if necessary (see Chapter 3B). Cleaning of the fuel strainer inside the tank is also advised after a particularly high mileage has been covered, although no interval is specified. It is also necessary if fuel starvation is suspected. Remove the fuel pump from the tank to access the strainer (see Chapter 3B). Flush the strainer through. Check the gauze for damage.

5 On 2005 and 2006 YBR models, make sure the fuel tap is OFF, then unscrew the filter holder on the bottom of the tap. Drain any residual fuel. Check the condition of the filter and replace it with a new one if necessary. Cleaning of the fuel tap strainer inside the tank is also advised after a particularly high mileage has been covered, although no interval is specified. It is also necessary if fuel starvation is suspected and the filter is good. Remove the fuel tap from the tank to access the strainer (see Chapter 3A). Flush the strainer through. Check the gauze for damage and replace it with a new one if necessary.

7 Throttle and choke cables

Throttle cable

Note: On 2010-on YBR models, a throttle opening and a throttle closing cable are fitted. Adjustment is made to the opening cable as described, the closing cable is not adjustable.

1 With the engine off, make sure the throttle grip rotates smoothly and freely from fully closed to fully open with the front wheel turned at various angles. The grip should return automatically from fully open to fully closed when released.

2 If the throttle sticks, this is probably due to a cable fault. Remove the cable (see Chapter 3A or 3B) and lubricate it (see Section 13). Check

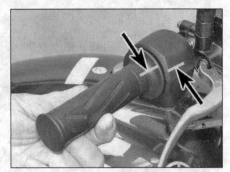

7.4 Throttle cable freeplay is measured in terms of twistgrip rotation

that the inner cable slides freely and easily in the outer cable. If not, replace the cable with a new one.

3 With the cable removed, make sure the throttle twistgrip rotates freely on the handlebar – dirt combined with a lack of lubrication can cause the action to be stiff. If necessary, on 2005 and 2006 YBR-ED models and on Custom models remove the handlebar end-weight, then on all models slide the twistgrip off the handlebar. Clean any old grease from the bar and the inside of the tube. Smear some new grease of the specified type onto the bar, then refit the twistgrip. When re-fitting the end-weight on those YBR models, make sure there is a 1 to 2 mm gap between the grip and the weight. Install the cable, making sure it is correctly routed (see Chapter 3A or 3B). If this fails to improve the operation of the throttle, the cable must be replaced with a new one. Note that in very rare cases the fault could lie in the carburettor or throttle body (see Chapter 3A or 3B).

4 With the throttle operating smoothly, and after the idle speed has been checked and if necessary adjusted (Section 5), check for a small amount of freeplay in the cable, measured in terms of the amount of twistgrip rotation before the throttle opens, and compare the amount to that listed in this Chapter's Specifications **(see illustration)**. If it's incorrect, adjust the cable to correct it as follows.

5 Adjust freeplay using the adjuster in the upper (handlebar) end of the cable **(see illustrations)**. Slide the rubber boot off the adjuster. Loosen the locknut and turn

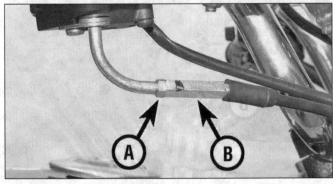

7.5a Adjuster locknut (A) and adjuster (B) – early YBR and all Custom models

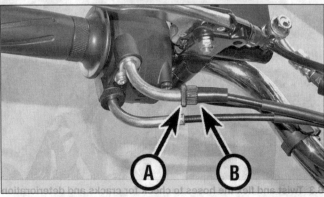

7.5b Adjuster locknut (A) and adjuster (B) – 2010-on YBR models

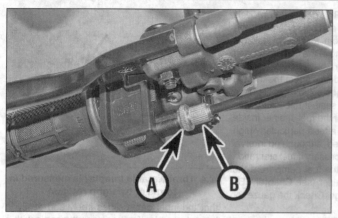

7.5c Adjuster locknut (A) and adjuster (B) – XT models

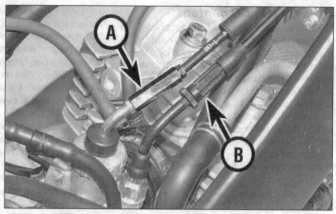

7.6 Throttle cable adjuster (A), choke cable adjuster (B) – carburettor models

the adjuster in or out as required until the specified amount of freeplay is obtained (see this Chapter's Specifications), then retighten the locknut and fit the boot.

6 On carburettor models there is another adjuster in the cable just before it reaches the carburettor **(see illustration)** – if necessary remove the fuel tank (see Chapter 3A), then reset this in the same way to obtain the correct amount of freeplay.

7 If the cable cannot be adjusted as specified, replace it with a new one (see Chapter 3A or 3B). Check that the throttle twistgrip operates smoothly and snaps shut quickly when released.

⚠️ *Warning: Turn the handlebars all the way through their travel with the engine idling. Idle speed should not change. If it does, the cables may be routed incorrectly. Correct this condition before riding the bike.*

Choke cable – XT models

8 With the engine off, make sure the choke lever moves smoothly and freely.

9 If it is stiff or stuck, this is probably due to a cable fault. Remove the cable (see Chapter 3A) and lubricate it (see Section 13). Check that the inner cable slides freely and easily in the outer cable. If not, replace the cable with a new one.

10 If the choke is still stiff or stuck with a new or lubricated cable, the fault is in the plunger in the carburettor. Remove the plunger for inspection (see Chapter 3A).

11 Check for a small amount of freeplay in the lever before the choke opens. If there is none the choke could be permanently on, and if there is too much the choke might not open enough to be effective. If necessary remove the fuel tank to access the adjuster (see Chapter 3A). Loosen the locknut and turn the adjuster in or out as required until there is a small amount of freeplay then retighten the locknut and install the fuel tank **(see illustration 7.6)**.

8 Brake system

Brake system check

1 A routine general check of the brake system will ensure that any problems are discovered and remedied before the rider's safety is jeopardised.

2 Make sure all brake component fasteners are tight. Check the brake lever and pedal for improper or rough action, excessive play, bends, and other damage. Replace any

damaged parts with new ones (see Chapter 6). Clean and lubricate the lever and pedal pivots if their action is stiff or rough (see Section 13).

3 Check the brake pads and shoes for wear (see below), and make sure the fluid level in the reservoir(s) is correct (see *Pre-ride checks*). Look for leaks at the hose connections and check for cracks in the hoses and unions **(see illustration)**. If the lever or pedal is spongy, bleed the brakes (see Chapter 6).

4 Make sure the brake light comes on when the front brake lever is pulled in. If not, first check the bulb (see Chapter 8). If the bulb is good, check the switch (see Chapter 8) – the switch is not adjustable.

5 Make sure the brake light is activated just before the rear brake takes effect. On YBR models the switch is adjustable – if adjustment is necessary, remove the right-hand side cover (see Chapter 7). Hold the switch and turn the adjuster ring on the switch body until the brake light is activated when required **(see illustration)**. If the brake light comes on too late or not at all, turn the ring clockwise (when looked at from the top) so the switch threads out of the bracket. If the brake light comes on too soon or is permanently on, turn the ring anti-clockwise so the switch threads into the bracket. If the switch doesn't operate the brake light, check it (see Chapter 8).

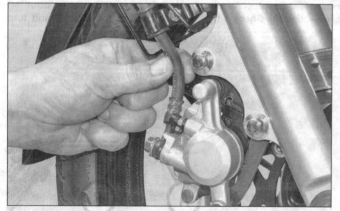

8.3 Twist and flex the hoses to check for cracks and deterioration

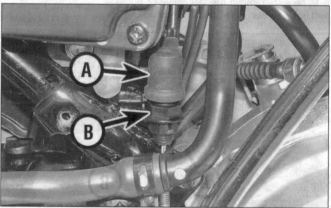

8.5 Hold the rear brake light switch body (A) and turn the adjuster ring (B) as required

8.6 Measure the amount of brake pedal freeplay

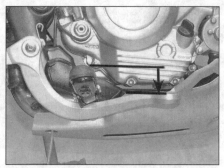

8.7a Check the height of the rear brake pedal

8.7b Slacken the locknut (A) and turn the pushrod (B) to adjust pedal height

On XT models the switch is actuated hydraulically and cannot be adjusted. If the brake light fails to operate properly, and the bulb is good, check the switch (see Chapter 8).

6 On YBR models check the amount of freeplay in the rear brake pedal before the brake comes on – it should be as specified at the beginning of the Chapter **(see illustration)**. If not adjust it by turning the adjuster nut on the end of the brake rod as required until the freeplay is correct **(see illustration 1.9a)**. Refer to Step 12 and now check the amount of brake shoe wear. After adjustment check that there is no brake drag, then adjust the rear brake light switch (Step 5).

7 On XT models the height of the rear brake pedal in relation to the top of the footrest should

be as specified at the beginning of the Chapter, or to suit the rider's preference if required **(see illustration)**. To adjust the height slacken the clevis locknut on the master cylinder pushrod, then turn the pushrod using a spanner on the hex at the top of the rod until the pedal is at the desired height **(see illustration)**. On completion tighten the locknut.

Brake pad wear check

8 On 2005 and 2006 YBR models remove the inspection plug from the front brake caliper.
9 On all models, visually check the amount of friction material remaining on each pad **(see illustrations)**. Yamaha specify a minimum thickness of 1 mm. **Note:** On YBR models the pads have wear indicator grooves. The pads have worn to their limit when the grooves are

no longer visible. Replace the pads with new ones before they have worn to the minimum thickness (see Chapter 6). On twin piston calipers also check that the pads are wearing evenly – uneven wear is indicative of a sticking piston, in which case the caliper should be overhauled (see Chapter 6).
10 If the pads are dirty or if you are in doubt as to the amount of friction material remaining, remove them for inspection (see Chapter 6). Yamaha specify a minimum thickness of 1 mm. If the pads are excessively worn, check the brake disc (see Chapter 6).

Brake shoe wear check – YBR models

11 Make sure the amount of rear brake pedal freeplay is correct (Step 6).
12 Apply the brake and check the position of the wear indicator on the top of the brake arm in relation to the wear limit line on the brake plate **(see illustration)**. If the indicator has reached the limit line replace the brake shoes with new ones (see Chapter 6). With the shoes removed check the drum as described in Chapter 6. Note that the larger triangular pointer on the brake plate indicates the extent of drum wear, but is only effective with new shoes – with the brake pedal freeplay correctly set (Step 6), and with new shoes, if the pointer on the arm aligns with the triangle the drum is worn (but back this up by measurement as in Chapter 6 before ever buying a new wheel).

8.9a Front brake pad friction material (arrowed) – 2008 YBR model

8.9b Front brake pad friction material (arrowed) – 2009 XT-X model

8.9c Rear brake pad friction material (arrowed) – XT models

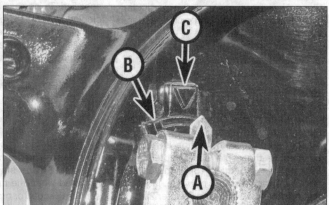

8.12 Brake shoe wear indicator (A) and limit line (B). The pointer (C) is the brake drum wear indicator

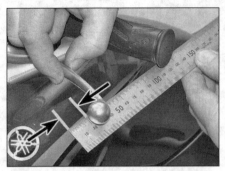

9.3 Measure the amount of freeplay at the clutch lever end as shown

9.4 Slacken the lockring and turn the adjuster in or out as required

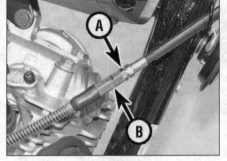

9.6 Slacken the locknut (A) and turn the adjuster (B) in or out as required

Brake fluid change

13 The brake fluid should be changed at the prescribed interval or whenever a master cylinder or caliper overhaul is carried out. Refer to Chapter 6, Section 11 for details. Ensure that all the old fluid is pumped from the hydraulic system and that the level in the fluid reservoir is checked and the brakes tested before riding the motorcycle. For 2010-on YBR125 ED models, Yamaha recommends that the master cylinder and caliper seals are renewed at the same service interval.

Brake hoses

14 The hoses will deteriorate with age and should be replaced with new ones regardless of their apparent condition (see Chapter 6).
15 Always replace the banjo union sealing washers with new ones when fitting new hoses. Refill the system with new brake fluid and bleed the system as described in Chapter 6.

Brake caliper and master cylinder seals

16 Brake system seals will deteriorate over a period of time and lose their effectiveness, leading to sticky operation of the brake master cylinder or the piston(s) in the brake caliper, or fluid loss. On 2010-on YBR-ED models, Yamaha recommends that the master cylinder and caliper internal components are renewed every two years. No interval is specified for other models but is advised after a high mileage has been covered and particularly if fluid leakage or a sticking caliper action is apparent (see Chapter 6).

9 Clutch

1 Check that the clutch lever operates smoothly and easily.
2 If the clutch lever operation is heavy or stiff, remove the cable (see Chapter 2) and lubricate it (see Section 13). If the cable is still stiff, replace it with a new cable (see Chapter 2). Install the lubricated or new cable (see Chapter 2).
3 With the cable operating smoothly, check that it is correctly adjusted. Periodic adjustment is necessary to compensate for wear in the clutch

plates and stretch of the cable. Check that the amount of freeplay at the clutch lever end is within the range specified at the beginning of the Chapter **(see illustration)**.
4 If adjustment is required, pull the rubber boot off the adjuster in the lever bracket. Loosen the adjuster lockring, then turn the adjuster in or out until the required amount of freeplay is obtained **(see illustration)**. To increase freeplay, thread the adjuster into the lever bracket. To reduce freeplay, thread the adjuster out of the bracket.
5 Make sure that the slot in the adjuster and the lockring, are not aligned with the slot in the lever bracket – these slots are to allow removal of the cable, and if they are all aligned while the bike is in use a there is a possibility that the cable could jump out. Also make sure the adjuster is not threaded too far out of the bracket so that it is only held by a few threads – this will leave it unstable and the threads could be damaged. Tighten the lockring on completion, then refit the rubber boot.
6 On YBR models, if all the adjustment has been taken up at the lever, thread the adjuster all the way into the bracket to give the maximum amount of freeplay, then back it out one turn – this resets the adjuster to its start point. Now set the correct amount of freeplay using the adjuster located near the top of the engine on the right-hand side **(see illustration)**. Slacken the locknut, then turn the adjuster as required until the freeplay at the lever end is as specified. To increase freeplay turn the adjuster clockwise, and to reduce freeplay turn the adjuster anti-clockwise. Tighten the locknut on completion. Subsequent adjustments can now be made using the lever adjuster only.

10 Sidestand, centrestand and starter safety circuit

1 Check the stand springs for damage and distortion. The springs must be capable of retracting the stand fully and holding it retracted when the motorcycle is in use. If a spring is sagged or broken it must be replaced with a new one.
2 Lubricate the stand pivot regularly (see Section 13).

3 Check the stand and its mount for bends and cracks. Stands can often be repaired by welding.
4 On 2005 and 2006 YBR models the starter safety circuit, comprising the neutral switch and the clutch switch, prevents the engine from being started unless it is in neutral, or if it is in gear unless the clutch lever is pulled in. Check the circuit is working correctly.
5 On 2007-on YBR models and all XT models the starter safety circuit, comprising the neutral switch, the clutch switch and the sidestand switch, prevents the engine from being started unless it is in neutral, or if it is in gear unless the clutch lever is pulled in and the sidestand is up. Check the circuit is working correctly.
6 If the circuit does not operate as described, check the neutral switch, the clutch switch, the sidestand switch (where fitted), the circuit diode, and the wiring between them (see Chapter 8).

11 Suspension

1 The suspension components must be maintained in top operating condition to ensure rider safety. Loose, worn or damaged suspension parts decrease the motorcycle's stability and control.

Front suspension check

2 While standing alongside the motorcycle, apply the front brake and push on the handlebars to compress the forks several times **(see illustration)**. See if they move

11.2 Compress and release the front suspension

11.8 Checking for play in the swingarm bushes

11.9 Checking for play in the rear shock mountings

up-and-down smoothly without binding. If binding is felt, the forks should be disassembled and inspected (see Chapter 5).

3 Inspect the fork inner tubes for scratches, corrosion and pitting which will cause premature seal failure – if the damage is excessive, new tubes should be fitted (see Chapter 5).

4 Inspect the area above the dust seal for signs of oil leakage, then carefully lever the seal up using a flat-bladed screwdriver and inspect the area around the fork seal. If leakage is evident, the seals must be replaced with new ones (see Chapter 5). If there is evidence of corrosion between the seal retaining ring and its groove in the fork outer tube spray the area with a penetrative lubricant, otherwise the ring will be difficult to remove if needed. Press the dust seal back into the top of the fork outer tube on completion.

5 Check the tightness of the fork clamp bolts in the yokes, and on YBR models the fork top bolts, to be sure none have worked loose, referring to the torque settings specified at the beginning of Chapter 5.

Rear suspension check

6 Inspect the rear shock absorber(s) for fluid leakage and tightness of the mountings. If leakage is found, the shock must be replaced with a new one (see Chapter 5).

7 With the aid of an assistant to support the bike, compress the rear suspension several times. It should move up-and-down freely without binding. If any binding is felt, the worn or faulty component must be identified and checked (see Chapter 5). The problem could be due to either the shock absorber(s) or the swingarm pivot.

8 Support the motorcycle on its centrestand (YBR models) or on an auxiliary stand (XT models) so that the rear wheel is off the ground. Grab the swingarm and rock it from side-to-side – there should be no discernible movement at the rear **(see illustration)**. If there's a little movement or a slight clicking can be heard, inspect the tightness of the

swingarm and shock absorber mounting bolts and nuts, referring to the torque settings specified at the beginning of Chapter 5, and re-check for movement.

9 Next, grasp the top of the rear wheel and pull it upwards – there should be no discernible freeplay before the shock absorber(s) compresses **(see illustration)**. Any freeplay felt in either check indicates worn bushes in the shock absorber or swingarm. The worn components must be identified and replaced with new ones (see Chapter 5).

10 To make an accurate assessment of the swingarm bushes, remove the rear wheel (see Chapter 6) and the bolt securing the shock absorber(s) to the swingarm (see Chapter 5). Grasp the rear of the swingarm with one hand and place your other hand at the junction of the swingarm and the frame. Try to move the rear of the swingarm from side-to-side. Any wear (play) in the bushes should be felt as movement between the swingarm and the frame at the front. If there is any play the swingarm will be felt to move forward and backward at the front (not from side-to-side). If there is any play in the swingarm remove it for inspection (see Chapter 5).

Front fork oil change

11 Although there is no set interval for

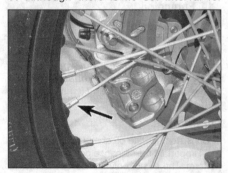

12.1 Turn the adjuster (arrowed) to set spoke tension

changing the fork oil, note that the oil will degrade over a period of time and lose its damping qualities. Refer to Chapter 5 for details of fork removal, oil draining and refilling. The forks do not need to be completely disassembled to change the oil.

Rear suspension lubrication

12 Remove the swingarm, clean and re-grease the pivot bolt, spacers and bushes (see Chapter 5).

12 Wheels, wheel bearings and tyres

Wire spoke wheels

1 Visually check the spokes for damage and corrosion. A broken or bent spoke must be replaced with a new one immediately because the load taken by it will be transferred to adjacent spokes which may in turn fail. Check the tension in each spoke by tapping each one lightly with a screwdriver and noting the sound produced – each should make the same sound of the correct pitch. Properly tensioned spokes will make a sharp pinging sound, loose ones will produce a lower pitch dull sound and tight ones will be higher pitched. If a spoke needs adjustment turn the adjuster at the rim using a spoke adjustment tool or an open-ended spanner **(see illustration)**.

2 Unevenly tensioned spokes will promote rim misalignment – refer to information on wheel runout in Chapter 6 and seek the advice of a Yamaha dealer or wheel building specialist if the wheel needs realigning, which it may well do if many spokes are unevenly tensioned. Check front and rear wheel alignment as described in Chapter 6. Check that any wheel balance weights are fixed firmly to the wheel rim. If you suspect that a weight has fallen off, have the wheel rebalanced by a motorcycle tyre specialist.

Cast wheels

3 Cast wheels are virtually maintenance free, but they should be kept clean and checked periodically for cracks and other damage. Also check the wheel runout and alignment (see Chapter 6). Never attempt to repair damaged cast wheels; they must be replaced with new ones if damaged. Check that any wheel balance weights are fixed firmly to the wheel rim. If you suspect that a weight has fallen off, have the wheel rebalanced by a motorcycle tyre specialist.

Tyres

4 Check the tyre condition, pressure and tread depth thoroughly – see *Pre-ride checks*.
5 Make sure the valve cap is in place and tight. Check the valve for signs of damage. If tyre deflation occurs and it is not due to a slow puncture the valve core may be loose or it could be leaking past the seal – remove the cap and make sure the core is tight; if it is tight then it could be leaking – unscrew the core from the valve housing using a core removal tool and thread a new one in its place.

Wheel bearings

6 Wheel bearings will wear over a considerable mileage and should be checked periodically to avoid handling problems.
7 Support the motorcycle upright using an auxiliary stand so that the wheel being examined is off the ground. When checking the front wheel bearings turn the handlebars to full lock on one side so you have something to push against. Check for any play in the bearings by pushing and pulling the wheel against the hub **(see illustration)**. Also rotate the wheel and check that it turns smoothly and without any grating noises.
8 If any play is detected in the hub, or if the wheel does not rotate smoothly (and this is not due to brake or transmission drag), remove the wheel and inspect the bearings for wear or damage (see Chapter 6).

13 General lubrication

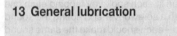

Pivot points

1 Since the controls, cables and various other components of a motorcycle are exposed to the elements, they should be checked and lubricated periodically to ensure safe and trouble-free operation.
2 The footrest pivots, clutch and brake lever pivots, brake pedal pivot and sidestand and centrestand (where fitted) pivots should be lubricated frequently. In order for the lubricant to be applied where it will do the most good, the component should be disassembled (see Chapters 5 and 6). The lubricant recommended by Yamaha for each application is listed at the beginning of the Chapter. If an aerosol lubricant is being used, it can be applied to the pivot joint

12.7 Checking for play in the front wheel bearings

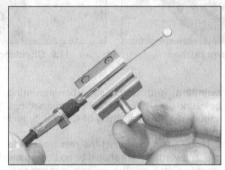

13.3b . . . and tighten the screw to seal it in . . .

gaps and will usually work its way into the areas where friction occurs, so less disassembly of the component is needed (however it is always better to do so and clean off all corrosion, dirt and old lubricant first). If motor oil or light grease is being used, apply it sparingly as it may attract dirt (which could cause the controls to bind or wear at an accelerated rate).

Cables

Special tool: *A cable lubricating adapter is necessary for this procedure* **(see illustration 13.3c)**.
3 To lubricate the cables, disconnect the relevant cable at its upper end, then lubricate it with a pressure adapter and aerosol lubricant **(see illustrations)**. See Chapter 3A or 3B for throttle and choke cable removal procedures, and Chapter 2 for the clutch cable.

14 Engine oil

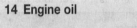

 Warning: Be careful when draining the oil, as the exhaust pipe, the engine, and the oil itself can cause severe burns.

Oil change

1 Consistent routine oil changes are the single most important maintenance procedure you can perform. The oil not only lubricates the internal parts of the engine, transmission and clutch, but it also acts as a coolant, a cleaner, a sealant,

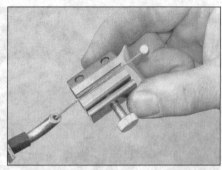

13.3a Fit the cable into the adapter . . .

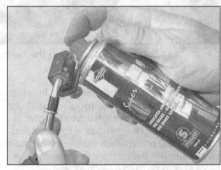

13.3c . . . then apply the lubricant using the nozzle provided inserted in the hole in the adapter

and a protector. Because of these demands, the oil takes a terrific amount of abuse and should be replaced as specified with new oil of the recommended grade and type.

> **HAYNES HiNT**
>
> *Saving a little money on the difference in cost between a good oil and a cheap oil won't pay off if the engine is damaged.*

2 Before changing the oil, warm up the engine so the oil will drain easily. Place the bike on its sidestand on level ground. The oil drain plug is on the left-hand side of the engine. On XT models remove the sump guard (see Chapter 7).
3 Position a clean drain tray below the engine. Unscrew the oil filler cap to vent the crankcase and to act as a reminder that there is no oil in the engine **(see illustration)**.

14.3 Unscrew the oil filler cap to act as a vent

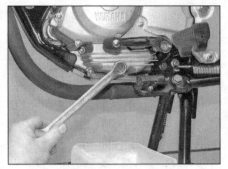

14.4a Unscrew the oil drain plug . . .

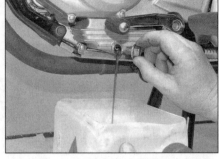

14.4b . . . and allow the oil to completely drain

4 Unscrew the oil drain plug and allow the oil to flow into the drain tray **(see illustrations)**. Check the condition of the sealing washer on the drain plug and replace it with a new one if it is damaged or worn – it is highly advisable to use a new one whatever the condition of the old one. You may have to cut the old one off, depending on the type fitted.

5 When the oil has completely drained, fit the plug into the engine, preferably using a new sealing washer, and tighten it to the torque setting specified at the beginning of the Chapter **(see illustration)**. Do not overtighten it as the threads in the engine are easily damaged.

6 Refill the engine to the proper level using the recommended type and amount of oil (see *Pre-ride checks*). With the motorcycle vertical, the oil level should lie between the upper and lower level lines on the dipstick (see *Pre-ride checks*). Check the condition of the O-ring on the filler cap and replace it with a new one if it is damaged or worn. Install the filler cap **(see illustration 14.3)**.

7 Start the engine and let it run for two or three minutes. Shut it off, wait a few minutes, then check the oil level. If necessary, add more oil to bring the level close to the upper line, but do not go above it.

8 Check around the drain plug for leaks. If a leak is evident and a new washer was not used, you will have to drain the oil again and fit a new washer. If a new washer was used then make sure the plug is tightened to the correct torque setting using a torque wrench. If one is

not available tighten the plug a little more but take great care not to overtighten it and strip the threads – if in doubt ask a dealer to check using a torque wrench. On XT models install the sump guard (see Chapter 7).

9 The old oil drained from the engine cannot be re-used and should be disposed of properly. Check with your local refuse disposal company, disposal facility or environmental agency to see whether they will accept the used oil for recycling. Don't pour used oil into drains or onto the ground.

> **HAYNES HINT** *Check the old oil carefully – if it is very metallic coloured, then the engine is experiencing wear from break-in (new engine) or from insufficient lubrication. If there are flakes or chips of metal in the oil, then something is drastically wrong internally and the engine will have to be disassembled for inspection and repair. If there are pieces of fibre-like material in the oil, the clutch is experiencing excessive wear and should be checked.*

Oil strainer

10 After a significant mileage has been covered, or if there has been internal engine damage or there is evidence of oil sludge after draining the oil (see **Haynes Hint**), the strainer should be removed and cleaned. Drain the engine oil (see Steps 2 to 5).

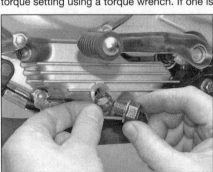

14.5 Install the drain plug using a new sealing washer and tighten it to the specified torque

14.12 Withdraw the strainer and clean the mesh

11 Remove the clutch cover (see Chapter 2).
12 Withdraw the strainer from its slot in the bottom of the engine, noting which way round it fits **(see illustration)**.
13 Wash the strainer in solvent making sure all debris is removed from the mesh. Check the mesh for holes and damage and replace it with a new one if necessary.
14 Coat the rubber rim of the strainer with clean oil, then slide it into the grooves in its chamber, making sure the thinner edge goes in first.
15 Install the clutch cover (see Chapter 2). Refill the engine with oil (see Steps 6 to 8).

15 Nuts and bolts

1 Since vibration of the machine tends to loosen fasteners, all nuts, bolts, screws, etc. should be periodically checked for proper tightness.
2 Pay particular attention to the following, referring to the relevant Chapter:
   Spark plug (Chapter 1).
   Engine oil drain plug (Chapter 1).
   Lever and pedal bolts (Chapter 5).
   Footrest and stand bolts (Chapter 5).
   Engine mounting bolts/nuts (Chapter 2).
   Shock absorber bolts/nut; swingarm pivot bolt/nut (Chapter 5).
   Handlebar clamp bolts (Chapter 5).
   Front fork clamp bolts (top and bottom yoke), and fork top bolts on YBR models (Chapter 5).
   Steering stem nut (Chapter 5).
   Front axle nut on YBR models, axle bolt on XT models (Chapter 6).
   Rear axle nut (Chapter 6).
   Front and rear sprocket bolts/nuts (Chapter 6).
   Brake caliper and master cylinder mounting bolts (Chapter 6).
   Brake hose banjo bolts and caliper bleed valves (Chapter 6).
   Brake disc bolts (Chapter 6).
   Exhaust system bolts/nuts (Chapter 3A and 3B).
3 If a torque wrench is available, use it along with the torque settings given at the beginning of this and other Chapters.

16 Steering head bearings

Freeplay check and adjustment

1 Steering head bearings can become dented, rough or loose during normal use of the machine. In extreme cases, worn or loose steering head bearings can cause steering wobble – a condition that is potentially dangerous.

16.4 Checking for play in the steering head bearings

16.7a Slacken the fork clamp bolt (arrowed) on each side . . .

16.7b . . . then unscrew the steering stem nut . . .

Check

2 Raise the front wheel off the ground using an auxiliary stand placed under the engine. Always make sure that the bike is properly supported and secure.

3 Point the front wheel straight-ahead and slowly move the handlebars from lock to lock. Any dents or roughness in the bearing races will be felt and if the bearings are too tight the bars will not move smoothly and freely. Again point the wheel straight-ahead, and tap the front of the wheel to one side. The wheel should 'fall' under its own weight to the limit of its lock, indicating that the bearings are not too tight (take into account the restriction that cables and wiring may have). Check for similar movement to the other side.

4 Next, grasp the bottom of the forks and gently pull and push them forward and backward **(see illustration)**. Any looseness or freeplay in the steering head bearings will be felt as front-to-rear movement of the forks. If play is felt, adjust the bearings as described below.

> **HAYNES HINT** *Make sure you are not mistaking any movement between the bike and stand, or between the stand and the ground, for freeplay in the bearings. Do not pull and push the forks too hard – a gentle movement is all that is needed.*

Adjustment – YBR models

5 As a precaution, remove the fuel tank (see Chapter 3A or 3B) – though not actually necessary, this will prevent the possibility of damage should a tool slip.

6 Remove the instrument cluster (see Chapter 8). Displace the handlebars from the top yoke and support them clear on some rag (see Chapter 5).

7 Slacken fork clamp bolts in the top yoke **(see illustration)**. Unscrew the steering stem nut and remove it along with its washer **(see illustration)**.

8 Gently ease the top yoke upwards off the fork tubes and position it clear, using a rag to protect the tank or other components **(see illustration)**.

9 Remove the tabbed lock washer, noting how it fits **(see illustration)**. Unscrew and

remove the locknut, using either a C-spanner, a peg spanner or a drift located in one of the notches if required – though it should only be finger-tight **(see illustration)**. Remove the rubber washer **(see illustration)**.

10 To adjust the bearings as specified by Yamaha, a special service tool (Pt. No. 90890-01403) and a torque wrench are required. If the tool is available, first slacken the adjuster nut, then tighten it to the initial torque setting specified at the beginning of the Chapter, making sure the torque wrench arm is at 90° to the tool arm **(see illustration)**. Now slacken the nut a 1/4 turn, then tighten it to the final torque setting specified. Check that the steering is still able to move freely from side to side, but that all freeplay is eliminated.

11 If the Yamaha tool is not available, use a C-spanner located in one of the notches to slacken the adjuster nut slightly until pressure

16.8 . . . and lift the yoke off the forks

16.9a Remove the lockwasher . . .

16.9b . . . the locknut . . .

16.9c . . . and the rubber washer

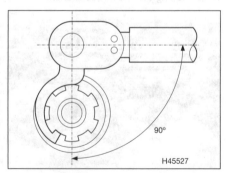

16.10 Setting the steering head bearing adjuster nut using the Yamaha tool – YBR models

16.11 Using a C-spanner to tighten the head bearing adjuster nut

16.13a Make sure the rubber cap on the top of each side of the headlight bracket locates in the hole in the yoke (arrowed)

is just released, then tighten it until all freeplay is removed, then tighten it a little more **(see illustration)**. This pre-loads the bearings. Now slacken the nut, then tighten it again, setting it so that all freeplay is just removed, yet the steering is able to move freely from side to side. To do this tighten the nut only a little at a time, and after each tightening repeat the checks outlined above (Steps 2 to 4) until the bearings are correctly set. The object is to set the adjuster nut so that the bearings are under a very light loading, just enough to remove any freeplay.

Caution: Take great care not to apply excessive pressure because this will cause premature failure of the bearings.

12 With the bearings correctly adjusted, fit the rubber washer, then the locknut **(see illustrations 16.9c and b)**. Tighten the locknut finger-tight, then tighten it further until its notches align with those in the adjuster nut. If necessary, counter-hold the adjuster nut and tighten the locknut using a C-spanner until the notches align, but make sure the adjuster nut does not turn as well. Fit the tabbed lock washer so that the tabs fit into the notches in both the locknut and adjuster nut **(see illustration 16.9a)**.

13 Fit the top yoke onto the steering stem, locating the rubber-capped tops of the headlight bracket in the holes in the underside

(see illustration). Fit the washer and steering stem nut and tighten the nut to the torque setting specified at the beginning of the Chapter **(see illustration)**. Now tighten both the fork clamp bolts to the specified torque setting **(see illustration 16.7a)**.

14 Install the handlebars (see Chapter 5) and the instrument cluster (see Chapter 8).

15 Check the bearing adjustment as described above and re-adjust if necessary.

16 Install the fuel tank if removed (see Chapter 3A or 3B).

Adjustment – XT models

17 As a precaution, remove the fuel tank (see Chapter 3A) – though not actually necessary, this will prevent the possibility of damage should a tool slip.

18 Slacken the fork clamp bolts in the top yoke **(see illustration 16.7a)**. Remove the plug from the steering stem nut, then slacken the nut **(see illustration)**.

19 Using a slim C-spanner or a suitable drift located in one of the notches in the adjuster nut under the top yoke, turn the adjuster nut, either clockwise to tighten the head bearings or anti-clockwise to loosen them, and only moving it a small amount at a time **(see illustration)**. After each small adjustment recheck the freeplay as described above (Steps 2 to 4), before making further

adjustments. The object is to set the adjuster nut so that the bearings are under a very light loading, just enough to remove any freeplay, but not so much that the steering does not move freely from side-to-side as described in the check procedure above.

Caution: Take great care not to apply excessive pressure because this will cause premature failure of the bearings.

20 If the bearings cannot be correctly adjusted, disassemble the steering head and check the bearings and races (see Chapter 5).

21 With the bearings correctly adjusted, tighten the steering stem nut to the torque setting specified at the beginning of the chapter. Tighten the fork clamp bolts to the specified torque. Fit the plug **(see illustration 16.18)**.

22 Check the bearing adjustment as described above and re-adjust if necessary.

23 Install the fuel tank if removed (see Chapter 3A).

Lubrication

24 Over a considerable time the grease in the bearings will be dispersed or will harden allowing the ingress of dirt and water.

25 The steering head should be disassembled periodically and the bearings cleaned and re-greased (see Chapter 6, Sections 9 and 10).

16.13b Tighten the nut to the specified torque

16.18 Remove the plug then slacken the nut (arrowed)

16.19 Steering head bearing adjuster nut (arrowed)

17 Air induction system

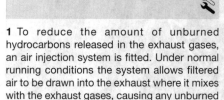

1 To reduce the amount of unburned hydrocarbons released in the exhaust gases, an air injection system is fitted. Under normal running conditions the system allows filtered air to be drawn into the exhaust where it mixes with the exhaust gases, causing any unburned particles of the fuel in the mixture to be burnt. This process changes a considerable amount of hydrocarbons and carbon monoxide into relatively harmless carbon dioxide and water.

2 On 2005 and 2006 YBR models the control valve, mounted under the fuel tank, is actuated by a vacuum taken off the intake duct between the carburettor and engine. Under normal operating conditions, the valve is open allowing air from the filter housing to be drawn through via a reed valve and into the air passage through the cylinder head to the exhaust port. The reed valve prevents the flow of exhaust gases back up the cylinder head passage and into the air filter housing. On early XT models the system is basically the same but the air is drawn directly into the top of the exhaust downpipe rather than through the cylinder head and into the exhaust port. Later XT models have the same system as the YBR **(see illustration)**.

3 On 2007-on YBR models air is drawn constantly from the air filter housing directly into the front of the exhaust silencer via a reed valve that prevents the flow of exhaust gases back into the air filter housing **(see illustration)**.

4 The system is not adjustable and requires little maintenance. Remove the fuel tank to access and inspect the components (see Chapter 3A or 3B). Check that the hoses are not kinked or pinched, are in good condition and are securely connected at each end. Replace any hoses that are cracked, split or generally deteriorated with new ones.

5 Refer to Chapter 3A or 3B for further information on the system and for checks if it is believed to be faulty.

18 Battery

Note: *A standard type battery is fitted to 2005 and 2006 YBR models, and a maintenance free (MF) battery is fitted to all other models. It is possible however that the standard battery on 2005 and 2006 YBR models has been replaced with a maintenance free (MF) battery at some point, in which case see Step 10 only. It is also possible that models fitted with an MF battery have had a standard battery fitted. The batteries are easy to distinguish – standard ones have removable caps across the top and electrolyte level lines (marked UPPER and LOWER or MAX and MIN), while MF batteries*

17.2 Air induction system control valve (arrowed) and hoses – later XT models

do not, and are usually marked MF on the front. Identify the type of battery fitted on your bike before proceeding.

Standard battery

1 On YBR models remove the left-hand side panel (see Chapter 7). On XT models remove the seat (see Chapter 7).

2 The electrolyte level is visible through the translucent battery case – it should be between the UPPER and LOWER level marks **(see illustration)**.

3 If the electrolyte is low, remove the battery (see Chapter 8). Remove the cell caps and fill each cell to the upper level mark with distilled water **(see illustration)**. Do not use tap water (except in an emergency), and do not overfill. The cell holes are quite small, so it may help to use a clean plastic squeeze bottle with a small spout to add the water. Fit the cell caps.

4 The battery case should be kept clean to prevent current leakage, which can discharge the battery over a period of time (especially when it sits unused). Wash the outside of the case with a solution of baking soda and water. Rinse the battery thoroughly, then dry it.

5 Look for cracks in the case and replace the battery if any are found. If acid has been spilled on the frame or battery box, neutralise it with a baking soda and water solution, dry it thoroughly, then touch up any damaged paint.

6 If the motorcycle sits unused for long periods of time, remove the battery and charge it once every month to six weeks (see Chapter 8).

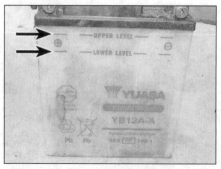

18.2 Make sure the level of the electrolyte is between the lines

17.3 Air induction system control valve (arrowed) and hoses – YBR models with FI

7 The condition of the battery can be assessed by measuring its specific gravity and open-circuit voltage (see Chapter 8).

8 Check the battery terminals and leads for corrosion. If corrosion is evident, clean the terminals and lead ends with a wire brush or knife and emery paper. Apply a thin coat of petroleum jelly (Vaseline) or a dedicated battery terminal spray to the connections to slow further corrosion.

9 Install the battery (see Chapter 8).

Maintenance free battery

Note: *Do not attempt to remove the battery caps to check the electrolyte level or battery specific gravity. Removal will damage the caps, resulting in electrolyte leakage and battery damage.*

10 On YBR models remove the left-hand side panel (see Chapter 7). On XT models remove the seat (see Chapter 7).

11 Check the battery terminals and leads for tightness and corrosion. If corrosion is evident, clean the terminals and lead ends with a wire brush or knife and emery paper. Apply a thin coat of petroleum jelly (Vaseline) or a dedicated battery terminal spray to the connections to slow further corrosion.

12 If the machine is not in regular use, disconnect the battery and give it a refresher charge every month to six weeks (see Chapter 8).

13 The condition of the battery can only be assessed by measuring its open-circuit voltage (see Chapter 8).

18.3 Top up using distilled water if necessary

Chapter 2
Engine, clutch and transmission

Contents

Degrees of difficulty

Easy, suitable for novice with little experience	**Fairly easy,** suitable for beginner with some experience	**Fairly difficult,** suitable for competent DIY mechanic	**Difficult,** suitable for experienced DIY mechanic	**Very difficult,** suitable for expert DIY or professional

Specifications

General

Type	Four-stroke single
Capacity	123.7 cc
Bore	54.0 mm
Stroke	54.0 mm
Compression ratio	10.0 to 1
Cylinder compression	170 psi (12 Bar)
Cooling system	Air cooled
Lubrication	Wet sump, trochoid pump
Clutch	Wet multi-plate
Transmission	Five-speed constant mesh
Final drive	Chain and sprockets

Camshafts and followers

Intake lobe height	
Standard	25.881 to 25.981 mm
Service limit (min)	25.851 mm
Exhaust lobe height	
Standard	25.841 to 25.941 mm
Service limit (min)	25.811 mm
Runout (max)	0.03 mm
Rocker arm bore diameter	
Standard	10.000 to 10.015 mm
Service limit (min)	10.030 mm
Rocker arm shaft diameter	
Standard	9.981 to 9.991 mm
Service limit (min)	9.95 mm
Rocker arm-to-shaft clearance	
Standard	0.009 to 0.034 mm
Service limit (min)	0.080 mm

Cylinder head

Warpage (max)	
2005 to 2009 YBR-ED models, all YBR Custom models	0.05 mm
2010-on YBR-ED and all XT models	0.03 mm

Valves, guides and springs

Valve clearances	see Chapter 1
Stem diameter	
Intake valve	
Standard	4.975 to 4.990 mm
Service limit (min)	
2005 to 2009 YBR-ED, all YBR Custom and XT models	4.945 mm
2010-on YBR-ED models	4.950 mm
Exhaust valve	
Standard	4.960 to 4.975 mm
Service limit (min)	
2005 to 2009 YBR-ED, all YBR Custom and XT models	4.930 mm
2010-on YBR-ED models	4.935 mm
Guide bore diameter – intake and exhaust valves	
Standard	5.000 to 5.012 mm
Service limit (max)	
2005 to 2009 YBR-ED, all YBR Custom and XT models	5.045 mm
2010-on YBR-ED models	5.042 mm
Stem-to-guide clearance	
Intake valve	
Standard	0.010 to 0.037 mm
Service limit	0.08 mm
Exhaust valve	
Standard	0.025 to 0.052 mm
Service limit	0.10 mm
Valve stem runout (max)	0.010 mm
Head diameter	
Intake valve	25.9 to 26.1 mm
Exhaust valve	21.9 to 22.1 mm
Face width	
Intake valve	
2005 to 2009 YBR-ED, all YBR Custom and XT models	1.10 to 3.00 mm
2010-on YBR-ED models	1.40 to 3.00 mm
Exhaust valve	1.70 to 2.80 mm
Seat width (in cylinder head)	
Standard	0.9 to 1.1 mm
Service limit (max)	1.6 mm
Margin thickness	
Intake valve	0.4 to 0.8 mm
Exhaust valve	0.8 to 1.2 mm
Valve spring free length – intake and exhaust valves	
YBR models	
Standard	47.06 mm
Service limit (min)	44.71 mm
XT models	
Standard	38.78 mm
Service limit (min)	37.0 mm
Valve spring tilt (max)	
YBR models	2.1 mm
XT models	1.7 mm

Cylinder bore

YBR models	
Standard	54.024 to 54.056 mm
Service limit (max)	54.156 mm
XT models	
Standard	54.000 to 54.018 mm
Ovality (out-of-round) (max)	0.01 mm
Taper (max)	0.05 mm
Cylinder compression	
Standard	170.7 psi (12 Bar)
Maximum	191.2 psi (13.4 Bar)
Minimum	148.5 psi (10.4 Bar)

Piston

Piston diameter (measured 4.5 mm up from skirt, at 90° to piston pin axis)
YBR models . . . . 53.997 to 54.029 mm
XT models
   Standard . . . . 53.977 to 53.996 mm
   Oversize 2005 models* . . . . +0.5 and +1.0 mm
   Oversize 2006 and 2007 models* . . . . +0.25, +0.5, +0.75 and +1.0 mm
Piston-to-bore clearance
Standard
   YBR models . . . . 0.019 to 0.035 mm
   XT models . . . . 0.020 to 0.028 mm
   Service limit (min) . . . . 0.15 mm*
Piston pin diameter
   Standard . . . . 14.991 to 15.000 mm
   Service limit (min) . . . . 14.971 mm
Piston pin bore diameter in piston
   Standard . . . . 15.002 to 15.013 mm
   Service limit (max) . . . . 15.043 mm
Piston pin-to-piston pin bore clearance
YBR models
   Standard . . . . 0.002 to 0.022 mm
   Service limit . . . . 0.072 mm
XT models . . . . 0.009 to 0.013 mm

*On 2005 to 2007 XT models, if the piston-to-bore clearance exceeds the service limit, the cylinder can be rebored and an oversize piston and rings fitted. Check what sizes are available before the rebore. Following rebore, the oversize piston-to-bore clearance must be the same as the standard specification

Piston rings – YBR models

Ring end gap (installed)
Top ring
   Standard . . . . 0.15 to 0.30 mm
   Service limit (max)
      2005 to 2009 ED models and all Custom models . . . . 0.55 mm
      2010-on ED models . . . . 0.40 mm
Second ring
   Standard . . . . 0.30 to 0.45 mm
   Service limit (max)
      2005 to 2009 ED models and all Custom models . . . . 0.80 mm
      2010-on ED models . . . . 0.55 mm
Oil ring side-rail
   Standard . . . . 0.20 to 0.70 mm
Ring-to-groove clearance
Top ring
   Standard
      2005 to 2009 ED models and all Custom models . . . . 0.035 to 0.070 mm
      2010-on ED models . . . . 0.030 to 0.070 mm
   Service limit (max) . . . . 0.12 mm
Second ring
   Standard . . . . 0.020 to 0.060 mm
   Service limit (max) . . . . 0.12 mm

Piston rings – XT models

Ring end gap (installed)
Top and second rings
   Standard . . . . 0.15 to 0.30 mm
   Service limit (max) . . . . 0.40 mm
Oil ring side-rail
   Standard . . . . 0.20 to 0.70 mm
Ring-to-groove clearance
Top ring
   Standard . . . . 0.030 to 0.070 mm
   Service limit (max) . . . . 0.12 mm
Second ring
   Standard . . . . 0.020 to 0.060 mm
   Service limit (max) . . . . 0.12 mm

Clutch

Friction plates
    YBR models 4
    XT models. 5
Plain plates
    YBR models 3
    XT models. 4
Friction plate thickness
    Standard
        2005 to 2009 YBR-ED, all YBR Custom and XT models . . . . 2.92 to 3.08 mm
        2010-on YBR-ED models . . . . 3.0 mm
    Service limit (min) . . . . 2.80 mm
Plain plate thickness
    YBR models . . . . 1.6 mm
    XT models
        Standard. . . . . 1.05 to 1.35 mm
        Service limit (min) . . . . 1.0 mm
Plain plate warpage (max)
    2005 to 2009 YBR-ED, all YBR Custom models . . . . 0.20 mm
    2010-on YBR-ED models and all XT models . . . . 0.05 mm
Spring free length
    YBR models
        Standard. . . . . 29.30 mm
        Service limit (min) . . . . 27.84 mm
    XT models
        Standard. . . . . 31.0 mm
        Service limit (min) . . . . 29.0 mm

Oil pump

	Standard	Service limit (max)
Inner rotor tip-to-outer rotor clearance (max)		
YBR-ED 2005 to 2009 and all YBR Custom models	0.07 mm	0.15 mm
YBR-ED 2010-on models	Less than 0.15 mm	0.23 mm
XT models.	0.15 mm	0.20 mm
Outer rotor-to-body clearance		
YBR models	0.13 to 0.19 mm	0.26 mm
XT models.	0.06 to 0.10 mm	0.15 mm
Rotor end-float		
YBR models	0.06 to 0.10 mm	0.17 mm
XT models.	0.06 to 0.10 mm	0.15 mm

Transmission

Gear ratios (no. of teeth)
    Primary reduction . . . . 3.400 to 1 (68/20)
    Final reduction
        YBR-ED models . . . . 3.214 to 1 (45/14)
        YBR Custom models . . . . 3.071 to 1 (43/14)
        XT-R models . . . . 3.571 to 1 (50/14)
        XT-X models . . . . 3.429 to 1 (48/14)
    1st gear. . . . . 2.643 to 1 (37/14)
    2nd gear. . . . . 1.778 to 1 (32/18)
    3rd gear . . . . 1.316 to 1 (25/19)
    4th gear . . . . 1.045 to 1 (23/22)
    5th gear . . . . 0.875 to 1 (21/24)
Input shaft set length (see text)
    Manufacturer's method of measurement (to recessed face) . . . . 83.25 to 83.45 mm
    Our method of measurement (to outer rim) . . . . 85.55 to 85.75 mm
    Depth of recess . . . . 2.3 mm
Shaft runout (max) . . . . 0.03 mm

Crankshaft and connecting rod

Crankshaft runout (max). . . . . 0.03 mm
Crankshaft width (see text). . . . . 46.95 to 47.00 mm
Connecting rod big-end side clearance
    Standard. . . . . 0.15 to 0.45 mm
    Service limit (max) . . . . 0.80 mm
Connecting rod big-end radial clearance
    Standard. . . . . 0.010 to 0.021 mm
    Service limit (max) . . . . 0.05 mm

Torque settings

Air induction system pipe bolts	10 Nm
Cam chain tensioner blade bolt	10 Nm
Cam chain tensioner cap bolt	8 Nm
Cam chain tensioner mounting bolts	10 Nm
Camshaft/rocker shaft retainer bolt	10 Nm
Camshaft sprocket cover bolts	10 Nm
Camshaft sprocket bolt	
2005 to 2009 YBR-ED, all YBR Custom and XT models	20 Nm
2010-on YBR-ED models	26 Nm
Clutch cover bolts	10 Nm
Clutch nut	60 Nm
Clutch spring bolts	6 Nm
Crankcase bolts	10 Nm
Cylinder head 8 mm bolts	22 Nm
Cylinder head 6 mm bolts	10 Nm
Engine mounting bolt nuts	
YBR models	
Front engine bracket-to-frame	55 Nm
All others	38 Nm
XT models	
Swingarm pivot bolt	60 Nm
All others	23 Nm
Footrest/sidestand assembly rear bolts (YBR models)	23 Nm
Intake duct bolts	10 Nm
Kickstart nut	50 Nm
Oil pressure check bolt	7 Nm
Primary drive gear nut	70 Nm
Starter clutch bolts	30 Nm
Stopper arm bolt	10 Nm
Valve clearance adjuster access caps	18 Nm

1 General information

The engine/transmission unit is an air-cooled single cylinder of unit construction. The two valves are operated by rocker arms actuated by a single overhead camshaft which is chain driven off the left-hand end of the crankshaft. The crankcase divides vertically.

The crankcase incorporates a wet sump, pressure-fed lubrication system which uses a single rotor trochoidal oil pump that is gear-driven off the right-hand end of the crankshaft. Oil is filtered by a rotary filter on the crankshaft.

The alternator is on the left-hand end of the crankshaft. The crankshaft position sensor triggers for the ignition timing are on the outside of the alternator rotor, and the sensor is mounted in the alternator cover along with the stator.

Power from the crankshaft is routed to the transmission via the clutch. The clutch is of the wet, multi-plate type and is gear-driven off the crankshaft. The clutch is operated by cable. The transmission is a five-speed constant-mesh unit. Final drive to the rear wheel is by chain and sprockets.

There is a kickstart mechanism to supplement the electric starter motor on all machines except 2010-on YBR125 ED models.

2 Component access

Operations possible with the engine in the frame

The components and assemblies listed below can be removed without having to remove the engine from the frame. If however, a number of areas require attention at the same time, removal of the engine is recommended.

Camshaft and rockers
Cylinder head
Cylinder block and piston
Cam chain, tensioner and blades
Clutch
Oil pump and filter
Kickstart mechanism

Gearchange mechanism
Alternator
Starter clutch
Starter motor

Operations requiring engine removal

It is necessary to remove the engine from the frame to gain access to the following components.

Crankshaft, connecting rod and bearings
Transmission shafts and bearings
Selector drum and forks
Balancer shaft

3 Engine wear assessment

Cylinder compression check

Special tool: *A compression gauge is required to perform this test.*

1 Poor engine performance may be caused by leaking valves, incorrect valve clearances, a leaking head gasket, or a worn piston, piston rings or cylinder. A cylinder compression check will highlight these conditions and can also indicate the presence of excessive carbon deposits in the cylinder head.

2 The only tools required are a compression gauge (there are two types, one with a threaded adapter to fit the spark plug hole in the cylinder head, the other has a rubber seal which is pressed into the spark plug hole to create a seal – the threaded adapter type is preferable), and a spark plug socket. Depending on the outcome of the initial test, a squirt-type oil can may also be needed.

3 Make sure the valve clearances are correctly set (see Chapter 1). Make sure the cylinder head bolts are tightened to the correct torque setting (see Section 9).

4 Run the engine until it is at normal operating temperature. Remove the spark plug (see Chapter 1). Fit the plug back into the plug cap and ground the plug against the engine away from the plug hole – if the plug is not grounded the ignition system could be damaged.

5 Fit the gauge into the spark plug hole – if the rubber cone type is used keep the gauge pressed onto the hole throughout the test to maintain a good seal **(see illustration)**.

6 With the ignition switch ON, the throttle held fully open and the spark plug grounded, turn the engine over on the starter motor until the gauge reading has built up and stabilised **(see illustrations)**. Alternatively you could turn the engine over several times using the kickstart (where fitted).

7 Compare the reading on the gauge to the cylinder compression figure specified at the beginning of the Chapter.

8 If the reading is low, it could be due to a worn cylinder bore, piston or rings, failure of the head gasket, or worn valve seats. To determine which is the cause, pour a small quantity of engine oil into the spark plug hole to seal the rings, then repeat the compression test. If the figures are noticeably higher the cause is a worn cylinder, piston or rings. If there is no change the cause is probably a leaking head gasket or worn valve seats, but could also be due to a holed piston or broken ring(s).

9 In the unlikely event that the reading is higher than specified there could be a build-up of carbon deposits in the combustion chamber. Remove the cylinder head and scrape all deposits off the piston and the cylinder head.

Engine oil pressure check

10 If there is any doubt about the performance of the engine lubrication system an oil pressure check must be carried out. The check provides useful information about the state of wear of the engine.

11 There is no oil pressure switch or level sensor, and therefore no oil pressure or level warning light in the instrument cluster.

12 Check the engine oil level and make sure it is correct, and make sure the correct grade oil is being used (see *Pre-ride checks*). Make sure there is no obvious oil leakage from anywhere around the engine, and that the drain plug is tight (see Chapter 1). Remove the oil pressure check bolt from the cylinder head **(see illustration)**. Have some rag to hand.

13 Start the engine and allow it idle, and

watch the pressure check hole – oil should come out of the hole quite soon after starting the engine. When the oil appears stop the engine. If no oil has appeared after one minute stop the engine immediately.

14 If no oil came out during the test, the pressure is significantly lower than it should be or non-existent, either the oil pump or its drive mechanism is faulty, the filter is blocked, an oil passage is blocked, or there is other engine damage. Begin diagnosis by checking the oil strainer (see Chapter 1), then the filter and pump (see Section 18). If those items check out okay, the engine needs to be overhauled to clean out all oil passages.

15 Fit the oil pressure check bolt into the cylinder head and tighten it to the torque setting specified at the beginning of the Chapter.

---

4 Engine removal and installation

Caution: The engine isn't particularly heavy, but the aid of an assistant is advised during this process.

Removal

1 Support the bike on its centrestand where fitted, or using an auxiliary stand, making sure it is on level ground. Work can be made easier by raising the machine to a suitable working height on an hydraulic ramp or a suitable platform. Make sure the motorcycle is secure and will not topple over, and tie the front brake lever to the handlebar to prevent it rolling forwards. On XT models the swingarm pivot bolt goes through the engine's rear mounting brackets and so must be removed; to prevent the swingarm moving make sure the bike is supported so the weight of the bike is not on the rear wheel, and if the wheel is off the ground place a support under it, but make sure it is not compressing the suspension.

2 On XT models remove the sump guard (see Chapter 7).

3 If the engine is dirty, particularly around its mountings, wash it thoroughly. This will make work much easier and rule out the possibility of caked on lumps of dirt falling into some vital component.

4 Drain the engine oil (see Chapter 1).

5 Disconnect the leads from the battery (see Chapter 8).

6 Remove the fuel tank (see Chapter 3A or 3B).

7 Remove the carburettor or throttle body and fuel injector, according to model (see Chapter 3A or 3B). Plug the intake on the engine with clean rag.

8 Remove the exhaust system (see Chapter 3A or 3B).

9 On 2005 and 2006 YBR models, and where fitted on XT models, release the clamp and detach the air induction system hose from the

3.5 Thread the gauge hose adapter into the spark plug hole

3.6b ... until the reading on the gauge has stabilised

3.6a Hold the throttle open and turn the engine over ...

3.12 Unscrew the oil pressure check bolt (arrowed)

4.9a Release the clamp (arrowed) and detach the hose

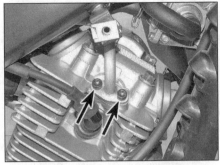

4.9b If required unscrew the bolts (arrowed) and remove the pipe

4.10 Pull the cap off the spark plug

pipe on the cylinder head **(see illustrations)**. If required unscrew the bolts and remove the pipe. Discard the gasket.

10 Pull the spark plug cap off the plug and secure the lead clear of the engine **(see illustration)**.

11 Create some slack in the clutch cable (see Chapter 1). Draw the cable out of the bracket on the engine and free the end from the release arm **(see illustrations 16.2a and b)**. Position the cable clear of the engine.

12 Remove the front sprocket (see Chapter 6).

13 Disconnect the alternator, crankshaft position (CKP) sensor and neutral switch wiring connectors **(see illustrations)**.

14 On 2007-on YBR models disconnect the sidestand switch wiring connector and the engine temperature (ET) sensor wiring connector **(see illustrations)**.

15 Make a mark where the slot in the gearchange lever aligns with the shaft.. Unscrew the pinch bolt and slide the lever off the shaft **(see illustration)**.

16 If required, remove the starter motor (see Chapter 8). If you want to leave the starter motor in situ, pull back the rubber cover on its terminal, then undo the screw and disconnect the lead **(see illustration)**. On YBR models remove the lead guard from the underside of the engine **(see illustration)** – it is secured by two of the crankcase bolts, so after removing the guard refit the bolts and tighten them lightly. Secure the lead clear of the engine.

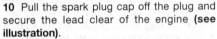

4.13a Alternator, CKP sensor and neutral switch connectors – YBR models

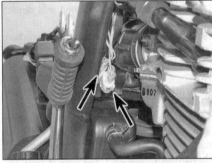

4.13b Alternator and CKP sensor connectors (arrowed) – 2008-on XT models

4.14a Disconnect the sidestand switch connector (arrowed) . . .

4.14b . . . and the ET sensor connector

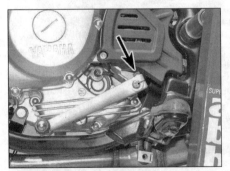

4.15 Make an alignment mark on the shaft then unscrew the bolt (arrowed) and slide the arm off

4.16a Undo the screw and detach the lead

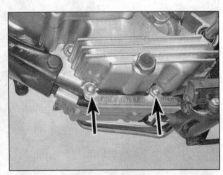

4.16b Unscrew the bolts (arrowed) and remove the guard

4.17 Unscrew the bolt (arrowed) and detach the lead

4.18 Release the clamp (arrowed) and detach the hose

4.19a Unhook the spring from the pedal (arrowed)

17 Unscrew the earth lead bolt and detach the lead **(see illustration)**.

18 Detach the crankcase breather hose from the engine **(see illustration)**.

19 On YBR models unhook the brake light switch spring from the brake pedal **(see illustration)**. Thread the rear brake adjuster nut off the end of the rod, then press the pedal down and draw the rod out of the arm **(see illustrations)**. Remove the pivot bush from the arm if required for safekeeping **(see illustration)**. Unscrew the rider's footrest/

sidestand assembly rear bolts, then unscrew the nut on the right-hand end of the lower rear engine mounting bolt **(see illustration)**. Withdraw the bolt and remove the footrest/ sidestand assembly from under the engine **(see illustration)**.

20 Position an hydraulic or mechanical jack under the engine with a block of wood between the jack head and sump. Make sure the jack is centrally positioned so the engine will not topple in any direction when the last mounting bolt is removed. Raise the jack to take the

weight of the engine, but make sure it is not lifting the bike and taking the weight of that as well. The idea is to support the engine so that there is no pressure on any of the mounting bolts once they have been slackened, so they can be easily withdrawn. Note that it may be necessary to alter the position of the jack as some of the bolts are removed to relieve the stress transferred to the other bolts. Continue according to the relevant sub-section below.

YBR models

Note: *Check which side the engine mounting*

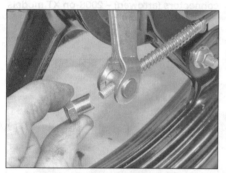

4.19b Thread the nut off . . .

4.19c . . . and draw the rod out of the arm

4.19d Remove the bush from the arm

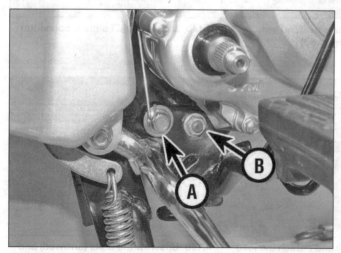

4.19e Unscrew the bolt (A) on each side, then unscrew the nut (B)

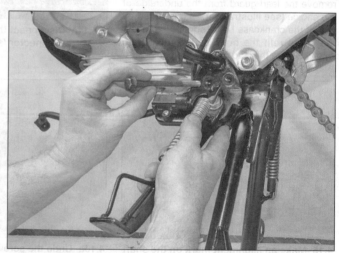

4.19f Withdraw the bolt and remove the footrest/stand assembly

4.21a Unscrew the nuts (arrowed) . . .

4.21b . . . then withdraw the bolts and remove the bracket

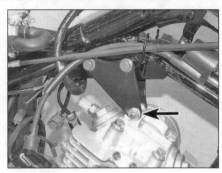

4.22a Unscrew the nut (arrowed) . . .

bolts and bracket bolts are fitted, and keep any washers with their bolts.

21 Unscrew the nuts from the engine front mounting bolts and the bolts securing the front bracket to the frame **(see illustrations)**. Withdraw the bolts and remove the bracket **(see illustrations)**.

22 Unscrew the nut on the engine upper mounting bolt and withdraw the bolt **(see illustrations)**.

23 Unscrew the nut on the upper rear mounting bolt **(see illustration)**.

24 Check that the engine is properly supported by the jack. Check that all wiring, cables and hoses are free and clear.

25 Withdraw the upper rear mounting bolt **(see illustration)**. Carefully lower the jack, supporting the engine and keeping it clear of the frame. With the aid of an assistant remove the jack from under the engine and remove the engine (see *Caution* on page 2•6).

XT models

Note: *Check which side the engine mounting*

bolts and bracket bolts are fitted, and keep any washers (where fitted) with their bolts.

26 Unscrew the nut on the engine lower front mounting bolt, and remove the washer **(see illustration)**. Withdraw the bolt, with its washer.

27 Unscrew the nuts on the bolts securing the front brackets to the engine and frame, and remove the washers **(see illustration)**. Withdraw the bolts, with their washers, and remove the brackets.

28 Unscrew the nut on the swingarm

4.22b . . . and withdraw the bolt

4.23 Unscrew the nut (arrowed)

4.25 Withdraw the bolt and remove the engine

4.26 Unscrew the nut (arrowed) and withdraw the bolt

4.27 Unscrew the nuts (arrowed), withdraw the bolts and remove the brackets

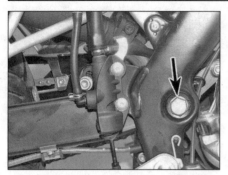

4.28 Swingarm pivot bolt (arrowed)

pivot bolt, and remove the washer **(see illustration)**.

29 Check that the engine is properly supported by the jack. Check that all wiring, cables and hoses are free and clear.

30 Withdraw the swingarm pivot bolt, along with its washer, then with the aid of an assistant carefully lift the engine out to the right-hand side, keeping it clear of the frame (see *Caution* on page 2•6).

31 If required, unscrew the nuts on the left-hand end of the bolts securing the rear brackets to the engine, and remove the washers. Withdraw the bolts, with their washers, and remove the brackets.

Installation

32 On XT models, if removed, fit the rear brackets onto the engine and insert the bolts, with their washers. Fit the nuts, with their washers, and tighten them to the torque setting specified at the beginning of the Chapter.

33 Manoeuvre the engine into position in the frame and support it with a jack. Align all the mounting bolt holes, making sure that all cables and wiring are correctly routed and do not get trapped. Note that it may be necessary to adjust the jack as some of the bolts are installed and tightened to realign the other bolt holes.

34 Referring to the relevant illustrations in the removal procedure, fit all the mounting bolts and brackets, and on YBR models the rider's footrest/sidestand assembly, inserting the bolts from the same side from which they were removed, and not forgetting any washers on XT models. On XT models make sure the swingarm pivots are correctly aligned with the engine and frame before inserting the pivot bolt. Fit all the nuts and tighten them finger-tight. Now, in reverse order of their slackening and removal (i.e. rear first, then upper, then front), tighten the nuts on the mounting bolts and brackets to the torque settings specified at the beginning of the Chapter, counter-holding the bolt heads to prevent them turning. On YBR models also tighten the footrest/sidestand assembly rear bolts to the specified torque.

35 Remove the jack from under the engine.

36 The remainder of the installation procedure

is the reverse of removal, noting the following points, and referring to the relevant illustrations in the removal procedure:

● When fitting the gearchange lever onto the gearchange shaft, align the slit in the arm with the mark on the shaft.
● Use a new gasket on the exhaust pipe.
● If removed on 2005 and 2006 YBR models and where fitted on XT models, fit the air induction system pipe onto the cylinder head using a new gasket and tighten the bolts to the torque setting specified at the beginning of the Chapter. Fit the hose onto the pipe and secure it with the clamp.
● Make sure all wires, cables and hoses are correctly routed and connected, and secured by any clips or ties.
● Refill the engine with oil to the correct level (see Chapter 1 and *Pre-ride checks*).
● Adjust the throttle and clutch cable freeplay (see Chapter 1).
● Adjust the drive chain (see Chapter 1).
● On YBR models fit the rear brake rod pivot bush and rod into the arm on the brake plate and thread the nut onto the rod. Hook the brake light switch spring onto the brake pedal. Adjust the rear brake pedal (see Chapter 1).
● Start the engine and check that there are no oil leaks. Adjust the idle speed (see Chapter 1).

5 Engine overhaul information

1 Before beginning the engine overhaul, read through the related procedures to familiarise yourself with the scope and requirements of the job. Overhauling an engine is not all that difficult, but it is time consuming. Check on the availability of parts and make sure that any necessary special tools are obtained in advance.

2 Most work can be done with a decent set of typical workshop hand tools, although a number of precision measuring tools are required for inspecting parts to determine if they are worn.

3 To ensure maximum life and minimum trouble from a rebuilt engine, everything must be assembled with care in a spotlessly clean environment.

Disassembly

4 Before disassembling the engine, thoroughly clean and degrease its external surfaces. This will prevent contamination of the engine internals, and will also make the job a lot easier and cleaner. A high flash-point solvent, such as paraffin (kerosene) can be used, or better still, a proprietary engine degreaser such as Gunk. Use old paintbrushes and toothbrushes to work the solvent into the various recesses of the casings. Take care to exclude solvent

or water from the electrical components and intake and exhaust ports.

 Warning: The use of petrol (gasoline) as a cleaning agent should be avoided because of the risk of fire.

5 When clean and dry, position the engine on the workbench, leaving suitable clear area for working. Gather a selection of small containers, plastic bags and some labels so that parts can be grouped together in an easily identifiable manner. Also get some paper and a pen so that notes can be taken. You will also need a supply of clean rag, which should be as absorbent as possible.

6 Before commencing work, read through the appropriate section so that some idea of the necessary procedure can be gained. When removing components note that great force is seldom required, unless specified (checking the specified torque setting of the particular bolt being removed will indicate how tight it is, and therefore how much force should be needed). In many cases, a component's reluctance to be removed is indicative of an incorrect approach or removal method – if in any doubt, re-check with the text.

7 When disassembling the engine, keep 'mated' parts together that have been in contact with each other during engine operation. These 'mated' parts must be reused or replaced as an assembly.

8 A complete engine stripdown should be done in the following general order with reference to the appropriate Sections.

Remove the camshaft
Remove the cylinder head
Remove the cylinder block and piston
Remove the starter motor (see Chapter 8)
Remove the clutch
Remove the oil pump
Remove the gearchange mechanism
Remove the kickstart mechanism (where fitted)
Remove the alternator and starter clutch (see Chapter 8)
Remove the cam chain and tensioner blade
Separate the crankcase halves
Remove the selector drum and forks
Remove the transmission shafts
Remove the crankshaft and balancer shaft

Reassembly

9 Reassembly is accomplished by reversing the general disassembly sequence.

6 Cam chain tensioner

Note: *The cam chain tensioner can be removed with the engine in the frame.*

Removal

1 Slacken the tensioner cap bolt **(see illustration)**.

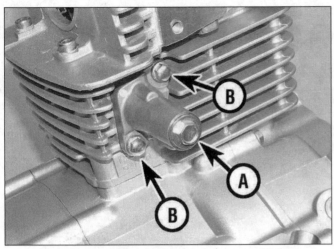

6.1 Tensioner cap bolt (A) and mounting bolts (B)

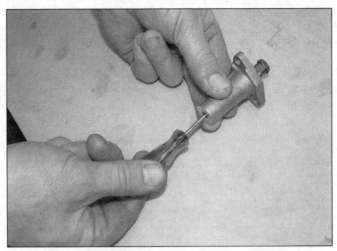

6.6 Insert the screwdriver and retract the plunger

6.9a Install the tensioner using a new gasket . . .

6.9b . . . and tighten the mounting bolts to the specified torque

6.10 Fit the cap with a new sealing washer

2 Unscrew the tensioner mounting bolts and withdraw the tensioner from the engine.

3 Remove the gasket and discard it – a new one must be used on installation. Do not attempt to dismantle the tensioner.

4 Remove all traces of old gasket from the tensioner and cylinder block mating surfaces.

Inspection

5 Unscrew the tensioner cap bolt. Discard the sealing washer as a new one must be used.

6 Insert a small flat-bladed screwdriver in the end of the tensioner so that it engages the slotted plunger (see illustration). Hold a finger pressed on the end of the plunger and turn the screwdriver clockwise until the plunger is fully retracted. Remove the screwdriver and release the plunger. The plunger should move smoothly when wound into the tensioner and spring back out freely when released.

Installation

7 Ensure the tensioner and cylinder block mating surfaces are clean and dry.

8 Insert a small flat-bladed screwdriver in the end of the tensioner so that it engages the slotted plunger (see illustration 6.6). Turn the screwdriver clockwise until the plunger is fully retracted and hold it in this position.

9 Fit a new gasket onto the tensioner body (see illustration). Fit the tensioner and insert the bolts with their washers and tighten them to the torque setting specified at the beginning of the Chapter, all the time keeping a hold on the screwdriver (see illustration). Release and remove the screwdriver.

10 Fit a new sealing washer onto the tensioner cap bolt, then tighten the bolt to the specified torque (see illustration).

7 Camshaft and rocker arms

Note: *The camshaft and rockers can be removed with the engine in the frame.*

Removal

1 Remove the spark plug (see Chapter 1).

2 Unscrew the camshaft sprocket cover bolts and remove the cover (see illustration). Unscrew the valve clearance adjuster access caps from the front and back of the cylinder head (see illustration). Discard the O-rings – new ones must be used.

3 Unscrew the timing inspection cap and

7.2a Unscrew the bolts (arrowed) and remove the sprocket cover

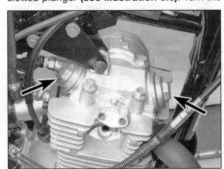

7.2b Unscrew the adjuster access caps (arrowed)

7.3 Remove the crankshaft end cap (A) and the timing inspection cap (B)

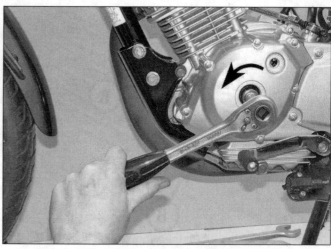

7.4a Turn the engine anti-clockwise using the nut . . .

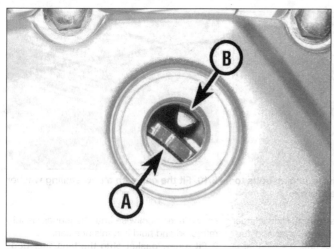

7.4b . . . until the line (A) on the rotor aligns with the pointer (B) . . .

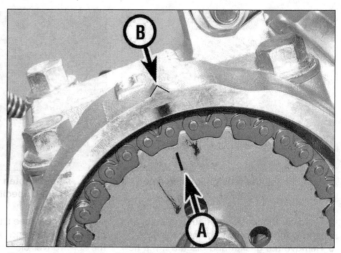

7.4c . . . and the line (A) on the camshaft sprocket aligns with the pointer (B)

the crankshaft end cap from the alternator cover on the left-hand side of the engine **(see illustration)**. Check the condition of the cap O-rings and replace them with new ones if necessary.

4 The engine must be turned to position the piston at top dead centre (TDC) on its

compression stroke so that the valves are closed. Turn the engine anti-clockwise using a suitable socket on the alternator rotor nut until the index line on the rotor (which on YBR models comes just before the ignition timing H mark – do not get them mixed up) aligns with the pointer inside the inspection hole,

and the index line on the camshaft sprocket is above the centre of the sprocket and aligned with the pointer on the top of the cylinder head **(see illustrations)**. There should now be some freeplay in each rocker arm (i.e. they are not contacting the valve stem). If the index line on the sprocket is below the centre, rotate the engine anti-clockwise one full turn (360°) until the index line on the rotor again aligns with the pointer inside the inspection hole – the index line on the sprocket will now be above the centre.

5 Remove the cam chain tensioner (see Section 6).

6 Counter-hold either the alternator rotor nut or the cam chain sprocket, using a suitable holding tool in the holes, and unscrew the bolt securing the sprocket **(see illustration)**. Slip the sprocket off the end of the camshaft, noting how it locates, and disengage it from the chain **(see illustration)**. Prevent the chain from dropping down its tunnel by securing it with a piece of wire.

7.6a Unscrew the bolt . . .

7.6b . . . and remove the sprocket

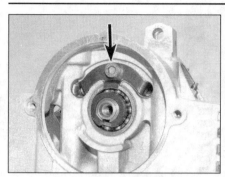

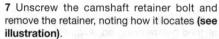

7.7 Unscrew the bolt (arrowed) and remove the retainer

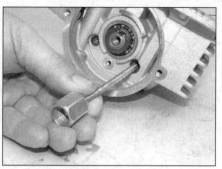

7.8a Thread the adapter into the end of the shaft . . .

7.8b . . . then fit the slide hammer and draw the shaft out

7 Unscrew the camshaft retainer bolt and remove the retainer, noting how it locates **(see illustration)**.

8 Mark each rocker arm according to its location in the holder. To remove the rocker arm shafts you need a slide-hammer to pull them out. Thread a 6 mm adapter with a 1 mm pitch thread into the end of the rocker arm shaft being removed, then fit the slide-hammer attachment **(see illustrations)**. Hold the rocker arm and draw the shaft out. If you don't have the necessary tools you can trying using a normal bolt and a pair of pliers on the bolt, rotating the shaft as you do to ease removal, but on the model photographed the shafts were too tight for this method. Slide the rocker arm back onto its shaft to prevent mixing up – both shafts and rocker arms are identical and are therefore interchangeable, but mark them according to their location so they can be installed in their original position. Repeat the procedure for the other rocker arm and shaft.

9 Thread the cam chain sprocket bolt partially into the end of the camshaft and use it to draw the camshaft out of the cylinder head **(see illustration)**.

10 While the camshaft is out, do not rotate the crankshaft – the chain may drop down and bind between the crankshaft and case, which could damage these components. Place a rag over the cylinder head.

Inspection

11 Clean the camshaft, rockers and shafts.

Blow the camshaft oil passages out with compressed air.

12 Check the camshaft bearings, one on the shaft and one in the head **(see illustrations)** – they must run smoothly, quietly and freely, and there shouldn't be excessive play between the inner and outer races, or between the inner race and the camshaft, or between the outer race and the cylinder head. Replace worn or damaged components with new ones.

13 Check the camshaft lobes for heat discoloration (blue appearance), score marks, chipped areas, flat spots and pitting. Measure the height of each lobe with a micrometer **(see illustration)** and compare the results to the minimum height listed in this Chapter's Specifications. If damage is noted or wear is excessive, the camshaft must be replaced with a new one.

14 Check the amount of camshaft runout by supporting each end on V-blocks, and

7.9 Pull the camshaft out using the sprocket bolt as a handle

measuring any runout using a dial gauge. If the runout exceeds the specified limit the camshaft must be replaced with a new one.

> **HAYNES HiNT** *Refer to Tools and Workshop Tips in the Reference section for details of how to read a micrometer and dial gauge.*

15 Check the rocker arms for heat discoloration (blue appearance), score marks, chipped areas, flat spots and pitting where they contact the camshaft lobes **(see illustration)**. Similarly check the bottom of each clearance adjuster and the top of each valve stem. If damage is noted or wear is excessive, the rocker arms, camshaft and valves must be replaced with new ones as required.

16 Check for freeplay between each rocker

7.12a Check the bearing (arrowed) on the camshaft . . .

7.12b . . . and the bearing (arrowed) in the head

7.13 Measure the height of the camshaft lobes with a micrometer

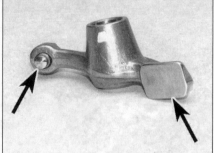

7.15 Check the contacting surfaces on the rocker arms and adjusters (arrowed)

7.16a Check for freeplay between the arm and the shaft . . .

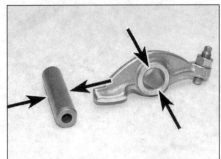

7.16b . . . and measure the internal diameter of the bore and the external diameter of the shaft (arrowed)

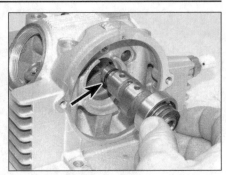

7.19a Grease the O-ring (arrowed) and insert the camshaft . . .

arm and its shaft **(see illustration)**. The arms should move freely with a light fit but no appreciable freeplay. If necessary measure the internal diameter of the arm bores and the corresponding diameter of the shaft to determine the extent of wear **(see illustration)**. Replace the arms and/or shafts with new ones if they are worn beyond their specifications. Check that the fork shaft holes in the holder are neither worn nor damaged.

17 Except in cases of oil starvation, the cam chain should wear very little. If the chain has stretched excessively, which makes it difficult to maintain proper tension, or if it is stiff or the links are binding or kinking, replace it with a new one. Refer to Section 8 for replacement. Check the sprocket for wear, cracks and other damage, and replace it with a new one if necessary. If the sprocket teeth are worn,

the cam chain is also worn, and so probably is the sprocket on the crankshaft. If severe wear is apparent, the entire engine should be disassembled for inspection.

18 Inspect the cam chain guide and tensioner blade (see Section 8).

Installation

19 Lubricate the camshaft bearings with clean engine oil and the camshaft lobes with molybdenum disulphide oil. Where fitted smear some grease onto the O-ring on the inner end. Slide the camshaft fully into the head and locate its inner end in the bearing in the head, then push the shaft in until the O-ring (where fitted) is felt to locate **(see illustrations)** – to aid installation if necessary thread the sprocket bolt into the camshaft **(see illustration 7.9)** then tap the end of the

bolt, but make sure the camshaft is correctly aligned before doing so. Align the camshaft so the cut-out for the cam chain sprocket is pointing down **(see illustration)**.

20 Lubricate each rocker shaft and arm with molybdenum disulphide oil (a 50/50 mixture of molybdenum disulphide grease and engine oil). Position each rocker arm in its location in the head, with the adjuster on the outside and the contact faces on the inner ends located against the camshaft lobes, and slide its shaft all the way through **(see illustration)** – if the shaft is tight thread an M6 x 1 bolt in its end and tap the end of the bolt, but make sure everything is correctly aligned before doing so **(see illustration)**.

21 Make sure both rocker shafts and the camshaft are fully inserted in the head. Apply some threadlock to the retainer bolt, then fit the retainer and tighten the bolt to the torque setting specified at the beginning of the Chapter **(see illustration)**.

22 Check that the index line on the alternator rotor aligns with the pointer inside the inspection hole **(see illustration 7.4b)**. Make sure the sprocket locating cut-out in the camshaft is at the bottom **(see illustration 7.19c)**.

23 Engage the cam chain sprocket with the chain, making sure the crankshaft does not rotate, that the front run of the chain between the sprockets is tight and that any slack is in the rear run so it will be taken up by the tensioner, that the index line on the camshaft sprocket is above the centre of the sprocket

7.19b . . . pushing it in to locate it in the bearing

7.19c Align the cut-out (arrowed) as shown

7.20a Slide the shaft into the head and through the rocker . . .

7.20b . . . threading a bolt into the shaft so you can tap it into place if necessary

7.21 Fit the retainer plate, making sure it locates correctly

7.23 Fit the sprocket into the chain and onto the camshaft as described

7.24 Secure the sprocket with its bolt

7.25 Feeding the chain around the sprocket as shown makes it easy to gauge how many teeth you are moving it by

and aligned with the pointer on the top of the cylinder head, and fit the sprocket onto the flange, locating the projection on the inner face of the sprocket in the cut-out in the end of the camshaft **(see illustration)**.

24 Fit the camshaft sprocket bolt with its washer and lightly tighten it **(see illustration)**.

25 Use a piece of wooden dowel or other suitable tool to press on the back of the cam chain tensioner blade via the tensioner bore in the cylinder block; this will ensure that any slack in the cam chain is taken up and transferred to the rear run of the chain. At this point check that the timing marks are still in **exact** alignment as described in Step 4 **(see illustrations 7.4b and c)**. Note that it is easy to be slightly out (one tooth on the sprocket) without the marks appearing drastically out of alignment. If the marks are out, unscrew the sprocket bolt and slide the sprocket off the camshaft, then reposition the sprocket in the chain as required, fit the sprocket back into the chain and onto the camshaft, and check the marks again **(see illustration)**.

Caution: If the marks are not aligned exactly as described, the valve timing will be incorrect and the valves may strike the pistons, causing extensive damage to the engine.

26 Install the cam chain tensioner (see Section 6).

27 Turn the engine anti-clockwise through two full turns and check again that all the timing marks still align (see Step 4) **(see illustrations 7.4a, b and c)**.

7.29b Fit the sprocket cover using a new O-ring (arrowed) smeared with grease

7.28 Tighten the sprocket bolt to the specified torque

28 Counter-hold the alternator rotor nut and tighten the camshaft sprocket bolt to the specified torque setting **(see illustration)**. Check the valve clearances and adjust them if necessary (see Chapter 1).

29 Fit the access caps using new O-rings smeared with grease and tighten them to the torque setting specified at the beginning of the Chapter **(see illustration)**. Fit the sprocket cover using a new O-ring smeared with grease and tighten the bolts to the specified torque **(see illustration)**.

30 Fit the timing inspection cap and crankshaft end cap using new O-rings if required, and smear the O-rings with grease **(see illustration)**.

31 Install the spark plug (see Chapter 1). Check and adjust the idle speed (see Chapter 1).

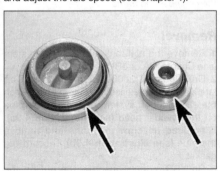

7.30 Fit the caps using new O-rings (arrowed) if required and smear them with grease

7.29a Fit each access cap using a new O-ring (arrowed) smeared with grease

8 Cam chain, tensioner blade and guide blade

Note: *The cam chain and its blades can be removed with the engine in the frame.*

Removal

Cam chain

1 Remove the camshaft sprocket (see Section 7).

2 Remove the alternator rotor and starter clutch (see Chapter 8).

3 Draw the cam chain off the crankshaft sprocket and out of the engine **(see illustration)**.

8.3 Removing the cam chain

8.6a Unscrew the bolt (arrowed) . . .

8.6b . . . and withdraw the blade

8.6c Note the collar fitted into the pivot

8.8 Draw the guide blade out, noting how it locates

8.11a Make sure the bottom locates in its seat . . .

8.11b . . . and the lugs locate in the cut-outs

Tensioner blade

4 Remove the cylinder head (see Section 9).
5 Remove the alternator rotor and starter clutch (see Chapter 8).
6 Unscrew the tensioner blade bolt, then draw the blade out of the top of the cylinder block **(see illustrations)**. Note the pivot collar **(see illustration)**.

Guide blade

7 Remove the cylinder head (see Section 9).
8 Draw the guide blade out of the top of the cylinder block, noting how it locates **(see illustration)**.

Inspection

Cam chain

9 Check the chain for binding, kinks and any obvious damage and replace it with a new one if necessary. Check the camshaft and crankshaft sprocket teeth for wear and replace the cam chain, camshaft sprocket and crankshaft sprocket with a new set if necessary – the drive sprocket on the crankshaft is pressed on, so the crankshaft will have to be taken to a workshop or dealer equipped with an hydraulic press to remove it and to fit a new one.

Tensioner and guide blades

10 Check the sliding surface and edges of the blades for excessive wear, deep grooves, cracking and other obvious damage, and replace them with new ones if necessary.

Installation

11 Installation of the chain and blades is the reverse of removal. Make sure the bottom of the guide blade sits in its seat and the lugs near its top locate in the cut-outs in the cylinder block **(see illustrations)**. Lubricate the tensioner blade pivot collar with clean oil **(see illustration 8.6c)**. Apply threadlock to the bolt and tighten it to the torque setting specified at the beginning of the Chapter.

9 Cylinder head

Note: *The cylinder head can be removed with the engine in the frame.*

Removal

1 Remove the fuel tank and exhaust system (see Chapter 3A or 3B).
2 On 2005 and 2006 YBR models and on late XT models, release the clamp and detach the air induction system hose from the pipe on the cylinder head **(see illustration 4.9a)**. If required unscrew the bolts and remove the pipe **(see illustration 4.9b)**. Discard the gasket.
3 On YBR models unscrew the nut on the end of the engine upper mounting bolt and withdraw the bolt **(see illustrations 4.22a and b)**. Unscrew the nuts on the ends of the bolts

securing the upper brackets to the frame, then withdraw the bolts and remove the brackets, noting how they fit. Remember which side the bolts are fitted from so they are installed the same way.
4 Remove the camshaft sprocket (see Section 7, Steps 1 to 6). If required also remove the camshaft and rocker arms, but note that you can do this after removing the head.
5 Unscrew the bolts securing the intake duct to the cylinder head **(see illustration)**. Move the duct within the limits possible to make sure it is not stuck. On fuel injected YBR models note the plate fitted between the duct and the head, and remove it if loose.
6 Unscrew the cylinder head bolts 1/4 a turn at a time in a criss-cross pattern until they are all loose, then remove them, noting the washers fitted with the 8 mm bolts **(see**

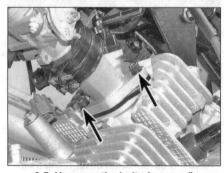

9.5 Unscrew the bolts (arrowed)

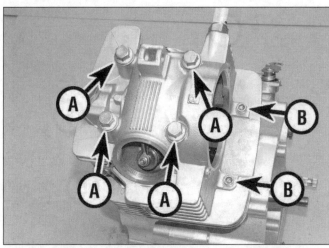

9.6 Cylinder head 8 mm bolts (A) and 6 mm bolts (B)

9.7 Carefully lift the head up off the block

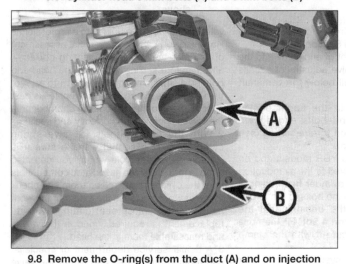

9.8 Remove the O-ring(s) from the duct (A) and on injection models the plate (B)

9.12 Fit the dowels (arrowed) then lay the new gasket on the block

illustration). Discard the washers as new ones should be used.

7 Hold the cam chain up and the intake duct/carburettor or throttle assembly back and pull the cylinder head up off the block, then pass the cam chain down through the tunnel **(see illustration)**. Do not let the chain fall into the engine – lay it over the front of the block and secure it with a piece of wire. If the head is stuck, tap around the joint faces with a soft-faced mallet. Do not attempt to free it by inserting a screwdriver between the head and block mating surfaces – you'll damage them.

8 Remove the cylinder head gasket and discard it as a new one must be used **(see illustration 9.12)**. If they are loose, remove the dowels from the cylinder block or the underside of the cylinder head. On carburettor models remove the O-ring from the intake duct, and on injection models remove the O-ring from the plate, and if the plate is loose remove it and the O-ring between it and the duct **(see illustration)**.

9 Check the cylinder head gasket and the mating surfaces on the cylinder head and cylinder block for signs of leakage, which

could indicate warpage. Refer to Section 10 and check the cylinder head gasket surface for warpage.

10 Clean all traces of old gasket material from the cylinder head and cylinder block. If a scraper is used, take care not to scratch or gouge the soft aluminium. Be careful not to let any of the gasket material fall into the cylinder bore or the oil passages.

Installation

11 Lubricate the cylinder bore with engine oil. If removed, fit the dowels into the cylinder block **(see illustration 9.12)**. Make sure the cam chain guide blade is correctly seated (see Section 8).

12 Ensure both cylinder head and cylinder block mating surfaces are clean. Lay the new head gasket over the cam chain and blades and onto the block, locating it over the dowels and making sure all the holes are correctly aligned **(see illustration)**. Never reuse the old gasket.

13 Carefully fit the cylinder head over the cam chain blades and onto the block, feeding the cam chain up through the tunnel as you

do, and making sure it locates correctly onto the dowels **(see illustration 9.7)**. Secure the chain in place with a piece of wire to prevent it from falling back down.

14 Apply engine oil to the threads, under the heads and onto both sides of the new sealing washers on the 8 mm bolts. Fit the bolts with their washers and tighten them finger-tight **(see illustration)**. Apply a suitable

9.14a Fit the 8 mm bolts with new sealing washers . . .

9.14b . . . and apply sealant to the threads of the 6 mm bolts

9.14c Tighten the bolts as described in the numerical sequence shown

sealant to the threads of the 6 mm bolts, then tighten them finger-tight **(see illustration)**. Now tighten the bolts evenly and a little at a time in the numerical sequence shown to the torque settings specified at the beginning of the Chapter – the 8 mm bolts are numbered 1 to 4 and the 6 mm bolts are 5 and 6 **(see illustration)**.

15 On carburettor models fit a new O-ring smeared with grease into the groove in the intake duct, then fit the intake duct onto the head and tighten the bolts to the specified torque setting. On fuel injection models fit a new O-ring smeared with grease into the groove in the intake duct, then fit the plate, then fit a new O-ring smeared with grease onto the plate, then fit the intake duct onto the head and tighten the bolts to the specified torque setting **(see illustrations 9.8 and 9.5)**.

16 Install the camshaft and rocker arms

if removed and not already done, then the camshaft sprocket (see Section 7).

17 Pour a small amount of engine oil into the head via one of the valve adjustment access holes so it fills the well below the camshaft lobes.

18 On YBR models fit the upper engine mounting brackets and bolts and tighten the nuts to the specified torque setting **(see illustration 4.22b and a)**.

19 On 2005 and 2006 YBR models and on late XT models, if removed fit the air induction system pipe onto the cylinder head using a new gasket and tighten the bolts to the torque setting specified at the beginning of the Chapter **(see illustration 4.9b)**. Fit the hose onto the pipe and secure it with the clamp **(see illustration 4.9a)**.

20 Install the exhaust system and fuel tank (see Chapter 3A or 3B).

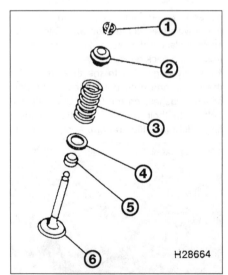

10.5 Valve components

1 Collets	4 Spring seat
2 Spring retainer	5 Valve stem oil seal
3 Valve spring	6 Valve

10 Cylinder head and valve overhaul

1 Because of the complex nature of this job and the special tools and equipment required, most owners leave servicing of the valves,

10.6a Make sure the compressor locates correctly both on the top of the spring retainer . . .

valve seats and valve guides to a professional. However, you can make an initial assessment of whether the valves are seating correctly, and therefore sealing, by tilting the head and pouring a small amount of solvent into each of the valve ports in turn. If the solvent leaks past either valve into the combustion chamber area the valve is not seating correctly and sealing.

2 With the correct tools (a valve spring compressor is essential – make sure it is suitable for motorcycle work), you can also remove the valves and associated components from the cylinder head, clean them and check them for wear to assess the extent of the work needed, and, unless seat cutting or guide replacement is required, grind in the valves and reassemble them in the head.

3 A dealer service department or specialist can replace the guides and re-cut the valve seats.

4 After the valve service has been performed, be sure to clean the head very thoroughly before installation to remove any metal particles or abrasive grit that may still be present from the valve service operations. Use compressed air, if available, to blow out all the holes and passages.

Disassembly

5 Before proceeding, arrange to label and store the valves along with their related components in such a way that they can be returned to their original locations without getting mixed up **(see illustration)**. Labelled plastic bags or a plastic container with two compartments are ideal.

6 Compress the valve spring on the first valve with a spring compressor, making sure it is correctly located onto each end of the valve assembly – on the top of the valve the adaptor needs to be about the same size as the spring retainer – if it is too small it will be difficult to remove and install the collets **(see illustration)**. On the underside of the head make sure the plate on the compressor only contacts the valve and not the soft aluminium

10.6b . . . and on the bottom of the valve

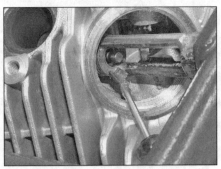

10.7a Remove the collets . . .

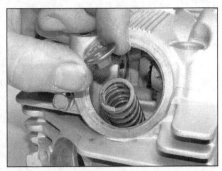

10.7b . . . the spring retainer . . .

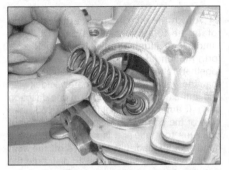

10.7c . . . the spring . . .

10.7d . . . and the valve

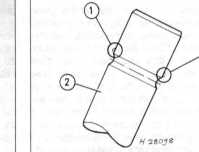

10.7e If the valve stem (2) won't pull through the guide, deburr the area above the collet groove (1)

of the head (see illustration) – if the plate is too big for the valve, use a spacer between them. Do not compress the spring any more than is absolutely necessary.

7 Remove the collets, using a magnet or a screwdriver with a dab of grease on it (see illustration). Carefully release the valve spring compressor and remove the spring retainer, noting which way up it fits, the spring and the valve (see illustrations). If the valve binds in the guide and won't pull through, push it back into the head and deburr the area around the collet groove with a very fine file or whetstone (see illustration).

8 Pull the valve stem seal off the top of the valve guide with pliers and discard it (the old seals should never be reused) (see illustration). Remove the spring seat noting which way up it fits (see illustration).

9 Repeat the procedure for the other valve. Remember to keep the parts for each valve together so they can be reinstalled in the same location.

10 Clean the cylinder head with solvent and dry it thoroughly. Compressed air will speed the drying process and ensure that all holes and recessed areas are clean. Note: Do not use a wire brush mounted in a drill motor to clean the combustion chamber as the head material is soft and may be scratched or eroded away by the wire brush.

11 Clean all of the valve springs, collets, retainers and spring seats with solvent and dry them thoroughly. Do the parts from one valve at a time so that no mixing of parts occurs.

12 Scrape off any deposits that may have formed on the valve, then use a motorised wire brush to remove deposits from the valve heads and stems. Again, make sure the valves do not get mixed up.

Inspection

13 Inspect the head very carefully for cracks and other damage. If cracks are found, a new head is required.

14 Using a precision straight-edge and a

feeler gauge set to the warpage limit listed in the specifications at the beginning of the Chapter, check the head gasket mating surface for warpage. Take six measurements, one along each side and two diagonally across. If the head is warped beyond the limit specified at the beginning of this Chapter, consult a Yamaha dealer or take it to a specialist repair shop for an opinion, though be prepared to have to buy a new one.

15 Examine the valve seats in the combustion chamber. If they are pitted, cracked or burned, the head will require work beyond the scope of the home mechanic. Measure the valve seat width and compare it to this Chapter's Specifications (see illustration). If it exceeds the service limit, or if it varies around its circumference, overhaul is required.

16 Working on one valve and guide at a time, measure the valve stem diameter

10.8a Pull the seal off the valve stem . . .

10.8b . . . then remove the spring seat

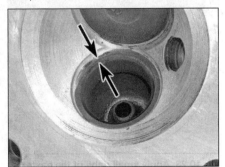

10.15 Measure the valve seat width

10.16a Measure the valve stem diameter with a micrometer

10.16b Measure the valve guide with a small bore gauge, then measure the bore gauge with a micrometer

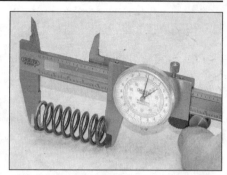

10.19 Measure the free length of the valve springs and check them for bend

(see illustration). Clean the valve's guide using a guide reamer to remove any carbon build-up. Now measure the inside diameter of the guide (at both ends and in the centre of the guide) with a small bore gauge, then measure the gauge with a micrometer (see illustration). Measure the guide at the ends and at the centre to determine if they are worn in a bell-mouth pattern (more wear at the ends). Subtract the stem diameter from the valve guide diameter to obtain the valve stem-to-guide clearance. If the stem-to-guide clearance is greater than listed in this Chapter's Specifications, replace whichever component is beyond its specification limits with a new one – take the head to a specialist for valve guide replacement. If the valve guide is within specifications, but is worn unevenly, it should be replaced with a new one. Repeat for the other valve.

17 Carefully inspect each valve face, stem and collet groove area for cracks, pits and burned spots.

18 Rotate the valve and check for any obvious indication that it is bent, in which case it must be replaced with a new one. Check the end of the stem for pitting and excessive wear. The presence of any of the above conditions indicates the need for valve servicing.

19 Check the end of the valve spring for wear and pitting. Measure the spring free length and compare them to the specifications (see illustration). If any spring is shorter than specified it has sagged and must be replaced with a new one. Also place the spring upright on a flat surface and check it for bend by

placing a ruler against it, or alternatively lay it against a set square. If the bend in any spring exceeds the specified limit, it must be replaced with a new one.

20 Check the spring seats, retainers and collets for obvious wear and cracks. Any questionable parts should not be reused, as extensive damage will occur in the event of failure during engine operation.

21 If the inspection indicates that no overhaul work is required, the valve components can be reinstalled in the head.

Reassembly

22 Unless a valve service has been performed, before installing the valves in the head they should be ground in (lapped) to ensure a positive seal between the valves and seats. This procedure requires coarse and fine valve grinding compound and a valve grinding tool (either hand-held or drill driven – note that some drill-driven tools specify using only a fine grinding compound). If a grinding tool is not available, a piece of rubber or plastic hose can be slipped over the valve stem (after the valve has been installed in the guide) and used to turn the valve.

23 Apply a small amount of coarse grinding compound to the valve face (see illustration). Smear some molybdenum disulphide oil (a 50/50 mixture of molybdenum disulphide grease and engine oil) to the valve stem, then slip the valve into the guide (see illustration 10.27). Note: Make sure each valve is installed in its correct guide and be careful not to get any grinding compound on the valve stem.

24 Attach the grinding tool to the valve and rotate the tool between the palms of your hands (see illustration). Use a back-and-forth motion (as though rubbing your hands together) rather than a circular motion (i.e. so that the valve rotates alternately clockwise and anti-clockwise rather than in one direction only). If a motorised tool is being used, take note of the correct drive speed for it – if your drill runs too fast and is not variable, use a hand tool instead. Lift the valve off the seat and turn it at regular intervals to distribute the grinding compound properly. Continue the grinding procedure until the valve face and seat contact area is of uniform width, and unbroken around the entire circumference (see illustration and 10.15).

25 Carefully remove the valve and wipe off all traces of grinding compound, making sure none gets in the guide. Use solvent to clean the valve and wipe the seat area thoroughly with a solvent soaked cloth.

26 Repeat the procedure with fine valve grinding compound, then use solvent to clean the valve and flush the guide, and wipe the seat area thoroughly with a solvent soaked cloth. Repeat the entire procedure for the other valve. On completion thoroughly clean the entire head again, then blow through all passages with compressed air. Make sure all traces of the grinding compound have been removed before assembling the head.

27 Coat the valve stem with molybdenum disulphide oil (a 50/50 mixture of molybdenum disulphide grease and engine oil), then slide it into its guide, rotating it slowly to avoid

10.23 Apply small dabs of the paste around the circumference of the valve

10.24a Using a valve lapping tool

10.24b Make sure the contact areas are as described

10.27 Lubricate the valve stem and fit it into the guide

10.29a Fit a new valve stem seal . . .

10.29b . . . and press it squarely into place using a deep socket of the appropriate size

damaging the seal (see illustration). Check that the valve moves up-and-down freely in the guide.

28 Working on one valve at a time, lay the spring seat in place in the cylinder head with its shouldered side facing up (see illustration 10.8b).

29 Fit a new valve stem seal onto the guide, using finger pressure, a stem seal fitting tool or an appropriate size deep socket, to push the seal squarely onto the end of the valve guide until it is felt to clip into place (see illustrations).

30 Next, install the spring, with the closer-wound coils facing down into the cylinder head (see illustration 10.7c). Fit the spring retainer, with its shouldered side facing down so that it fits into the top of the spring (see illustration 10.7b).

31 Apply a small amount of grease to the collets to help hold them in place. Compress the valve spring with a spring compressor, making sure it is correctly located onto each end of the valve assembly (see Step 6) (see illustrations 10.6a and b). Do not compress the spring any more than is necessary to slip the collets into place. Locate each collet in turn into the groove in the valve stem using a screwdriver with a dab of grease on it (see illustration 10.7a). Carefully release the compressor, making sure the collets seat and lock in the retaining groove (see illustration).

32 Repeat the procedure for the other valve.

33 Support the cylinder head on blocks so

the valves can't contact the work surface, then tap the end of each valve stem lightly to make sure the collets have seated in their grooves.

 HAYNES HiNT *Check for proper sealing of the valves by pouring a small amount of solvent into each of the valve ports. If the solvent leaks past any valve into the combustion chamber the valve grinding operation on that valve should be repeated.*

34 After the cylinder head and camshaft have been installed, check the valve clearances and adjust as required (see Chapter 1).

11 Cylinder block

Note: *The cylinder block can be removed with the engine in the frame.*

Removal

1 Remove the cylinder head (see Section 9).

2 Draw the cam chain guide blade out of the top of the block, noting how it locates (see illustration 8.8).

3 Hold the cam chain up and pull the cylinder block up off the crankcase, supporting the piston so the connecting rod does not knock against the engine, then pass the cam chain

down through the tunnel (see illustration). Do not let the chain fall into the engine – lay it over the front and secure it with a piece of wire. If the block is stuck, tap around the joint faces with a soft-faced mallet. Do not attempt to free it by inserting a screwdriver between the block and crankcase mating surfaces – you'll damage them.

4 Remove the base gasket and discard it as a new one must be used. If they are loose, remove the dowels from the crankcase or the underside of the cylinder block (see illustration 11.12). Remove the O-ring from the underside of the cylinder block and discard it (see illustration).

5 Stuff some clean rag into the cam chain tunnel and around the connecting rod to protect and support it and the piston and to prevent anything falling into the engine.

6 Clean all traces of old gasket material from the cylinder block and crankcase. If a scraper is used, take care not to scratch or gouge the soft aluminium. Be careful not to let any of the gasket material fall into the engine.

Inspection

7 Check the cylinder wall carefully for scratches and score marks.

8 Using a telescoping bore gauge and a micrometer, check the dimensions of the cylinder to assess the amount of wear, taper and ovality. Measure near the top (but below the level of the top piston ring at TDC), centre and bottom (but above the level of the oil ring at BDC) of the bore, both parallel to and

10.31 Make sure each collet has located in its groove in the top of the valve stem

11.3 Carefully lift the block up off the crankcase

11.4 Remove the O-ring (arrowed)

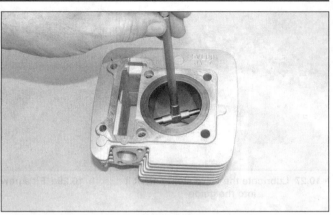

11.8a Measure the cylinder bore in the directions shown . . .

11.8b . . . using a telescoping gauge, then measure the gauge with a micrometer

across the crankshaft axis **(see illustrations)**. Compare the results to the specifications at the beginning of the Chapter. On 2005 to 2007 XT models, if the cylinder is worn, oval or tapered beyond the service limit it can be re-bored – oversize sets of pistons and rings are available (see *Specifications* at the beginning of this Chapter). Note that the person carrying out the re-bore must be aware of the piston-to-bore clearance. On all other models, a new cylinder, piston and ring set will have to be fitted.

9 If the precision measuring tools are not available, take the cylinder block to a Yamaha dealer or specialist motorcycle repair shop for assessment and advice.

Installation

10 Check that the mating surfaces of the cylinder block and crankcase are free from oil or pieces of old gasket.

11 If removed, fit the dowels into the crankcase and push them firmly home **(see illustration 11.12)**.

12 Remove the rags from around the piston and the cam chain tunnel, taking care not to let the connecting rod fall against the rim of the crankcase. Lay the new base gasket in place, locating it over the dowels **(see illustration)**. The gasket can only fit one way, so if all the holes do not line up properly it is the wrong way round. Never re-use the old gasket.

13 Fit a new O-ring smeared with grease over

the liner and onto the underside of the block **(see illustration)**.

14 Ensure the piston ring end gaps are positioned correctly before fitting the cylinder block (see Section 13) **(see illustration 13.10)**. If possible, have an assistant to support the cylinder block while the piston rings are fed into the bore.

15 Rotate the crankshaft so that the piston is at its highest point (top dead centre). It is useful to place a support under the piston so that it remains at TDC while the block is fitted, otherwise the downward pressure will turn the crankshaft and the piston will drop. Lubricate the cylinder bore, piston and piston rings with clean engine oil.

16 Carefully lower the block onto the piston until the crown fits into the bore, holding the underside of the piston if you are not using a support to prevent it dropping, and making sure it enters the bore squarely and does not get cocked sideways **(see illustration 11.3)**. Feed the cam chain up the tunnel and slip a piece of wire through it to prevent it falling back into the engine. Keep the chain taut to prevent it becoming disengaged from the crankshaft sprocket.

17 Carefully compress and feed each ring into the bore as the cylinder is lowered **(see illustration)**. If necessary, use a soft mallet to gently tap the cylinder down, but do not use force if it appears to be stuck as the piston and/or rings will be damaged.

18 When the piston and rings are correctly located in the bore, remove the support if used then press the cylinder block down onto the base gasket, making sure the dowels locate.

19 Hold the block down and turn the crankshaft to check that everything moves as it should.

20 Install the cam chain guide blade, making sure the bottom of the blade sits in its seat and the lugs near its top locate in the cut-outs in the cylinder block **(see illustrations 8.8 and 8.11a and b)**.

21 Install the cylinder head (see Section 9).

12 Piston

Note: *The piston can be removed with the engine in the frame.*

Removal

1 Remove the cylinder block (see Section 11). Check that the holes into the crankcase and the cam chain tunnel are completely blocked with rag.

2 Note that the piston crown is marked with an arrow that points to the front (exhaust side) of the engine (though the mark is likely to be invisible until the piston is cleaned).

3 Carefully prise out the circlip on one side of the piston using needle-nose pliers or a small flat-bladed screwdriver inserted into the notch

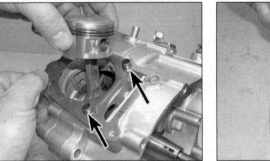

11.12 Lay the new gasket over the dowels (arrowed) and onto the crankcase

11.13 Fit a new O-ring around the liner

11.17 Carefully feed each ring into the bore as you lower the block

12.3a Prise out the circlip using a suitable tool in the notch . . .

12.3b . . . then push out the pin and separate the piston from the rod

12.10 Measure the piston ring-to-groove clearance with a feeler gauge

(see illustration). Push the piston pin out from the other side to free the piston from the connecting rod **(see illustration)**. Remove the other circlip and discard them as new ones must be used.

> *If the piston pin is a tight fit in the piston bosses, heat the piston using a heat gun – this will expand the piston sufficiently to release its grip on the pin. If the piston pin is particularly stubborn, extract it using a drawbolt tool, but be careful not to mark the pin's bearing surfaces in the piston.*

4 Using your thumbs or a piston ring removal and installation tool, carefully remove the rings from the pistons **(see illustrations 13.9, 13.8a and b, 13.6c, b and a)**. Do not nick or gouge the piston in the process. Carefully note which way up each ring fits and in which groove as they must be installed in their original positions if being re-used. The upper surface of the top and second rings should have a manufacturer's mark so they cannot be fitted upside down **(see illustration 13.8a)**.
5 Scrape all traces of carbon from the top of the piston. A hand-held wire brush or a piece of fine emery cloth can be used once most of the deposits have been scraped away. Do not, under any circumstances, use a wire brush mounted in a drill motor to remove deposits from the piston; the piston material

is soft and will be eroded away by the wire brush.
6 Use a piston ring groove cleaning tool to remove any carbon deposits from the ring grooves. If a tool is not available, a piece broken off an old ring will do the job. Be very careful to remove only the carbon deposits. Do not remove any metal and do not nick or gouge the sides of the ring grooves.
7 Once the deposits have been removed, clean the piston with solvent and dry it thoroughly. Make sure the oil return holes below the oil ring groove are clear.

Inspection

8 Carefully inspect the piston for cracks around the skirt, at the pin bosses and at the ring lands. Normal piston wear appears as even, vertical wear on the thrust surfaces. If the skirt is scored or scuffed, the engine may have been suffering from overheating and/or abnormal combustion, which caused excessively high operating temperatures. Also check that the circlip grooves are not damaged.
9 A hole in the top of the piston, in one extreme, or burned areas around the edge of the piston crown, indicate that pre-ignition or knocking under load have occurred. If you find evidence of any problems the cause must be corrected or the damage will occur again (see *Fault Finding* in the Reference section).
10 Measure the piston ring-to-groove

clearance by laying each piston ring in its groove and slipping a feeler gauge in beside it **(see illustration)**. Make sure you have the correct ring for the groove (see Step 4). Check the clearance at three or four locations around the groove. If the clearance is greater than specified, replace both the piston and rings as a set. If new rings are being used, measure the clearance using the new rings. If the clearance is greater than that specified, the piston is worn and must be replaced with a new one.
11 Check the piston-to-bore clearance by measuring the bore (see Section 11), then measure the piston 4.5 mm up from the bottom of the skirt and at 90° to the piston pin axis **(see illustration)**. Refer to the Specifications at the beginning of the Chapter and subtract the piston diameter from the bore diameter to obtain the clearance. If it is greater than the specified figure, the piston must be replaced with a new one (assuming the bore itself is within limits).
12 Apply clean engine oil to the piston pin, insert it into the piston and check for any freeplay between the two **(see illustration)**. Measure the pin external diameter at each end, and the pin bore in the piston **(see illustration)**. Calculate the difference to obtain the piston pin-to-piston pin bore clearance. Compare the result to the specifications at the beginning of the Chapter. If the clearance is greater than specified, replace the components that are worn beyond their specified limits. Repeat the check and measurements between the middle

12.11 Measure the piston diameter with a micrometer at the specified distance from the bottom of the skirt

12.12a Fit the pin into the piston and check for any freeplay

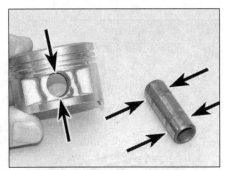

12.12b Measure the external diameter of each end of the pin and the internal diameter of the bore in the piston on each side

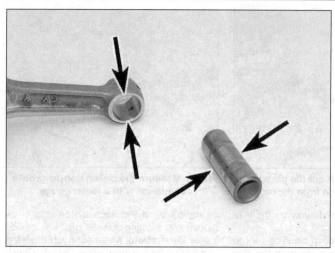

12.12c Measure the external diameter of the middle of the pin and the internal diameter of the small-end of the connecting rod

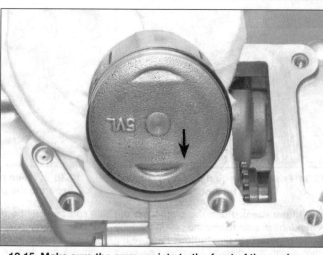

12.15 Make sure the arrow points to the front of the engine . . .

of the pin and the connecting rod small-end **(see illustration)**.

Installation

13 Inspect and install the piston rings (see Section 13).
14 Lubricate the piston pin, the piston pin bore and the connecting rod small-end bore with molybdenum disulphide oil (a 50/50 mixture of molybdenum disulphide grease and clean engine oil).
15 When fitting the piston onto the connecting rod make sure the arrow on the piston

crown faces the exhaust side (front) of the engine **(see illustration)**.
16 Fit a *new* circlip into one side of the piston (do not reuse old circlips). Line up the piston on the connecting rod with the arrow pointing to the front and insert the piston pin from the other side **(see illustrations)**. Secure the pin with the other *new* circlip **(see illustration)**. When fitting the circlips, compress them only just enough to fit them in the piston, and make sure they are properly seated in their grooves with the open end away from the removal notch.

17 Install the cylinder block (see Section 11).

13 Piston rings

Inspection

1 It is good practice to replace the piston rings with new ones when an engine is being overhauled. Before installing the new rings, check the end gaps with the rings installed in the bore, as follows.
2 Insert the top ring into the top of the bore and square it up with the bore walls by pushing it in with the top of the piston **(see illustration)**. The ring should be about 20 mm below the top edge of the bore. Slip a feeler gauge between the ends of the ring and compare the measurement to the specifications at the beginning of the Chapter **(see illustration)**.
3 If the gap is larger or smaller than specified, double check to make sure that you have the correct ring before proceeding; excess end gap is not critical unless it exceeds the service limit.
4 If the service limit is exceeded with new rings, check the bore for wear (see Section 11). If the gap is too small, the ring ends may come in contact with each other during engine operation, which can cause serious damage.
5 Repeat the procedure for the second (middle) ring but not the oil control ring side-rails and expander ring.

Installation

6 Install the oil control ring (lowest on the piston) first. It is composed of three separate components, namely the expander and the upper and lower side-rails. Slip the expander into the groove, making sure the ends don't overlap, then fit the lower side-rail **(see**

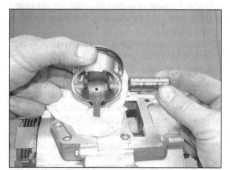

12.16a . . . then fit the piston pin through the piston and rod

12.16b Use new circlips and make sure they locate correctly

13.2a Fit the ring in its bore and set it square using the piston . . .

13.2b . . . then measure the end gap using a feeler gauge

13.6a Fit the oil ring expander in its groove . . .

13.6b . . . then fit the lower side rail . . .

13.6c . . . and the upper side rail on each side of it

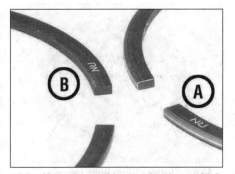

13.8a Note the marking on the rings which must face up, and identify the rings by their different profiles – top ring (A) has a chamfer on the upper outer rim, second ring (B) does not

13.8b Install the middle ring . . .

13.9 . . . and the top ring as described

illustrations). Do not use a piston ring installation tool on the side-rails as they may be damaged. Instead, place one end of the side-rail into the groove between the expander and the ring land. Hold it firmly in place and slide a finger around the piston while pushing the rail into the groove. Next, fit the upper side-rail in the same manner (see illustration).

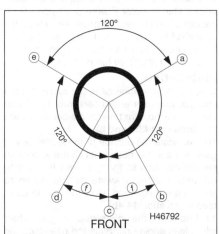

13.10 Piston ring installation details - stagger the ring end gaps as shown

a Top ring
b Upper side rail
c Oil ring expander
d Lower side rail
e Second ring
f 20 mm at piston edge

Check that the ends of the expander have not overlapped.

7 After the three oil ring components have been installed, check to make sure that both the upper and lower side-rails can be turned smoothly in the ring groove.

8 The upper surface of the top and second rings should be marked in some way, and note their different profiles (see illustration). Install the second (middle) ring next. Make sure that the identification mark near the end gap is facing up. Fit the ring into the middle groove in the piston (see illustration). Do not expand the ring any more than is necessary to slide it into place. To avoid breaking the ring, use a piston ring installation tool.

9 Finally, install the top ring in the same manner into the top groove in the piston (see illustration). Make sure the identification mark near the end gap is facing up.

14.3 Undo the screws (arrowed) and remove the retainer and the idle/reduction gear

10 Once the rings are correctly installed, check they move freely without snagging and stagger their end gaps as shown (see illustration).

14 Starter clutch and gears

Note: The starter clutch can be removed with the engine in the frame. If the engine has been removed, ignore the steps which do not apply.

Check

1 The operation of the starter clutch can be checked while it is in situ. Remove the starter motor (see Chapter 8). Check that the idle/reduction gear is able to rotate freely clockwise as you look at it via the starter motor aperture, but locks when rotated anti-clockwise. If not, the starter clutch is faulty and should be removed for inspection.

Removal

2 Remove the alternator rotor (see Chapter 8) – the starter clutch is bolted to the back of it. If the starter driven gear does not come away in the starter clutch, slide it off the end of the crankshaft, followed by the thrust washer.

3 Undo the idle/reduction gear retainer screws and remove the retainer (see illustration). Slide the gear off the shaft (see illustration 14.11a).

Inspection

4 With the rotor face down on a workbench, check that the starter driven gear rotates freely anti-clockwise and locks against the

14.4a Check the operation of the clutch as described

14.4b Withdraw the driven gear

14.5a Check the rollers and hub for wear and damage

14.5b Remove the rollers . . .

14.5c . . . plungers and springs

14.6a Starter clutch bolts (arrowed) . . .

rotor clockwise **(see illustration)**. If it doesn't, remove the starter driven gear, rotating it anti-clockwise if possible **(see illustration)**.

5 Check the condition of the rollers and the corresponding surface on the driven gear hub **(see illustration)**. If the rollers are damaged, marked or flattened at any point, remove them along with the plungers and springs, noting

how they fit, and replace them with new ones **(see illustrations)**.

6 To remove the starter clutch from the back of the alternator rotor hold the rotor using a holding strap and unscrew the three bolts **(see illustration)**. Discard the bolts – new ones should be used. On installation apply a suitable non-permanent thread locking

compound to the bolts and tighten them to the torque setting specified at the beginning of the Chapter. Stake the ends of the bolts as shown using a punch **(see illustration)**.

7 Check the bush in the starter driven gear hub and its bearing surface on the crankshaft **(see illustration)**. If the bush shows signs of excessive wear (the groove in the surface of the bush for holding the oil will be barely visible) replace the driven gear with a new one.

8 Check the teeth of the idle/reduction gear and the corresponding teeth of the starter driven gear and starter motor drive shaft. Replace the gears and/or starter motor if worn or chipped teeth are discovered on related gears. Also check the gear shaft for damage, and check that the gear is not a loose fit on it. Check the shaft ends and the bore and plate they run in for wear.

Installation

9 Apply clean engine oil to the rollers. Fit the springs, plungers and rollers into the starter clutch, making sure they locate correctly **(see illustrations 14.5c and b)**.

10 Lubricate the outside of the starter driven gear hub and the bush in its centre with clean engine oil, then fit the gear into the clutch, rotating it anti-clockwise as you do so to spread the rollers and allow the hub to enter **(see illustration 14.4b)**.

11 Lubricate the idle/reduction gear shaft with clean engine oil. Slide the gear onto the shaft, meshing the teeth of the larger inner gear with those of the starter motor shaft **(see illustration)**. Fit the retainer and tighten its screws **(see illustration)**.

12 Install the alternator rotor (see Chapter 8), making sure the teeth on the starter driven gear mesh with those on the idle/reduction gear.

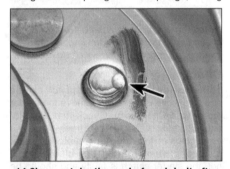

14.6b . . . stake the end of each bolt after tightening (arrow)

14.7 Check the bush (arrowed) for wear

14.11a Slide the gear onto the lubricated shaft (arrowed). . .

14.11b . . . then fit the retainer

15.4a Unscrew the nut (arrowed)

15.4b Make an alignment mark then draw the lever off

15.5 Unscrew the bolts (arrowed) and remove the cover

15 Clutch

Note: *The clutch can be removed with the engine in the frame. If the engine has been removed, ignore the steps which don't apply.*

Removal

1 Drain the engine oil (see Chapter 1).
2 Remove the starter motor (see Chapter 8).
3 On YBR models support the bike on its centre stand or an auxiliary stand. Unhook the brake light switch spring from the brake pedal **(see illustration 4.19a)**. Thread the rear brake adjuster nut off the end of the rod, then press the pedal down and draw the rod out of the arm **(see illustrations 4.19b and c)**. Remove the pivot bush from the arm for safekeeping **(see illustration 4.19d)**. Unscrew the rider's footrest/sidestand assembly rear bolts, then unscrew the nut on the right-hand end of the lower rear engine mounting bolt **(see illustration 4.19e)**. Withdraw the bolt and twist the footrest/sidestand assembly round until the heel plate is clear of the clutch cover **(see illustration 4.19f)**. If you prefer to remove the footrest/sidestand assembly completely you must first remove the exhaust system (see Chapter 3A or 3B) and either disconnect the sidestand switch wiring connector or displace the switch from the sidestand bracket (see Chapter 8).
4 Where fitted, unscrew the nut retaining the kickstart lever **(see illustration)**. Make an

alignment mark between the lever and the shaft, then draw it off **(see illustration)**.
5 Working evenly in a criss-cross pattern, unscrew the clutch cover bolts **(see illustration)** – if the engine is in the frame, note the earth lead secured by the lower rear bolt **(see illustration 4.17)**. Remove the cover, being prepared to catch any residual oil. Remove the gasket and discard it **(see illustration 15.31a)**. Remove the two dowels from either the cover or the crankcase if they are loose.
6 Working in a criss-cross pattern, gradually slacken the clutch spring bolts until pressure is released **(see illustration)**. To prevent the clutch from turning, cover it with a rag and hold it securely – the bolts are not very tight. If available, have an assistant hold the clutch while you unscrew the bolts. Remove the bolts, springs and the pressure plate/short pushrod assembly **(see illustrations 15.28 and 15.27)**. Using a magnet draw the pushrod ball bearing out of the transmission input shaft – you may need to tip the bike to the right, but take care when doing so **(see illustration 15.25)**. There is also a long pushrod inside the shaft but this will only come out of the left-hand end, which means the transmission shafts have to be removed (see Section 25 if required).
7 Grasp the complete clutch plate assembly and draw it out **(see illustration 15.24a)**. Unless the plates are being replaced with new ones, keep the assembly together. If you are going to remove the primary drive gear, refer to Section 17 and slacken its nut now.
8 Bend the clutch nut lockwasher tab off the

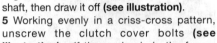

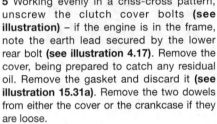

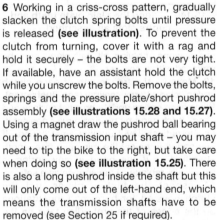

15.8b ... then lock or hold the clutch and unscrew the nut - this shows a commercially available holding tool

15.6 Unscrew the bolts (arrowed) as described

nut **(see illustration)**. To unscrew the clutch nut, the input shaft must be locked – this can be done in several ways: if the engine is in the frame, engage 5th gear and have an assistant hold the rear brake on hard with the rear tyre in firm contact with the ground;. alternatively, and if the engine has been removed, the Yamaha service tool (Pt. No. 90890-04086) or a commercially available clutch holding tool (as shown) can be used to stop the clutch centre from turning **(see illustration)**. Unscrew the nut and remove the washer **(see illustrations 15.23b and a)**. Check the condition of the washer and replace it with a new one if necessary – Yamaha specify to use a new one.
9 Slide the clutch centre off the shaft **(see illustration 15.22b)**. Slide the outer thrust washer off the shaft **(see illustration 15.22a)**.
10 Slide the clutch housing off the shaft **(see illustration)**. On YBR models slide the inner

15.8a Bend back the lockwasher tab ...

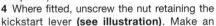

15.10 Draw the clutch housing off the shaft

15.11 Measuring clutch friction plate thickness

15.12 Check the plain plates for warpage

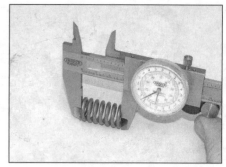

15.13 Measure the free length of the clutch springs and check them for bend

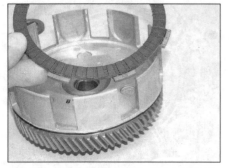

15.14a Check the friction plate tabs and housing slots . . .

15.14b . . . and the plain plate teeth and centre slots as described

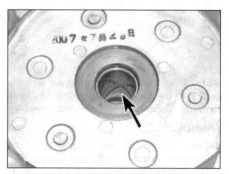

15.15 Check the bearing surfaces on the bush (arrowed) and the shaft

thrust washer off the shaft (see illustration 15.20). On XT models slide the inner thrust washer and the conical washer off the shaft.

Inspection

11 After an extended period of service the clutch friction plates will wear and promote clutch slip. Measure the thickness of each friction plate using a Vernier calliper (see illustration). If any plate has worn to or beyond the service limit given in the Specifications at the beginning of the Chapter, or if any of the plates smell burnt or are glazed, the friction plates must be replaced with a new set.

12 The plain plates should not show any signs of excess heating (bluing). Check for warpage using a flat surface and feeler gauges (see illustration). If any plate exceeds the maximum permissible amount of warpage, or

shows signs of bluing, all plain plates must be replaced with a new set.

13 Measure the free length of each clutch spring using a Vernier caliper (see illustration). Place each spring upright on a flat surface and check it for bend by placing a ruler against it, or alternatively lay it against a set square. If any spring is below the minimum free length specified or if the bend in any spring is excessive, replace all the springs as a set.

14 Inspect the friction plates and the clutch housing for burrs and indentations on the edges of the protruding tabs on the plates and/or the slots in the housing (see illustration). Similarly check for wear between the inner teeth of the plain plates and the slots in the clutch centre (see illustration). Wear of this nature will cause clutch drag and slow disengagement during gear changes as the plates will snag when the pressure plate is

lifted. With care a small amount of wear can be corrected by dressing with a fine file, but if this is excessive the worn components should be replaced with new ones.

15 Inspect the bearing surfaces of the clutch housing bush and the input shaft (see illustration). If there are any signs of wear, pitting or other damage the affected parts must be replaced with new ones.

16 Check the pressure plate, pushrod assembly and ball bearing for signs of wear or damage (see illustration). Replace any parts necessary with new ones.

17 Check the release mechanism in the left-hand side of the engine for a smooth action (see illustration). If the action is stiff or rough, detach the cable (see Section 16), then withdraw the shaft and remove the spring, noting how its ends locate (see illustration). Check the contacting surface of

15.16 Check the pressure plate assembly

15.17a Check the action of the release mechanism shaft

15.17b Withdraw the shaft along with the spring

15.17c Remove the circlip . . .

15.17d . . . then lever out the seal . . .

15.17e . . . and press a new one into place

15.17f Make sure the spring ends locate correctly

15.18 Check the primary drive and driven gears for wear and damage

15.20 Slide the inner thrust washer onto the shaft

the shaft for wear and damage. Clean and check the oil seal and the shaft bore in the cover. The seal can be replaced by removing the circlip, then levering the old one out with a seal hook or screwdriver and pressing the new one in, using a suitable socket to drive it in if necessary, and securing it with the circlip, preferably using a new one as Yamaha specify (see illustrations). Lubricate the shaft with molybdenum disulphide oil (a 50/50 mixture of molybdenum disulphide grease and engine oil) and the seal lips with grease before installing the shaft and fitting the spring. Make sure the return spring ends locate correctly (see illustration).

18 Check the teeth of the primary driven gear on the back of the clutch housing and the corresponding teeth of the primary drive gear on the crankshaft (see illustration). Replace the clutch housing and/or primary drive gear with a new one if worn or chipped teeth are discovered – refer to Section 17 for the primary drive gear. Check for any rotational

play between the primary driven gear and the clutch housing and replace the housing with a new one if any is evident. On machines fitted with a kickstarter, check the teeth on the kickstart mechanism driven gear and the corresponding teeth on the idle gear and the slider gear (see Section 20).

Installation

19 Remove all traces of old gasket from the crankcase and clutch cover surfaces.
20 On YBR models slide the inner thrust washer onto the shaft (see illustration). On XT models slide the conical washer then the inner thrust washer onto the shaft.
21 Smear the bush in the centre of the clutch housing with clean engine oil (see illustration 15.15). Slide the housing onto the shaft making sure that the teeth of the primary driven gear and kickstart driven gear on the back of the housing engage with those of the primary drive gear and kickstart idle gear (see

15.21 Make sure related gears engage correctly

illustration). Note: *Kickstart gears are not fitted to 2010-on YBR models.*
22 Slide the outer thrust washer onto the shaft, followed by the clutch centre (see illustrations).
23 Fit the lockwasher, locating its locking tab in the cut-out (see illustration). Thread

15.22a Fit the thrust washer onto the splines . . .

15.22b . . . then slide the clutch centre on

15.23a Locate the washer tab in the cut-out (arrowed)

15.23b Thread the nut on . . .

15.23c . . . and tighten it to the specified torque

15.23d Bend the tab up against the nut

15.24a Fit a friction plate first . . .

15.24b . . . then a plain plate and so on

15.25 Push the ball into the shaft

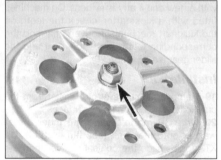

15.26 Leave the locknut (arrowed) loose

the clutch nut on. **(see illustration)** Using the method employed on removal to lock the input shaft, tighten the nut to the torque setting specified at the beginning of the Chapter **(see illustration)**. Bend the rim of the washer up against one of the flats on the nut to lock it **(see illustration)**. If you need to tighten the primary drive gear nut, do so now (Section 17).

24 Coat each clutch plate with engine oil. Build up the plates in the housing, starting with a friction plate, then a plain plate, then alternating friction and plain plates until all are installed **(see illustrations)**.

25 Push the ball bearing into the hole in the shaft **(see illustration)**.

26 If removed fit the short pushrod, its holder, the washer and the locknut into the pressure plate **(see illustration 15.16)** – leave the locknut loose as the position of the pushrod will need to be adjusted **(see illustration)**.

27 Fit the pressure plate, inserting the pushrod in the shaft, and making sure the castellations locate in the clutch centre **(see illustration)**. Hold the pressure plate and check for any gaps between the clutch plates – there should be none; if there are, it means the pressure plate has not located properly.

28 Fit the clutch springs and bolts and tighten the bolts evenly and a little at a time in a criss-cross sequence to the specified torque **(see illustration)**.

15.27 Slide the rod into the shaft and engage the castellations

15.28 Fit the springs and tighten the bolts as described

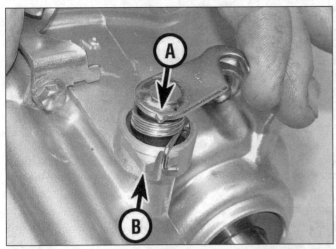

15.29a Make sure the pointer (A) aligns with the projection (B)

15.29b Slacken the locknut (A) if loose and turn the pushrod (B) as required until the marks align

15.31a Locate the new gasket over the dowels (arrowed) . . .

15.31b . . . then fit the cover

29 Push the release mechanism arm in until all freeplay is taken up – the pointer on the arm should align with the projection on the shaft bore in the crankcase **(see illustration)**. If they do not align, counter-hold the outer end of the short pushrod using a screwdriver and slacken the locknut (if tight), then turn the pushrod as required until the marks do align when the arm is pushed in **(see illustration)**. Hold the pushrod so it can't turn and tighten the locknut. Re-check the alignment marks with the lever pushed in. This setting is important as there must be some freeplay between the rods when the clutch is engaged. Reconnect the cable (Section 16).

30 Refer to Section 20, Step 8 and fit a new kickstart shaft oil seal (where applicable) and crankshaft oil seal, into the clutch cover.

31 Fit the two dowels into the crankcase if removed, then fit a new gasket, locating it over the dowels **(see illustration)**. Fit the cover **(see illustration)**. Install all the bolts finger-tight, not forgetting the earth lead if the engine is in the frame **(see illus-**

tration 4.17), then tighten them evenly and a little at a time in a criss-cross pattern to the specified torque.

32 If applicable, slide the kickstart onto the shaft, getting it as close as possible to the clutch cover without actually touching it **(see illustration)**. Fit the nut and tighten it to the specified torque.

33 On YBR models locate the footrest/

15.32 Align the marks and slide the lever on, securing it with the nut

sidestand assembly then insert the bolts and fit the nut onto the engine lower rear mounting bolt **(see illustrations 4.19f and e)**. Tighten the nut and the bolts to the torque settings specified at the beginning of the Chapter. If removed install the exhaust system (see Chapter 3A or 3B). Fit the pivot bush and rear brake rod into the arm on the brake plate and thread the nut onto the rod **(see illustrations 4.19d, c and b)**. Hook the brake light switch spring onto the brake pedal **(see illustration 4.19a)**. Adjust the rear brake pedal (see Chapter 1).

34 Install the starter motor (See Chapter 8).

35 Fill the engine with the correct amount and type of oil (see Chapter 1 and *Pre-ride checks*).

16 Clutch cable

1 Pull the rubber boot off the adjuster at the handlebar end of the cable. Fully slacken the

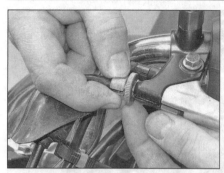

16.1 Pull back the boot, slacken the lockring and turn the adjuster in

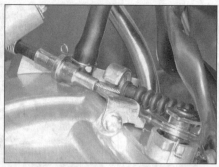

16.2a Draw the cable out of the bracket . . .

16.2b . . . and detach the end from the arm

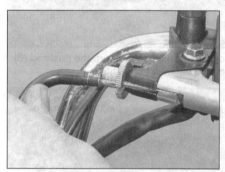

16.3a Free the outer cable from the adjuster . . .

16.3b . . . and the inner cable from the lever

lockring, then thread the adjuster fully in **(see illustration)**. This provides freeplay in the cable and resets the adjuster to the beginning of its span.

2 Draw the cable out of the bracket on the engine and detach the end from the release arm **(see illustrations)**.

3 Align the slots in the adjuster and lockring at the handlebar end of the cable with that in the lever bracket, then pull the outer cable end from the socket in the adjuster and release the inner cable from the lever **(see illustrations)**. Remove the cable from the machine, noting its routing.

HAYNES HiNT *Before removing the cable from the bike, tape the lower end of the new cable to the upper end of the old cable. Slowly pull the lower end of the old cable out, guiding the new cable down into position. Using this method will ensure the cable is routed correctly.*

4 Installation is the reverse of removal. Apply grease to the cable ends. Make sure the cable is correctly routed through its guides. Adjust the amount of clutch lever freeplay (see Chapter 1).

17 Primary drive gear

Removal

1 Remove the clutch plates (see Section 15, Steps 1 to 7).

2 To unscrew the primary drive gear nut wedge a stout piece of rag or rolled up strap, or if available a piece of aluminium plate as shown (DO NOT use steel), between the teeth of the primary drive and driven gears where they mesh at the top – this will lock them together to prevent them turning **(see illustration)**. Slacken the primary drive gear nut. Remove the rag, strap or plate.

3 Remove the remainder of the clutch assembly (Section 15).

4 Unscrew the primary drive gear nut and remove the washer, then slide the gear off the end of the crankshaft, noting how it locates on the Woodruff key **(see illustration)**. Remove the key from its slot **(see illustration 17.7a)**.

5 Refer to Section 18 for removal of the oil filter and pump.

17.2 Using a piece of aluminium plate to jam the gears while unscrewing the nut (arrowed)

17.4 Unscrew the nut and remove the washer and the gear

17.7a Fit the key into its slot . . .

17.7b . . . then fit the gear with the side with the larger chamfer facing in . . .

17.7c . . . locating it over the key

Installation

6 Make sure the oil pump and filter are installed (see Section 18).

7 Fit the Woodruff key into its slot in the crankshaft **(see illustration)**. Align the cut-out in the gear with the key, then slide the gear onto the shaft, with its marked side facing out and more chamfered side facing in, so it locates over the key **(see illustrations)**. Fit the washer and tighten the nut finger-tight **(see illustration 17.4)**.

8 Fit the clutch housing and clutch centre and tighten the clutch nut (see Section 15, Steps 19 to 23).

9 Wedge the stout piece of rag, strap or aluminium plate where the primary drive and driven gear teeth mesh at the bottom and tighten the primary drive gear nut to the torque setting specified at the beginning of the Chapter **(see illustration)**.

10 Install the remainder of the clutch assembly (see Section 15).

18 Oil filter, strainer and oil pump

Note: *The oil pump can be removed with the engine in the frame. If the engine has been removed, ignore the steps which don't apply.*

Removal

1 Remove the primary drive gear (see Section 17).

2 Slide the oil filter off the shaft, noting how it fits **(see illustration)**. Slide the oil pump drive gear off, on XT models followed by the washer **(see illustration)**.

3 Turn the driven gear to align the holes with the pump screws, then undo the screws and

remove the pump **(see illustration)**. Remove the gasket and discard it – a new one must be used.

4 Withdraw the oil strainer **(see illustration)**.

Inspection

Note: *Before removing the rotors from the oil pump, mark the outer faces to serve as a guide to which way round to fit the rotors on installation. Refitting the rotors in their original positions will ensure that mated surfaces continue to run together.*

5 Remove the E-clip and washer(s) from the outer end of the shaft **(see illustration)**. Slide the gear off the shaft then remove the drive pin and the washer **(see illustrations 18.17d, c, b and a)**.

6 Undo the screw securing the cover to the pump body, then remove the cover, and the locating pins if loose **(see illustration)**. Withdraw the shaft and the drive pin **(see**

17.9 Wedge the plate as shown and tighten the nut to the specified torque

18.2a Slide the filter off . . .

18.2b . . . followed by the drive gear

18.3 Align the holes, undo the screws (arrowed) and remove the pump

18.4 Withdraw the strainer

18.5 Remove the e-clip, the washers and the drive gear

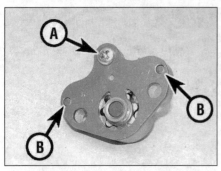

18.6 Undo the screw (A) and remove the cover, and the pins (B) if loose

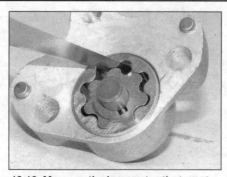

18.10 Measure the inner rotor tip-to-outer rotor clearance as shown

18.11 Measure the outer rotor-to-body clearance as shown

18.12 Measure rotor end-float as shown

18.15 Fit the pin into the shaft and the shaft into the rotors

18.16 Fit the cover, locating the pins in the holes

illustration 18.15). Remove the inner and outer rotors, noting which way round they fit.

7 Clean all the components in solvent.

8 Check the rotary filter cracks, damage and wear and replace it with a new one if necessary. Check the strainer for holes or tears in its gauze and damage to the rim and replace it with a new one if necessary.

9 Inspect the pump body and rotors for scoring and wear. If any damage, scoring or uneven or excessive wear is evident, replace the components with new ones.

10 Fit the inner and outer rotors into the pump body with the marks made on removal facing out. Fit the shaft into the inner rotor **(see illustration 18.15)**. Measure the clearance between the inner rotor tip and the outer rotor with a feeler gauge and compare it to the service limit listed in the specifications at the beginning of the Chapter **(see illustration)**. If the clearance

measured is greater than the maximum listed, replace the rotors with new ones.

11 Measure the clearance between the outer rotor and the pump body with a feeler gauge and compare it to the maximum clearance listed in the specifications at the beginning of the Chapter **(see illustration)**. If the clearance measured is greater than the maximum listed, replace the outer rotor and pump body with new ones.

12 Lay a straight-edge across the rotors and the pump body and, using a feeler gauge, measure the rotor end-float (the gap between the rotors and the straight-edge **(see illustration)**. If the clearance measured is greater than the maximum listed, replace the rotors and pump body with new ones.

13 Check the pump drive and driven gears, shaft and drive pins for wear and damage, and replace them with new ones if necessary.

14 If the pump is good, make sure all the components are clean, then lubricate them with new engine oil.

15 Fit the outer rotor into the pump body with the mark facing out. Fit the inner rotor into the outer rotor with the mark facing out. Slide the shorter drive pin through the inner hole in the shaft **(see illustration)**. Fit the shaft through the rotors and pump housing, locating the drive pin ends in the cut-outs in the inner rotor.

16 Fit the cover locating pins if removed. Fit the cover onto the pump body and tighten the screws **(see illustration)**.

17 Fit the washer onto the outer end of the shaft, then fit the drive pin **(see illustrations)**. Slide the driven gear onto the shaft with the cut-outs for the drive pin facing in, and locate the drive pin ends in the cut-outs **(see illustration)**. Fit the washer(s), with the outer rim of the spring washer away from the gear

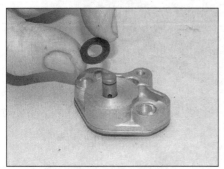

18.17a Fit the washer . . .

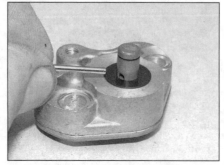

18.17b . . . and the drive pin . . .

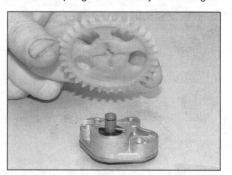

18.17c . . . then fit the gear onto the pin

18.17d Fit the washers . . .

18.17e . . . making sure the spring washer sits as shown

18.17f Slide the e-clip into the groove

18.19a Use a new gasket . . .

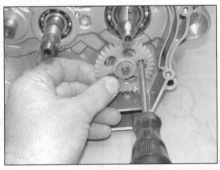

18.19b . . . and align the holes to get on the screws

18.22 Make sure the filter is the correct way round

face (see illustrations). Fit the E-clip into its groove (see illustration).
18 Rotate the pump shaft by hand and check it turns the rotors smoothly and freely. Fill the pump with clean engine oil via the holes in the cover.

Installation

19 Fit the pump using a new gasket and tighten the screws (see illustrations).
20 On YBR models slide the drive gear onto the crankshaft with the mark facing out (see illustration 18.2b).
21 On XT models slide the washer onto the crankshaft with the H mark facing out. Slide the drive gear onto the shaft with its grooved side facing in.
22 Slide the rotary filter onto the shaft, with the deeper face on the inside (see illustration), and aligning it so the tab locates in the cut-out (see illustration 18.2a).

23 Fit the oil strainer (see illustration 18.4).
24 Install the primary drive gear (see Section 17).

19 Gearchange mechanism

Note: The gearchange mechanism can be removed with the engine in the frame. If the engine has been removed, ignore the steps which don't apply.

Removal

1 Make sure the transmission is in neutral. Remove the clutch (see Section 15).
2 Make a mark where the slot in the gearchange lever aligns with the shaft. Unscrew the pinch bolt and slide the lever off the shaft (see illustration 4.15).

3 Wrap a single layer of thin insulating tape around the gearchange shaft splines to protect the oil seal lips as the shaft is removed.
4 Note how the gearchange shaft centralising spring ends fit on each side of the locating pin in the casing, and how the pawls on the selector arm locate onto the pins on the cam plate end of the selector drum. Grasp the shaft/arm assembly and withdraw it from the crankcase (see illustration).
5 Unhook the stopper arm spring (see illustration). Note how the roller locates in the neutral detent on the selector drum cam. Unscrew the stopper arm bolt and remove the arm, the washer and the spring, noting how they fit.
6 If the crankcases are being separated, or if otherwise required, undo the cam plate screw, locking the selector drum with a holding tool as shown or using a suitable tool wedged between the plate and the crankcase (see illustration).

19.4 Withdraw the shaft/arm assembly, noting how it fits

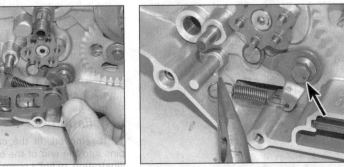

19.5 Unhook the spring, then unscrew the bolt (arrowed) and remove the arm

19.6a Hold the cam plate to prevent it turning and unscrew the bolt

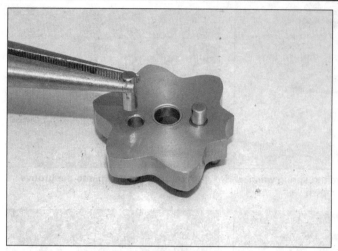

19.6b Remove the plate locating pins

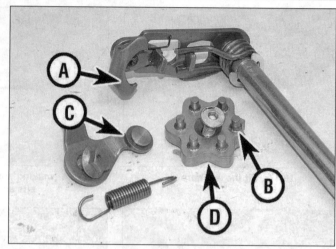

19.7 Check the selector arm pawls (A) and cam plate pins (B), and the stopper arm roller (C) and cam plate detents (D)

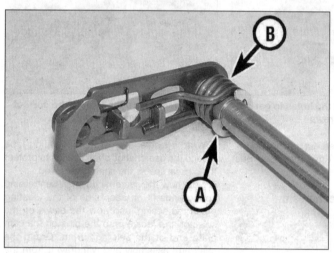

19.8 Release the e-clip (A) to free the centralising spring (B)

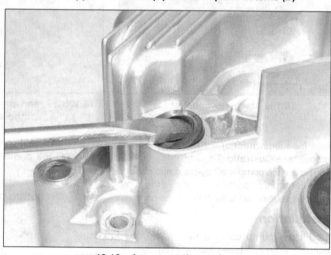

19.10a Lever out the seal . . .

Remove the plate, noting that there are two pins that locate the plate on the end of the selector drum – take care as they could drop out. Remove them from the drum for safekeeping (see illustration).

Inspection

7 Check the selector arm for cracks, distortion and wear of its pawls, and check for any corresponding wear on the pins on the selector drum cam plate (see illustration).

Also check the stopper arm roller and the detents in the cam plate for any wear or damage, and make sure the roller turns freely. Replace any components that are worn or damaged with new ones. If required (and not already done), refer to Step 6 for removal of the cam plate, and to Step 11 for installation.
8 Inspect the shaft centralising spring and the stopper arm return spring for fatigue, wear or damage. If any is found, they must be replaced with new ones. To replace the shaft spring,

release the E-clip, then slide it off the end of the shaft (see illustration). Fit the new spring, locating the ends on each side of the tab, then fit the E-clip, using a new one if necessary.
9 Check the gearchange shaft is straight and look for damage to the splines. If the shaft is bent you can attempt to straighten it, but if the splines are damaged the shaft must be replaced with a new one.
10 Check the condition of the shaft oil seal in the left-hand side of the crankcase. If it is damaged, deteriorated or shows signs of leakage it must be replaced with a new one, though it is advisable to fit a new one whatever the apparent condition. Lever out the old seal with a seal hook or screwdriver (see illustration). Press or drive the new seal squarely into place using your fingers, a seal driver or suitable socket (see illustration).

Installation

11 If removed, fit the cam plate locating pins into the end of the selector drum (see illustration 19.6b). Locate the cam plate onto the pins (see illustration). Apply a suitable non-permanent thread locking compound

19.10b . . . and press a new one into place

19.11a Fit the cam plate onto the pins . . .

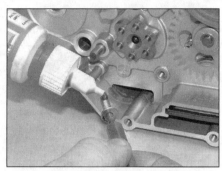

19.11b ... then threadlock the bolt ...

19.11c ... and tighten it to the specified torque

19.12a Threadlock the bolt and fit the stopper arm

19.12b This is how the stopper arm should be positioned

19.14 Make sure everything is correctly located

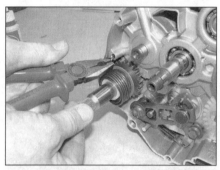

20.3 Removing the kick start assembly – hold the spring end to prevent it uncoiling

to the cam plate screw and tighten it **(see illustration)** – lock the drum with a holding tool as on removal **(see illustration)**.

12 Apply a suitable non-permanent thread locking compound to the stopper arm bolt. Fit the stopper arm and tighten the bolt to the torque setting specified at the beginning of the Chapter **(see illustration)**. Hook the stopper arm spring onto its post **(see illustration)**.

13 Check that the shaft centralising spring is properly positioned **(see illustration 19.8)**. Apply some grease to the lips of the gearchange shaft oil seal in the left-hand side of the crankcase. Slide the shaft into place and push it all the way through the case until the splined end comes out the other side, and locate the selector arm pawls onto the pins on the selector drum and the centralising spring ends onto each side of the locating pin in the crankcase **(see illustration 19.4)**.

14 Check that all components are correctly

positioned **(see illustration)**. Install the clutch (see Section 15).

15 Remove the insulating tape from around the gearchange shaft splines. Slide the gearchange lever onto the shaft, aligning its slit with the punch mark **(see illustration 4.15)**. Fit the pinch bolt and tighten it.

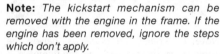

20 Kickstart mechanism – except 2010-on YBR-ED models

Note: *The kickstart mechanism can be removed with the engine in the frame. If the engine has been removed, ignore the steps which don't apply.*

Removal

1 Remove the clutch (see Section 15).

2 Release the outer circlip securing the idle gear and remove the outer washer, the gear,

the inner washer, and if required the inner circlip **(see illustrations 20.10e to a)**. Discard the circlips – Yamaha specify to use new ones.

3 Note how the return spring ends locate, then hold the end in the crankcase with pliers and remove the kickstart assembly **(see illustration)**.

Inspection

4 Clean all the components in solvent.

5 Check the teeth on the slider gear and the helical splines between the slider gear and the shaft for wear and damage **(see illustration)**. Also check the idle gear teeth and the driven gear teeth on the back of the clutch housing. Check the bush in the idle gear for wear **(see illustration)**.

6 Check the return spring and kick spring for wear and damage. If a spring gauge is available, check the force that can be applied to the kick spring before it spins in its groove in the gear **(see illustration)** – it should be 8 to 12 N.

7 If any components are worn or damaged

20.5a Check the gears and splines for wear and damage . . .

20.5b ... and check the bush (arrowed)

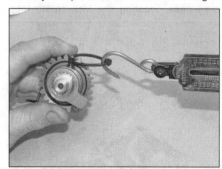

20.6 Check the force applied as the kick spring turns in the groove

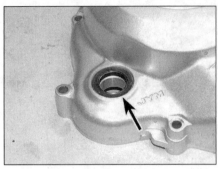

20.8a Check the kickstart shaft oil seal (arrowed) . . .

20.8b . . . and the crankshaft oil seal (arrowed)

20.9a Locate the kick spring loop in the recess (arrowed) . . .

20.9b . . . and the return spring end in the hole as you fit the shaft

20.10a Fit the inner circlip . . .

20.10b . . . the inner washer . . .

they must be replaced with new ones. Remove the spacer, return spring, washer, slider gear and kick spring from the shaft, noting how they all fit. On reassembly make sure the bent end of the kick spring faces in **(see illustration 20.5a)**. Make sure the notch in the spacer for the return spring faces in and that the spring end locates in it.

8 Check the condition of the shaft oil seals (one for the kickstart shaft and one for the crankshaft) in the clutch cover **(see illustrations)**. If they are damaged, deteriorated or shows signs of leakage they must be replaced with new ones (though it is best to fit new ones whatever the apparent condition) – lever out the old seal with a seal hook or screwdriver. Press or drive the new seal squarely into place using your fingers, a seal driver or suitable socket.

Installation

9 Fit the kickstart mechanism onto the crankcase, locating the kick spring loop

in the recess, and tensioning the return spring to locate its free end in the hole **(see illustrations)**.

10 If removed fit the idle gear inner circlip into its groove, then fit the inner washer, the gear with its marked side facing out, the outer washer and the outer circlip **(see illustrations)** – Yamaha specify to use new circlips.

11 Install the clutch (see Section 15).

21 Crankcase separation and reassembly

Note: *To separate the crankcase halves, the engine must be removed from the frame.*

Separation

1 To access the crankshaft and connecting rod assembly, balancer shaft, transmission shafts, selector drum and forks, and their

bearings, the crankcase must be split into its two halves.

2 Before the crankcases can be separated the following components must be removed:

Starter motor (Chapter 8)
Neutral switch (Chapter 8)
Camshaft (Section 7)
Cylinder head (Section 9)
Cam chain and blades (Section 8)
Cylinder block (Section 11)
Piston (Section 12)
Alternator (Chapter 8)
Starter clutch (Section 14)
Clutch (Section 15)
Primary drive gear (Section 17)
Oil filter, strainer and pump (Section 18)
Gearchange mechanism (Section 19)
Kickstart mechanism (Section 20)

3 On 2010-on YBR models (not fitted with a kickstart) remove the outer circlip, collar and inner circlip from the right-hand end of the transmission output shaft.

20.10c . . . the idle gear . . .

20.10d . . . the outer washer . . .

20.10e . . . and the outer circlip

4 Make a cardboard template punched with holes to match all the bolts in the each crankcase half – as each crankcase bolt is removed, store it in its relative position in the template **(see illustration)**. This will ensure all bolts are installed in the correct location on reassembly. Unscrew the crankcase bolts evenly, a little at a time and in a criss-cross sequence until they are finger-tight, then remove them, noting the one that secures the clutch cable holder – there are two bolts in the right-hand side and eight in the left **(see illustrations)**. **Note:** *As each bolt is removed, store it in its relative position in a cardboard template of the crankcase halves. This will ensure all bolts and washers are returned to their original locations on reassembly.*

5 Holding both halves of the crankcase place the engine on its left-hand side, laying it on wooden blocks so the shaft ends are clear of the bench. Carefully lift the right crankcase half off the left half – use a screwdriver inserted in the two leverage points to initially separate the halves, along with a soft-faced mallet if necessary to tap around the joint and on the right-hand ends of the crankshaft and transmission input shaft to ensure they remain in the left-hand crankcase **(see illustration)**. **Note:** *If the halves do not separate easily, make sure all fasteners have been removed. Do not try and separate the halves by levering against the crankcase mating surfaces as they are easily scored and will leak oil in the future if damaged.* The right-hand crankcase half will come away leaving the crankshaft, balancer shaft, transmission shafts and selector drum and forks in the left-hand half.

6 Remove the two locating dowels from the crankcase if they are loose – they could be in either half **(see illustration 21.11)**.

7 Refer to Sections 22 to 27 for the removal and installation of the components housed within the crankcases.

Reassembly

8 Remove all traces of sealant from the crankcase mating surfaces.

9 Refer to Sections 22 to 27 and double check that all components and their bearings, and the transmission output shaft oil seal, are in place in the left-hand crankcase half, and that all bearings are in the right-hand half.

10 Generously lubricate the crankshaft and

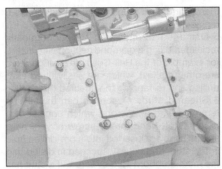

21.4a Make a cardboard template like the one shown to store the bolts

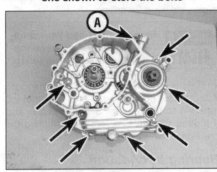

21.4c Left-hand crankcase bolts (arrowed) – note the clutch cable holder (A)

21.4b Right-hand crankcase bolts (arrowed)

21.5 Carefully separate the crankcase halves

transmission shaft bearings and gears and the selector fork shafts and fork ends and the tracks in the selector drum with clean engine oil, then use a rag soaked in high flash-point solvent to wipe over the mating surfaces of both crankcase halves to remove all traces of oil.

11 If removed, fit the two locating dowels into the right-hand crankcase half **(see illustration)**.

12 Apply a small amount of suitable sealant (Yamaha-Bond 1215 or equivalent RTV sealant – ask your dealer) to the mating surface of the right-hand crankcase half as shown, avoiding the oil passages in the top and front of the crankcase **(see illustration)**.

Caution: Apply the sealant only to the mating surfaces. Do not apply an excessive amount as it will ooze out when the case halves are assembled and may obstruct oil passages. Do not apply the sealant close to any of the oil passages.

13 Check again that all components are in position **(see illustration)**. Carefully fit the

right-hand crankcase half down onto the left-hand half, making sure the shaft ends and dowels all locate correctly **(see illustration 21.5)**.

14 Check that the right-hand crankcase half is correctly seated. Clean the threads of all the crankcase bolts, then apply some sealant to them. Fit the two bolts into the right-hand crankcase and tighten them finger-tight **(see illustration 21.4a)**. Grasp both halves of the crankcase and turn the engine over.

Caution: The crankcase halves should fit together without being forced. If the casings are not correctly seated, remove the right-hand crankcase half and investigate the problem. Do not attempt to pull them together using the crankcase bolts as the casing will crack and be ruined.

15 Install the eight left-hand crankcase bolts, fitting the clutch cable holder with the uppermost bolt, and tighten them finger-tight **(see illustration and 21.4b)**. Set the engine upright. Now tighten all the bolts evenly and a little at a

21.11 Make sure the dowels (arrowed) are fitted

21.12 Apply the sealant to the perimeter mating surface, making sure none blocks the oil passages (arrowed)

21.13 Make sure all components and assemblies are correctly installed

time in a criss-cross sequence to the torque setting specified at the beginning of the Chapter.

16 With all crankcase fasteners tightened, check that the crankshaft, balancer shaft and transmission shafts rotate smoothly and easily. Check that the transmission shafts rotate freely and independently in neutral, then rotate the selector drum by hand (you will need to fit the cam plate – see Section 19) and select each gear in turn whilst rotating the input shaft. If there are any signs of undue stiffness, tight or rough spots, or of any other problem, the fault must be rectified before proceeding further.

17 Install all other removed assemblies in a reverse of the sequence given in Steps 3 and 2.

22 Crankcases and bearings

Crankcases

1 After the crankcases have been separated, remove the crankshaft and balancer shaft, the selector drum and forks and the transmission shafts, referring to the relevant Sections of this Chapter.

2 Clean the crankcases thoroughly with new solvent and dry them with compressed air. Blow out all oil passages with compressed air.

3 Remove all traces of old gasket sealant from the mating surfaces. Clean up minor damage to the surfaces with a fine sharpening stone or grindstone.

Caution: Be very careful not to nick or gouge the crankcase mating surfaces or oil leaks will result. Check both crankcase halves very carefully for cracks and other damage.

4 Small cracks or holes in aluminium castings can be repaired with an epoxy resin adhesive as a temporary measure or with one of the low temperature welding kits. Permanent repairs can only be done by TIG (tungsten inert gas or heli-arc) welding, and only a specialist in this process is in a position to advise on the economy or practical aspect of such a repair.

If any damage is found that can't be repaired, replace the crankcase halves as a set.

5 Damaged threads can be economically reclaimed using a diamond section wire insert, for example of the Heli-Coil type (though there are other makes), which are easily fitted after drilling and re-tapping the affected thread.

6 Sheared studs or screws can usually be removed with extractors, which consist of a tapered, left-hand thread screw of very hard steel. These are inserted into a pre-drilled hole in the stud, and usually succeed in dislodging the most stubborn stud or screw. If a stud has sheared above its bore line, it can be removed using a conventional stud extractor which avoids the need for drilling.

 Refer to Tools and Workshop Tips for details of installing a thread insert and using screw extractors.

7 Install all components and assemblies, referring to the relevant Sections of this and the other Chapters, before reassembling the crankcase halves.

Bearing information

8 The crankshaft, balancer shaft, and transmission shaft bearings should all be replaced with new ones as part of a complete engine overhaul, or individually as required due to wear or failure.

9 Bearing failure occurs mainly because of lack of lubrication, the presence of dirt or other foreign particles, overloading the engine, break-up of one or more of the bearing components due to fatigue, or corrosion. Regardless of the cause of bearing failure, it must be corrected before the engine is reassembled to prevent it from happening again.

10 The bearings should rotate smoothly, freely and quietly, there should be no rough spots, and there should be no excessive play between the inner and outer races, or between the inner race and the shaft it fits on, or between the outer race and its housing in the crankcase.

11 Dirt and other foreign particles get into the engine in a variety of ways. They may be left in the engine during assembly or they may pass through filters or breathers, then get into the oil and from there into the bearings. Metal chips from machining operations and normal engine wear are often present. Abrasives are sometimes left in engine components after reconditioning operations, especially when parts are not thoroughly cleaned using the proper cleaning methods. The best prevention for this cause of bearing failure is to clean all parts thoroughly and keep everything spotlessly clean during engine reassembly. Regular oil changes are also recommended.

12 Lack of lubrication or lubrication breakdown has a number of interrelated causes. Excessive heat (which thins the oil), overloading and oil leakage all contribute to lubrication breakdown. Blocked oil passages will starve a bearing of lubrication and destroy it.

13 Riding habits can have a definite effect on bearing life. Full throttle low, speed operation, or labouring the engine, puts very high loads on bearings. Short trip riding leads to corrosion of bearings, as insufficient engine heat is produced to drive off the condensed water and corrosive gases produced. These products collect in the engine oil, forming acid and sludge. As the oil is carried to the engine bearings, the acid attacks and corrodes the bearing material.

14 Incorrect bearing installation during engine assembly will lead to bearing failure as well. To avoid bearing problems, clean all parts thoroughly before reassembly, and lubricate the new bearings with clean engine oil during installation.

Bearing removal and installation

Note: *If the correct bearing removal and installation tools are not available take the crankcases and crankshaft to a Yamaha dealer for removal and installation of the bearings – do not risk damaging either the cases or the crankshaft.*

Crankshaft (main) bearings

15 If the crankshaft (main) bearings have failed, excessive rumbling and vibration will be felt when the engine is running **(see illustrations)**.

22.15a Crankshaft (main) bearing (A), balancer shaft bearing (B), transmission input shaft bearing (C) and output shaft bearing (D) – **right-hand crankcase half**

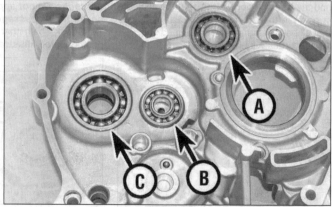

22.15b Balancer shaft bearing (A), transmission input shaft bearing (B) and output shaft bearing (C) – **left-hand crankcase half**

16 Separate the crankcase halves (Section 21) and remove the crankshaft (Section 23).

17 To remove the right-hand main bearing from the crankcase, heat the bearing housing with a hot air gun, then tap the bearing out from the outside of the crankcase using a bearing driver or a suitable socket (**see illustration 22.15a**).

18 Smear the outside of the new bearing with clean oil and fit it with its marked side towards the inside of the engine, then heat the housing again and drive the bearing squarely in until it seats using a driver or socket that bears only on the outer race.

19 Before removing the left-hand bearing from the crankshaft check with a Yamaha dealer as to the availability of parts (**see illustration**) – the crankshaft may be available as a complete built-up assembly with the bearing fitted, and it is worth mentioning that if the bearing is worn it is quite likely that the connecting rod big-end bearing is also worn. Balance up the respective costs of the complete unit if available with the cost of the individual parts, and bear in mind that removal and installation of the bearing also means removing and installing the cam chain sprocket and that you will need a good bearing puller, or possibly an hydraulic press, for the procedure. If a new connecting rod or big-end bearing is required you will need the help of a specialist to separate and reset the crankshaft webs on the crankpin.

20 To remove the left-hand main bearing from the crankshaft, use an external bearing puller to draw it and the cam chain sprocket off.

21 Smear the inside of the new bearing with clean oil and fit it with its marked side towards the crankshaft, then heat the bearing inner race and drive or press the bearing squarely on until it seats using a tubular driver that bears only on the inner race. Drive the cam chain sprocket onto the shaft and against the bearing.

Connecting rod (big-end) bearing

22 If the connecting rod (big-end) bearing has failed, there will be a pronounced knocking noise when the engine is running, particularly under load and increasing with engine speed. Refer to Section 23, Step 6 for checks that can be made.

23 See Step 19.

Balancer shaft bearings

24 If the balancer bearings have failed, excessive rumbling and vibration will be felt when the engine is running (**see illustrations 22.15a and b**).

25 Separate the crankcase halves (Section 21) and remove the balancer shaft (Section 24).

26 To remove the right-hand bearing from the crankcase, heat the bearing housing with a hot air gun, then tap the bearing out from the outside of the crankcase using a bearing driver or a suitable socket.

27 Smear the outside of the new bearing with clean oil and fit it with its marked side towards

22.19 Left-hand crankshaft (main) bearing (arrowed)

the inside of the engine, then heat the housing again and drive the bearing squarely in until it seats using a driver or socket that bears only on the outer race.

28 To remove the left-hand bearing from the crankcase, heat the bearing housing with a hot air gun until the bearing drops out. If it doesn't come out, an expanding knife-edge bearing puller with slide-hammer attachment is required. Heat the bearing housing with a hot air gun, then fit the expanding end of the puller behind the bearing, then turn the puller to expand it and lock it. Attach the slide-hammer to the puller, then hold the crankcase firmly down and operate the slide-hammer to jar the bearing out.

29 Smear the outside of the new bearing with clean oil and fit it with its marked side towards the inside of the engine, then heat the housing again and drive the bearing squarely in until it seats using a driver or socket that bears only on the outer race.

Transmission shaft bearings

30 If the transmission bearings have failed, excessive rumbling and vibration will be felt when the engine is running (**see illustrations 22.15a and b**).

31 Separate the crankcase halves (Section 21) and remove the transmission shafts and the output shaft oil seal (Section 25).

32 Unscrew the two bolts securing the input shaft bearing retainer plate on the inside of the right-hand crankcase .

33 To remove the input shaft bearing from the right-hand crankcase and the output shaft bearings from each crankcase, heat the bearing housing with a hot air gun, then tap the bearing out from the outside of the crankcase using a bearing driver or a suitable socket.

34 Smear the outside of the new bearing with clean oil and fit it with its marked side towards the inside of the engine, then heat the housing again and drive the bearing squarely in until it seats using a driver or socket that bears only on the outer race.

35 To remove the input shaft bearing from the left-hand crankcase, heat the bearing housing with a hot air gun until the bearing drops out. If it doesn't come out, an expanding knife-edge bearing puller with slide-hammer attachment is required. Heat the bearing housing with a hot

air gun, then fit the expanding end of the puller behind the bearing, then turn the puller to expand it and lock it. Attach the slide-hammer to the puller, then hold the crankcase firmly down and operate the slide-hammer to jar the bearing out.

36 Smear the outside of the new bearing with clean oil and fit it with its marked side towards the inside of the engine, then heat the housing again and drive the bearing squarely in until it seats using a driver or socket that bears only on the outer race.

37 Apply a suitable non-permanent thread locking compound to the bearing retainer plate bolts, then fit the plate and tighten the screws (**see illustration 22.15a**).

23 Crankshaft and connecting rod

Note: *To remove the crankshaft the engine must be removed from the frame and the crankcase halves separated. The connecting rod is an integral part of the crankshaft assembly which comes as a pressed-up unit – individual components are not available.*

Removal

1 Remove the engine from the frame (see Section 4) and separate the crankcase halves (see Section 21).

2 Remove the balancer shaft (see Section 24).

3 Yamaha advise the crankshaft should be pressed out of the left-hand crankcase using Yamaha tool part No. 90890-01135 or a suitable commercial equivalent. Set the tool up as shown, making sure it is central to the shaft axis, then heat the area around the bearing housing with a hot air gun to ease removal and turn the bolt to press the crankshaft out, making sure you are ready to support it once it is free (**see illustration**). It was however found that if the crankcase was hot enough the crankshaft could be removed with only a small amount of persuasion with a hammer via a nut

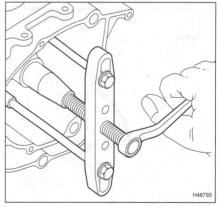

23.3a Removing the crankshaft using the Yamaha special tool

23.3b Removing the crankshaft using the Haynes method

23.4 Balancer drive gear (arrowed)

23.6 Measuring the connecting rod side clearance

threaded onto the end **(see illustration)** – DO NOT hit directly onto the threaded end of the crankshaft and DO NOT use excessive force. If you do not have the tools or experience required take the crankcase to a dealer or specialist.

Inspection

4 Clean the crankshaft with solvent. If available, blow the crank dry with compressed air. Check the balancer drive gear for wear or damage **(see illustration)**. If any of the gear teeth are excessively worn, chipped or broken, the crankshaft must be replaced with a new one. If wear or damage is found, also inspect the driven gear on the balancer shaft **(see illustration 24.3)**. Similarly check the cam chain sprocket.

5 Place the crankshaft on V-blocks and check for runout using a dial gauge. Take a reading at each end of the crankshaft and compare it to the maximum runout specified at the beginning of the Chapter. If the runout exceeds the limit, the crankshaft must be replaced with a new one.

6 Measure the connecting rod side clearance (the gap between the connecting rod big-end and the crankshaft web) with a feeler gauge **(see illustration)**. If the clearance is greater than the service limit listed in this Chapter's Specifications, replace the crankshaft with a new one.

7 Hold the crankshaft still and check for any radial (up and down) play in the big-end bearing by pushing and pulling the rod against the crank **(see illustration)**. If a dial gauge is

available measure the amount of radial play and compare the reading to the maximum specified at the beginning of the Chapter. If the play exceeds the limit, the crankshaft must be replaced with a new one.

8 Refer to Section 12 and check the connecting rod small-end and piston pin for wear.

9 Have the rod checked for twist and bend by a Yamaha dealer if you are in doubt about its straightness.

10 Refer to Section 22 and check the crankshaft (main) bearings.

11 Measure the width of the crankshaft from between the outer edge of each web **(see illustration)**. Replace the crankshaft assembly with a new one if it is not within the specified limits.

Installation

12 Yamaha advise the crankshaft be drawn or pressed into the left-hand crankcase. To draw it in as Yamaha specify you need Yamaha tools part Nos. 90890-01274, 01275, 01278 and 04081. Set the tool up as shown, making sure it is central to the shaft axis, then heat the area around the bearing housing with a hot air gun to ease installation and draw the crankshaft in until it seats **(see illustration)**. An alternative is to press it in, but again you need specialized tooling for this. However we found that if the crankcase was hot enough and by also using a freeze spray on the bearing the crankshaft

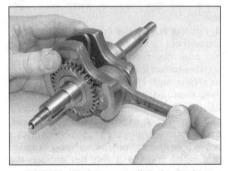

23.7 Check for any radial play in the big-end bearing

23.11 Check the width of the crankshaft as shown

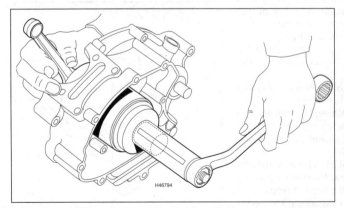

23.12a Installing the crankshaft using the Yamaha special tool

23.12b Heat the bearing housing and use freeze spray on the bearing . . .

23.12c ... then locate the crankshaft, making sure the connecting rod is correctly positioned ...

23.12d ... and use a hammer and socket to drive it in until it seats

fitted with only a small amount of persuasion with a hammer via a suitable socket bearing on the balancer drive gear **(see illustrations)** – DO NOT hit on the end of the crankshaft and DO NOT use excessive force. When installing the crankshaft make sure the connecting rod is positioned so it sits in the opening for the cylinder bore. If you do not have the tools or experience required take the crankcase and crankshaft to a dealer or specialist.

13 Install the balancer shaft (see Section 24).

14 Reassemble the crankcase halves (see Section 21).

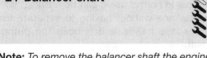

24 Balancer shaft

Note: *To remove the balancer shaft the engine must be removed from the frame and the crankcases separated.*

Removal

1 Remove the engine from the frame (see Section 4) and separate the crankcase halves (see Section 21).

2 Turn the crankshaft and balancer shaft until

the punch marks on their respective gears are aligned – this is how they must be positioned on installation **(see illustration)**. Lift the balancer shaft out of the crankcase **(see illustration)**. On 2005 and 2006 YBR models discard the O-ring on each end of the shaft – new ones must be fitted.

Inspection

3 Clean the balancer shaft with solvent. If available, blow it dry with compressed air. Check the balancer driven gear for wear or damage **(see illustration)**. If any of the gear teeth are excessively worn, chipped or broken, the gear must be replaced with a new one. If wear or damage is found, also inspect the drive gear on the crankshaft **(see illustration 23.4)**.

4 Refer to Section 22 and check the balancer shaft bearings.

Installation

5 On 2005 and 2006 YBR models fit a new O-ring smeared with grease into the groove on each end of the shaft.

6 Carefully fit the balancer shaft into the left-hand crankcase, locating the shaft end in the bearing, and aligning the punch mark on the its driven gear tooth with that on the drive

gear tooth on the crankshaft as shown – turn the crankshaft as required for alignment **(see illustrations 24.2b and a)**.

7 Check that the crankshaft and balancer shaft rotate freely and easily.

8 Reassemble the crankcase halves (see Section 21).

25 Transmission shaft and oil seal removal and installation

Note: *To remove the transmission shafts the engine must be removed from the frame and the crankcases separated.*

Removal

1 Remove the engine from the frame and separate the crankcase halves (see Section 21).

2 Remove the selector drum and forks (see Section 27).

3 Grasp the input shaft and output shaft together and lift both shafts out of the crankcase – hold the bottom pinion on the output shaft to prevent it dropping off, and note that the long pushrod for the clutch will

24.2a Align the punch marks ...

24.2b ... then lift the balancer shaft out

24.3 Check the driven gear (arrowed)

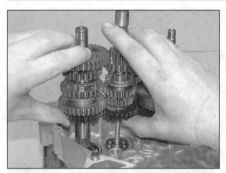

25.3 Lift the transmission shafts out together

25.4 Remove and discard the oil seal

25.7 Drive the new seal into place using a seal driver or socket

25.8 Do not forget the pushrod

25.9 Join the shafts so all related gears are engaged

25.16 Tilt the seal and lever it out

drop out of the input shaft **(see illustration)**. If the shafts are stuck, use a soft-faced hammer and gently tap on their ends. Note that there is a thrust washer on the left-hand end of the output shaft which may stick to the bearing or fall off as you remove the shafts – retrieve the washer and fit it back onto the shaft **(see illustration 26.32)**.

4 Prise the output shaft oil seal out of the left-hand crankcase using a seal hook or screwdriver **(see illustration)**. Discard the seal as a new one must be used.

5 If necessary, the transmission shafts can be disassembled and inspected for wear or damage (see Section 26).

6 Refer to Section 22 and check the transmission shaft bearings.

Installation

7 Grease the lips of the new seal. Press or drive the seal into its housing until its outer face is level with the inner rim of the chamfered edge as shown **(see illustration and 25.17c)**.

8 Make sure the thrust washer is on the left-hand end of the output shaft and that it stays in place when installing the shafts – stick it in place with some oil or grease if it is likely to fall off **(see illustration 26.32)**. Make sure the clutch pushrod is inserted into the left-hand end of the input shaft **(see illustration)**.

9 Join the shafts together on the bench so their related gears are engaged **(see illustration)**. Grasp the shafts together, holding the pinion on the left-hand end of the

output shaft to prevent it dropping off, and making sure the pushrod does not drop out of the input shaft, and fit them into the left-hand crankcase, locating the shaft ends in the bearings **(see illustration 25.3)**.

10 Make sure both transmission shafts are correctly seated and their related pinions are correctly engaged.

11 Install the selector drum and forks (see Section 27).

12 Position the gears in the neutral position and check the shafts are free to rotate easily and independently (i.e. the input shaft can turn whilst the output shaft is held stationary) before proceeding further. Also check that each gear can be selected by turning the input shaft with one hand and the selector drum with the other.

13 Reassemble the crankcase halves (see Section 21).

Output shaft oil seal

14 If there is evidence of leakage from the oil seal in normal use it can be replaced with a new one without having to separate the crankcase halves and remove the output shaft.

15 Remove the front sprocket (see Chapter 6).

16 Push one side of the seal in so it tilts, then prise out the other side **(see illustration)**.

17 Wrap some insulating tap around the end of the shaft **(see illustration)**. Grease the lips of the new seal. Slide the seal over the shaft and press it into its housing **(see illustration)**.

25.17a Wrap some tape around the shaft . . .

25.17b . . . then slide the seal into place . . .

25.17c . . . setting it as shown

Press or drive the seal in until its outer face is level with the inner rim of the chamfered edge as shown **(see illustration)**.

26 Transmission shaft overhaul

1 Remove the transmission shafts from the crankcase (see Section 25). Always disassemble the transmission shafts separately to avoid mixing up the components **(see illustrations)**.

Input shaft

Disassembly

2 Before disassembly measure the set length of the shaft between the outer faces of the

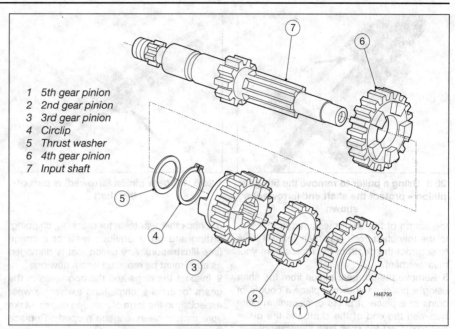

1 5th gear pinion
2 2nd gear pinion
3 3rd gear pinion
4 Circlip
5 Thrust washer
6 4th gear pinion
7 Input shaft

26.1a Transmission input shaft components

outer pinions as shown and record the result **(see illustration)** – when rebuilt the shaft must be exactly the same length. Note that the manufacturer's specification given at the beginning of the Chapter for the set length is measured between the centre of the outer face

of the large 5th gear pinion, which is recessed. However this can be difficult to measure, depending on the equipment available. Using a conventional Vernier gauge it is easier to use our method, which is to measure to the outer non-recessed rim – if you want to compare

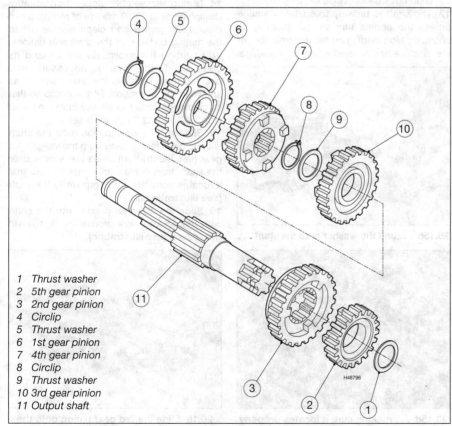

1 Thrust washer
2 5th gear pinion
3 2nd gear pinion
4 Circlip
5 Thrust washer
6 1st gear pinion
7 4th gear pinion
8 Circlip
9 Thrust washer
10 3rd gear pinion
11 Output shaft

26.1b Transmission output shaft components

HAYNES HINT

When disassembling the transmission shafts, place the parts on a long rod or thread a wire through them to keep them in order and facing the proper direction.

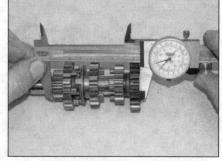

26.2 Measure the set length of the assembled shaft

26.3 Using a puller to remove the 5th gear pinion – protect the shaft end (arrowed) as shown

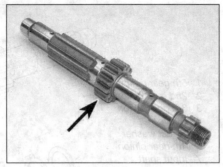

26.6 1st gear pinion (arrowed) is part of the shaft

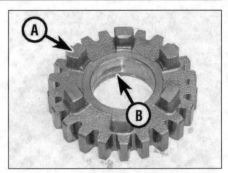

26.8 Check the gear teeth, the dogs (A) and the bearing surface (B) for wear and damage

the length of the shaft measured in this way to the manufacturer's way then you will have to subtract the depth of the recess from your measurement.

3 Remove the 5th gear pinion from the shaft using a puller as shown – place a couple of coins or a piece of brass or aluminium plate between the end of the shaft and the puller bolt to protect the shaft **(see illustration)**.

4 Slide the 2nd gear pinion and the 3rd gear pinion off the shaft **(see illustrations 26.17 and 26.16)**.

5 Remove the circlip securing the 4th gear pinion, then slide the thrust washer and the pinion off the shaft **(see illustrations 26.15c, b and a)**.

6 The 1st gear pinion is integral with the shaft **(see illustration)**.

Inspection

7 Wash all of the components in clean solvent and dry them off.

8 Check the gear teeth for cracking, chipping, pitting and other obvious wear or damage **(see illustration)**. Any pinion that is damaged as such must be replaced with a new one.

9 Inspect the dogs and the dog holes in the gears for cracks, chips, and excessive wear especially in the form of rounded edges. Make sure mating gears engage properly. Replace the paired gears as a set if necessary.

10 Check for signs of scoring or bluing on the pinions and shaft. This could be caused by overheating due to inadequate lubrication. Check that all the oil holes and passages are clear. Replace any damaged pinions with new ones.

11 Check that each pinion moves freely on the shaft but without undue freeplay.

12 The shaft is unlikely to sustain damage unless the engine has seized, placing an unusually high loading on the transmission, or the machine has covered a very high mileage.

Check the surface of the shaft, especially where a pinion turns on it, and replace the shaft if it has scored or picked up, or if there are any cracks. Damage of any kind can only be cured by replacement. Using V-blocks and a dial gauge check the shaft for runout – replace the shaft with a new one if it exceeds the specified limit.

13 Check the washer(s) and circlip(s) and replace any that are bent or appear weakened or worn. Use new ones if in any doubt about their condition. Note that it is good practice, and specified by Yamaha, to use new circlips when overhauling the transmission shafts.

Reassembly

14 During reassembly, apply molybdenum disulphide oil (a 50/50 mixture of molybdenum disulphide grease and clean engine oil) to the mating surfaces of the shaft and pinions. When fitting the circlip, do not expand its ends any further than is necessary, and position them between the raised splines as shown in the illustration. Fit the circlip so that its chamfered side faces away from the thrust side, i.e. towards the pinion it secures.

15 Slide the 4th gear pinion onto the shaft with its dogs facing away from the integral 1st gear **(see illustration)**. Slide the washer onto the shaft, then fit the circlip, making sure that it locates correctly in the groove in the shaft **(see illustrations)**.

16 Slide the 3rd gear pinion onto the shaft with the selector fork groove facing the 4th gear pinion **(see illustration)**.

26.15a Slide the 4th gear pinion . . .

26.15b . . . and the washer onto the shaft . . .

26.15c . . . and secure them with the circlip . . .

26.15d . . . making sure it locates properly in its groove

26.16 Slide the 3rd gear pinion onto the shaft . . .

17 Slide the 2nd gear pinion onto the shaft with its dogs facing the 3rd gear pinion **(see illustration)**.

18 Press the 5th gear pinion onto the end of the shaft with the recessed face away from the 2nd gear pinion and the raised section towards it **(see illustration)** – one way to do this is to use a vice with the shaft set up as shown, with the clutch nut threaded onto the right-hand end of the shaft to protect the threads, and a piece of brass or aluminium plate between the nut and the vice **(see illustration)**. On the left-hand end use a nut as shown or an old socket between the vice and the recessed face of the pinion – it must be large enough to fit over the shaft. Close the vice to press the gear on, making sure that you repeatedly measure the set length accurately (see Step 2) as the raised section on the inner face of the 5th gear pinion approaches the 2nd gear pinion – it must be positioned so that the set length of the shaft is as specified or as recorded before disassembly when measured as shown **(see illustration 26.2)**. If the length is too short the raised section on the inner face of the 5th gear pinion could press against the 2nd gear pinion and prevent it from turning freely. If you go too far, draw the 5th gear pinion back using the puller as on removal.

19 Check that all components have been correctly installed **(see illustration)**.

Output shaft

Disassembly

20 Slide the thrust washer off the left-hand end of the shaft, followed by the 5th gear pinion and the 2nd gear pinion **(see illustrations 26.32, 26.31 and 26.30)**.

21 Release the circlip securing the 1st gear pinion on the right-hand end of the shaft, then remove the washer **(see illustrations 26.29b and a)**.

22 Slide the 1st gear pinion off the shaft, followed by the 4th gear pinion **(see illustrations 26.28 and 27)**.

23 Release the circlip securing the 3rd gear pinion, then slide the washer and pinion off the shaft **(see illustrations 26.26c, b and a)**.

Inspection

24 Refer to Steps 7 to 13 above.

Reassembly

25 During reassembly, apply molybdenum disulphide oil (a 50/50 mixture of molybdenum disulphide grease and clean engine oil) to the mating surfaces of the shaft, pinions and bushes. When installing the circlips, do not expand the ends any further than is necessary. Install the stamped circlips so that their chamfered side faces away from the thrust side, i.e. towards the pinion it secures.

26 Slide the 3rd gear pinion onto the right-hand end of the shaft, with its dogs facing the right. Slide the washer onto the shaft, then fit the circlip, making sure it is locates correctly in its groove **(see illustrations)**.

26.17 . . . followed by the 2nd gear pinion

26.18a Fit the 5th gear pinion onto the shaft . . .

26.18b . . . and press it into place as described

26.19 The complete assembly should be as shown

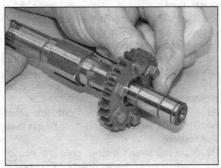

26.26a Slide the 3rd gear pinion onto the shaft . . .

26.26b . . . followed by the washer . . .

26.26c . . . and secure them with the circlip . . .

26.26d . . . making sure it locates in the groove

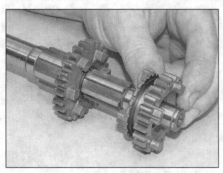

26.27 Slide the 4th gear pinion onto the shaft

26.28 Slide the 1st gear pinion onto the shaft

26.29a Slide the washer onto the shaft . . .

26.29b . . . then fit the circlip . . .

26.29c . . . making sure it locates in the groove

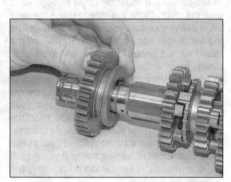

26.30 Slide the 2nd gear pinion onto the shaft

26.31 Slide the 5th gear pinion onto the shaft

27 Slide the 4th gear pinion onto the shaft, with its selector fork groove facing the 3rd gear pinion **(see illustration)**.

28 Slide the 1st gear pinion onto the shaft with the more recessed face and raised centre section facing the 4th gear pinion **(see illustration)**.

29 Slide the washer onto the shaft then fit the circlip, making sure it is locates correctly in its groove **(see illustrations)**.

30 Slide the 2nd gear pinion onto the left-hand end of the shaft with its selector fork groove facing the 3rd gear pinion **(see illustration)**.

31 Slide the 5th gear pinion onto the shaft with its dogs facing the 2nd gear pinion **(see illustration)**.

32 Slide the thrust washer onto the end of the shaft – smear it with grease to prevent it dropping off **(see illustration)**.

33 Check that all components have been correctly installed **(see illustration)**.

27 Selector drum and forks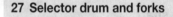

Note: *To remove the selector drum and forks the engine must be removed from the frame and the crankcases separated.*

Removal

1 Remove the engine (see Section 4) and separate the crankcase halves (see Section 21).

2 Before removing the selector forks, note that each fork carries an identification letter **(see illustration)**. The right-hand fork has R, the centre fork C, and the left-hand fork L, with all marks facing the right-hand side of the engine. If no letters are visible, mark them

26.32 Slide the thrust washer onto the shaft

26.33 The assembled shaft should be as shown

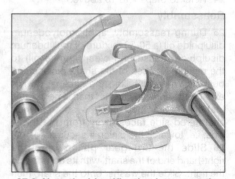

27.2 Note the identification letters on the forks

27.5 Check the fit of each fork in its pinion . . .

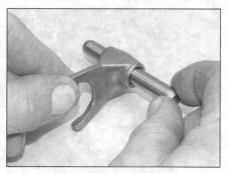

27.6 . . . and on its shaft

27.8 Check the guide pins and their grooves in the drum

yourself using a felt pen. The R and L forks fit into the output shaft and are carried on the longer shaft, and the C fork on the shorter shaft fits into the input shaft.

3 Support the output shaft selector forks and withdraw the shaft from the casing **(see illustration 27.13c)**. Pivot each fork out of its groove in the selector drum and remove them **(see illustrations 27.13b and a)**.

4 Withdraw the selector drum **(see illustration 27.12b)**. Support the input shaft selector fork and withdraw the shaft from the casing and remove the fork **(see illustration 27.11b and a)**. Once removed, slide the forks back onto the shafts to keep them in the correct order and way round.

Inspection

5 Inspect the selector forks for any signs of wear or damage, especially around the fork ends where they engage with the groove in the pinion. Check that each fork fits correctly in its pinion groove **(see illustration)**. Check closely to see if the forks are bent. If the forks are in any way damaged they must be replaced with new ones.

6 Check that the forks fit correctly on the shaft **(see illustration)**. They should move freely with a light fit but no appreciable freeplay. Replace the fork(s) and/or shaft(s) with new ones if they are worn beyond their specifications. Check that the fork shaft holes

27.11a Fit the input shaft fork . . .

in the casings are neither worn nor damaged.

7 Check each selector fork shaft is straight by rolling it along a flat surface. A bent rod will cause difficulty in selecting gears and make the gearchange action heavy. Replace the shaft with a new one if it is bent.

8 Inspect the selector drum grooves and selector fork guide pins for signs of wear or damage **(see illustration)**. If either component shows signs of wear or damage the fork(s) and drum must be replaced with new ones.

9 Check that the selector drum rotates freely in each crankcase half and has no sign of freeplay between it and the casing. Replace the drum and/or crankcases with new ones if they are worn.

27.11b . . . and shaft . . .

Installation

10 Lubricate the ends and bore of each fork and the fork shaft with oil before installing it.

11 Locate the input shaft fork, marked C, in its pinion groove, making sure it is the correct way up – see Step 2 **(see illustration)**. Slide the short shaft through the fork and into its bore **(see illustration)**.

12 Lubricate the selector drum left-hand end with clean engine oil. Slide the selector drum into position in the crankcase, aligning it so that the contact for the neutral switch pin points to the neutral switch hole in the crankcase **(see illustration)**, and lifting the fork and locating its guide pin in the centre track in the drum **(see illustration)**.

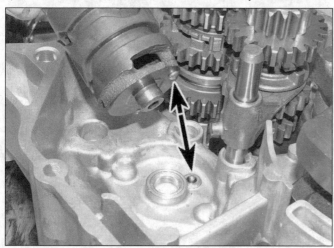

27.12a . . . then fit the drum, aligning it as shown . . .

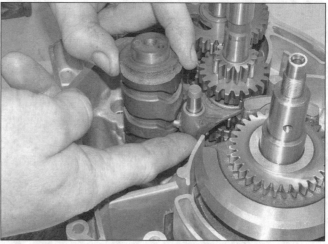

27.12b . . . and locating the fork guide pin in its track

27.13a Fit the fork marked L . . .

27.13b . . . and the fork marked R . . .

27.13c . . . then locate their guide pins in the tracks and fit the shaft

13 Locate the output shaft forks in their pinion groove, making sure they are the correct way round and up – see Step 2 **(see illustrations)**. Pivot each fork round to locate its guide pin in its groove in the selector drum **(see illustration)**. Slide the long shaft through the output shaft forks and into its bore in the crankcase.

14 Reassemble the crankcase halves (see Section 21).

28 Running-in procedure

1 Make sure the engine oil level is correct (see *Pre-ride checks*). Make sure there is fuel in the tank.

2 Turn the engine kill switch to the ON position and shift the gearbox into neutral. Turn the ignition ON. On carburettor models set the choke.

3 Start the engine and allow it to run at a moderately fast idle until it reaches operating temperature.

4 If a lubrication failure is suspected, carry out an oil pressure check as described in Section 3 of this Chapter. If an engine is run without oil, even for a short period of time, severe damage will occur.

5 Check carefully that there are no oil leaks and make sure the transmission and controls, especially the brakes, function properly before road testing the machine.

6 Treat the machine gently for the first few miles to make sure oil has circulated throughout the engine and any new parts installed have started to seat.

7 Even greater care is necessary if a new piston and rings or a new cylinder have been fitted, and the bike will have to be run in as when new. This means greater use of the transmission and a restraining hand on the throttle until at least 300 miles (500 km) have been covered. There's no point in keeping to any set speed limit – the main idea is to keep from labouring the engine, not using more than 1/2 throttle, keeping engine speed below 6000 rpm, but making sure you vary engine speed and load within those limits. Gradually increase performance up to the 300 miles (500 km) mark, and do not run the engine for more than an hour without letting it cool down for five to ten minutes. Between 300 and 600 miles (500 to 1000 km) use more throttle (up to 3/4), but not full throttle, and keep engine speed below 7500 rpm. Experience is the best guide, since it's easy to tell when an engine is running freely.

8 Upon completion of the road test, and after the engine has cooled down completely, recheck the valve clearances (see Chapter 1) and check the engine oil level (see *Pre-ride checks*).

Chapter 3A
Fuel system and exhaust –
2005 and 2006 YBR models and all XT models

Contents

Degrees of difficulty

Easy, suitable for novice with little experience 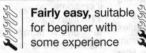	**Fairly easy,** suitable for beginner with some experience	**Fairly difficult,** suitable for competent DIY mechanic	**Difficult,** suitable for experienced DIY mechanic

Very difficult, suitable for expert DIY or professional

Specifications

Fuel

Grade	Unleaded, 91 RON (Research Octane Number)
Fuel tank capacity	
YBR models	
Total (inc. reserve)	13.0 litres
Reserve	approx 3.0 litres
XT models	
Total (inc. reserve)	10.0 litres
Reserve (when fuel warning light comes on)	approx. 2.0 litres

Carburettor

YBR models

Type	Mikuni VM22SH
ID mark	3D91 00
Fuel level	6 to 7 mm below float chamber mating surface
Float height	21.8 mm
Idle speed	see Chapter 1
Pilot screw setting (no. of turns out)	1 1/2
Main jet	97.5
Needle	5EJ7-2
Needle jet	N-7M
Pilot jet	15
Heater resistance	4.5 to 9.2 ohms @ 20°C

XT models

Type	Mikuni VM2059
ID mark	3D6
Fuel level	7.5 mm below float chamber mating surface
Float height	18.9 mm
Idle speed	see Chapter 1
Pilot screw setting (no. of turns out)	1 1/4
Main jet	105
Needle	5EJ9-2
Needle jet	N-7M
Pilot jet	12.5
Heater resistance	approx. 11 ohms

Torque wrench settings

Air induction system pipe bolts	10 Nm
Carburettor flange bolts (YBR models)	10 Nm
Downpipe flange bolts	10 Nm
Intake duct bolts	10 Nm
Silencer mounting bolt	
YBR models	22 Nm
XT models	40 Nm

---

1 General information and precautions

General information

The fuel system consists of the fuel tank, the fuel tap with integral strainer, fuel hose, carburettor and control cables.

The carburettor has a slide type throttle valve (piston). For cold starting, on YBR models the choke lever is on the left-hand side of the carburettor, and on XT models the choke lever is incorporated in the left-hand switch housing and is connected to the carburettor by cable.

Air is drawn into the carburettor via an air filter fitted in a housing behind the carburettor.

YBR models have a fuel gauge in the instrument cluster, actuated by a level sensor inside the fuel tank – when the needle hits the red zone there is approximately 3 litres of fuel left (see Chapter 8 for details).

XT models have a low fuel warning light in the instrument cluster, actuated by a level sensor inside the fuel tank and part of the fuel tap – when the light comes on there is approximately 2 litres of fuel left (see Chapter 8 for details).

Precautions

⚠️ **Warning: Petrol (gasoline) is extremely flammable, so take extra precautions when you work on any part of the fuel system. Don't smoke or allow open flames or bare light bulbs near the work area, and don't work in a garage where a natural gas-type appliance is present. If you spill any fuel on your skin, rinse it off immediately with soap and water. When you perform any kind of work on the fuel system, wear safety glasses and have a fire extinguisher suitable for a class B type fire (flammable liquids) on hand.**

Always perform service procedures in a well-ventilated area to prevent a build-up of fumes.

Never work in a building containing a gas appliance with a pilot light, or any other form of naked flame. Ensure that there are no naked light bulbs or any sources of flame or sparks nearby.

Do not smoke (or allow anyone else to smoke) while in the vicinity of petrol (gasoline), or of components containing petrol. Remember the possible presence of vapour from these sources and move well clear before smoking.

Check all electrical equipment belonging to the house, garage or workshop where work is being undertaken (see the *Safety First!* section of this manual). Remember that certain electrical appliances such as drills, cutters etc. create sparks in the normal course of operation and must not be used near petrol (gasoline) or any component containing it. Again, remember the possible presence of fumes before using electrical equipment.

Always mop up any spilt fuel and safely dispose of the rag used.

Any stored fuel that is drained off during servicing work must be kept in sealed containers that are suitable for holding petrol (gasoline), and clearly marked as such; the containers themselves should be kept in a safe place. Note that this last point applies equally to the fuel tank if it is removed from the machine; also remember to keep its filler cap closed at all times.

Read the *Safety first!* section of this manual carefully before starting work.

---

2 Fuel tank and fuel tap

⚠️ *Warning: Refer to the precautions given in Section 1 before starting work.*

YBR models

Fuel tank draining

1 Turn the fuel tap off. Have a rag ready to catch any residual fuel, release the fuel hose clamp and detach the hose from the tap.

2 Connect a drain hose to the fuel outlet union on the tap and insert its end in a container suitable and large enough for storing the fuel. Turn the fuel tap to the 'RES' position and allow the tank to drain. When the tank has drained, turn the tap to the 'OFF' position.

Fuel tank removal

3 Turn the fuel tap off.

4 Remove the side covers, the seat, and the air ducts (see Chapter 7).

5 Have a rag ready to catch any residual fuel, then release the fuel hose clamp and detach the hose from the tap.

6 Disconnect the fuel level sensor wiring connector.

7 Unscrew the fuel tank bolt and remove the washer and rubber support **(see illustration)**. Draw the tank back and remove it.

8 Inspect the tank mounting rubbers for signs of damage or deterioration and replace them with new ones if necessary.

Fuel tank installation

9 Installation is the reverse of removal, noting the following:
- Make sure the tank rubbers are correctly fitted and the washer is fitted on the rear mounting bolt.
- Make sure the fuel hose is fully pushed onto the tap union and is secured by the clamp.
- Turn the fuel tap ON and check that there is no sign of fuel leakage, then turn it off.

Fuel tap removal

10 Remove the fuel tank and drain it as described in Step 2, then turn it over and rest it on some rag.

11 Undo the screws securing the tap to the tank and withdraw the tap. Note the washers. Remove the O-ring and discard it as a new one must be used.

12 Clean the strainer in a high flash point solvent and remove any particles caught in the gauze. If there any tears or holes replace the tap with a new one. If the tap has been leaking you can disassemble it and check for worn or damaged parts. Replace any damaged parts with new ones if available, or otherwise fit a new tap.

Fuel tap installation

13 Fit a new O-ring into the groove in the tap.

14 Fit the tap, making sure the O-ring stays in place. Fit the screws with the washers and tighten them.

15 Install the fuel tank (see above).

XT models

Fuel tank draining

16 Have a rag ready to catch any residual fuel, then release the fuel hose clamp and detach the hose from the tap **(see illustration 2.19)**. Also detach the vacuum hose.

2.7 Unscrew the bolt and remove the washer and rubber support

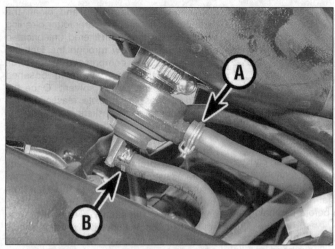

2.19 Release the clamps and detach the fuel hose (A) and the vacuum hose (B)

2.20 Disconnect the wiring connector (arrowed)

17 Connect a drain hose to the fuel outlet union on the tap and insert its end in a container suitable and large enough for storing the fuel. Gradually apply a vacuum to the tap union (connect a hose to the union and suck on its end) until fuel starts to flow, then allow the tank to drain. When the tank has drained, release the vacuum and detach the hose.

Fuel tank removal

18 Remove the seat and fuel tank panels (see Chapter 7).
19 Have a rag ready to catch any residual fuel, then release the fuel hose clamp and detach the hose from the tap **(see illustration)**. Also detach the vacuum hose.

20 Disconnect the fuel level sensor wiring connector **(see illustration)**.
21 Undo the fuel tank screws **(see illustrations)**.
22 Draw the tank back and remove it.
23 Remove the collars from the tank mounting bolt grommets. Check the grommets and tank support rubbers for signs of damage or deterioration – replacing them with new ones if necessary. If required remove the tank filler cap, then lift the tank cover off **(see illustrations)**. Replace the filler cap.

Fuel tank installation

24 Installation is the reverse of removal, noting the following:

● Make sure the tank support rubbers are correctly fitted and the collars are in the mounting bolt grommets.
● Make sure the hoses are fully pushed onto their unions, and are secured by their clamps **(see illustration 2.19)**.
● Start the engine and check that there is no sign of fuel leakage, then turn it off.

Fuel tap removal

25 Remove the fuel tank and drain it as described in Step 17, then turn it over and rest it on some rag.
26 Slacken the clamp screw then carefully pull the tap out of the tank **(see illustrations)**.

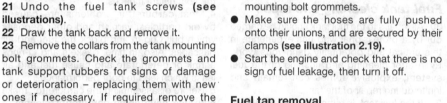

2.21a Undo the screw (arrowed) at the front . . .

2.21b . . . and the two (arrowed) at the back

2.23a Remove the filler cap . . .

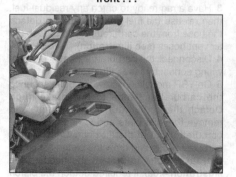

2.23b . . . and lift off the cover

2.26a Slacken the clamp (arrowed) . . .

2.26b . . . and withdraw the tap

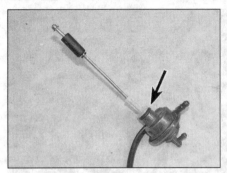

2.27 Fit a new O-ring (arrowed)

Remove the O-ring and discard it as a new one must be used **(see illustration 2.27)**.

Fuel tap Installation

27 Fit a new O-ring into the groove in the tap **(see illustration)**.
28 Fit the tap into the tank and tighten the clamp screw.
29 Install the fuel tank (see above).

Fuel tank cleaning and repair

30 All repairs to the fuel tank should be carried out by a professional who has experience in this critical and potentially dangerous work. Even after cleaning and flushing of the fuel system, explosive fumes can remain and ignite during repair of the tank.
31 If the fuel tank is removed from the bike, it should not be placed in an area where sparks or open flames could ignite the fumes coming out of the tank. Be especially careful inside garages where a natural gas-type appliance

is located, because the pilot light could cause an explosion.

3 Carburettor overhaul general information

1 Poor engine performance, hesitation, hard starting, stalling, flooding and backfiring are all signs that carburettor maintenance may be required.
2 However these symptoms are often caused by ignition or electrical system malfunctions, or mechanical problems within the engine. Try to establish for certain that the carburettor is in need of maintenance before beginning an overhaul.
3 Check the fuel tap, strainer, the fuel hose, the intake duct on the cylinder head and its joint clamps, the air filter, the ignition system, the spark plug, and valve clearances before assuming that a carburettor overhaul is required. Also check the fuel level, and adjust the float height if necessary.
4 Most carburettor problems are caused by dirt particles, varnish and other deposits which build up in and block the fuel and air passages. Also, in time, gaskets and O-rings shrink or deteriorate and cause fuel and air leaks which lead to poor performance.
5 Before disassembling the carburettor, make sure you have some carburettor cleaner, a supply of clean rags, some means of blowing out the carburettor passages and a clean place to work.
6 When overhauling the carburettor,

disassemble it completely and clean the parts thoroughly with the carburettor cleaning solvent and dry them with filtered, unlubricated compressed air. Blow through the fuel and air passages with compressed air to force out any dirt that may have been loosened but not removed by the solvent. Once the cleaning process is complete, reassemble the carburettor using new gaskets and O-rings.
7 If the engine runs extremely rough at idle or continually stalls, and an overhaul does not cure the problem (and it definitely is a carburation problem), the idle screw may require adjustment. First check that the screw is set to the correct number of turns out from its fully seated position (see Specifications), and reset if necessary. Note that any adjustment from the specified position should be done in conjunction with an exhaust gas CO analyser to ensure that the machine does not exceed emissions regulations – a dealer or tuning shop will have one. Due to the increased emphasis on controlling exhaust emissions, regulations have been formulated which prevent adjustment of the air/fuel mixture, and the pilot screws in some markets have a limiter cap fitted to prevent tampering.

4 Carburettor removal and installation

⚠ **Warning: Refer to the precautions given in Section 1 before starting work.**

Removal

1 On YBR models remove the right-hand side cover (see Chapter 7), and for best access the fuel tank (see Section 2). Detach the AIS system hose and the crankcase breather hose from the air filter housing. Fully slacken the clamp screw securing the air duct to the carburettor – note the orientation of the clamp. Unscrew the air filter housing bolts and draw the housing out.
2 On XT models remove the fuel tank. Release the clamps securing the air duct to the air filter housing and carburettor and remove the duct **(see illustration)**. If required draw the mesh filter out of the filter housing **(see illustration)**.
3 Have a rag ready to catch any residual fuel, then release the fuel hose clamp and detach the hose from the carburettor. Also detach the air vent hoses **(see illustration)**.
4 Disconnect the carburettor heater element wiring connectors **(see illustration)**.
5 On YBR models unscrew the bolts securing the carburettor flange to the intake duct. Detach the carburettor from the duct and remove the joint plate and O-rings. Ease the carburettor out of the air duct. Unscrew the carburettor cap and draw the piston assembly out, taking care to protect the needle **(see illustration 4.6a)**. If required detach the piston from the throttle cable (see Section 7, Step 3).

4.2a Release the clamps and remove the duct . . .

4.2b . . . and if required the mesh filter

4.3 Detach the air vent hoses (arrowed)

4.4 Disconnect the wiring connectors (arrowed)

4.6a Unscrew the cap and draw the piston out

4.6b Unscrew the nut and draw the choke plunger out

4.6c Release the clamp and remove the carburettor

Note: *Keep the carburettor level to prevent fuel spillage from the float chamber.*

6 On XT models unscrew the carburettor cap and draw the piston assembly out, taking care to protect the needle **(see illustration)**. If required detach the piston from the throttle cable (see Section 7, Step 3). Unscrew the choke plunger nut and draw the plunger assembly out **(see illustration)**. If required detach the plunger from the cable (see Section 7, Step 15). Check the condition of the O-rings and replace them with new ones if necessary **(see illustration 7.14)**. Fully slacken the clamp screw securing the carburettor to the intake duct and ease the carburettor out **(see illustration)**.

Caution: Stuff clean rag into each cylinder head intake after removing the carburettors, to prevent anything from falling in.

7 Place a suitable container below the float chamber, then slacken the drain screw and drain all the fuel from the carburettor **(see illustration)**. Tighten the screw once all the fuel has been drained.

8 If required detach the vacuum hose(s) from the intake duct, then unscrew the bolts securing the duct to the cylinder head and remove it **(see illustration)**. Discard the O-ring.

Installation

9 Installation is the reverse of removal, noting the following.

● Check for cracks or splits in the air duct and intake duct, and replace them with

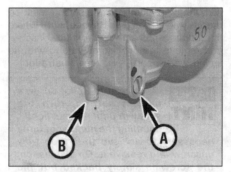

4.7 Float chamber drain screw (A) and drain (B)

new ones if necessary. If removed fit the intake duct using a new O-ring smeared with grease and tighten the bolts to the torque setting specified at the beginning of the Chapter. Connect the vacuum hose(s) **(see illustration 4.8)**.

● Refer to Section 7 for connection of the throttle cable, and on XT models the choke cable to the piston if required. Check the operation of the cable(s) and adjust them as necessary (see Chapter 1).

● On YBR models fit the joint plate using new O-rings smeared with grease, making sure it seats in the groove. Tighten the carburettor flange bolts to the torque setting specified at the beginning of the Chapter. Make sure the air duct is fully engaged on the carburettor when fitting the air filter housing, and tighten the clamp screw after the housing bolts.

4.8 Detach the hoses then undo the screws (arrowed) and remove the duct

● On XT models make sure the carburettor is fully engaged with the intake duct and air duct – if they are difficult to engage a squirt of WD40 or a smear of grease will ease entry. Make sure the clamps are positioned correctly.

● Do not forget to connect the heater element wiring **(see illustration 4.4)**.

● Check the idle speed and adjust as necessary (see Chapter 1).

5 Carburettor overhaul and fuel level check

⚠ Warning: Refer to the precautions given in Section 1 before starting work.

Disassembly

1 Remove the carburettor (see Section 4).

2 On YBR models undo the choke lever screw and remove the lever, noting how it locates under the head of the plunger. Unscrew the choke plunger nut and draw the plunger assembly out. Undo the air cut-off valve cover screws and remove the cover, spring and diaphragm, and the small air passage O-ring.

3 If required remove the heater element (see Section 6).

4 Detach the overflow hose from the float chamber **(see illustration)**. Undo the screws securing the chamber to the base of the carburettor and remove it **(see illustration)**. Remove the rubber seal or gasket (according

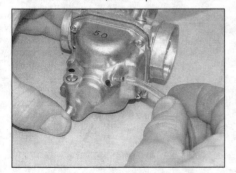

5.4a Detach the overflow hose

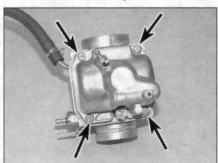

5.4b Undo the screws (arrowed) and remove the float chamber

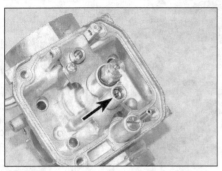

5.6 Unscrew and remove the pilot jet (arrowed)

5.7a Remove the dish . . .

5.7b . . . then unscrew the main jet (arrowed) . . .

to model) and discard it – a new one should be fitted.

5 Withdraw the float pivot pin and remove the float **(see illustration 5.28c)**. Unhook the needle valve from the tab on the float, noting how it fits **(see illustration 5.28a)**.

6 Unscrew and remove the pilot jet **(see illustration)**.

7 On XT models remove the dish from the main jet **(see illustration)**. Unscrew the main jet **(see illustration)**. Unscrew the emulsion tube **(see illustration)**. If required push the needle jet down from the venturi and remove it **(see illustrations)**.

8 On YBR models unscrew the main jet. Unscrew the emulsion tube and remove the O-ring and needle jet.

9 Undo the needle valve seat holder screw and remove the holder **(see illustration)**. Withdraw the seat and remove the O-ring.

10 The pilot screw can be removed from the carburettor, but note that its setting must be precisely noted first **(see Haynes Hint)**. Where fitted remove the anti-tamper plug. Unscrew and remove the pilot screw, along with its spring, washer and O-ring **(see illustration)**.

> **HAYNES HiNT** *To record the pilot screw's current setting, turn the screw in until it seats lightly, counting the number of turns necessary to achieve this, then fully unscrew and remove it. On installation, the screw is simply backed out the number of turns you've recorded.*

11 Repeat Step 10 for the idle speed adjuster screw if required **(see illustration)**.

Cleaning

Caution: Use only a dedicated carburettor

cleaner or petroleum-based solvent for carburettor cleaning. Do not use caustic cleaners. Never clean the jets or passages with a piece of wire or a drill bit, as they will be enlarged, causing the fuel and air metering rates to be upset.

12 Clean the carburettor body and individual components according to the instructions on the cleaner container.

13 Loosen and remove the varnish and other deposits using a nylon-bristle brush. Rinse then dry with compressed air, blowing out all of the fuel and air passages.

Inspection

14 Inspect the choke plunger and its spring for wear and damage and replace with new ones if necessary. Check the plunger bore and make sure the plunger moves smoothly up and down in it. Remove any dirt and corrosion from the bore if necessary.

5.7c . . . and the emulsion tube

5.7d Push the needle jet (arrowed) down . . .

5.7e . . . and remove it

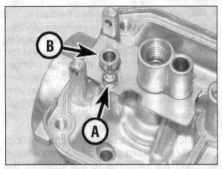

5.9 Undo the screw (A) and remove the holder and the needle valve seat (B)

5.10 Pilot screw (arrowed)

5.11 Idle speed adjuster screw (arrowed)

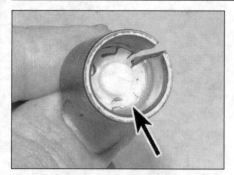

5.18 Release the needle holder (arrowed) from the piston

5.19 Check the tip of the needle valve for wear

5.24a Fit the seat . . .

15 If removed, check the tapered portion of the pilot screw and the spring and O-ring for wear or damage. Similarly check the idle speed adjuster screw. Replace any worn or damaged component with a new one if necessary.

16 Check the carburettor body, float chamber, jet housings and cap for cracks, distorted sealing surfaces and other damage. If any defects are found, replace the faulty component with a new one, although replacement of the entire carburettor may be necessary (check with a dealer on the availability of separate components).

17 Insert the piston in the carburettor and check that it moves up and down smoothly. Check the surface of the piston and its bore for wear. If the piston doesn't move smoothly or there is excessive wear, replace the piston and/or carburettor with new ones as necessary.

18 Check the needle is straight. Replace it with a new one if it is bent, or if the tip is worn – release the needle from the piston and remove the washer, circlip and needle seat if not also replacing these, noting their positions, and fit them onto the new needle in the same way **(see illustration)**. Fit the needle into the piston.

19 Check the tip of the float needle valve and the valve seat **(see illustration)**. Check the spring loaded rod in the valve operates correctly. If either is worn or damaged replace them with a new set.

20 Check the float for damage. This will usually be apparent by the presence of fuel inside the float. If it is damaged, replace it with a new one.

21 On YBR models check the air cut-off valve

5.24b . . . and secure it with the holder

5.26a Thread the emulsion tube into its bore . . .

components, particularly looking for any holes or splits in the diaphragm – holding it up to a light will help reveal any. Make sure the spring is not distorted.

Reassembly

Note: *When reassembling the carburettors, use new O-rings and a new float chamber seal or gasket. Do not overtighten the carburettor jets and screws, as they are easily damaged.*

22 Install the pilot screw (if removed) along with its spring, washer and O-ring, turning it in until it seats lightly **(see illustration 5.10)**. Now turn the screw out the number of turns previously recorded on removal. Fit a new anti-tamper plug where necessary. If you are not sure of the previous setting, set the pilot screw to the number of turns out specified at the beginning of the Chapter according to your model.

23 Repeat Step 22 for the idle speed adjuster screw if removed **(see illustration 5.11)** –

there is no specified setting for this, so if the previous setting was not recorded you will have to make final adjustments to the idle speed after reassembling and installing the carburettor – refer to Chapter 1.

24 Fit the float needle valve seat with its O-ring and secure it with the holder **(see illustrations)**.

25 On YBR models fit the needle jet then fit the emulsion tube with its O-ring. Screw the main jet into the emulsion tube.

26 On XT models fit the needle jet, making sure it is the correct way round and locates up into the venturi **(see illustrations 5.7e and d)**. Fit the emulsion tube with its O-ring and screw it in, then screw the main jet into it **(see illustrations)**. Fit the dish **(see illustration 5.7a)**.

27 Screw the pilot jet into the carburettor **(see illustration)**.

28 Hook the float needle valve onto the tab on the float **(see illustration)**. Fit the float

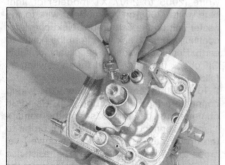

5.26b . . . then thread the main jet into the tube

5.27 Screw the pilot jet into its bore

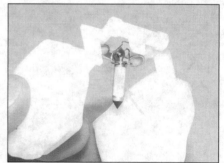

5.28a Hook the needle valve onto the float . . .

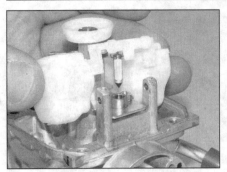

5.28b . . . then fit the float . . .

5.28c . . . and insert the pin

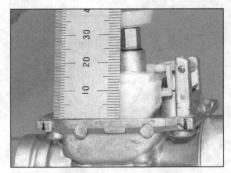

5.29a Checking float height

onto the carburettor, making sure the needle valve locates in the seat, then insert the pivot pin **(see illustrations)**.

29 To check the float height, hold the carburettor upside down and measure the height of the upper surface of the float above the chamber mating surface with an accurate ruler **(see illustration)**. The height should be as specified at the beginning of the Chapter. If not, first make sure the needle valve tip and seat are not worn, in which case replace them with new ones. If necessary adjust the float height by carefully bending the tab for the needle valve **(see illustration)** – bend the tab down to increase height and up to reduce it.

30 Fit the rubber seal or gasket (according to model) onto the float chamber, making sure it is seated properly. Fit the chamber onto the carburettor and tighten the screws **(see illustration)**. Connect the overflow hose to its union **(see illustration 5.4a)**.

31 If removed install the heater element (see Section 6).

32 On YBR models fit the air cut-off valve O-ring onto the air passage. Fit the diaphragm with its tip innermost, then fit the spring and the cover. Insert the choke plunger assembly and tighten the nut. Fit the choke lever, locating its end under the plunger head.

33 Install the carburettor (see Section 4).

Fuel level check

Note: *The fuel level is checked with the carburettor installed.*

34 To check the fuel level, position the

motorcycle on level ground and support it using the centrestand or an auxiliary stand so the carburettor is vertical.

35 Yamaha can provide a fuel level gauge (part No. 90890-01312), or alternatively a suitable length of clear plastic tubing can be used. Attach the gauge or tubing to the drain on the bottom of the float chamber and position its open end vertically alongside and above the level of the carburettor's float chamber gasket surface.

36 On YBR models, turn the tap to ON or RES as appropriate. Slacken the drain screw and allow the fuel to flow into the tube **(see illustration 4.7)**. The level at which the fuel stabilises in the tubing indicates the level of the fuel in the float chamber. Refer to the Specifications at the beginning of the Chapter and measure the level relative to the mating surface of the float chamber with the carburettor body. Tighten the drain screw, then detach the tube, catching the fuel in rag.

37 On XT models detach the vacuum hose from the fuel tap. Slacken the drain screw **(see illustration 4.7)** and allow the fuel to flow into the tube – at this stage there will only be the residual fuel from the float chamber, so apply a vacuum to the fuel tap by connecting a hose to the vacuum stub union and sucking on its end. Fuel will start to flow into the chamber and the level in the tube will rise. The level at which the fuel stabilises indicates the level of the fuel in the float chamber. Refer to the Specifications at the beginning of the Chapter and measure the level relative to the mating surface of the float chamber with the

carburettor body. Tighten the drain screw, then detach the tube, catching the fuel in a rag. Reconnect the vacuum hose to the tap.

38 If the level was incorrect, remove the carburettor (see Section 4), then remove the float chamber (see Steps 4 and 5 – there is no need to remove the needle valve seat), and adjust the float height by carefully bending the float tab a little at a time until the correct height is obtained (Step 29). **Note:** *With the float held the same way up as it is when installed, bending the tab up lowers the fuel level – bending it down raises the fuel level.*

6 Carburettor heater system

⚠️ *Warning: Refer to the precautions given in Section 1 before starting work.*

1 The carburettor has a heater unit controlled by a thermo sensor. Before checking the system, check all the wiring and connectors in the circuit for breaks and loose connections, referring to the Wiring Diagrams at the end of Chapter 8. Disconnect the thermo sensor wiring connector (see Step 3 for access). With the ignition switch on, check for battery voltage at the brown (YBR models) or blue (XT models) wire terminal on the loom side of the connector using a voltmeter. If there is no voltage check the wiring back to the ignition switch. If there is voltage check for continuity in the yellow (YBR models), blue/white (2005 to 2007 XT models) or light blue/white (2008-on XT models) wire to the heater unit on the carburettor. Next check for continuity in the black wire from the heater to earth. Repair the wiring if necessary, or if it is OK check the heater and thermo switch as follows.

2 To test the heater, disconnect the wiring connectors **(see illustration 4.4)**. Using an ohmmeter or multimeter set to the ohms x 1 scale, connect the positive (+ve) probe to the tip of the heater and the negative (-ve) probe to the hex on the base. The resistance should be as specified at the beginning of the Chapter. If not, replace the heater with a new one.

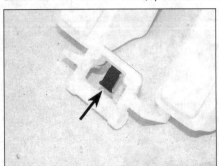

5.29b Carefully bend the tab (arrowed) a small amount to adjust float height

5.30 Fit the float chamber using a new gasket or seal

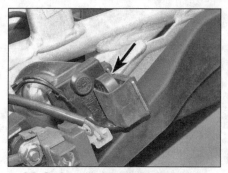

6.3 Carburettor heater thermoswitch (arrowed) – XT shown

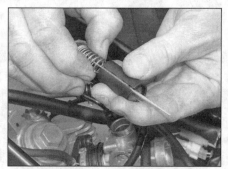

7.3a Release the cable end from the piston and remove the spring

7.3b Lever the E-clip out of its slot . . .

3 To access the thermo sensor, on YBR models remove the seat, and on XT models remove the left-hand side cover (see Chapter 7). Remove the sensor from its holder and unplug the wiring connector **(see illustration)**. To properly check the action of the sensor you will need a thermometer in a container of water that can be gently warmed up and cooled down, effectively to simulate increasing and decreasing air temperatures – just the sensing head of the sensor should be immersed. Connect the probes of a continuity tester or multimeter (set to test continuity) to the terminals of the sensor.

4 In the 'heating up phase', the meter reading should show continuity below 16°C, indicating that the sensor is closed (ON). As the temperature reaches around 16°C, the sensor's contacts should open and show no continuity (OFF) on the meter. In the 'cooling down phase', the meter should continue to show no continuity until the temperature drops to around 11°C, whereupon the sensor's contacts should close and show continuity (ON) on the meter. If the meter readings are obtained at much different temperatures (allow a variance of +/-3°C), or if it remains constantly ON or OFF at all temperatures,

then the sensor is faulty and must be replaced with a new one.

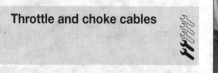

7   Throttle and choke cables

Warning: Refer to the precautions given in Section 1 before proceeding.

Throttle cable
Removal

1 On YBR models remove the right-hand air duct and the right-hand side cover (see Chapter 7), and if required for best access the fuel tank (see Section 2). On XT models remove the fuel tank (see Section 2).

2 Unscrew the carburettor cap and draw the piston assembly out, taking care to protect the needle **(see illustration 4.6a)**.

3 Hold the piston spring up, then detach the cable end from the piston and remove the spring **(see illustration)**. Release the E-clip and draw the cable out of the carburettor cap **(see illustrations)**.

4 Withdraw the cable from the machine,

7.3c . . . and draw the cable out of the cap

carefully noting its correct routing – you can tie string to the end which can be drawn through with the cable and used as a guide to draw the new cable in when installing it.

5 On YBR models undo the screw securing the cable retainer to the switch housing on the handlebar **(see illustration)**. Undo the switch housing screws and detach the top half. Detach the cable end from the pulley in the housing, then draw the cable out of the housing **(see illustration)**.

6 On XT models undo the throttle housing screws and detach the top half **(see**

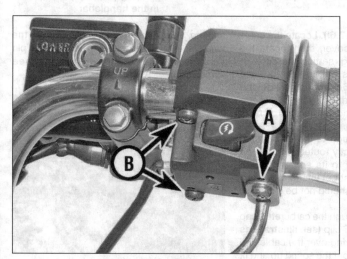

7.5a Undo the retainer screw (A) then the housing screws (B)

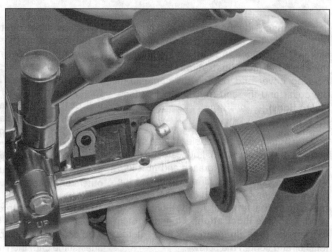

7.5b Split the housing and detach the cable end from the pulley

7.6a Undo the screws (arrowed) . . .

7.6b . . . and detach the top of the housing

7.6c Slide the twistgrip off . . .

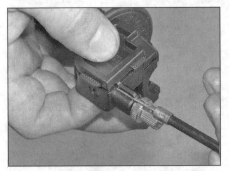

7.6d . . . then align the slots and slip the cable out

7.6e Detach the cover and free the cable from it . . .

7.6f . . . and the pulley

7.7a Fit the cable into the housing . . .

7.7b . . . and then into the pulley

7.7c Locate the peg (arrowed) in the hole in the handlebar

illustrations). Slide the twistgrip and housing off the handlebar (see illustration). Align the slits in the adjuster and its lockring and slip the cable out (see illustration). Release the housing cover and detach the cable from the cover and the end from the pulley (see illustrations).

Installation

7 On YBR models fit the cable into the switch housing (see illustration). Lubricate the cable end with multi-purpose grease and fit it into the throttle pulley (see illustration). Fit the housing halves onto the handlebar, locating the peg in the top half in the hole in the handlebar (see illustration). Fit and tighten the screws (see illustration 7.5a). Fit the retainer and tighten the screw.

8 On XT models lubricate the cable end with multi-purpose grease and fit it into the throttle

pulley (see illustration 7.6f). Locate the cable in its channel in the cover, then locate the cover onto the housing, setting the cable in the adjuster, and press the cover into place (see illustrations 7.6e and d). Slide the twistgrip onto the handlebar, then fit the top half of the housing and tighten the screws (see illustrations 7.6a).

9 Feed the cable through to the carburettor, making sure it is correctly routed – if used on removal, tie the string to its end and pull it through. The cable must not interfere with any other component and should not be kinked or bent sharply.

10 Feed the cable through the carburettor cap and secure it with the E-clip (see illustrations 7.3c and b). Fit the spring over the cable and against the cap, then hold the spring up and fit the cable end into the piston (see illustration 7.3a). Fit the piston into the carburettor,

making sure it is correctly aligned so the long slot in its side locates over the guide pin and the needle locates in the jet (see illustration).

7.10 Make sure the piston is correctly aligned

7.14 Free the cable end (A) from the plunger. Replace the O-rings (B) with new ones if necessary

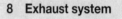

7.17a Draw the outer cable from the socket . . .

11 On YBR modes install the fuel tank if removed (see Section 2), and the right-hand air duct and the right-hand side cover (see Chapter 7). On XT models install the fuel tank (see Section 2).

12 Adjust the cable freeplay (see Chapter 1). Operate the throttle to check that it opens and closes freely. Turn the handlebars back and forth to make sure the cable doesn't cause the steering to bind.

13 Start the engine and check that the idle speed does not rise as the handlebars are turned. If it does, the throttle cable is routed incorrectly. Correct the problem before riding the motorcycle.

Choke cable (XT models)

Removal

14 Remove the fuel tank (see Section 2).

15 Unscrew the choke plunger nut and withdraw the plunger from the carburettor body **(see illustration 4.6b)**. Hold the plunger spring up, then detach the cable end from the plunger, remove the spring and draw the cable out **(see illustration)**. Check the condition of the O-rings and replace them with new ones if necessary.

16 Withdraw the cable from the machine, carefully noting its correct routing – you can tie string to the end which can be drawn through with the cable and used as a guide to draw the new cable in when installing it.

17 Pull the rubber boot off the clutch/choke lever bracket. Free the cable end from the lever **(see illustrations)**.

Installation

18 Fit the cable end into the lever **(see illustrations 7.17c, b and a)**. Fit the rubber boot.

19 Feed the cable through to the carburettor, making sure it is correctly routed – if used on removal tie the string to its end and pull it through. The cable must not interfere with any other component and should not be kinked or bent sharply.

20 Feed the cable through the plunger cap and spring and fit it into the plunger **(see illustration 7.14)**. Fit the choke plunger into the carburettor body and tighten the nut **(see illustrations 4.6b)**.

21 Adjust the cable freeplay (see Chapter 1). Operate the choke to check that it opens and closes freely. Turn the handlebars back and forth to make sure the cable doesn't cause the steering to bind.

22 Start the engine and check that the idle speed does not rise as the handlebars are turned. If it does, the choke cable is routed incorrectly. Correct the problem before riding the motorcycle.

8   Exhaust system

> **Warning: If the engine has been running the exhaust system will be very hot. Allow the system to cool before carrying out any work.**
>
> **Note:** *Before starting work on the exhaust system spray all the mounting bolts, and if they are to be removed the heat shield bolts, with penetrating fluid – many of them are exposed and are prone to corrosion.*

YBR models

Removal

1 Unscrew the bolts securing the downpipe to the cylinder head **(see illustration)**.

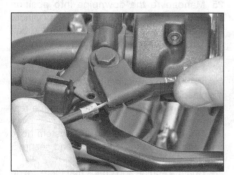

7.17b . . . then open the lever . . .

7.17c . . . and detach the inner cable end

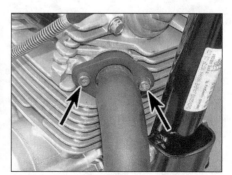

8.1 Unscrew the bolts (arrowed)

8.2 Unscrew the bolt . . .

8.3 . . . and remove the exhaust

8.7 Fit a new gasket into the port

2 Support the exhaust, then unscrew the silencer mounting bolt **(see illustration)**.

3 Detach the downpipe from the cylinder head and remove the exhaust system **(see illustration)**.

4 Remove the gasket from the port in the cylinder head and discard it – a new one must be fitted **(see illustration 8.7)**.

5 If required remove the heat shields – note the washers fitted on each side of the shields.

Installation

6 If removed fit the heat shields – fit a washer on each side of the shield with each bolt, and apply a thread locking compound to the bolts.

7 Fit a new gasket into the cylinder head port **(see illustration)** – apply a smear of grease to keep it in place if necessary.

8 Manoeuvre the exhaust system into position and locate the head of the downpipe in its port in the cylinder head. Align the silencer mounting and secure the bolt finger-tight.

9 Fit the downpipe bolts and tighten them evenly and a bit at a time to the torque setting specified at the beginning of the Chapter. Tighten the silencer bolt to the specified torque.

10 Run the engine and check that there are no exhaust gas leaks.

XT models

Removal – silencer

11 Slacken the clamp bolt securing the silencer to the downpipe **(see illustration)**.

12 Support the silencer, then unscrew the mounting bolt and carefully draw the silencer off the downpipe **(see illustration)**.

13 Check the condition of the sealing ring and replace it with a new one if necessary.

14 If required remove the heat shield – note the washers fitted on each side of the shield.

Removal – downpipe

15 Remove the sump guard (see Chapter 7). On early models release the AIS system hose clamp and detach the hose from its union on the downpipe.

16 Slacken the clamp bolt securing the silencer to the downpipe **(see illustration 8.11)**. Unscrew the bolt securing the rear of the downpipe **(see illustration)**.

17 Unscrew the bolts securing the downpipe to the cylinder head **(see illustration)**.

18 Detach the downpipe from the cylinder head and manoeuvre it down off the silencer.

19 Remove the gasket from the port in the cylinder head and discard it – a new one must be fitted **(see illustration 8.7)**. Check the condition of the downpipe-to-silencer sealing ring and replace it with a new one if necessary.

Installation – silencer

20 If removed fit the heat shield – fit a washer on each side of the shield with each bolt, and apply a thread locking compound to the bolts.

21 Manoeuvre the silencer onto the downpipe. Align the silencer mounting and tighten the bolt to the torque setting specified at the beginning of the Chapter **(see illustration 8.12)**.

22 Tighten the clamp bolt **(see illustration 8.11)**.

23 Run the engine and check that there are no exhaust gas leaks.

Installation – downpipe

24 Fit a new gasket into the cylinder head port **(see illustration 8.7)** – apply a smear of grease to keep it in place if necessary.

25 Manoeuvre the downpipe into position and locate the head in its port in the cylinder head and the rear on the silencer. Fit the bolt securing the rear of the downpipe and tighten it finger-tight **(see illustration 8.16)**.

26 Fit the downpipe bolts and tighten them evenly and a bit at a time to the torque setting specified at the beginning of the Chapter **(see illustration 8.17)**. Tighten the downpipe rear bolt.

27 On early models fit the AIS system hose onto its union on the downpipe and secure it with the clamp.

28 Run the engine and check that there are no exhaust gas leaks.

29 Install the sump guard (see Chapter 7).

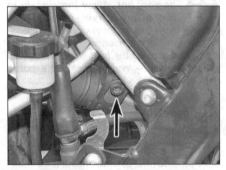

8.11 Slacken the clamp bolt (arrowed) . . .

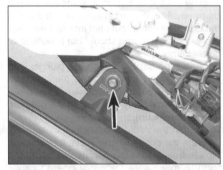

8.12 . . . then unscrew the mounting bolt (arrowed) and remove the silencer

8.16 Unscrew the bolt (arrowed)

8.17 Unscrew the bolts (arrowed)

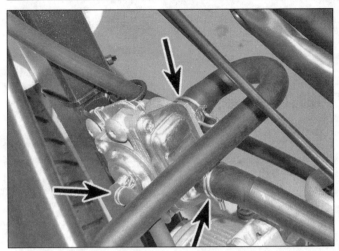

9.6a Release the clamps (arrowed) and detach the hoses

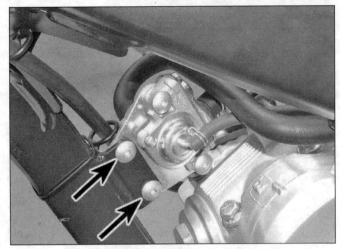

9.6b Undo the screws and remove the valve

9   Air induction system (AIS)

Function and check

1 The air induction system uses negative exhaust gas pulses to suck fresh air from the filter housing into the exhaust port or downpipe (according to model), where it mixes with hot combustion gases. The extra oxygen causes continued combustion, allowing unburnt hydrocarbons to burn off, thereby reducing emissions. The control valve incorporates a reed valve and an air cut-off valve. The air cut-off valve, which has a diaphragm actuated on by a vacuum sourced from the intake duct to the cylinder head, is open during normal running allowing the flow of air into the valve, and shuts off the flow during deceleration, preventing backfiring. The reed valve controls the flow of air out of the control valve and prevents exhaust gases flowing back into it.
2 Refer to Chapter 1 for routine checks of the system.
3 If the control valve is thought to be faulty, remove it (see below). Yamaha provide no test details for the valve, and it comes as a unit with no individual parts available. However in theory with no vacuum applied to the vacuum hose union, it should be possible to blow air into the hose union from the air filter and it should exit via the reed valve through the union for the hose to the cylinder head. If you then apply a vacuum it should not be possible to blow air through. If not, the control valve is faulty. Also it should not be possible to blow air through in the opposite direction via the

cylinder head hose union and for it to exit via the air filter hose union. If you can, then the reed valve is faulty.
4 The tests described above enable a basic check of the system, but as there are no specifications for the vacuum required to open the air cut-off valve and the pressure required to open the reed valves, a valve assembly that does not behave as described should not automatically be condemned as faulty. Take it to a Yamaha dealer for testing, or substitute it with a known good one.

Control valve removal

5 Remove the fuel tank (see Section 2).
6 Release the clamps securing the air inlet hose, the vacuum hose, and the outlet hose and detach them from their unions, noting which fits where **(see illustration)**. Unscrew the bolts and remove the control valve **(see illustration)**.
7 To replace any hoses or pipes, release the clamps securing them and disconnect them at each end.
8 Make sure all the hoses are correctly routed and securely connected at each end and held by their clamps.

10 Catalytic converter

General information

1 A catalytic converter is incorporated in the exhaust system to minimise the level of exhaust pollutants released into the atmosphere. It is an open-loop system with no feedback to the ECU.

2 The catalytic converter consists of a canister containing a fine mesh impregnated with a catalyst material, over which the hot exhaust gases pass. The catalyst speeds up the oxidation of harmful carbon monoxide, unburned hydrocarbons and soot, effectively reducing the quantity of harmful products released into the atmosphere via the exhaust gases.

Precautions

3 The catalytic converter is a reliable and simple device which needs no maintenance in itself, but there are some facts of which an owner should be aware if the converter is to function properly for its full service life.
● DO NOT use leaded or lead replacement petrol (gasoline) – the additives will coat the precious metals, reducing their converting efficiency and will eventually destroy the catalytic converter.
● Always keep the ignition and fuel systems well-maintained in accordance with the manufacturer's schedule – if the fuel/air mixture is suspected of being incorrect have it checked on an exhaust gas analyser.
● If the engine develops a misfire, do not ride the bike at all (or at least as little as possible) until the fault is cured.
● DO NOT use fuel or engine oil additives – these may contain substances harmful to the catalytic converter.
● DO NOT continue to use the bike if the engine burns oil to the extent of leaving a visible trail of blue smoke.
● Avoid bump-starting the bike unless absolutely necessary.

Chapter 3B
Fuel system and exhaust – 2007-on YBR models

Contents

Degrees of difficulty

Easy, suitable for novice with little experience	**Fairly easy,** suitable for beginner with some experience	**Fairly difficult,** suitable for competent DIY mechanic	**Difficult,** suitable for experienced DIY mechanic	**Very difficult,** suitable for expert DIY or professional

Specifications

Fuel
Grade . . . .   Unleaded. Minimum 91 RON
Fuel tank capacity
  Total (inc. reserve)
    ED models . . . .   13.0 litres
    Custom models . . . .   12.0 litres
  Reserve
    2007 to 2009 ED and all Custom models . . . .   approx. 3.0 litres
    2010-on ED models . . . .   3.4 litres

Fuel injection system
Throttle body
  2007 to 2009 ED models
    Type . . . .   Mikuni AC26-4
    ID mark 3D92 00
  2010-on ED models
    Type . . . .   Mikuni AC26-1
    ID mark 51D1 00
  Custom models
    Type . . . .   Mikuni AC26-6
    ID mark 3D92 10
Idle speed . . . .   see Chapter 1
Crankshaft position (CKP) sensor resistance . . . .   248 to 372 ohms @ 20°C
Engine temperature (ET) sensor resistance
  @ 20°C . . . .   2.5 to 2.8 K-ohms
  @ 100°C . . . .   210 to 221 ohms
Fast idle (FID) solenoid resistance . . . .   31.5 to 38.5 ohms @ 25°C
Fuel injector resistance . . . .   12.5 ohms (see text)
Fuel pressure (at idle speed) . . . .   35 psi (2.5 Bar)
Intake air pressure (IAP) sensor output voltage . . . .   3.75 to 4.25 volts
Intake air temperature (IAT) sensor resistance
  2007 to 2009 ED models . . . .   2.4 to 2.9 K-ohms @ 20°C
  2010-on ED models and Custom models . . . .   5.7 to 6.3 K-ohms @ 20°C
Throttle position (TP) sensor input voltage . . . .   5 volts
Throttle position (TP) sensor output voltage (throttle closed) . . . .   0.63 to 0.73 volts
Tip-over (TO) sensor output voltage
  Sensor upright . . . .   0.4 to 1.4V
  Sensor tilted at 65° angle . . . .   3.7 to 4.4V

Torque settings

Engine temperature sensor	18 Nm
Exhaust system	
Silencer mounting bolt	24 Nm
Downpipe bolts	10 Nm
Fuel injector bolts	10 Nm
Fuel pump retaining ring bolts	4 Nm
Intake duct flange bolts	10 Nm

1 General information and precautions

Fuel system

The fuel supply system consists of the fuel tank, an internal and integrated fuel pump, filter, pressure regulator and level sensor, the fuel hose, fuel injector, throttle body, and throttle cable. The injection system supplies fuel and air to the engine via a single throttle body. The injector is operated by the Electronic Control Unit (ECU) using the information obtained from the sensors it monitors (refer to Section 5 for more information on the operation of the fuel injection system). Cold start idle speed is controlled by the ECU via the fast idle solenoid (FID).

Air is drawn into the throttle body via an air filter fitted in a housing behind the throttle body.

All models have a fuel gauge in the instrument cluster, actuated by a level sensor that is part of the fuel pump inside the fuel tank – when the needle enters the red zone there is approximately 3 litres of fuel left (see Chapter 8 for details).

Precautions

⚠ *Warning: Petrol (gasoline) is extremely flammable, so take extra precautions when you work on any part of the fuel system. Always remove the battery (see Chapter 8). Don't smoke or allow open flames or bare light bulbs near the work area, and don't work in a garage where a natural gas-type appliance is present. If you spill any fuel on your skin, rinse it off immediately with soap and water. When you perform any kind of work on the fuel system, wear safety glasses and have a fire extinguisher suitable for a class B type fire (flammable liquids) on hand.*

Residual pressure will remain in the fuel feed hose and fuel injector after the motorcycle has been used. Before disconnecting any fuel hose, ensure the ignition is switched OFF and have some rag handy to catch any fuel. It is vital that no dirt or debris is allowed to enter the fuel system. Any foreign matter could result in injector damage or malfunction. Ensure the ignition is switched OFF before disconnecting or reconnecting any fuel injection system wiring connector. If a connector is disconnected or reconnected with the ignition switched ON, the electronic control unit (ECU) may be damaged.

Always perform service procedures in a well-ventilated area to prevent a build-up of fumes.

Never work in a building containing a gas appliance with a pilot light, or any other form of naked flame. Ensure that there are no naked light bulbs or any sources of flame or sparks nearby.

Do not smoke (or allow anyone else to smoke) while in the vicinity of petrol (gasoline) or of components containing it. Remember the possible presence of vapour from these sources and move well clear before smoking.

Check all electrical equipment belonging to the house, garage or workshop where work is being undertaken (see the *Safety first!* section of this manual). Remember that certain electrical appliances such as drills, cutters etc, create sparks in the normal course of operation and must not be used near petrol (gasoline) or any component containing it. Again, remember the possible presence of fumes before using electrical equipment.

Always mop up any spilt fuel and safely dispose of the rag used.

Any stored fuel that is drained off during servicing work must be kept in sealed containers that are suitable for holding petrol (gasoline), and clearly marked as such; the containers themselves should be kept in a safe place. Note that this last point applies equally to the fuel tank if it is removed from the machine; also remember to keep its filler cap closed at all times.

Read the *Safety first!* section of this manual carefully before starting work.

2 Fuel tank

⚠ *Warning: Refer to the precautions given in Section 1 before starting work.*

Draining

1 The best way to drain the tank is to use a siphon pump, cheaply available at any good parts shop.

2 Remove the filler cap, insert the suction end of the pump in the tank and the expulsion end into a container suitable and large enough for storing the fuel, then pump away, moving the suction nozzle around all the extremities of the tank, until empty. Refit the filler cap.

Removal

3 On ED models remove the side covers, the seat, and the air ducts (see Chapter 7). On 2010-on models, note the location of the water drain funnel on the lower right-hand side of the tank **(see illustration)**. Draw the drain hose out from the front engine mounting bracket and the side panel support bracket, noting its routing **(see illustration)**. On Custom models remove the seat (see Chapter 7).

4 Make sure the fuel filler cap is secure. Unscrew the fuel tank bolt and remove the washer and rubber support **(see illustration)**. Lift the back of the tank and support it.

2.3a Location of the water drain funnel

2.3b Note the routing of the drain hose

2.4 Unscrew the bolt and remove the washer and rubber support

5 Disconnect the fuel pump wiring connector **(see illustration)**.

6 Have a rag ready to catch any residual fuel. Slide the orange connector cover down to reveal the clips, then press the clips in and pull the hose off its union **(see illustrations)**.

7 Draw the tank back and remove it.

8 Inspect the tank mounting rubbers for signs of damage or deterioration and replace them with new ones if necessary.

Installation

9 Installation is the reverse of removal, noting the following:

● Make sure the tank rubbers are correctly fitted and the plain and rubber washers are fitted with the bolt.

● Make sure the fuel hose is fully pushed on to the union until the clips locate, then push the connector cover up **(see illustration)**.

● Start the engine and check that there is no sign of fuel leakage, then turn it off.

Fuel tank cleaning and repair

10 All repairs to the fuel tank should be carried out by a professional who has experience in this critical and potentially dangerous work. Even after cleaning and flushing of the fuel system, explosive fumes can remain and ignite during repair of the tank.

11 If the fuel tank is removed from the bike, it should not be placed in an area where sparks or open flames could ignite the fumes coming out of the tank. Be especially careful inside garages where a natural gas-type appliance is located, because the pilot light could cause an explosion.

3 Fuel pressure check

Special Tool: *A fuel pressure gauge is required for this procedure.*

1 To check the fuel pressure, a suitable gauge and adapter hose (Yamaha Pt. Nos. 90890-03153 and 90890-03186) are needed.

2 Undo the screw securing the fuel hose connector security clamp and remove the clamp **(see illustration)**. Have a rag ready to catch any residual fuel. Slide the black connector cover up to reveal the clips, then

2.5 Disconnect the wiring connector

2.6b . . . and pull the hose off the union

2.6a Slide the cover down and press the clips in . . .

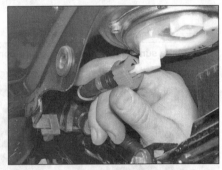

2.9 Make sure the hose clicks into place then push the cover up

press the clips in and pull the hose off its union on the fuel injector **(see illustrations)**.

3 Connect the gauge assembly between the hose and the injector.

4 Start the engine and check the pressure with the engine idling. It should be as specified at the beginning of this Chapter.

5 Turn the ignition OFF and remove the gauge assembly, using a rag to catch any residual fuel.

6 Push the fuel hose connector fully onto the union on the fuel injector until the clips locate, then push the connector cover down **(see illustration)**. Fit the security clamp and tighten the screw **(see illustration 3.2a)**.

3.2a Undo the screw (arrowed) and remove the clamp

3.2b Slide the cover up . . .

3.2c . . . press in the clips . . .

3.2d . . . and pull the hose off the union

3.6 Make sure the hose clicks into place then push the cover down

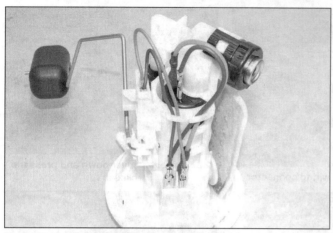

4.2 Make sure all the pump wiring and connectors are secure

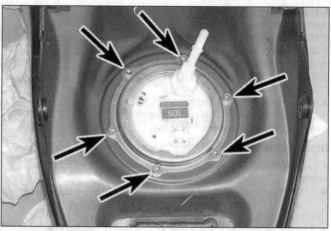

4.4a Unscrew the bolts (arrowed) and remove the ring

4.4b Carefully withdraw the pump . . .

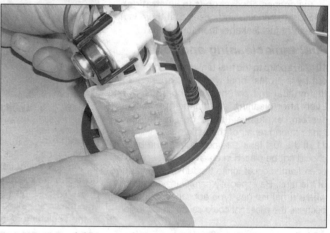

4.4c . . . and remove the sealing ring

7 If the pressure is too low, check for a leak in the fuel supply system, including the injector and its holder. If there is no leakage the pressure regulator could be faulty, the pick-up in the pump could be blocked, or the pump could be faulty. The pressure regulator is part of the pump. Refer to Section 4 to check the pump.

8 If the pressure is too high, either the pressure regulator or the fuel pump check valve is faulty or a fuel hose, the strainer or the injector could be clogged. Check the pump, fuel hose and injector.

4 Fuel pump

Check

1 The fuel pump is located inside the fuel tank. When the ignition is switched ON, it should be possible to hear the pump run for a few seconds until the system is up to pressure. If you can't hear anything, first make sure the battery is charged and the fuse is good (see Chapter 8).

2 Next refer to Section 2 and disconnect the pump wiring connector **(see illustration**

2.5)**. Using a voltmeter check for voltage at the brown wire terminal in the loom side of the pump connector with the ignition ON. If there is voltage check for continuity in the yellow wire to the ECU wiring connector. If there is a fault in either case check the wiring, connectors and terminals in the pump circuit for physical damage or loose or corroded connections and rectify as necessary (see Electrical system fault finding and the *Wiring Diagrams* in Chapter 8). If the pump still will not run, remove it (see below) and check that all its wiring and connectors are secure **(see illustration)**. If they are replace the pump with a new one. If all appears to be fine so far, check the ignition switch (see Chapter 8). If no fault can be found it is possible the ECU is faulty (see Chapter 4).

Removal

3 Disconnect the battery (see Chapter 8). Drain and remove the fuel tank (see Section 2). Place the tank upside down on a suitable work surface, resting it on plenty of rag.

4 Note which way the fuel hose union points. Unscrew the pump bolts and remove the retaining ring **(see illustration)**. Carefully withdraw the pump from the tank, taking

care not to snag the sensor float arm **(see illustration)**. Remove the pump seal and discard it – a new one must be fitted **(see illustration)**. Do not disassemble the pump.

Installation

5 Make sure the strainer is clean **(see illustration)**. Ensure the pump and tank mating surfaces are clean and dry. Fit a new sealing ring onto the base of the pump, making sure it is the correct way round as shown, and locating the tabs in the cut-outs **(see illustrations)**.

6 Carefully manoeuvre the pump assembly

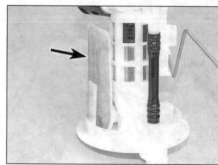

4.5a Make sure the strainer (arrowed) is clean

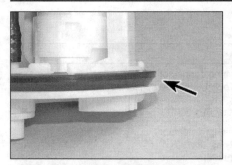

4.5b Make sure the sealing ring is the correct way up . . .

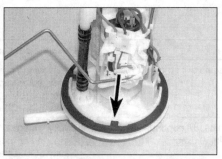

4.5c . . . and locate each tab in its cut-out

4.6a Fit the retaining ring, locating the cut-out over the projection (arrowed)

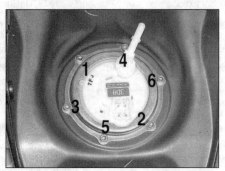

4.6b Tighten the bolts in the correct numerical sequence to the specified torque

into the tank, aligning the fuel hose union so it points just to the left of forward (to the right with the tank upside down) on ED models, and to the rear on Custom models (see illustration 4.4b). Fit the retaining ring, locating the cut-out in its inner rim over the projection on the pump base (see illustration). Fit the bolts and tighten them evenly and a little at a time in the numerical sequence shown to the torque setting specified at the beginning of the Chapter (see illustration) – note that the sequence is relative to the position of the fuel hose union, rather than the position of the fuel tank.

7 Install the fuel tank. Pour in some fuel and check there is no leakage around the pump.

8 Connect the battery (see Chapter 8).

5 Fuel injection system description

1 The fuel injection system consists of the fuel circuit and the electronic control circuit.

2 The fuel circuit consists of the tank with internal integrated pump/pressure regulator/strainer/ level sensor, the fuel hose, the throttle body and injector. Fuel is pumped under pressure from the tank to the injector via the strainer and pressure regulator. Operating pressure is maintained by the pump and pressure regulator. The injector sprays pressurised fuel into the intake duct where it mixes with air controlled by the throttle body and vaporises, before entering the cylinder where it is compressed and ignited by the spark plug.

3 The electronic control circuit consists of the electronic control unit (ECU), which operates and co-ordinates both the fuel injection and

ignition systems, and the various sensors which provide the ECU with information on engine operating conditions.

4 The electronic control unit (ECU) monitors signals from the following sensors:
● Intake air temperature (IAT) sensor*
● Intake air pressure (IAP) sensor*
● Throttle position (TP) sensor*
● Ignition timing (crankshaft position or CKP) sensor
● Engine temperature (ET) sensor
● Tip-over (TO) sensor
*The IAT, IAP and TP sensors are all integrated into one unit on the throttle body.

5 Based on the information it receives, the ECU calculates the appropriate ignition and fuel requirements of the engine. By varying the length of the electronic pulse it sends to the injector, the ECU controls the length of time the injector is held open and thereby the amount of fuel that is supplied to the engine. Fuel supply varies according to the engine's needs for starting, warming-up, idling, cruising and acceleration. In the event of the machine falling over, the tip-over sensor cuts power to the fuel and ignition systems.

6 The fuel injection system has its own fault diagnosis function (Section 6). In the event of a problem the engine trouble warning light in the instrument cluster comes on or flashes and any fault codes are stored in the ECU. The ECU will determine whether the engine can still be run safely. If it can, a back-up mode substitutes the sensor signal with a fixed signal, restricting performance but allowing the bike to be ridden home or to a dealer. When this occurs, the engine trouble warning light in the instrument cluster

will come on and stay on. In some cases the engine will continue to run after the fault has been registered, but once stopped the engine will not be able to be restarted. If the fault is serious, the fuel injection system will be shut down and the engine will not run. When this occurs, the engine trouble warning light will flash while the start switch is being pressed.

7 After the engine has been stopped, the appropriate self-diagnostic fault code will appear on the warning light. See Section 6 for fault diagnosis.

6 Fuel injection system fault diagnosis

Note: *The engine trouble warning light comes on for three seconds when the ignition is first turned ON. If the light does not come on, check the bulb (see Chapter 8).*

1 The system incorporates a self-diagnostic function whereby most faults, when they occur, are identified by a fault code which is displayed on the engine trouble warning light in the instrument cluster after the engine has been stopped. The codes are stored in the ECU memory until a deletion operation is performed (see Steps 4 and 5). In the case of a minor fault in the injection system, the warning light will come on and stay on and the engine will continue to run, and may be able to be restarted (depending on the fault), enabling the machine to be ridden, although performance will be significantly reduced. In the case of a major fault the warning light will flash while the start switch is being pressed, or if already running the engine will stop and not be able to be restarted – this applies to fault codes 19, 30, 33, 39, 41 and 50 (refer to the table below). Certain faults may not activate the warning light and are not subject to a fault code, but will be recorded as a diagnostic code. If the engine does not run correctly and no warning light and fault code are shown, and no fault can be traced or identified by its symptoms, and all the wiring and connectors have been checked (see Section 7, Step 1), take the bike to a Yamaha dealer equipped with the FI diagnostic tool.

2 All fault codes are two digit numbers. The first number of any code is indicated by long (1 second) flashes with 1.5 second intervals, the number of flashes representing the number of the code. The second number of any code is indicated by short (0.5 second) flashes with 0.5 second intervals, the number of flashes representing the number of the code. For example fault code 15 comprises one long flash and five short flashes, and fault code 43 comprises four long flashes and three short flashes. If there is more than one code the lowest number is indicated first.

3 Compare the fault code displayed with those in the table below to identify the faulty component, then refer to Section 7 or the relevant Chapter as indicated in the table and check the component as described.

Fuel injection system fault codes

Fault code	Fault symptoms	Possible causes
12	Crankshaft position sensor – engine will stop and will not restart	Faulty wiring or wiring connector Damaged or improperly installed sensor or timing trigger on generator rotor Faulty ECU (Chapter 4)
13	Intake air pressure sensor – engine will continue to run and can be restarted, air pressure signal fixed	Faulty wiring or wiring connector Damaged or faulty sensor Faulty ECU (Chapter 4)
14	Intake air pressure sensor – engine will continue to run and can be restarted, air pressure signal fixed	Aperture between sensor and intake blocked Faulty ECU (Chapter 4)
15	Throttle position sensor – engine will continue to run and can be restarted	Faulty wiring or wiring connector Damaged, faulty or improperly installed sensor Faulty ECU (Chapter 4)
16	Throttle position sensor – engine will continue to run and can be restarted	Throttle position sensor stuck Faulty ECU (Chapter 4)
19	No signal from black/white wire between ignition switch and ECU – engine will not run	Faulty wiring or wiring connector Faulty ignition switch or sidestand switch (Chapter 8) Faulty ECU (Chapter 4)
22	Intake air temperature sensor – engine will continue to run and can be restarted, intake air temperature signal fixed	Faulty wiring or wiring connector Damaged, faulty or improperly installed sensor Faulty ECU (Chapter 4)
28	Engine temperature sensor – engine will continue to run and can be restarted, engine temperature signal fixed	Faulty wiring or wiring connector Damaged, faulty or improperly installed sensor Faulty ECU (Chapter 4)
30	Tip-over sensor – engine will not run	Machine overturned Faulty ECU (Chapter 4)
33	Ignition coil – engine will not run	Faulty wiring or wiring connector Damaged or faulty ignition coil (Chapter 4) Faulty ignition cut-off circuit (Chapters 1 and 8) Faulty ECU (Chapter 4)
39	Fuel injector – engine will not run	Faulty wiring or wiring connector Damaged, faulty or improperly installed injector Faulty ECU (Chapter 4)
41	Tip-over sensor – engine will not run	Faulty wiring or wiring connector Damaged, faulty or improperly installed sensor Faulty ECU (Chapter 4)
44	Error reading from or writing to ECU EE-PROM – engine will continue to run and can be restarted	Faulty ECU (Chapter 4)
46	Abnormal power supply to FI system – engine will continue to run and can be restarted	Faulty wiring or wiring connector Faulty charging system (Chapter 8)
50	ECU malfunction – fault code may not be displayed, engine will not run	Faulty wiring or wiring connector Faulty ECU (Chapter 4)

4 Once the fault has been corrected and the system has been reinstated as described in the relevant part of Section 7, confirm that the fault code is no longer displayed by turning the ignition switch OFF and then ON again. If the code is no longer displayed the repair is complete.

5 If you want to delete the fault code from the ECU memory the diagnostic tool must be used – take the bike to a Yamaha dealer.

7 Fuel injection system sensors

1 If a fault is indicated in any of the system components, first check the wiring and connectors between the appropriate component and the ECU (refer to *Electrical system fault finding* at the beginning of Chapter

8, and to the *Wiring diagrams* at the end of Chapter 8). A continuity test of all wires will locate a break or short in any circuit. Inspect the terminals inside the wiring connectors and ensure they are not loose, bent or corroded. Spray the inside of the connectors with a proprietary electrical terminal cleaner before reconnection.

2 It is possible to undertake most checks on system components using a multimeter and

7.5 CKP sensor wiring connector (arrowed)

comparing the results with the specifications at the beginning of the Chapter. **Note:** *Different meters may give slightly different results to those specified even though the component being tested is not faulty – do not consign a component to the bin before having it double-checked.* However, some faults will only become evident when a component is tested with specialised equipment, in which case the checks should be undertaken by a Yamaha dealer.

3 If after a thorough check the source of a fault has not been identified, it is possible that the ECU itself is faulty. Yamaha provides no test specifications for the ECU. In order to determine conclusively that the unit is defective, it should be substituted with a known good one. If the problem is rectified, the original unit is faulty.

Crankshaft position (CKP) sensor

Check

4 Make sure the ignition is OFF. Remove the left-hand side cover (see Chapter 7).

5 The crankshaft position sensor is in the alternator cover on left-hand side of the engine. Trace the wiring from the top of the cover and disconnect it at the 2-pin connector **(see illustration)**. Using an ohmmeter or multimeter set to the ohms x 100 scale,

measure the resistance between the terminals on the sensor side of the connector. If the result is not as specified, replace the sensor with a new one (Step 7).

6 If the result is good, and you have checked the wiring and connectors as described in Step 1, remove the alternator cover (see Chapter 8) and check whether the sensor head is fouled or the sensor has come loose on its mountings **(see illustration)**.

Removal and installation

7 Make sure the ignition is OFF. Remove the alternator cover, then remove the stator and CKP sensor from it (see Chapter 8) – the stator and CKP sensor come as an integrated assembly along with the wiring sub-loom, including the neutral switch wire.

8 After installing the new sensor, turn the engine over on the starter motor to reinstate the system, then check the fault code has been erased by turning the ignition switch OFF and then ON again. If the code is no longer displayed the repair is complete.

Intake air pressure sensor

9 Make sure the ignition is OFF. Remove the left-hand side cover (see Chapter 7).

10 The sensor is part of the throttle body sensor assembly, containing the intake air pressure and temperature sensors and the throttle position sensor, and is on the left-hand side of the throttle body **(see illustration)**.

11 For fault code 13, first check the wiring and connectors as in Step 1. Next, using a voltmeter or multimeter set to the volts (DC) scale, insert the positive (+) probe of the meter into the pink/white wire terminal in the back of the connector, with the connector still connected, and insert the negative (-) probe into the black/blue terminal. Turn the ignition ON and measure the sensor output voltage. Turn the ignition OFF.

12 If the voltage is not as specified, replace the throttle body with a new one – the sensor assembly is part of it and is not available

separately, though it may be worth asking a Yamaha parts supplier.

13 For fault code 14, make sure the throttle body and sensor assembly are clean and the aperture to the sensor is not blocked.

14 After installing the new throttle body, for fault code 13 turn the ignition switch ON, and for fault code 14 run the engine at idle speed, to reinstate the system, then check the fault code has been erased by turning the ignition switch OFF and then ON again. If the code is no longer displayed the repair is complete.

Intake air temperature sensor

15 Make sure the ignition is OFF. Remove the left-hand side cover (see Chapter 7).

16 The sensor is part of the throttle body sensor assembly, containing the intake air pressure and temperature sensors and the throttle position sensor, and is on the left-hand side of the throttle body **(see illustration 7.10)**.

17 First check the wiring and connectors as in Step 1. Next, disconnect the wiring connector from the sensor assembly **(see illustration 7.10)**. Using an ohmmeter or multimeter set to the K-ohms scale, connect the positive (+) probe to the brown/white wire terminal in the sensor socket and the negative (-) probe to the black/blue wire terminal and measure the resistance.

18 If the resistance is not as specified, replace the throttle body with a new one – the sensor assembly is part of it and is not available separately, though it is worth asking a Yamaha parts supplier.

19 After installing the new throttle body, turn the ignition switch ON to reinstate the system, then check the fault code has been erased by turning the ignition switch OFF and then ON again. If the code is no longer displayed the repair is complete.

Throttle position sensor

20 Make sure the ignition is OFF. Remove the left-hand side cover (see Chapter 7).

7.6 Check the sensor head (A) and bolts (B)

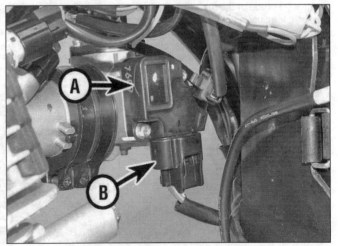

7.10 Throttle body sensor assembly (A) and its wiring connector (B)

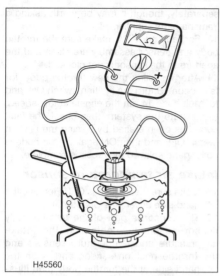

7.27 Engine temperature sensor test set-up

21 The sensor is part of the throttle body sensor assembly, containing the intake air pressure and temperature sensors and the throttle position sensor, and is on the left-hand side of the throttle body **(see illustration 7.10)**.
22 First check the wiring and connectors as in Step 1. Also make sure the sensor assembly is not loose on the throttle body, and that the throttle twistgrip turns smoothly and freely from fully closed to fully open.
23 Next, using a voltmeter or multimeter set to the volts (DC) scale, insert the positive (+) probe of the meter into the blue wire terminal in the back of the connector, with the connector still connected, and insert the negative (-) probe into the black/blue terminal. Turn the ignition ON and measure the sensor input voltage. If the voltage is not as specified, and the blue wire between the sensor and the ECU is OK, the ECU could be faulty. Turn the ignition OFF.
24 To check the output voltage, insert the positive (+) probe of the meter into the yellow/blue wire terminal in the back of the connector, with the connector still connected, and insert the negative (-) probe into the black/blue terminal. Turn the ignition ON and measure the sensor output voltage. Now slowly open the

throttle and check that the voltage increases steadily. If the voltage in the closed position is not as specified, or if it does not rise or rises abruptly when opened, replace the throttle body with a new one – the sensor assembly is part of it and is not available separately, though it is worth asking a Yamaha parts supplier.
25 After installing the new throttle body, for fault code 15 turn the ignition switch ON, and for fault code 16 run the engine first at idle speed and then quickly open and close the throttle so the engine races but does not exceed the red line, to reinstate the system, then check the fault code has been erased by turning the ignition switch OFF and then ON again. If the code is no longer displayed the repair is complete.

Engine temperature sensor

Check

26 Remove the sensor from the cylinder head (see Step 30).
27 Fill a small heatproof container with water and place it on a stove. Using an ohmmeter, connect the positive (+) probe of the meter to the green/red wire terminal on the sensor, and the negative (-) probe to the black/blue wire terminal. Using some wire or other support suspend the sensor in the coolant so that just the sensing head and thread are submerged, and with the head about 40 mm above the bottom of the container **(see illustration)**. Also place a thermometer capable of reading temperatures up to 130°C in the water so that its bulb is close to the sensor. **Note:** *Neither component should be allowed to directly touch the container.*

 ⚠ *Warning: This must be done very carefully to avoid the risk of personal injury.*

28 Begin to heat the coolant, stirring it gently. When the temperature reaches 20°C, check the resistance – it should be as specified at the beginning of the Chapter. When the temperature reaches 100°C, the resistance should again be as specified at the beginning of the Chapter. If no meter readings are obtained, or they are different by a significant margin, then the sensor is faulty and must be replaced with a new one.
29 After installing the new sensor, turn the

ignition switch ON to reinstate the system, then check the fault code has been erased by turning the ignition switch OFF and then ON again. If the code is no longer displayed the repair is complete.

Removal and installation

 ⚠ *Warning: The engine must be completely cool before carrying out this procedure.*

30 Disconnect wiring connector from the sensor **(see illustration)**. Unscrew and remove the sensor. Remove the sealing washer and discard it – a new one must be fitted.
31 Install the sensor using a new sealing washer and tighten it to the torque setting specified at the beginning of the Chapter. Connect the wiring.

Tip-over sensor

Check

32 Make sure the ignition is OFF. Remove the seat (see Chapter 7).
33 First check the wiring and connectors as in Step 1 **(see illustration)**. Also make sure the sensor is not loose on its mounts **(see illustration)**.
34 Displace the sensor (see Step 37) leaving the wiring connected.
35 Using a voltmeter or multimeter set to the volts (DC) scale, insert the positive (+) probe of the meter into the yellow/green wire terminal in back of the connector, with the connector still connected, and insert the negative (-) probe into the black/blue terminal. Turn the ignition ON. Hold the sensor in its normal position when the bike is upright with the UP mark facing up, then tilt it 65° to one side and then the other. Turn the ignition OFF.
36 If the voltage is not as specified when the sensor is upright and tilted over, replace the sensor with a new one. Note the top surface of the sensor is marked UP.

Removal and installation

37 Make sure the ignition is OFF. Remove the seat (see Chapter 7). On 2010-on ED models, access to the sensor is improved by removing the upper centre section of the seat cowling. Undo the bolts securing the sensor, noting the washers **(see illustration 7.33b)**. Displace the sensor and disconnect the wiring connector. Note the top surface of the sensor is marked

7.30 Disconnect the sensor wiring connector

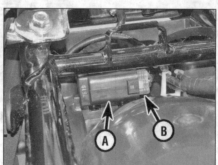

7.33a Tip-over sensor (A) and its wiring connector (B) . . .

7.33b . . . and mounting bolts (arrowed)

8.2a Free the hose from its clip (arrowed)

8.2b Detach the AIS hose (arrowed) . . .

8.2c . . . and the breather hose (arrowed)

8.3a Slacken the clamp (arrowed) . . .

8.3b . . . then undo the bolts (arrowed) . . .

8.3c . . . and remove the housing

UP – make sure this mark is on top when installing the sensor.

Fuel injector

38   Refer to Section 9.

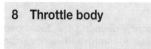

8   Throttle body

> **Warning: Refer to the precautions given in Section 1 before starting work.**

Removal

Note: *The throttle body can be removed by itself leaving the injector and intake duct bolted to the cylinder head, or you can remove the throttle body/intake duct/injector assembly as one – follow the relevant Steps.*

1 Remove the right-hand side cover (see Chapter 7), and for best access the fuel tank (see Section 2).

2 Free the AIS system hose from its clip on the air intake duct **(see illustration)**. Detach the AIS system hose and the crankcase breather hose from the air filter housing **(see illustrations)**.

3 Fully slacken the clamp screw securing the air duct to the throttle body – note the orientation of the clamp **(see illustration)**. Unscrew the air filter housing bolts and draw the housing out **(see illustrations)**.

4 If you are removing the intake duct and injector along with the throttle body, and if the fuel tank has been removed and the fuel hose does not have to be disconnected for any particular reason, it can stay connected to the injector. If the tank has not been removed, undo the screw securing the fuel

hose connector security clamp and remove the clamp **(see illustration 3.2a)**. Have a rag ready to catch any residual fuel. Slide the black connector cover up to reveal the clips, then press the clips in and pull the hose off its union **(see illustrations 3.2b, c and d)**. Also disconnect the fuel injector wiring connector **(see illustration)**.

5 Disconnect the fast idle solenoid wiring connector **(see illustration 10.2)**. Disconnect the throttle body sensor assembly wiring connector **(see illustration 7.10)**.

6 Detach the throttle cable (Section 11).

7 If you are removing the throttle body by itself, loosen the clamp screw securing the throttle body in the intake duct **(see illustration)**. Ease the throttle body out of the adapter and remove it **(see illustration)**.

8 If you are removing the intake duct and injector along with the throttle body, unscrew

8.4 Disconnect the injector wiring connector (arrowed)

8.7a Slacken the clamp screw (arrowed) . . .

8.7b . . . and remove the throttle body

8.8 Unscrew the bolts (arrowed) and remove the throttle body assembly

8.15 Fit new O-rings (arrowed) and make sure the joint plate is correctly positioned

the duct flange bolts, noting the washers, and remove the throttle body/intake duct/injector assembly along with the joint plate **(see illustration)**. Discard the O-rings on the duct flange and plate **(see illustration 8.15)** – new ones must be used.

Caution: Do not snap the throttle valve from fully open to fully closed once the cable has been disconnected because this can lead to engine idle speed problems.

Caution: Tape over or stuff clean rag into the intake duct or cylinder head (according to what has been removed) to prevent anything from falling in.

9 Check the intake duct rubber joint for signs of cracking or deterioration and replace it with a new one if necessary – slacken the clamp screw (s) to release it. Make sure the mating surfaces are clean before refitting, and locate the tab on the flat front side of the joint between the tabs on the intake duct, and the tab on the raised rear side between the tabs on the throttle body **(see illustrations 8.7a and b)**.

10 Do not remove the sensor assembly from the throttle body.

Cleaning and inspection

Caution: Use only a dedicated cleaner or petroleum-based solvent for cleaning. Do not use caustic cleaners.

11 Clean the throttle body according to the instructions on the cleaner container.

12 Loosen and remove any varnish and other deposits using a nylon-bristle brush – do not use any metallic or pointed tool to clean

passages. Rinse then dry with compressed air, blowing out all of the passages.

13 Check the throttle body and intake duct for cracks, distorted sealing surfaces and other damage. If any defects are found, replace the faulty component with a new one.

14 Make sure the butterfly valve moves smoothly and returns under spring pressure. Make sure valve is not distorted or loose on its shaft.

Installation

15 Installation is the reverse of removal, noting the following:

● Remove the tape/plug from the intake adapter or cylinder head.

● Make sure the rubber joint is correctly located with the tab on the flat front side between the tabs on the intake duct, and make sure the throttle body is pushed all the way into the joint with the tab on the raised rear side between the tabs on the throttle body, before tightening the clamp **(see illustrations 8.7a and b)**.

● Fit new O-rings smeared lightly with grease into the grooves in the intake duct flange and joint plate, and fit the joint plate with the protruding tab on the lower right-hand side **(see illustration)**. Tighten the intake duct flange bolts to the torque setting specified at the beginning of the Chapter.

● Make sure the wiring connectors are securely connected.

● Push the fuel hose connector fully onto the union on the fuel injector until the clips locate, then push the connector

cover down **(see illustration 3.6)**. Fit the security clamp and tighten the screw **(see illustration 3.2a)**.

● Check the operation of the throttle and adjust the cable as necessary (see Chapter 1).

● Run the engine and check that the fuel system is working correctly before taking the machine out on the road.

9 Fuel injector

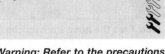

⚠️ *Warning: Refer to the precautions given in Section 1 before starting work.*

Check

1 First refer to Section 7, Step 1, and check the wiring and connectors.

2 Disconnect the injector wiring connector **(see illustration 8.4)**. Connect an ohmmeter or multimeter set to the ohms x 1 scale between the terminals on the injector side of the connector and check for a resistance – Yamaha do not specify a figure but one we tested showed 12.5 ohms **(see illustration)**. If your measurement is much higher or there is no resistance the injector is probably faulty.

3 If the resistance is as specified check for battery voltage at the brown wire terminal in the loom side of the connector with the ignition ON. If there is no voltage check the wire between the connector and the ignition switch, then check the switch itself (see Chapter 8).

Removal

4 Undo the screw securing the fuel hose connector security clamp and remove the clamp **(see illustration 3.2a)**. Have a rag ready to catch any residual fuel. Slide the black connector cover up to reveal the clips, then press the clips in and pull the hose off its union on the fuel injector **(see illustrations 3.2b, c and d)**.

5 Disconnect the fuel injector wiring connector **(see illustration 8.4)**.

6 Undo the bolt securing the injector **(see illustration)**. Draw the injector out of the intake duct along with the joint plate, noting how they locate **(see illustration)**.

9.2 Checking injector resistance

9.6a Unscrew the bolt (arrowed) . . .

9.6b . . . and remove the injector

9.7 Remove the O-ring (arrowed) and fit a new one on installation

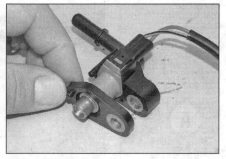

9.8 Fit the joint plate as shown and described

10.2 Fast idle solenoid wiring connector (arrowed)

7 Remove the O-ring from the injector – a new one must be used **(see illustration)**.

Installation

8 Installation is the reverse of removal, noting the following:

● Fit a new O-ring smeared lightly with clean engine oil onto the injector **(see illustration 9.7)**.

● Fit the joint plate with the pin facing away from the injector, and locate the pin on the injector housing in the hole in the plate **(see illustration)**. Locate the pin on the plate in the hole in the intake duct.

● Apply some threadlock to the threads of the bolt and tighten it to the torque setting specified at the beginning of the Chapter.

● Push the fuel hose connector fully onto the union on the fuel injector until the clips locate, then push the connector cover down **(see illustration 3.6)**. Fit the security clamp and tighten the screw **(see illustration 3.2a)**.

● Make sure the wiring connector is securely connected **(see illustration 8.4)**.

● Run the engine and check that the fuel system is working correctly, with no leaks before taking the machine out on the road.

10 Fast idle solenoid (FID)

⚠ **Warning: Refer to the precautions given in Section 1 before starting work.**

Check

1 First refer to Section 7, Step 1, and check

10.5 Undo the screws (arrowed) and remove the solenoid

the wiring and connectors between the solenoid on top of the throttle body and the ECU and ignition switch.

2 Disconnect the wiring connector from the solenoid **(see illustration)**. Connect an ohmmeter or multimeter set to the ohms x 1 scale between the terminals on the solenoid and check for a resistance – it should be as

11.2a Slacken the locknut (arrowed)

11.2c Release the cable from the bracket

specified at the beginning of the Chapter. If your measurement is much higher or there is no resistance the solenoid is probably faulty.

3 If the resistance is as specified check for battery voltage at the brown wire terminal in the loom side of the connector with the ignition ON. If there is no voltage check the wire between the connector and the ignition switch, then check the switch itself (see Chapter 8).

Removal and installation

4 Disconnect the wiring connector from the solenoid **(see illustration 10.2)**.

5 Undo the screws and detach the solenoid from the throttle body, noting how it locates **(see illustration)**.

6 Installation is the reverse of removal.

11 Throttle cable

⚠ **Warning: Refer to the precautions given in Section 1 before proceeding.**

Removal

1 Remove the right-hand air duct and the right-hand side cover (see Chapter 7), and if required for best access the fuel tank (see Section 2).

2 Slacken the locknut securing the cable elbow in the bracket on the throttle body **(see illustration)**. On 2010-on ED models, slacken the locknuts on the opening and closing cable elbows **(see illustration)**. Draw the cable(s) out of the bracket, then detach the cable end(s) from the pulley **(see illustrations)**.

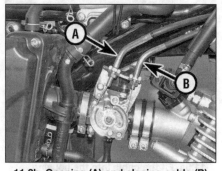

11.2b Opening (A) and closing cable (B) elbows – 2010-on ED models

11.2d Detach the cable from the pulley

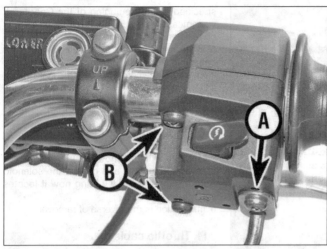

11.4a Cable retainer screw (A) – 2007 to 2009 ED and all Custom models. Note the housing screws (B)

11.4b Undo the opening cable retainer screw – 2010-on ED models

11.4c Closing cable retaining ring – 2010-on ED models

11.4d Detach the top half of the housing

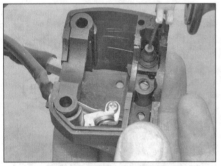

11.5a Fit the cable into the housing . . .

11.5b . . . and then into the pulley

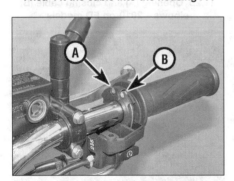

11.5c Throttle opening cable (A) and closing cable (B) – 2010-on ED models

11.5d Locate the peg (arrowed) in the hole in the handlebar

3 Withdraw the cable from the machine, carefully noting its correct routing – you can tie string to the end which can be drawn through with the cable and used as a guide to draw the new cable in when installing it.

4 Undo the screw securing the cable retainer to the switch housing on the handlebar **(see illustrations)**. On 2010-on models, unscrew the closing cable retaining ring **(see illustration)**. Undo the switch housing screws and detach the top half **(see illustration)**. Detach the cable end from the pulley in the housing, then draw the cable out of the housing.

Installation

5 Fit the cable into the switch housing **(see illustration)**. Lubricate the cable end with multi-purpose grease and fit it into the throttle pulley **(see illustration)**. On 2010-on ED models, ensure that the opening cable is fitted at the front of the housing and into the front hole on the pulley. Fit the housing halves onto the handlebar, locating the peg in the top half in the hole in the handlebar **(see illustration)**. Fit and tighten the screws **(see illustration 11.4a)**. Fit the retainer and tighten the screw. On 2010-on ED models, tighten the closing cable retaining ring **(see illustration 11.4c)**.

6 Feed the cable through to the throttle body, making sure it is correctly routed – if used on removal tie the string to its end and pull it through. The cable must not interfere with any other component and should not be kinked or bent sharply.

7 Lubricate the cable nipple with multi-purpose grease. Hold the throttle pulley open and fit the cable end **(see illustration 11.2c)**. Locate the cable elbow in its bracket and tighten the nut **(see illustrations 11.2b and a)**.

8 Adjust the cable freeplay (see Chapter 1). Operate the throttle to check that it opens and closes freely. Turn the handlebars back and forth to make sure the cable doesn't cause the steering to bind.

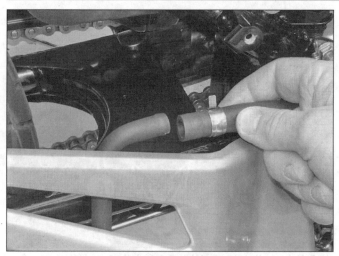

12.1 Detach the hose from its union

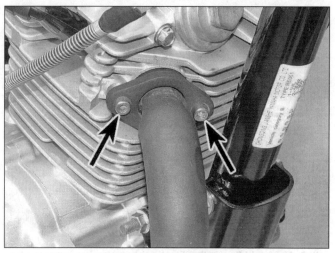

12.2 Unscrew the bolts (arrowed)

9 Start the engine and check that the idle speed does not rise as the handlebars are turned. If it does, the throttle cable is routed incorrectly. Correct the problem before riding the motorcycle.

10 Install the fuel tank if removed (see Section 2). Install the right-hand air duct and the right-hand side cover (see Chapter 7).

12 Exhaust system

 Warning: If the engine has been running the exhaust system will be very hot. Allow the system to cool before carrying out any work.
Note: *Before starting work on the exhaust system spray all the nuts, mounting bolts and clamp bolts with penetrating fluid – many of them are exposed and are prone to corrosion.*

Removal

1 Release the AIS system hose clamp and detach the hose from its union on the silencer **(see illustration)**.

2 Unscrew the bolts securing the downpipe to the cylinder head **(see illustration)**.
3 Support the exhaust, then unscrew the silencer mounting bolt **(see illustration)**.
4 Detach the downpipe from the cylinder head and remove the exhaust system **(see illustration)**.
5 Remove the gasket from the port in the cylinder head and discard it – a new one must be fitted.
6 If required remove the heat shields – note the washers fitted on each side of the shields.

Installation

7 If removed fit the heat shields – fit a washer on each side of the shield with each bolt, and apply a thread locking compound to the bolts.
8 Fit a new gasket into the cylinder head port **(see illustration)**. If necessary, apply a smear of grease to the gasket to keep it in place.
9 Manoeuvre the exhaust system into position and locate the head of the downpipe in its port in the cylinder head. Align the silencer mounting and secure the bolt finger-tight.
10 Fit the downpipe bolts and tighten them evenly and a bit at a time to the torque setting specified at the beginning of the Chapter.

Tighten the silencer bolt to the specified torque.
11 Fit the AIS system hose onto its union on the silencer and secure it with the clamp.
12 Run the engine and check that there are no exhaust gas leaks.

13 Air induction system (AIS)

Function and check

1 The air induction system uses negative exhaust gas pulses to suck fresh air from the filter housing into the exhaust silencer, where it mixes with hot combustion gases. The extra oxygen causes continued combustion, allowing unburnt hydrocarbons to burn off, thereby reducing emissions. The reed valve fitted in the hose controls the flow of air and prevents exhaust gases flowing back into it.
2 Refer to Chapter 1 for routine checks of the system.
3 If the reed valve is thought to be faulty, remove it (see below). If the valve is working correctly it should be possible to blow air

12.3 Unscrew the bolt . . .

12.4 . . . and remove the exhaust

12.8 Fit a new gasket into the port

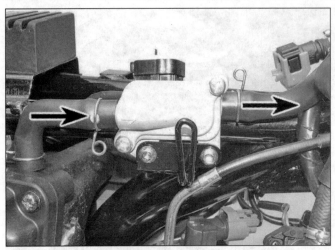

13.3 Air should flow in the direction shown and as indicated by the arrow cast on the cover

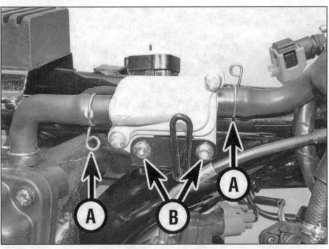

13.5 Release the clamps (A) and detach the hoses, then unscrew the bolts (B) and remove the valve

into the hose union from the air filter and it should exit through the union for the hose to the silencer **(see illustration)**. It should not be possible to blow air through in the opposite direction. If you can, then the reed valve is faulty, but before discarding it remove the cover and check for any build-up of carbon or other deposits that may be preventing the reed to seat and seal correctly. Clean the valve up and visually check that there isn't a gap between the reed and its seat.

Reed valve

4 Remove the fuel tank (see Section 2).

5 Release the clamps securing the air inlet and outlet hoses and detach them from their unions, noting which fits where **(see illustration)**. Unscrew the bolts and remove the control valve.

6 To replace any hoses or pipes, release the clamps securing them and disconnect them at each end.

7 Fit the reed valve with the arrow pointing to the front of the bike, in the direction of airflow through it. Make sure all the hoses are correctly routed and securely connected at each end and held by their clamps.

14 Catalytic converter

General information

1 A catalytic converter is incorporated in the exhaust system to minimise the level of exhaust pollutants released into the atmosphere. It is an open-loop system with no feedback to the ECU.

2 The catalytic converter consists of a canister containing a fine mesh impregnated with a catalyst material, over which the hot exhaust gases pass. The catalyst speeds up the oxidation of harmful carbon monoxide, unburned hydrocarbons and soot, effectively reducing the quantity of harmful products released into the atmosphere via the exhaust gases.

Precautions

3 The catalytic converter is a reliable and simple device which needs no maintenance in itself, but there are some facts of which

an owner should be aware if the converter is to function properly for its full service life.

● DO NOT use leaded or lead replacement petrol (gasoline) – the additives will coat the precious metals, reducing their converting efficiency and will eventually destroy the catalytic converter.

● Always keep the ignition and fuel systems well-maintained in accordance with the manufacturer's schedule – if the fuel/air mixture is suspected of being incorrect have it checked on an exhaust gas analyser.

● If the engine develops a misfire, do not ride the bike at all (or at least as little as possible) until the fault is cured.

● DO NOT use fuel or engine oil additives – these may contain substances harmful to the catalytic converter.

● DO NOT continue to use the bike if the engine burns oil to the extent of leaving a visible trail of blue smoke.

● Avoid bump-starting the bike unless absolutely necessary.

Chapter 4
Ignition system

Contents

Degrees of difficulty

Easy, suitable for novice with little experience	**Fairly easy,** suitable for beginner with some experience	**Fairly difficult,** suitable for competent DIY mechanic	**Difficult,** suitable for experienced DIY mechanic	**Very difficult,** suitable for expert DIY or professional

Specifications

Spark plug

Type and gap	see Chapter 1

Ignition timing

At idle

YBR models	7° BTDC @ 1400 rpm
XT models	0° BTDC @ 1400 rpm

Crankshaft position (CKP) sensor

Crankshaft position (CKP) sensor resistance

YBR models	248 to 372 ohms @ 20°C
XT models	192 to 288 ohms @ 20°C

Ignition coil

Primary winding resistance

2005 and 2006 YBR models	0.32 to 0.48 ohms @ 20°C
2007-on YBR models	2.16 to 2.64 ohms @ 20°C
XT models	0.27 to 0.33 ohms @ 20°C

Secondary winding resistance (without plug cap)

2005 and 2006 YBR models	5.68 to 8.52 K-ohms @ 20°C
2007-on YBR models	8.64 to 12.96 K-ohms @ 20°C
XT models	2.84 to 3.48 K-ohms @ 20°C
Spark plug cap resistance	approx 5 K-ohms @ 20°C

Torque wrench settings

Timing inspection cap	6 Nm

1 General information

All models are fitted with a fully transistorised electronic ignition system which, due to its lack of mechanical parts, is totally maintenance-free. The system comprises a set of triggers, a crankshaft position (CKP) sensor, electronic control unit (ECU), and ignition coil (refer to *Wiring Diagrams* at the end of Chapter 8 for details).

The ignition triggers, which are on the alternator rotor on the left-hand end of the crankshaft, magnetically operate the crankshaft position sensor as the crankshaft rotates. The sensor sends a signal to the electronic control unit, which then supplies the ignition coil with the power necessary to produce a spark at the plug. The ECU incorporates an electronic advance system.

The system has a starter safety circuit, comprising the neutral switch, the clutch switch, and on 2007-on YBR models and all XT models the sidestand switch, that prevents the engine from being started unless it is in neutral, or if it is in gear unless the clutch lever is pulled in, and on 2007-on YBR models and all XT models the sidestand is up.

Because of their nature, the individual ignition system components can be checked but not repaired. If ignition system troubles occur, and the faulty component can be isolated, the only cure for the problem is to replace the part with a new one. Keep in mind that most electrical parts, once purchased, cannot be returned. To avoid unnecessary expense, make very sure the faulty component has been positively identified before buying a replacement part.

Note that the ignition timing can be checked but not adjusted.

2 Ignition system check

⚠ *Warning: The energy levels in electronic systems can be very high. On no account should the ignition be switched on whilst the plug or plug cap are being held. Shocks from the HT circuit can be most unpleasant. Secondly, it is vital that the engine is not turned over or run with the plug cap removed, and that the plug is soundly earthed (grounded) when the system is checked for sparking. The ignition system components can be seriously damaged if the HT circuit becomes isolated.*

1 As no means of adjustment is available, any failure of the system can be traced to failure of a system component or a simple wiring fault. Of the two possibilities, the latter is by far the most likely. In the event of failure, check the system in a logical fashion, as described. First make sure the battery is fully charged and fuse has not blown (see Chapter 8).

2 Next pull the cap off the spark plug **(see illustration)**. Fit a spare spark plug that is known to be good into the cap and lay the plug against the cylinder head with the threads contacting it. If necessary, hold the spark plug with an insulated tool.

⚠ *Warning: Do not remove the spark plug from the engine to perform this check – atomised fuel being pumped out of the open spark plug hole could ignite, causing severe injury! Make sure the plug is securely held against the engine – if it is not earthed when the engine is turned over, the ECU could be damaged.*

3 Check that the transmission is in neutral, then turn the ignition switch ON, and turn the engine over on the starter motor. If the system is in good condition a regular, fat blue spark should be evident at the plug electrodes. If the spark appears thin or yellowish, or is non-existent, further investigation will be necessary. Turn the ignition off.

4 The ignition system must be able to produce a spark which is capable of jumping at least a 6 mm gap. Simple ignition spark gap testing tools are commercially available – follow the manufacturer's instructions **(see illustration)**.

5 If the test results are good the entire ignition system can be considered good. If the spark appears thin or yellowish, or is non-existent, further investigation is necessary.

6 Ignition faults can be divided into two categories, namely those where the ignition system has failed completely, and those which are due to a partial failure. The likely faults are listed below, starting with the most probable source of failure. Work through the list systematically, referring to the subsequent sections for full details of the necessary checks and tests, and to the *Wiring Diagrams* at the end of Chapter 8. **Note:** *Before checking the following items ensure that the battery is fully charged and that the fuse is in good condition.*

● Loose, corroded or damaged wiring connections, broken or shorted wiring between any of the component parts of the ignition system (see Chapter 8).
● Faulty HT lead or spark plug cap, faulty spark plug, dirty, worn or corroded plug electrodes, or incorrect gap between electrodes.
● Faulty ignition switch (see Chapter 8).
● Faulty neutral, clutch or sidestand switch, or safety circuit diodes (see Chapter 8).
● On fuel injection models faulty tip-over sensor (see Chapter 3B).
● Faulty crankshaft position sensor or damaged trigger.
● On XT models faulty charge coil (see Chapter 8).
● Faulty ignition coil.
● Faulty electronic control unit (ECU).

7 If the above checks don't reveal the cause of the problem, have the ignition system tested by a Yamaha dealer.

3 Ignition coil and spark plug cap

Check

1 On YBR models remove the fuel tank (see Chapter 3A or B) – the coil is mounted between the top of the engine and the frame **(see illustration)**. On XT models remove the seat (see Chapter 7) – to locate the coil trace the HT lead from the spark plug. Check the coil visually for loose or damaged connectors and terminals, loose mountings, cracks and other damage.

2 Make sure the ignition is off.

2.2 Pull the cap off the spark plug

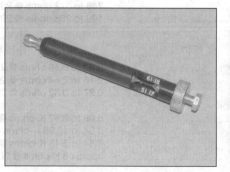

2.4 A typical spark gap testing tool

3.1 Ignition coil (arrowed) – YBR models

3.3 Disconnect the coil primary wiring connectors (arrowed)

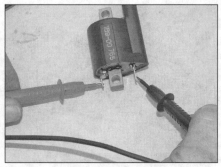

3.4 Testing the coil primary resistance on 2007-on YBR models

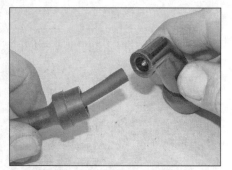

3.5a To test the coil secondary resistance unscrew the cap from the lead . . .

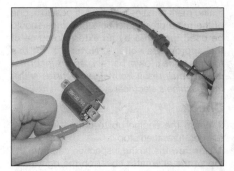

3.5b . . . and connect the multimeter leads between the primary circuit terminal and the spark plug lead end

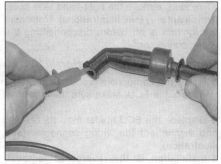

3.6 Measuring the resistance of the spark plug cap

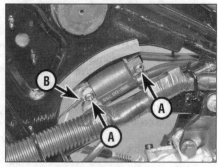

3.10 Coil mounting bolts (A) and earth wire (B) – YBR models

3 Disconnect the primary wiring connector(s) **(see illustration)**. Pull the cap off the spark plug **(see illustration 2.2)**.

4 Set an ohmmeter or multimeter to the ohms x 1 scale and measure the resistance between the primary terminal on the coil and one of the coil mounting bolts on 2005 and 2006 YBR models and all XT models, and between the two primary terminals on the coil on 2007-on YBR models **(see illustration)**. This will give a resistance reading of the primary windings of the coil and should be consistent with the value given in the Specifications at the beginning of the Chapter.

5 To check the condition of the secondary windings, set the meter to the K-ohm scale. Unscrew the plug cap from the end of the HT lead **(see illustration)**. On 2005 and 2006 YBR models and all XT models connect one meter probe to the primary terminal on the

coil, and insert the other in the end of the HT lead. On 2007-on YBR models connect one meter probe to one of the primary terminals on the coil, and insert the other in the end of the HT lead **(see illustration)**. If the reading obtained is not within the range shown in the Specifications, the coil is defective.

6 If the readings are as specified, measure the resistance of the spark plug cap by connecting the meter probes between the HT lead socket and the spark plug contact **(see illustration)**. If the reading obtained is not as specified, replace the spark plug cap with a new one.

Removal and installation

7 On YBR models remove the fuel tank (see Chapter 3A or 3B) – the coil is mounted between the top of the engine and the frame **(see illustration 3.1)**. On XT models remove

the seat (see Chapter 7) – trace the HT lead from the spark plug to locate the coil.

8 Disconnect the primary wiring connector(s) from the coil **(see illustration 3.3)**. Pull the cap off the spark plug **(see illustration 2.2)**.

9 Unscrew the two bolts and remove the coil, noting the earth wire on YBR models **(see illustration)**.

10 Installation is the reverse of removal.

4 Crankshaft position (CKP) sensor

Check

1 Make sure the ignition is OFF. On YBR models remove the left-hand side cover (see Chapter 7).

2 The crankshaft position sensor is in the alternator cover on left-hand side of the engine. Trace the wiring from the top if the cover and disconnect it at the 2-pin connector **(see illustrations)**. Check the wiring and connectors for loose or broken wires and terminals. Using an ohmmeter or multimeter set to the ohms x 100 scale, measure the resistance between the terminals on the sensor side of the connector. If the result is not as specified, replace the sensor with a new one (Step 4).

3 If the result is good, and you have checked the wiring and connectors, remove the alternator cover (see Chapter 8) and check

4.2a CKP sensor wiring connector (arrowed) – YBR models

4.2b CKP sensor wiring connector (arrowed) – XT models

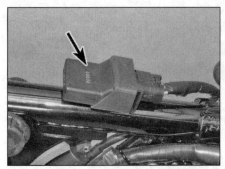

5.2a ECU – 2005 to 2012 YBR125 ED and Custom models

5.2b ECU – 2013-on YBR125 ED models

5.2c ECU – XT models

whether the sensor has come loose on its mounts.

Removal and installation

4 Make sure the ignition is OFF. Remove the alternator cover, then remove the stator and CKP sensor from it (see Chapter 8) – the stator and CKP sensor come as an integrated assembly along with the wiring sub-loom, including the neutral switch wire.

5 Electronic control unit (ECU)

Check

1 If the tests shown in the preceding or following Sections have failed to isolate the cause of an ignition fault, it is possible that the electronic control unit itself is faulty. No test details are available with which the unit can be tested. The best way to determine whether it is faulty is to substitute it with a known good one, if available. Otherwise, take the unit to a Yamaha dealer for assessment.

2 Before condemning the ECU make sure the wiring connector terminals are clean and none of the wires have broken – on 2005 to 2012 YBR125 ED and all Custom models remove the fuel tank (see Chapter 3A or 3B) to access the ECU; on 2013 YBR125 ED models, remove the seat (see Chapter 7); on

5.4 Separate the ECU from its holder

XT models, remove the right-hand side cover (see Chapter 7) **(see illustrations)**. Make sure the ignition is off before disconnecting the wiring connector.

Removal and installation

3 Follow the appropriate procedure in Step 2 to access the ECU. Make sure the ignition is off.

4 Displace the ECU holder from its bracket and disconnect the wiring connector **(see illustration)**.

5 Installation is the reverse of removal. Make sure the wiring connector is securely connected.

6 Ignition timing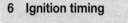

General information

1 Since no provision exists for adjusting the ignition timing and since no component is subject to mechanical wear, there is no need for regular checks: only if investigating a fault such as a loss of power or a misfire, should the ignition timing be checked.

2 The ignition timing is checked dynamically (engine running) using a stroboscopic lamp. The inexpensive neon lamps should be adequate in theory, but in practice may produce a pulse of such low intensity that the

6.4 Unscrew the timing inspection cap

timing mark remains indistinct. If possible, one of the more precise xenon tube lamps should be used, powered by an external source of the appropriate voltage. **Note:** *Do not use the machine's own battery, as an incorrect reading may result from stray impulses within the machine's electrical system.*

Check

3 Warm the engine up to normal operating temperature, then stop it.

4 Unscrew the timing inspection cap from the top of the alternator cover on the right-hand side of the engine **(see illustration)**.

5 The mark on the timing rotor which indicates the firing point at idle speed is an 'H' on YBR models and an I on XT models. The static timing mark with which this should align is the pointer in the inspection hole.

> **HAYNES HiNT** *The timing marks can be highlighted with white paint to make them more visible under the stroboscope light.*

6 Connect the timing light to the HT lead as described in the manufacturer's instructions.

7 Start the engine and aim the light at the inspection hole.

8 With the machine idling at the specified speed, the mark on the rotor should align with the static timing mark.

9 Slowly increase the engine speed whilst observing the mark – it should appear to move clockwise, increasing in relation to the engine speed until it reaches full advance (no identification mark).

10 As already stated, there is no means of adjustment of the ignition timing on these machines. If the ignition timing is incorrect, or suspected of being incorrect, one of the ignition system components is at fault, and the system must be tested as described in the preceding Sections of this Chapter.

11 Install the timing inspection cap using a new O-ring if required, and smear the O-ring with grease.

Chapter 5
Frame and suspension

Contents

Degrees of difficulty

Easy, suitable for novice with little experience 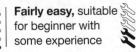	Fairly easy, suitable for beginner with some experience	Fairly difficult, suitable for competent DIY mechanic	Difficult, suitable for experienced DIY mechanic	Very difficult, suitable for expert DIY or professional

Specifications

Front forks

Fork oil type	10W fork oil
Fork oil capacity	
YBR ED models	
2005 to 2009 models	154 cc
2010-on models	163 cc
YBR Custom models	175.5 cc
XT models.	285 cc
Fork oil level*	
YBR ED models	
2005 to 2009 models	166 mm
2010-on models	142 mm
YBR Custom models	134 mm
XT models.	180 mm
Fork spring free length (min)	
YBR ED models	
Standard.	337 mm
Service limit	330.3 mm
YBR Custom models	
Standard.	347 mm
Service limit	340 mm
XT models.	495 ± 3 mm
Fork tube runout limit.	0.2 mm

*Oil level is measured from the top of the tube with the fork spring removed and the inner tube fully compressed.

Torque settings

Brake torque arm nut	19 Nm
Footrest assembly (YBR models)	
Lower rear engine mounting bolt nut	38 Nm
Rear bolts	23 Nm
Footrest bracket bottom bolts (YBR models)	26 Nm
Fork damper rod bolt	
YBR models	23 Nm
XT models	20 Nm
Fork top bolt (YBR models)	23 Nm
Fork clamp bolts	
YBR models	
Top yoke bolt	23 Nm
Bottom yoke bolt	32 Nm
XT models	
Top yoke bolt	20 Nm
Bottom yoke bolt	20 Nm
Handlebar clamp bolts	23 Nm
Rear shock absorber(s)	
YBR models	
Top nut	40 Nm
Bottom nut	32 Nm
XT models	
Top bolt/nut	45 Nm
Bottom bolt/nut	45 Nm
Silencer mounting bolt – YBR models	
2005 and 2006 ED models	22 Nm
2007-on ED and all Custom models	24 Nm
Steering head bearing adjuster nut – YBR models	
Initial setting	33 Nm
Final setting	22 Nm
Steering stem nut	
YBR models	110 Nm
XT models	30 Nm
Swingarm pivot bolt nut	
YBR models	59 Nm
XT models	60 Nm

1 General information

The steel frame uses the engine as a stressed member.

On YBR models front suspension is by oil-damped 30 mm forks, and rear suspension is by twin shock absorbers via a steel tube swingarm that pivots through the frame.

On XT models front suspension is by oil-damped 36 mm telescopic forks, and rear suspension is by a single shock absorber via a box-section steel swingarm that pivots through the frame.

2 Frame inspection and repair

1 The frame should not require attention unless accident damage has occurred. In most cases, fitting a new frame is the only satisfactory remedy for such damage. Frame specialists have the jigs and other equipment necessary for straightening a frame to the required standard of accuracy, but even then there is no simple way of assessing to what extent it may have been over-stressed.

2 After a high mileage, the frame should be examined closely for signs of cracking or splitting at the welded joints. Loose engine mounting bolts can cause ovaling or fracturing of the mounting points. Minor damage can often

3.1a Unhook the spring from the pedal (arrowed)

be repaired by specialised welding, depending on the extent and nature of the damage.

3 Remember that a frame that is out of alignment will cause handling problems. If, as the result of an accident, misalignment is suspected, it will be necessary to strip the machine completely so the frame can be thoroughly checked.

3 Footrests, brake pedal and gearchange lever

Footrests

YBR models

1 To remove the rider's footrest assembly, first remove the exhaust system (see Chapter 3A or 3B), the sidestand (see Section 4), and on 2007-on models the sidestand switch (see Chapter 8). Unhook the brake light switch spring from the brake pedal (see illustration). Thread the rear brake adjuster nut off the end of the rod, then press the pedal down and draw the rod out of the arm

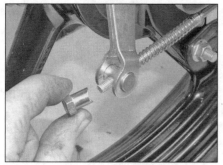

3.1b Thread the nut off . . .

3.1c . . . and draw the rod out of the arm

3.1d Remove the bush from the arm

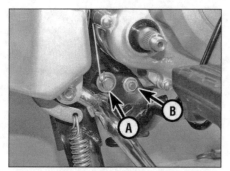

3.1e Unscrew the bolt (A) on each side,
then unscrew the nut (B)

3.1f Withdraw the bolt and remove the
footrest/stand assembly

3.2 Remove the e-clip (arrowed) and
washer and withdraw the pivot pin from
the top

(see illustrations). Remove the pivot bush from the arm if required for safekeeping (see illustration). Unscrew the rider's footrest assembly rear bolts, then unscrew the nut on the right-hand end of the lower rear engine mounting bolt (see illustration). Withdraw the bolt and remove the footrest assembly from under the engine (see illustration).

2 To remove a passenger footrest, remove the E-clip and washer from the bottom of the footrest pivot pin, then withdraw the pin and remove the footrest (see illustration). If required draw the rubber off the peg.

3 Installation is the reverse of removal. On the front tighten the lower rear engine mounting bolt nut and the footrest assembly rear bolts to the torque settings specified at the beginning of the Chapter. Fit the rear brake rod into the arm on the brake plate and thread the nut onto the rod. Hook the brake light switch spring onto the brake pedal. Adjust the rear brake pedal freeplay (see Chapter 1). On the rear apply a small amount of multi-purpose grease to the pivot pin.

XT models

4 To remove a rider's footrest, straighten and

remove the split pin from the bottom of the footrest pivot pin, then withdraw the pin and remove the footrest, noting how the return spring ends locate (see illustration). Discard the split pin. If required remove the rubber from the peg.

5 To remove a passenger footrest, straighten and remove the split pin from the bottom of the footrest pivot pin, then withdraw the pin and remove the footrest, collecting the detent ball, spring and the washer (see illustration). Discard the split pin.

6 Installation is the reverse of removal. Apply

3.4 Remove the split pin (A) and withdraw the pivot pin, noting
how the spring locates (B)

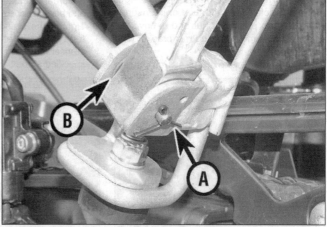

3.5 Remove the split pin (A), withdraw the pivot pin from the top,
and collect the ball and spring from the underside and the washer
(B) from the top side

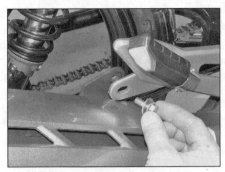

3.8a Unscrew the silencer mounting bolt . . .

3.8b . . . and the bottom footrest bracket bolt

3.8c Remove the pivot bolt nut and washer . . .

3.8d . . . and lift off the footrest bracket

3.10 Draw the pedal and spring off the pivot

3.11a Use pliers to locate the spring's inner end in the hole . . .

a small amount of multi-purpose grease to the pivot pin. Use new split pins on the pivot pins, and bend their ends round the pivot pin.

Brake pedal

YBR models

7 Place the bike on its sidestand or an auxiliary stand – the centrestand must be retracted.
8 Unscrew the silencer mounting bolt **(see illustration)**. Ensure no strain is placed on the exhaust system while the bolts is removed – if necessary, remove the exhaust system (see Chapter 3A or 3B). Unscrew the bottom bolt securing the right-hand passenger footrest bracket **(see illustration)**. Unscrew the swingarm pivot bolt nut and remove the washer, then remove the footrest bracket **(see illustration)**.
9 Unhook the brake light switch spring

from the brake pedal **(see illustration 3.1a)**. Straighten and remove the split pin securing the brake rod to the pedal, then remove the washer and draw the rod out.
10 Draw the pedal off its pivot along with the return spring, noting how its ends locate **(see illustration)**. Discard the split pin.
11 Installation is the reverse of removal, noting the following:
● Apply grease to the pedal pivot – clean off any old grease first.
● Use pliers to locate the inner end of the spring into its hole in the frame, and make sure both ends locate correctly **(see illustrations)**.
● Secure the brake rod using a new split pin and bend its ends around.
● Tighten the swingarm pivot bolt nut, the footrest bracket bottom bolt and the silencer mounting bolt to the torque settings specified at the beginning of the Chapter.

● Check the operation of the rear brake light switch (see Chapter 1).

XT models

12 Release and remove the pivot pin securing the brake pedal to the master cylinder pushrod and detach the pushrod from the pedal **(see illustration)**.
13 Unscrew the pedal pivot bolt and remove the pedal along with the return spring, noting how its ends locate, and the washer **(see illustration)**.
14 Check the condition of the pedal pivot bush and replace it with a new one if there is excess play between it and the pedal.
15 Installation is the reverse of removal, noting the following:
● Apply grease to the bush – clean off any old grease first.
● Make sure the return spring ends locate correctly **(see illustration 3.13)**.

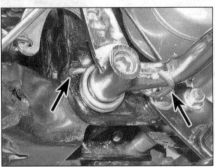

3.11b . . . and make sure both ends locate correctly (arrowed)

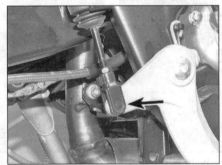

3.12 Release and withdraw the pin (arrowed) . . .

3.13 . . . then unscrew the bolt (arrowed) and remove the pedal

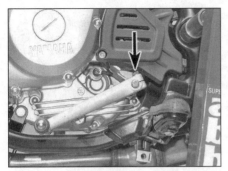

3.16 Unscrew the bolt (arrowed) and slide the lever off

4.2a On YBR models unhook the springs (arrowed)

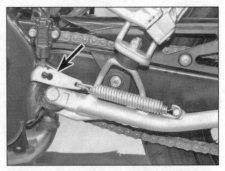

4.2b On XT models unhook the springs and spring plate (arrowed)

4.3a On YBR models unscrew the nut (A), then the bolt (B)

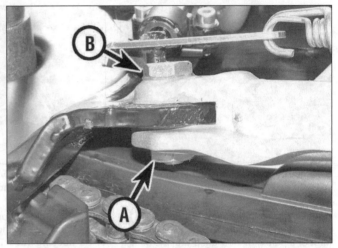

4.3b On XT models unscrew the nut (A), then the bolt (B)

Gearchange lever

Removal

16 Make a mark where the slot in the gearchange lever aligns with the shaft. Unscrew the pinch bolt and slide the lever off the shaft **(see illustration)**.

Installation

17 Installation is the reverse of removal – align the slit in the arm with the mark made on the shaft.

4 Sidestand and centrestand

Sidestand
Removal

1 Support the bike on its centrestand (YBR), or on an auxiliary stand (XT).
2 Unhook the stand springs, and on XT models the spring plate **(see illustrations)**.
3 Unscrew the nut from the pivot bolt **(see illustrations)**. Unscrew the pivot bolt and remove the stand.

Installation

4 Installation is the reverse of removal.

Apply grease to the pivot bolt shank. Do not overtighten the bolt, and check the stand pivots freely before fitting the nut. Counter-hold the bolt while tightening the nut **(see illustration 4.3b)**.
5 Reconnect the springs, and on XT models the spring plate, and check that they hold the stand securely up when not in use – an accident could occur if the stand extends while the machine is in motion. Check the operation of the sidestand switch on 2007-on YBR models (see Chapter 1).

Centrestand (YBR models)

Removal

6 Remove the rear brake pedal (see Section 3). For best access remove the exhaust system (see Chapter 3A or 3B).
7 Unhook the stand springs **(see illustration)**.
8 Unscrew the pivot bolt and remove the stand.

Installation

9 Installation is the reverse of removal. Apply grease to the pivot bolt shank. Check the stand pivots freely.
10 Reconnect the springs and check that they hold the stand securely up when not in

use – an accident could occur if the stand drops while the machine is in motion.

5 Handlebars and levers

1 As a precaution, remove the fuel tank (see Chapter 3A or 3B). Though not actually necessary, this will prevent the possibility of damage should a tool slip. Before removing the assemblies from the handlebars make a note of their position and alignment on the bar, making marks where necessary, so everything

4.7 Unhook the springs (arrowed)

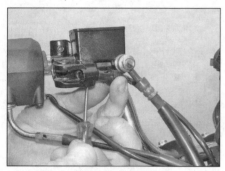

5.3a Release and withdraw the brake light switch

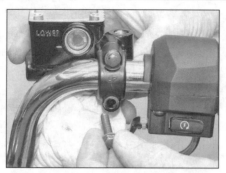

5.3b Unscrew the master cylinder clamp bolts and displace the assembly

5.4a Undo the screws (arrowed) and split the housing . . .

5.4b . . . then detach the cable and remove the twistgrip

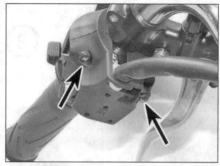

5.5 Undo the screws (arrowed) and split the housing

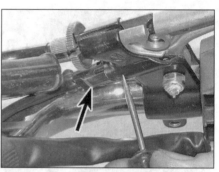

5.7 Release and withdraw the clutch switch (arrowed)

can be installed in the same position. Look for any existing alignment marks, usually in the form of a punch mark aligned with the mating surfaces of clamps.

Note: *If required, for example if the top yoke is being removed to access the steering head bearings, the handlebars can be displaced from the tops of the forks without detaching any of the assemblies from them – see Step 10 (YBR) or 18 (XT).*

Handlebar removal

YBR models

2 Remove the mirrors (see Chapter 7). Release any ties from the handlebars, noting what is secured and how it is routed. On 2005 and 2006 ED models and on Custom models remove the end-weight from each end of the handlebar.

3 Press the clip up on the underside of the brake light switch and draw the switch out of its housing **(see illustration)**. Unscrew the brake master cylinder assembly clamp bolts and position the assembly clear of the handlebar, wrapping it in some rag, and making sure no strain is placed on the hydraulic hose **(see illustration)**. Keep the master cylinder reservoir upright to prevent possible fluid leakage.

4 Undo the right-hand switch housing screws and detach the top half, then free the throttle cable from the twistgrip and slide the twistgrip off **(see illustrations)**.

5 Undo the left-hand switch housing screws and displace the switch **(see illustration)**.

6 Remove the grip from the left-hand end of the handlebar – if it has been glued on or is stuck feed a wooden or plastic tool up the inside and move it round the bar to release it.

You can squirt some aerosol lubricant into the gap between the grip and bar to aid removal of the grip, but be careful to protect your eyes from spray back! At worst you will have to cut the grip off and fit a new one.

7 Press the clip up on the underside of the clutch switch and draw the switch out of its housing **(see illustration)**.

8 Detach the clutch cable (see Chapter 2).

9 Unscrew the clutch lever bracket clamp bolt and slide the assembly off the handlebar **(see illustration)**.

10 Unscrew the handlebar clamp bolts and remove the clamps, then displace or remove the handlebars **(see illustrations)**.

XT models

11 Remove the mirrors (see Chapter 7). Release any ties from the handlebars, noting what is secured and how it is routed.

5.9 Unscrew the bolt (arrowed) and slide the clutch lever bracket off

5.10a Unscrew the clamp bolts (arrowed) . . .

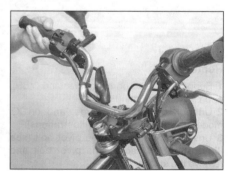

5.10b . . . and displace or remove the handlebars

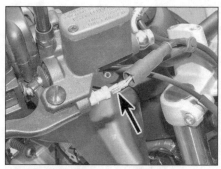

5.12a Disconnect the wiring connectors (arrowed)

5.12b Unscrew the bolts (arrowed) and displace the master cylinder assembly

5.13a Undo the screws (arrowed) . . .

5.13b . . . detach the top half of the housing . . .

5.13c . . . and slide the twistgrip off

5.14a Right-hand switch housing screws (arrowed)

12 Pull the rubber boot off the brake light switch and disconnect the wiring connectors **(see illustration)**. Unscrew the brake master cylinder assembly clamp bolts and position the assembly clear of the handlebar, wrapping it in some rag, and making sure no strain is placed on the hydraulic hose **(see illustration)**. Keep the master cylinder reservoir upright to prevent possible fluid leakage.

13 Undo the throttle housing screws and detach the top half, then slide the twistgrip assembly off the handlebar with the cable still attached **(see illustrations)**.

14 Undo the switch housing screws and displace the switches **(see illustrations)**.

15 Remove the grip from the left-hand end of the handlebar – if it has been glued on or is stuck feed a wooden or plastic tool up the inside and move it round the bar to release it. You can squirt some aerosol lubricant into the gap between the grip and bar to aid removal of the grip, but be careful to protect your eyes from spray back! At worst you will have to cut the grip off and fit a new one.

16 Pull the rubber boot off the clutch switch and disconnect the wiring connectors **(see illustration)**.

17 Unscrew the two clutch lever bracket clamp bolts and position the assembly clear of the handlebar, wrapping it in some rag **(see illustration)**.

18 Unscrew the handlebar clamp bolts and remove the clamps, then displace or remove the handlebars **(see illustration)**.

Handlebar installation

19 Installation is the reverse of removal, noting the following.
● Make sure the handlebars are central, and

5.14b Left-hand switch housing screws (arrowed)

align the punch mark with the clamp mating surfaces **(see illustration 5.19a or b)**.
● Fit the clamps with the larger section to the front, and tighten the front bolt first, then

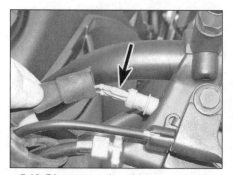

5.16 Disconnect the wiring connectors (arrowed)

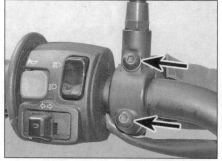

5.17 Unscrew the bolts (arrowed) and displace the clutch lever assembly

5.18 Unscrew the clamp bolts (arrowed) and displace or remove the handlebars

5.19a Handlebar alignment punch mark (arrowed) – YBR models

5.19b Handlebar alignment punch mark (arrowed) – XT models

5.19c Fit the larger section of clamp to the front of the handlebar

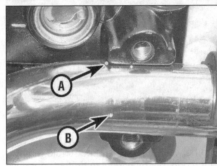

5.19d Align the master cylinder mating surface with the mark (A) and the side with the mark (B)

the rear, to the torque setting specified at the beginning of the Chapter (see illustration 5.19c).

● On YBR models make sure the front brake master cylinder bracket clamp is installed with the UP mark facing up and with the clamp mating surfaces aligned with the punch marks (see illustration 5.19d and 5.3b). Tighten the top clamp bolt first. Also align the clutch lever bracket clamp mating surfaces with the punch mark.

● When fitting the switch housings, where present locate the peg in the hole in the handlebar (see illustration 5.19e).

● When fitting the handlebar end-weights on 2005 and 2006 YBR ED models and on Custom models make sure there is a 1 to 2 mm gap between them and the grips.

Levers

YBR models

20 To remove the front brake lever, undo the lever pivot bolt locknut, then undo the pivot bolt and remove the lever and the spring (see illustrations).

21 To remove the clutch lever loosen the adjuster lockring then thread the adjuster into

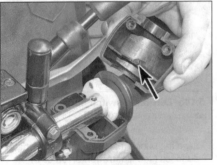

5.19e Locate the peg (arrowed) in the hole in the handlebar

5.20a Undo the nut . . .

5.20b . . . then undo the pivot screw . . .

5.20c . . . and remove the lever . . .

5.20d . . . and the spring

5.21a Slacken the lockring and thread the adjuster in

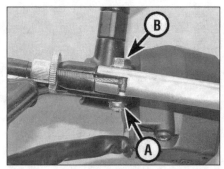

5.21b Unscrew the locknut (A) then undo the pivot screw (B) and remove the clutch lever

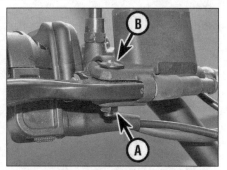

5.23a Unscrew the locknut (A) then undo the pivot screw (B) and remove the brake lever

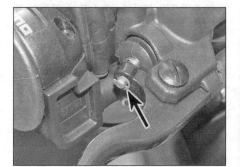

5.23b Release the e-clip (arrowed) and remove the pushrod piece

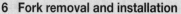

5.24 Unscrew the locknut (A) then undo and partially withdraw the pivot screw (B) and remove the lever

the bracket to provide freeplay in the cable **(see illustration)**. Undo the lever pivot bolt locknut, then undo the pivot bolt and remove the lever, detaching the cable nipple as you do **(see illustration)**.

22 Installation is the reverse of removal, noting the following.

● Apply silicone grease to the contact area between the front brake master cylinder pushrod tip and the brake lever.

● Apply lithium or molybdenum grease to the pivot bolt shafts and the contact areas between each lever and its bracket.

● Make sure the levers move smoothly and freely.

● Adjust clutch cable freeplay (see Chapter 1).

XT models

23 To remove the front brake lever, undo the lever pivot screw locknut, then undo the pivot screw and remove the lever **(see illustration)**. If required remove the E-clip and draw the pushrod piece out **(see illustration)**.

24 To remove the clutch lever loosen the adjuster lockring then thread the adjuster into the bracket to provide freeplay in the cable **(see illustration 5.21a)**. Undo the lever pivot bolt locknut, then undo and partially withdraw the pivot bolt and remove the lever, detaching the cable nipple as you do, and leaving the choke cable attached, unless otherwise required **(see illustration)**.

25 Installation is the reverse of removal, noting the following.

● Apply silicone grease to the contact area between the front brake master cylinder pushrod tip and the brake lever.

● Apply lithium or molybdenum grease to the pivot screw shafts and the contact areas between each lever and its bracket.

● Make sure the levers move smoothly and freely.

● Adjust clutch cable freeplay (see Chapter 1).

6 Fork removal and installation

Removal

1 Note the routing of the cables, brake hose and wiring around the forks.

2 On YBR models remove the front wheel (see Chapter 6) and the front mudguard (see Chapter 7). Tie the front brake caliper back so that it is out of the way. Where fitted, remove the bottom yoke cover **(see illustration)**. On 2014-on models, remove the fairing assembly (see Chapter 7).

3 On XT models remove the fairing, and to avoid the possibility of damage, the fuel tank panels (see Chapter 7). Remove the front wheel (see Chapter 6). Release the front brake hose and speed sensor wiring from the guide **(see illustration)**. Tie the front brake caliper back so that it is out of the way.

4 Working on one fork at a time, slacken

6.2 Unscrew the bolts (arrowed) and remove the cover

6.3 Undo the screws (arrowed) and free the hose and wiring

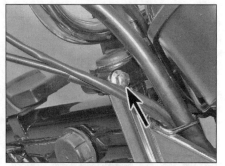

6.4 Slacken the fork clamp bolt (arrowed) in the top yoke

6.5a On YBR models remove the rubber cap . . .

6.5b . . . and slacken the fork top bolt now if the fork is to be disassembled

6.6a Bottom yoke fork clamp bolts (arrowed) – YBR shown

6.6b Draw the fork down and out of the yokes

the fork clamp bolt in the top yoke **(see illustration)**.

5 On YBR models, if the fork is to be disassembled, or if the fork oil is being changed, remove the rubber cap from the top

of the fork, then slacken the fork top bolt – you will need a 14 mm hex bit **(see illustrations)**.

6 Slacken the fork clamp bolt in the bottom yoke, and remove the fork by twisting it and pulling it down **(see illustrations)**.

 HAYNES HiNT *If the fork legs are seized in the yokes, spray the area with penetrating oil and allow time for it to soak in before trying again.*

Installation

7 Remove all traces of corrosion from the fork tube and the yokes. Make sure you install the forks the correct way round – On YBR models the right-hand fork has the lugs to carry the brake caliper, and on XT models it is the left-hand fork.

8 Slide the fork up through the bottom yoke and into the top yoke, making sure all cables, hoses and wiring are routed on the correct side of the fork **(see illustration 6.6b)**. Set the top of the fork inner tube flush with the top yoke. Tighten the clamp bolt in the bottom yoke to the torque setting specified at the beginning of the Chapter **(see illustration 6.6a)**.

9 On YBR models, if the fork has been dismantled or if the fork oil was changed, tighten the fork top bolt to the specified torque setting **(see illustration 6.5b)**. Fit the rubber cap **(see illustration 6.5a)**.

10 Tighten the fork clamp bolt in the top yoke to its specified torque setting **(see illustration 6.4)**.

11 Install the remaining components in a reverse of the removal procedure according to model (Step 2 or 3), also referring to the relevant Chapters.

12 Check the operation of the front forks and front brake before taking the machine out on the road.

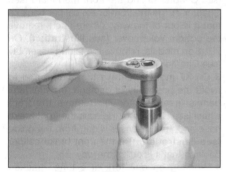

7.3a Unscrew the fork top bolt . . .

7.3b . . . and remove the spacer . . .

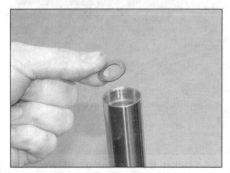

7.3c . . . the spacer seat . . .

7.3d . . . and the spring

7 Fork oil change

1 After a high mileage the fork oil will deteriorate and its damping and lubrication qualities will be impaired. Always change the oil in both fork legs.

2 Remove the fork – on YBR models make sure that the top bolt is loosened while the fork is still clamped in the bottom yoke (see Section 6).

3 On YBR models support the fork leg in an upright position and unscrew the fork top bolt from the top of the fork tube – the bolt is under pressure from the fork spring – use a ratchet tool so it does not need to be removed from the bolt as you unscrew it, and maintain some downward pressure on it, particularly as you come to the end of the threads, or alternatively hold the tool still and twist the fork tube to unthread it from the bolt **(see illustration)**. Slide the fork inner tube down into the outer tube and remove the spacer, the spacer seat and the spring as they become exposed **(see illustrations)**. Wipe any excess

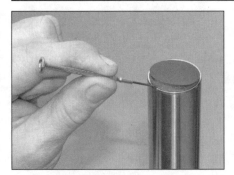

7.4a Prise out the top cap

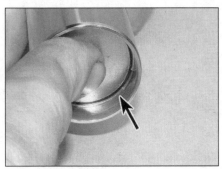

7.4b Push the top plug down, release the retaining ring (arrowed) . . .

7.4c . . . then remove the top plug, noting the O-ring (arrowed) . . .

oil off the spring and spacer. If the top bolt O-ring is damaged or deteriorated fit a new one **(see illustration 7.7)**.

4 On XT models support the fork leg in an upright position and carefully prise out the top cap **(see illustration)**. Press down on the top plug, noting it is under pressure from the fork spring, and release the retaining ring from its groove, then slowly release pressure on the top plug and remove it **(see illustrations)**. Slide the fork inner tube down into the slider and remove the spacer and the spring as they become exposed **(see illustration)**. Wipe any excess oil off the spring and spacer. If the O-ring is damaged or deteriorated fit a new one.

5 Invert the fork leg over a suitable container and pump the fork to expel as much oil as possible **(see illustration)**. Support the fork upside down in the container and allow it to drain for a few minutes.

6 Slowly pour in the specified quantity of the specified grade of fork oil, then pump the fork several times to distribute it evenly **(see illustration)**. Slide the inner tube down until it seats then measure the oil level from the top of the tube – if you don't have a narrow ruler use a piece of wooden dowel or steel rod with a piece of tape wrapped round it as an upper marker, then insert this into the fork so the tape is level with the inner tube and the bottom is in the oil, then remove and measure the distance between the tape and the oil mark **(see illustrations)**. Add or subtract oil until it is at the level specified at the beginning of this Chapter.

7 On YBR models fit the spring into the fork with its closer-wound coils at the top **(see**

illustration 7.3d). Draw the inner tube up until it is flush with the top of the spring, then fit the spacer seat **(see illustration 7.3c)**. Lift the tube some more and fit the spacer **(see illustration 7.3b)**. Smear some fork oil onto the top bolt O-ring **(see illustration)**. Fit the top bolt into the fork tube, compressing the spring as you do, and thread it in (making sure it does not cross-thread), keeping downward pressure on the spring, using a ratchet tool or by turning the tube while holding the bolt still as on removal **(see illustration 7.3a)**. **Note:** *The top bolt can be tightened to the specified torque setting at this stage if the tube is held between the padded jaws of a vice, but do not risk distorting the tube by doing so. A better method is to tighten the top bolt when the fork leg is being installed and is securely held in the bottom yoke.*

7.4d . . . and remove the spacer and the spring

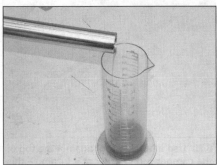

7.5 Invert the fork over a container and tip the oil out

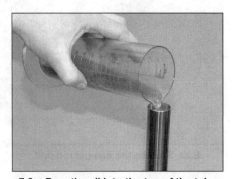

7.6a Pour the oil into the top of the tube and distribute it as described . . .

7.6b . . . then measure the level as described using a dipstick . . .

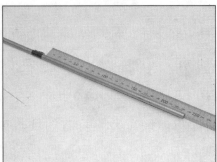

7.6c . . . and a ruler

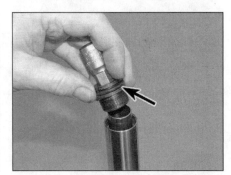

7.7 Smear the O-ring (arrowed) with oil before fitting the top bolt

8 On XT models fit the spring into the fork **(see illustration 7.3d)**. Draw the inner tube up until it is just above the top of the spring, then fit the spacer **(see illustration 7.4d)**. Lift the tube all the way. Smear some fork oil onto the top plug O-ring **(see illustration 7.4c)**. Fit the plug into the fork tube and press down on it, compressing the spring, and fit the retaining ring into its groove **(see illustration)**. Relax the pressure so the plug rests on the underside of the ring, which should remain secure in its groove. Fit the top cap **(see illustration)**.

9 Install the fork (see Section 6).

8 Fork overhaul

Disassembly

1 Remove the fork – on YBR models make sure that the top bolt is loosened while the leg is still clamped in the bottom yoke (see Section 6). Always dismantle the fork legs separately to avoid interchanging parts and thus causing an accelerated rate of wear. Store all components in separate, clearly marked containers.

2 Lay the fork flat on the bench, hold it down and slacken the damper rod bolt in the base

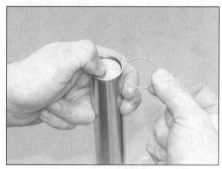

7.8a Press the plug down and fit the retaining ring into the groove

7.8b Press the cap into the top of the tube

of the outer tube **(see illustration)**. If the bolt does not slacken but instead the rod turns with the bolt inside the fork, try compressing the fork so that more pressure is exerted on the damper rod head, or if available use an air-ratchet. Otherwise, follow Step 3, then use the Yamaha holding tool (see your dealer), or on YBR-ED models a T70 Torx bit located in the shaped top of the damper rod on a long extension, and on all other models a broom handle or piece of wooden dowel rounded at the end, inserted in the fork and pressed against the top of the damper rod, to hold it **(see illustrations)**.

3 Refer to Section 7, Steps 3 to 5 and drain the oil form the fork.

4 Remove the damper rod bolt and its copper sealing washer from the bottom of the outer tube **(see illustration 8.17a)**. Discard the sealing washer as a new one must be used on reassembly. Tip the damper rod out **(see illustration)**.

5 Withdraw the inner tube from the outer tube **(see illustration)**. Carefully prise out the dust seal from the top of the outer tube **(see illustration)**. Discard the seal as a new one must be used.

6 Carefully remove the retaining clip, taking care not to scratch the surface of the tube **(see illustration)**.

7 Carefully prise the oil seal from the outer tube using either a seal hook or an internal puller with slide-hammer attachment **(see**

8.2a Slacken the damper rod bolt

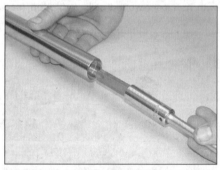

8.2b Use a holding tool against the top of the damper rod to prevent it turning – this shows a T70 Torx bit in an extension for YBR ED models

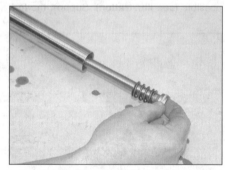

8.4 Tip the damper rod out of the inner tube

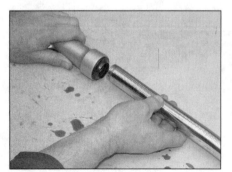

8.5a Draw the inner tube out of the outer tube . . .

8.5b . . . then prise out the dust seal using a flat-bladed screwdriver

8.6 Prise out the retaining clip using a flat-bladed screwdriver

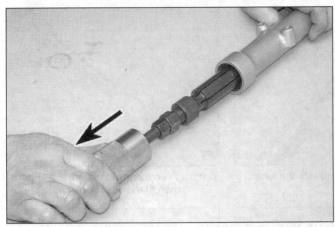

8.7a Locate the puller under the oil seal then expand the puller (arrowed) . . .

8.7b . . . and jar the seal out using the slide-hammer attachment

illustrations). If a seal hook is used take great care not to damage the rim of the tube.

8 Tip the damper rod oil lock piece out of the outer tube.

Inspection

9 Clean all parts in solvent and blow them dry with compressed air, if available. Check the inner fork tube for score marks, scratches, flaking of the chrome finish and excessive or abnormal wear. Look for dents in the outer tube and replace the tubes in both forks if any are found. Check the fork seal seat for nicks, gouges and scratches. If damage is evident, leaks will occur.

10 Check the fork tube for runout using V-blocks and a dial gauge. If the amount of runout exceeds the service limit specified, the tube should be replaced with a new one.

⚠ *Warning: If the tube is bent or exceeds the runout limit, it should not be straightened; replace it with a new one.*

11 Check the spring (both the main spring and the rebound spring on the damper rod) for cracks and other damage. Measure the main spring free length and compare the measurement to the specifications at the beginning of the Chapter **(see illustration).** If it is defective or sagged below the service limit

(YBR models) or less than the measurement given (XT models), replace the main springs in both forks with new ones. Never replace only one spring.

12 Check the damper rod, and in particular the ring around its head, for damage and wear, and replace it with a new one if necessary **(see illustration).** Check the oil lock piece for damage.

Reassembly

13 Smear the lips of the new oil seal with fork oil and press it squarely into its recess in the

top of the outer tube, with its markings face upwards, then use a seal driver or a suitable socket and drive it in until it seats and the retaining clip groove is visible above it **(see illustrations).**

> **HAYNES HiNT** *Place the old oil seal on top of the new one to protect it when driving the new seal into place.*

14 Once the seal is correctly seated, fit the retaining clip, making sure it is

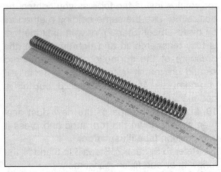

8.11 Measure the free length of the spring

8.12 Check the rod and spring for damage and the ring (arrowed) for wear

8.13a Fit the oil seal . . .

8.13b . . . and drive it into place . . .

8.13c . . . until it seats – the retaining ring groove (arrowed) will be exposed

8.14 Fit the seal retaining clip into its groove

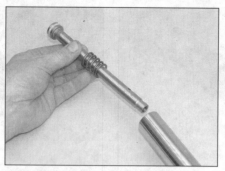

8.15a Fit the damper rod into the tube . . .

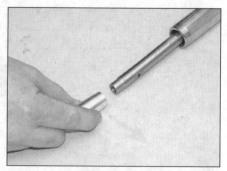

8.15b . . . so it protrudes from the bottom, then fit the oil lock piece. . .

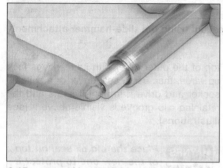

8.15c . . . and locate it in the bottom of the tube

8.16 Fit the inner tube into the outer tube

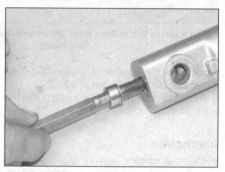

8.17a Fit the bolt using threadlock and a new sealing washer . . .

correctly located in its groove (see illustration).

15 If removed, fit the rebound spring onto the damper rod, and fit the ring into its groove in the head (see illustration 8.12). Slide the damper rod into the top of the inner tube and all the way down so it protrudes from the bottom (see illustrations). Fit the oil lock piece onto the bottom of the rod, then push the rod back into the tube so the oil lock piece fits into the bottom (see illustration).

16 Oil the inner tube with the specified fork oil. Insert the tube into the outer tube, twisting it as you do and making sure the lips of the seal do not turn inside, and push it fully down until it contacts the bottom (see illustration).

17 Lay the fork flat on the bench. Fit a new copper sealing washer onto the damper bolt and apply a few drops of a suitable non-permanent thread locking compound (see illustration). Fit the bolt into the bottom of the outer tube and tighten it to the specified torque setting (see illustration). If the damper rod rotates inside the tube as you tighten the bolt, either use the same holding method as on disassembly (Step 2), or wait until the fork is fully reassembled and tighten it then (the pressure of the spring on the damper rod should prevent it from turning, especially if you compress the fork – Step 20, but this is not guaranteed).

18 Lubricate the lips of the new dust seal then slide it down the fork tube and press it into position (see illustration).

19 Refer to Section 7, Steps 6 to 8 and fill the fork with oil and finish reassembly.

20 If the damper rod bolt requires tightening (see Step 17), place the fork upside down on the floor, using a rag to protect it, then have an assistant compress the fork so that maximum spring pressure is placed on the damper rod head while tightening the bolt to the specified torque setting.

21 Install the fork (see Section 6).

9 Steering stem

Removal

YBR models

1 Remove the fuel tank (see Chapter 3A or 3B).
2 Remove the front forks (see Section 6).
3 Remove the instrument cluster (see Chapter 8).
4 Trace the wiring from the ignition switch

8.17b . . . and tighten it to the specified torque

8.18 Fit the dust seal into the top of the outer tube

9.4a Ignition switch wiring connectors are inside the headlight shell – 2005 to 2013 models

9.4b Open the wiring boot –
2014-on models

9.5a Unscrew the wiring guide bolts
(arrowed) . . .

9.5b . . . noting how the right-hand one also
secures the brake hose holder (arrowed)

9.6 Unscrew the bracket bolts (arrowed) and remove the
headlight/turn signal assembly

9.7 Secure the handlebar/headlight/turn signal assembly to the
frame

and disconnect it at the connectors. On 2005 to 2013 models the connectors are located inside the headlight shell (see illustration). On 2014-on models, the wiring is located inside a protective boot – remove the fairing assembly for access (see Chapter 7). Unclip the boot and identify the ignition switch wiring (see illustration). Feed the wiring back to the switch, freeing it from any clips and ties and noting its routing.

5 Unscrew the wiring guide bolts and remove the guide and brake hose holder, noting how they fit (see illustrations).

6 Unscrew the headlight/turn signal assembly bracket bolts, then draw the assembly out, noting how the rubber bushes on the tops of the bracket locate in the holes in the underside of the top yoke (see illustration).

7 Displace the handlebars (see Section 5), then carefully fold the complete handlebar/headlight/turn signal assembly round to the right-hand side of the bike and tie it to the frame (see illustration).

8 Unscrew and remove the steering stem nut, and remove the washer (see illustration).

Lift the top yoke up off the steering stem and remove it (see illustration).

9 Remove the tabbed lock washer, noting how it fits (see illustration 9.26c). Unscrew and remove the locknut, using a C-spanner located in one of the notches if required – though it should only be finger-tight (see illustration 9.26b). Remove the rubber washer (see illustration 9.26a).

10 Support the bottom yoke and unscrew the bearing adjuster nut using a C-spanner (see illustration). Remove the bearing cover, then gently lower the bottom yoke and

9.8a Unscrew the nut and remove the
washer . . .

9.8b . . . then lift the yoke up off the stem

9.10a Unscrew the adjuster nut . . .

9.10b . . . and remove the bearing cover . . .

9.10c . . . then draw the bottom yoke/steering stem out of the steering head

9.11a Remove the inner race . . .

9.11b . . . and the upper bearing from the top of the head . . .

9.11c . . . and the lower bearing from the bottom of the stem

steering stem out of the frame **(see illustrations)**.

11 Remove the inner race and upper bearing from the top of the steering head **(see illustrations)**. Remove the lower bearing from the steering stem **(see illustration)**.

12 Wash all traces of old grease from the bearings and races using solvent or paraffin, then check them for wear or damage as described in Section 10. **Note:** *Do not attempt to remove the outer races from the steering head or the lower inner race from the steering stem unless they are to be replaced with new ones (see Section 10).*

XT models

13 Remove the front forks (see Section 6).

14 Remove the instrument cluster (see Chapter 8).

15 Disconnect the ignition switch wiring connector – free the wiring from any ties and note its routing.

16 Unscrew the bolt securing the headlight bracket to the bottom yoke **(see illustration)**.

17 Displace the handlebars (see Section 5) and secure the handlebar/headlight assembly clear.

18 Remove the plug from the steering stem, then unscrew and remove the steering stem

nut **(see illustration)**. Lift the top yoke up off the steering stem and remove it.

19 Support the bottom yoke and unscrew the bearing adjuster nut using a C-spanner **(see illustration)**. Remove the bearing cover, then gently lower the bottom yoke and steering stem out of the frame.

20 Remove the upper bearing from the top of the steering head. Remove the lower bearing from the steering stem.

21 Wash all traces of old grease from the bearings and races using solvent or paraffin, then check them for wear or damage as described in Section 10. **Note:** *Do not attempt*

9.16 Unscrew the headlight bracket bolt (arrowed)

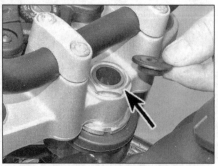

9.18 Remove the plug then unscrew the nut (arrowed)

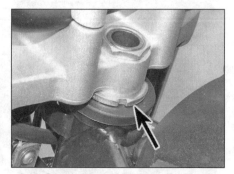

9.19 Steering head bearing adjuster nut (arrowed)

9.23a Fit the upper bearing . . .

9.23b . . . the inner race . . .

9.23c . . . the bearing cover . . .

to remove the races from the steering head or the steering stem unless they are to be replaced with new ones (see Section 10).

Installation

YBR models

22 Smear a liberal quantity of multi-purpose grease onto the bearing races and bearings. Fit the lower bearing onto the steering stem **(see illustration 9.11c)**.

23 Carefully lift the steering stem/bottom yoke up through the steering head and support it **(see illustration 9.10c)**. Fit the upper bearing and inner race into the top of the steering head, then fit the bearing cover **(see illustrations)**. Thread the adjuster nut onto the steering stem and tighten it finger-tight **(see illustration)**.

24 To adjust the bearings as specified by Yamaha, a special service tool (Pt. No.90890-

01403) and a torque wrench are required. If the tool is available, tighten the adjuster nut to the initial torque setting specified at the beginning of the Chapter, making sure the torque wrench arm is at 90° to the tool arm **(see illustrstion)**. Now slacken the nut a 1/4 turn, then tighten it to the final torque setting specified. Make sure that the steering stem is able to move freely from lock-to-lock yet all freeplay is eliminated.

25 If the Yamaha tool is not available, using either a C-spanner, a peg spanner or a drift located in one of the notches, tighten the adjuster nut until all freeplay is removed, then tighten it a little more **(see illustration)**. This pre-loads the bearings. Now slacken the nut, then tighten it again, setting it so that all freeplay is just removed, yet the steering is able to move freely from side to side.

Caution: Take great care not to apply

excessive pressure because this will cause premature failure of the bearings.

26 Fit the rubber washer, then the locknut **(see illustrations)**. Tighten the locknut finger-tight, then tighten it further until its notches align with those in the adjuster nut. If necessary, counter-hold the adjuster nut and tighten the locknut using a C-spanner until the notches align, but make sure the adjuster nut does not turn as well. Fit the tabbed lock washer so that the tabs fit into the notches in both the locknut and adjuster nut **(see illustration)**.

27 Fit the top yoke onto the steering stem **(see illustration 9.8b)**. Fit the steering stem nut with its washer and tighten it finger-tight **(see illustration 9.8a)**. Temporarily install one of the forks to align the top and bottom yokes, and secure it by tightening the bottom yoke clamp bolts only (see Section 6). Now tighten

9.23d . . . and the adjuster nut

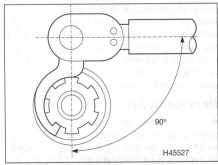

9.24 Setting the steering head bearing adjuster nut using the Yamaha tool – YBR models

9.25 Tightening the adjuster nut using a C-spanner

9.26a Fit the rubber washer . . .

9.26b . . . then tighten the locknut as described . . .

9.26c . . . and fit the tabs on the washer into the aligned notches

the steering stem nut to the torque setting specified at the beginning of the Chapter.

28 Install the remaining components in a reverse of the removal procedure, referring to the relevant Sections or Chapters where required, and to the torque settings specified at the beginning of the Chapter. Make sure the wiring, cables and brake hose are correctly routed. Make sure the rubber bushes are fitted on the headlight bracket and locate correctly in the holes in the underside of the top yoke **(see illustration)**.

29 Refer to the freeplay check procedure in Chapter 1 to make a final assessment of the bearings with the leverage and inertia of all components taken into account, and if necessary readjust.

XT models

30 Smear a liberal quantity of multi-purpose grease onto the bearing races and bearings. Fit the lower bearing onto the steering stem.

31 Carefully lift the steering stem/bottom yoke up through the steering head and support it. Fit the upper bearing into the top of the steering head, then fit the bearing cover. Thread the adjuster nut onto the steering stem and tighten it finger-tight.

32 Using either a C-spanner, a peg spanner or a drift located in one of the notches, tighten the adjuster nut until all freeplay is removed, then tighten it a little more **(see illustration 9.25)**. This pre-loads the bearings. Now slacken the nut, then tighten it again, setting it so that all freeplay is just removed, yet the steering is able to move freely from side to side.

Caution: Take great care not to apply excessive pressure because this will cause premature failure of the bearings.

33 Fit the top yoke onto the steering stem **(see illustration 9.8b)**. Fit the steering stem nut and tighten it finger-tight. Temporarily install one of the forks to align the top and bottom yokes, and secure it by tightening the bottom yoke clamp bolts only (see Section 6). Now tighten the steering stem nut to the torque setting specified at the beginning of the Chapter.

34 Install the remaining components in a reverse of the removal procedure, referring to the relevant Sections or Chapters where required, and to the torque settings specified at the beginning of the Chapter. Make sure the wiring, cables and brake hose are correctly routed.

9.28 Make sure the rubber bushes locate correctly

35 Refer to the freeplay check procedure in Chapter 1 to make a final assessment of the bearings with the leverage and inertia of all components taken into account, and if necessary readjust.

10 Steering head bearings

Inspection

1 Remove the steering stem (see Section 9).

2 Wash all traces of old grease from the bearings and races using paraffin or solvent, and check them for wear or damage.

3 The races should be polished and free from indentations **(see illustration)**. Inspect the bearing balls for signs of wear, damage or discoloration. If there are any signs of wear on any of the above components both upper and lower bearing assemblies must be replaced with a new set. Only remove the outer races in the steering head and the lower bearing inner race on the steering stem if they need to be replaced with new ones – do not reuse them once they have been removed.

Replacement

4 The outer races are an interference fit in the steering head – tap them from position using a suitable drift located on the exposed inner lip of the race **(see illustrations)**. Tap firmly and evenly around each race to ensure that it is driven out squarely. Curve the end of the drift slightly to improve access if necessary.

10.3 Check the races for wear and damage

5 Alternatively, remove the races using a slide-hammer type bearing extractor – these can often be hired from tool shops.

6 Press the new outer races into the head using a drawbolt arrangement **(see illustration)**, or drive them in using a large diameter tubular drift (to do this the bike must be solidly supported as all the force needs to be transmitted to the race). Make sure that the drawbolt washer or drift (as applicable) bears only on the outer edge of the race and does not contact the working surface. Alternatively, have the races installed by a Yamaha dealer equipped with the bearing race installation tools.

> **HAYNES HiNT** *Installation of new bearing outer races is made much easier if the races are left overnight in the freezer. This causes them to contract slightly making them a looser fit. Alternatively, use a freeze spray on the races just before you install them.*

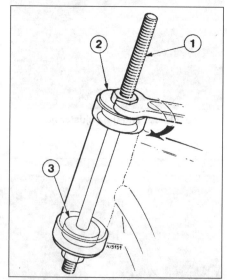

10.6 Drawbolt arrangement for fitting steering stem bearing races

1 *Long bolt or threaded bar*
2 *Thick washer*
3 *Guide for lower race*

10.4a Drive the bearing races out with a brass drift . . .

10.4b . . . locating it on the exposed inner rim of the race (arrowed)

7 Only remove the lower bearing inner race from the steering stem if a new one is being fitted. To remove the race, first thread the steering stem nut onto the top and position the yoke on its front for stability, then tap under it using a cold chisel – the nut will protect the threads from the transmitted force of the impact of the chisel (see illustration). Next use two screwdrivers placed on opposite sides to work the race free, using blocks of wood to improve leverage and protect the yoke (see illustration). If the race is firmly in place it will be necessary to use a puller (see illustration). Take the steering stem to a Yamaha dealer if required.

8 Where fitted remove the dust seal from the bottom of the stem and replace it with a new one. Smear the new one with grease.

9 Fit the new lower race onto the steering stem. Tap the new race into position using a length of tubing with an internal diameter slightly larger than the steering stem (see illustration).

10 Install the steering stem (see Section 9).

11 Rear shock absorber(s)

⚠️ **Warning: Do not attempt to disassemble this shock absorber. Improper disassembly could result in serious injury. No individual components are available for it.**

Removal

YBR models

1 Remove the exhaust system (see Chapter 3A or 3B).

2 Support the motorcycle on its centrestand or using an auxiliary stand so that no weight is transmitted through any part of the rear suspension – tie the front brake lever to the handlebar to ensure the bike can't roll forward. Position a support under the rear wheel or swingarm so that it does not drop when the second shock absorber is removed, but also making sure that the weight of the machine is off the rear suspension so that it is not compressed.

3 Unscrew the nuts and remove the washers securing the top and bottom of the shock absorber (see illustration).

4 Draw the shock absorber off its mounts (see illustration).

XT models

5 Remove the seat (see Chapter 7).

6 Remove the rear wheel (see Chapter 6).

7 Unscrew the three bolts securing the front of the rear mudguard and remove the collars (see illustration).

8 Unscrew the nut and withdraw the bolt securing the top of the shock absorber, noting the washers (see illustration).

9 Unscrew the nut and withdraw the bolt securing the bottom of the shock absorber,

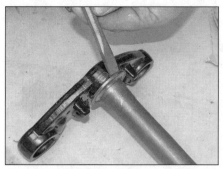
10.7a Remove the lower bearing race using a cold chisel . . .

10.7b . . . and screwdrivers . . .

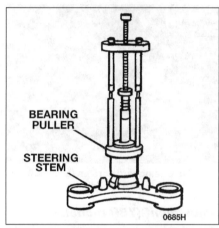
10.7c . . . or a puller if necessary

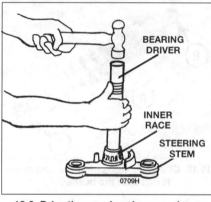
10.9 Drive the new bearing on using a suitable bearing driver or a length of pipe that bears only against the inner race and not against the ball cage

11.3 Unscrew the nut and remove the washer on each end . . .

11.4 . . . and remove the shock absorber

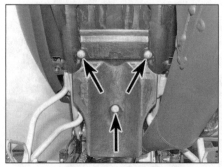
11.7 Unscrew the bolts (arrowed) and remove the collars

11.8 Unscrew the nut (arrowed) and withdraw the bolt

11.9a Unscrew the nut (arrowed) . . .

11.9b . . . withdraw the bolt . . .

11.9c . . . and remove the shock absorber

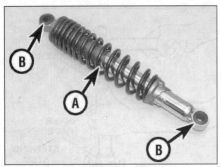

11.10 Check for signs of oil (A), and check for wear in the bushes (B)

12.2a Chainguard screws (arrowed) – YBR models

12.2b Chainguard screws (arrowed) – XT models

then pull the front of the rear mudguard back and draw the shock absorber out **(see illustrations)**.

Inspection

10 Inspect the shock absorber(s) for obvious physical damage and oil leakage, and the coil spring(s) for looseness, cracks or signs of fatigue **(see illustration)**.

11 Inspect the bushes in the shock absorber mounts and the mounts themselves for wear or damage.

Installation

12 Installation is the reverse of removal, noting the following:
● Apply multi-purpose grease to the shock absorber bushes.
● Tighten the bolts/nuts to the torque settings specified for your model at the beginning of the Chapter.

Adjustment (YBR models)

13 Preload can be adjusted by turning the stepped collar at the base of the shock absorber – use a rod in the hole provided to rotate the collar and make sure you set each shock to the same preload setting. The settings are numbered 1 to 5 on the collar, the indent for the current setting being engaged with the lug on the shock body. Position 2 is the standard setting. Position 1 indicates the maximum setting and position 5 the softest.

12 Swingarm

Removal

1 Support the motorcycle so that no weight

is transmitted through any part of the rear suspension – tie the front brake lever to the handlebar to ensure the bike can't roll forward.
2 Undo the screws securing the chainguard and remove it, noting how it fits **(see illustrations)**.
3 Remove the rear wheel (see Chapter 6).
4 On YBR models, remove the exhaust system (see Chapter 3A or 3B). Remove the shock absorbers (see Section 11). Remove the brake torque arm – remove the split pin from the inner end of the bolt, then unscrew the nut and remove the washer where fitted **(see illustration)**. Withdraw the bolt and remove the arm.
5 On XT models unscrew the bolt securing the brake hose guide to the right-hand side of the swingarm **(see illustration)**. Undo the screws securing the chain guide to the left-hand side **(see illustration)** – note the

12.4 Remove the split pin (arrowed), then unscrew the nut and withdraw the bolt

12.5a Unscrew the bolt (arrowed) to free the brake hose

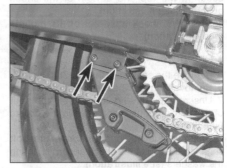

12.5b Undo the screws (arrowed) and remove the guide . . .

12.5c . . . take care not to lose the captive nuts

12.6 Withdraw the pivot bolt, bringing the bracket with it and remove the swingarm

12.8 Remove the slider if required – on YBR models note how the pegs locate in the holes to secure it

captive nuts on the back and remove them for safekeeping **(see illustration)**. Unscrew the nut and withdraw the bolt securing the bottom of the shock absorber to the swingarm, noting the washers **(see illustrations 11.9a and b)**.

6 On YBR models unscrew the bottom bolt securing the passenger footrest bracket on each side **(see illustration 3.8a)**. Unscrew the swingarm pivot bolt nut and remove the washer (where fitted), then remove the right-hand footrest bracket **(see illustration 3.8c or d)**. Withdraw the pivot bolt along with the left-hand footrest bracket, then manoeuvre the swingarm out of the frame **(see illustration)**.

7 On XT models unscrew the nut on the right-hand end of the swingarm pivot bolt and remove the washer. Withdraw the pivot bolt then manoeuvre the swingarm out of the frame.

8 Remove the chain slider from the front of the swingarm if required – on YBR models pull the pegs out of the holes in the swingarm, and on XT models unscrew the bolt, noting the collar **(see illustration)**. Check the condition of the slider and replace it with a new one if necessary. On XT models also check the lower guide fitted on the frame.

Inspection

9 Remove the pivot cap from each side (where fitted), noting any shims fitted with them **(see illustration)**.
10 Thoroughly clean the swingarm, removing all traces of dirt, corrosion and grease.
11 Inspect the swingarm closely, looking for obvious signs of wear such as heavy scoring, and cracks or distortion due to accident damage.
12 Check the pivot components (spacers, bushes and grease seals as fitted) **(see illustration)**. If necessary replace any worn

components with new ones – check with your dealer as to the availability of the bushes as you may have to fit a new swingarm if they are worn. Lever out the old grease seals where fitted and press new ones into place **(see illustrations)**.

13 Check the swingarm pivot bolt is straight by rolling it on a flat surface such as a piece of plate glass (first wipe off all old grease and remove any corrosion using wire wool). Replace the pivot bolt with a new one if it is bent.

12.9 Remove the pivot cap

12.12a Withdraw the spacer and check the bush in each pivot

12.12b Lever the old seal out . . .

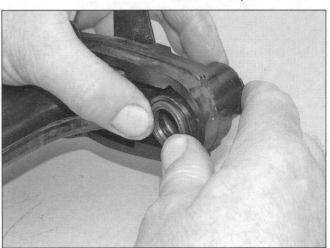

12.12c . . . and press the new one into place

12.14a Hold the straight-edge as shown and pull the swingarm against it to set the pivot and spacer flush . . .

12.14b . . . then measure the clearance between the pivot bolt and the bush

12.17 Fit the bottom bolt for the left-hand bracket

Installation

14 On YBR models, if any new pivot components have been fitted or a new swingarm is being fitted, the side clearance must first be measured, and adjusted using shims if necessary. Temporarily install the swingarm with the bushes, spacers and seals fitted but without the pivot caps, shims and passenger footrest brackets, and slide the pivot bolt through. Push each spacer fully into its bush so its inner end is against the frame. Now hold a straight-edge over the right-hand end of the pivot bolt and against the outside of the right-hand spacer, then draw the swingarm to the right so the pivot housing and spacer are flush with the straight-edge **(see illustrations)** – this sets all the clearance on the left-hand side, between the pivot bolt head and the bush. Measure this clearance, which is actually the amount of the protrusion of the spacer from the bush, using a feeler gauge blade as shown. The clearance should be 0.5 to 0.9 mm. If it is greater than this, fit

0.3 mm shims (available from Yamaha, part No. 5VL-F2127-00) as required into the pivot caps – if an even number of shims is required, fit the same number on each side; if an odd number is required, fit the greater number on the left-hand side.

15 If removed, install the chain slider, making sure it locates correctly **(see illustration 12.8)**. On XT models do not forget to fit the collar with the bolt.

16 Clean off all old grease, then lubricate the bushes and the pivot bolt with multi-purpose grease. Fit the spacers back into the bushes where removed, and on YBR models fit the pivot caps along with any shims **(see illustrations 12.12a and 12.9)**.

17 On YBR models fit the pivot bolt through the left-hand footrest bracket. Position the swingarm and loop the drive around the front. Slide the pivot bolt through from the left-hand side **(see illustration 12.6)**. Fit the bottom bolt into the footrest bracket to secure it **(see illustration)**. Fit the right-hand footrest bracket onto the end of the pivot bolt, then

fit swingarm pivot nut, with its washer (where fitted) and the bottom bolt **(see illustrations 3.8b and a)**. Tighten the pivot bolt nut to the torque setting specified at the beginning of the Chapter. Tighten the footrest bracket bottom bolts to the specified torque.

18 On XT models position the swingarm and loop the drive chain over the front. Slide the pivot bolt through from the left-hand side. Fit the nut with its washer and tighten it to the torque setting specified at the beginning of the Chapter.

19 Install the remaining components in reverse of the removal procedure. On XT models tighten the shock absorber bolt nut to its specified torque setting. On YBR models tighten the brake torque arm nut to its specified torque and secure it with a new split pin, bending the ends around the bolt **(see illustration 12.4)**.

20 Check and adjust the drive chain slack (see Chapter 1). Check the operation of the rear suspension and brake before taking the machine on the road.

Chapter 6
Brakes, wheels and final drive

Contents

Degrees of difficulty

Easy, suitable for novice with little experience 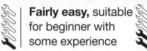	**Fairly easy,** suitable for beginner with some experience	**Fairly difficult,** suitable for competent DIY mechanic	**Difficult,** suitable for experienced DIY mechanic	**Very difficult,** suitable for expert DIY or professional

Specifications

Front brake

Brake fluid type	DOT 4
Brake pad friction material minimum thickness	1.0 mm
Caliper bore ID	
2005 and 2006 YBR models.	35.03 mm
2007-on YBR models	33.34 mm
XT-R models	32.0 mm
XT-X models	25.0 mm
Master cylinder bore ID	
2005 and 2006 YBR models.	12.7 mm
2007-on YBR models	11.0 mm
XT models.	11.0 mm
Disc thickness	
YBR models	
Standard	4.0 mm
Service limit (min)	3.5 mm
XT models	
Standard	3.5 mm
Service limit (min)	3.0 mm
Disc maximum runout	
YBR models	0.15 mm
XT models.	0.30 mm

Rear brake – YBR models

Drum internal diameter	
Standard	130.0 mm
Service limit	131.0 mm
Brake shoe lining minimum thickness	2.0 mm
Brake shoe spring free length	
2005 and 2006 models.	50.5 mm
2007-on models	52.0 and 48.0 mm

Rear brake – XT models

Brake fluid type	DOT 4
Brake pad friction material minimum thickness	1.0 mm
Caliper bore ID	32.0 mm
Master cylinder bore ID	12.7 mm
Disc thickness	
Standard	3.5 mm
Service limit (min)	3.0 mm
Disc maximum runout	0.30 mm

Wheels

Maximum wheel runout (front and rear)	
Axial (side-to-side)	0.5 mm
Radial (out-of-round)	1.0 mm

Tyres

Tyre pressures	see *Pre-ride* checks
Tyre sizes*	
YBR-ED models	
Front	2.75-18 42P – 2005 and 2006 tubed, 2007-on tubeless
Rear	90/90-18 57P – 2005 and 2006 tubed, 2007-on tubeless
YBR Custom models	
Front	3.00-18 47P tubeless
Rear	3.50-16 58P tubeless
XT-R models	
Front	90/90-21 54S tubed
Rear	120/80-18 62S tubed
XT-X models	
Front	100/80-17 52S tubed
Rear	130/70-17 62S tubed

Refer to the owners handbook or the tyre information label on the swingarm for approved tyre brands.

Final drive

Drive chain slack and lubricant	see Chapter 1
Drive chain type	
YBR models	DID 428V (118 links) O-ring chain
XT-R models	DID 428H (128 links) standard chain
XT-X models	DID 428H (126 links) standard chain

Sprocket sizes (No. of teeth)	YBR-ED	YBR Custom	XT-R	XT-X
Front (engine) sprocket	14	14	14	14
Rear (wheel) sprocket	45	43	50	48

Torque settings

Brake caliper bleed valves	6 Nm
Brake disc bolts	
YBR models	23 Nm
XT models	13 Nm
Brake hose banjo bolts	
2010-on YBR 125 ED models	
Hose to calliper bolt	25 Nm
Hose to master cylinder bolt	30 Nm
All other models	
Hose to caliper and master cylinder bolts	25 Nm
Brake torque arm nut – YBR models	19 Nm
Front axle nut – YBR models	59 Nm
Front axle – XT models	45 Nm
Front axle clamp bolt – XT models	20 Nm
Caliper mounting bolts	
YBR models	35 Nm
XT models	30 Nm
Caliper slider bolt (2005 and 2006 YBR models)	23 Nm
Front sprocket retainer plate bolts	
2010-on YBR125 ED models	6 Nm
All other models	10 Nm
Rear axle nut	
2005 and 2006 YBR models	91 Nm
2007-on YBR models	80 Nm
XT models	85 Nm
Rear sprocket bolts	
YBR models	40 Nm
XT models	30 Nm

1 General information

All models have an hydraulically operated single disc brake at the front. YBR models have a single piston sliding front caliper, XT-R models have a single opposed piston caliper, and XT-X models have a twin piston sliding caliper.

YBR models have a drum brake at the rear. XT models have an hydraulically operated single disc brake at the rear, with a single opposed piston caliper.

The drive to the rear wheel is by chain and sprockets.

YBR models have cast alloy wheels with tubed tyres. XT models have steel spoked wheels with tubed tyres.

Caution: Disc brake components rarely require disassembly. Do not disassemble components unless absolutely necessary. If an hydraulic brake hose is loosened or disconnected, the union sealing washers must be renewed and the system bled upon reassembly. Do not use solvents on internal brake components. Solvents will cause the seals to swell and distort. Use only clean DOT 4 brake fluid for cleaning. Use care when working with brake fluid as it can injure your eyes and it will damage painted surfaces and plastic parts.

2 Front brake pads

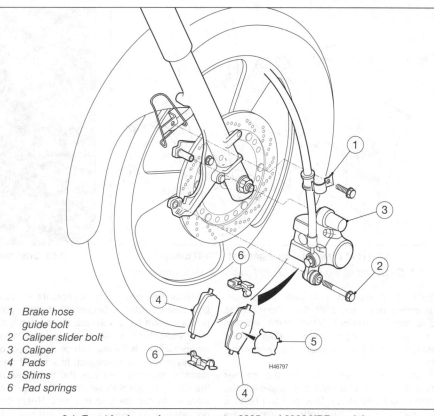

1 Brake hose guide bolt
2 Caliper slider bolt
3 Caliper
4 Pads
5 Shims
6 Pad springs

H46797

2.1 Front brake pad arrangement – 2005 and 2006 YBR models

![warning icon] *Warning: The dust created by the brake system is harmful to your health. Never blow it out with compressed air and don't inhale any of it. An approved filtering mask should be worn when working on the brakes.*

Note: *Do not operate the brake lever while the pads are out of the caliper.*

1 On 2005 and 2006 YBR models unscrew the brake hose guide bolt. Unscrew the caliper slider bolt. Pivot the caliper up and draw it off the bracket. Remove the pads from the bracket, noting how they fit. If required remove the shim from the back of each pad, noting how they fit **(see illustration)**.

2 On 2007-on YBR models unscrew the brake hose guide bolt **(see illustration)**. Unscrew the caliper mounting bolts and slide the caliper off the disc **(see illustration)**.

Remove the clips securing the pad pin **(see illustration)**. Withdraw the pin and remove the pads **(see illustrations 2.14b and a)**. Slide the caliper off the bracket **(see illustration)**.

2.2a Unscrew the bolt (arrowed) and free the guide

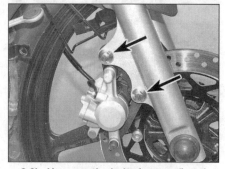

2.2b Unscrew the bolts (arrowed) and slide the caliper off the disc

2.2c Remove the clips . . .

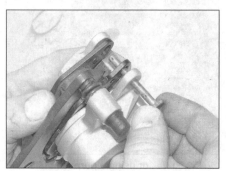

2.2d . . . then withdraw the pin

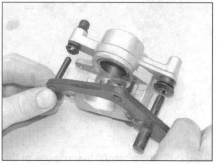

2.2e Slide the caliper off the bracket

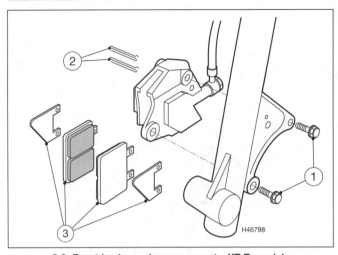

2.3 Front brake pad arrangement – XT-R models

1 Caliper mounting bolts   2 Pad pins   3 Pads and shims

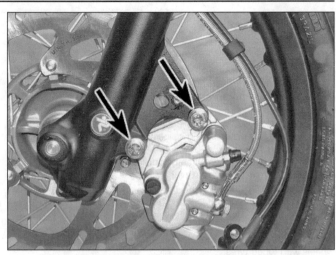

2.4a Unscrew the bolts (arrowed) and slide the caliper off the disc

3 On XT-R models unscrew the caliper mounting bolts and slide the caliper off the disc **(see illustration)**. Withdraw the pad pins and remove the pads. If required remove the shim from the back of each pad, noting how they fit.

4 On XT-X models unscrew the caliper mounting bolts and slide the caliper off the disc **(see illustration)**. Unscrew and remove the pad pins **(see illustration)**. Remove the pads **(see illustrations 2.16b and a)**. Slide the caliper off the bracket **(see illustration)**.

5 Inspect the surface of each pad for contamination and check that the friction material has not worn beyond its service limit (see Chapter 1, Section 8). If either pad is worn down to, or beyond, the service limit wear indicator (i.e. the wear indicator is no longer visible), is fouled with oil or grease, or heavily scored or damaged, fit a set of new pads. If required measure the thickness of the friction material to determine the extent of wear – the service limit is 1 mm. **Note:** *It is not possible to degrease the friction material; if the pads are contaminated in any way they must be replaced with new ones.*

6 If the pads are in good condition clean them carefully, using a fine wire brush which is completely free of oil and grease to remove all traces of road dirt and corrosion. Using a pointed instrument, dig out any embedded particles of foreign matter. If required, spray with a dedicated brake cleaner to remove any dust.

7 Check the condition of the brake disc (see Section 4).

8 Remove all traces of corrosion from the pad pin(s) and check for wear and damage. Fit new ones if necessary.

9 Clean around the exposed section of the piston(s) to remove any dirt or debris that could cause the seals to be damaged. If new pads are being fitted, now push the piston(s) all the way back into the caliper to create room for them; if the old pads are still serviceable push the piston(s) in a little way. To push the piston(s) back use finger pressure or a piece of wood as leverage, or place the old pads back in the caliper and use a metal bar or a screwdriver inserted between them, or use grips and a piece of wood, with rag or card to protect the caliper body **(see illustration)**. Alternatively obtain a proper piston-pushing tool from a good tool supplier **(see illustration)**. If there is too much brake fluid in the reservoir It may be necessary to remove the master cylinder reservoir cover, plate and diaphragm and siphon some out (see *Pre-ride) checks*. If a piston is difficult to push back, remove the bleed valve cap, then attach a length of clear hose to the bleed valve and place the open end in a suitable container, then open the valve and try again (see Section 11). Take great care not to draw any air into the system. If in doubt, bleed the brake afterwards.

10 If a piston appears seized, apply the brake lever and check whether the piston in question moves at all – on models with two pistons first block or hold the other piston using wood or cable-ties. If it moves out but can't be pushed back in, the chances are there is some hidden corrosion stopping it. If it doesn't move at

2.4b Unscrew the pad pins and remove the pads

2.4c Slide the caliper off the bracket

2.9a Push the piston(s) in using one of the methods described . . .

2.9b . . . or using a purpose built commercial tool

2.11a Make sure the boots (arrowed) are in good condition

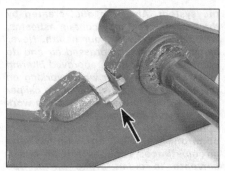

2.11b Make sure the pad guide (arrowed) . . .

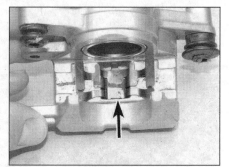

2.12 . . . and pad spring (arrowed) are correctly in place

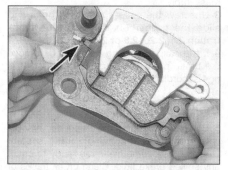

2.14a Make sure the projection on the pad locates correctly against the guide in the cut-out (arrowed)

2.14b Fit the pad onto the post then pivot it up into the caliper

2.14c Slide the caliper on to the disc and fit the bolts

all, or to fully clean and inspect the pistons, disassemble the caliper and overhaul it (see Section 3).

11 On all except XT-R models clean off all traces of corrosion and hardened grease from the slider pins on the bracket and from the boots in the caliper. Replace the rubber boots with new ones if they are damaged, deformed or deteriorated (see illustration). Make sure the each slider pin is tight. Apply a smear of silicone-based grease to the boots and slider pins. On 2005 and 2006 YBR models make sure the pad springs are correctly located on the bracket. On 2007-on YBR models make sure the pad guide is correctly located on the bracket (see illustration).

12 Make sure the pad spring is correctly located in the caliper (see illustration).

13 On 2005 and 2006 YBR models make sure the shim is correctly fitted on the back of each pad (see illustration 2.1). Smear some copper grease onto each shim. Fit the pads into the bracket with the friction material facing each side of the disc, making sure they locate correctly against the springs. Slide the caliper onto the bracket and pivot it down over the pads. Fit the slider bolt and tighten it to the torque setting specified at the beginning of the Chapter. Fit the brake hose guide.

14 On 2007-on YBR models slide the caliper onto the bracket, making sure each boot seats correctly around the base of its pin (see illustration 2.2e). Smear some copper grease onto the back of each pad, the inner pad locating post and the pad retaining pin.

Fit the outer pad, making sure it locates correctly against the guide on the bracket (see illustration). Fit the inner pad over the post and pivot it up into the caliper (see illustration). Press the pads up to align the holes and insert the pad pin (see illustration 2.2d). Secure the pin with the clips (see illustration 2.2c). Slide the caliper onto the disc making sure the pads locate correctly on each side (see illustration). Install the caliper mounting bolts and tighten them to the torque setting specified at the beginning of the Chapter. Fit the brake hose guide (see illustration 2.2a).

15 On XT-R models make sure the shim is correctly fitted on the back of each pad with the arrow pointing in the normal direction of disc rotation (see illustration 2.3). Smear some copper grease onto each shim. Fit

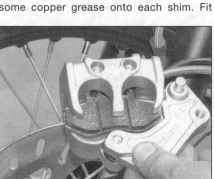

2.16a Fit the outer pad onto the caliper . . .

the pads into the caliper and push them up against the spring to align the holes, then insert the pad pins. Slide the caliper onto the disc making sure the pads locate correctly on each side. Install the caliper mounting bolts and tighten them to the torque setting specified at the beginning of the Chapter.

16 On XT-X models slide the caliper onto the bracket, making sure each boot seats correctly around the base of its pin (see illustration 2.4c). Smear some copper grease onto the back of each pad, the inner pad locating post and the pad retaining pins. Fit the outer pad, making sure it locates correctly (see illustration). Fit the inner pad against the post and pivot it up into the caliper (see illustration). Press the pads up to align the holes then insert and tighten the pad pins (see illustration 2.4b). Slide the caliper onto

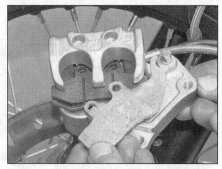

2.16b . . . then locate the inner pad against the post and pivot it up

2.16c Slide the caliper onto the disc and fit the bolts

the disc making sure the pads locate correctly on each side **(see illustration)**. Install the caliper mounting bolts and tighten them to the torque setting specified at the beginning of the Chapter.

17 Operate the brake lever until the pads contact with the disc. Check the level of fluid in the hydraulic reservoir and top-up if necessary (see *Pre-ride checks*).

18 Check the operation of the front brake before riding the motorcycle.

3 Front brake caliper

 Warning: If the caliper is in need of an overhaul all old brake fluid should be flushed from

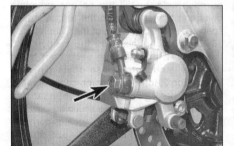

3.2a Brake hose banjo bolt (arrowed) – YBR models

3.2c Using a hose clamp to prevent fluid loss

the system. Also, the dust created by the brake system may contain asbestos, which is harmful to your health. Never blow it out with compressed air and do not inhale any of it. An approved filtering mask should be worn when working on the brakes. Overhaul of the brake caliper must be done in a spotlessly clean work area to avoid contamination and possible failure of the brake hydraulic system components. Do not, under any circumstances, use petroleum-based solvents to clean brake parts. Use clean DOT 4 brake fluid, dedicated brake cleaner or denatured alcohol only, as described. To prevent damage from spilled brake fluid, always cover paintwork when working on the braking system.*

Removal

Note: *If the caliper is being overhauled (usually due to sticking piston(s) or fluid leaks) read through the entire procedure first and make sure that you have obtained all the new parts required, including some new DOT 4 brake fluid.*

Note: *Do not operate the brake lever while the caliper is off the disc.*

1 If the caliper is just being displaced from the fork leg as part of the wheel removal procedure unscrew the mounting bolts and slide the caliper off the disc **(see illustration 2.1, 2.2b, 2.3 or 2.4a)** – on YBR models unscrew the brake hose guide bolt to give

3.2b Brake hose banjo bolt (arrowed) – XT-X models

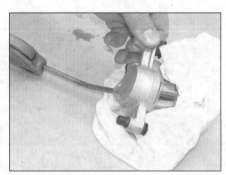

3.6 Apply compressed air to the fluid passage until the piston is displaced

more freedom of movement **(see illustration 2.2a)**. Tie the caliper back out of the way.

2 If the caliper is being completely removed or overhauled, unscrew the brake hose banjo bolt and detach the banjo union, noting its alignment with the caliper **(see illustrations)**. Wrap plastic foodwrap around the banjo union and secure the hose in an upright position to minimise fluid loss – on YBR models with a flexible hose (as opposed to braided on XT models) you can also use a hose clamp if available **(see illustration)**. Discard the sealing washers, as new ones must be fitted on reassembly.

3 Unscrew the caliper mounting bolts and slide the caliper off the disc **(see illustration 2.1, 2.2b, 2.3 or 2.4a)**.

4 If the caliper is being overhauled, remove the brake pads (see Section 2, Step 1, 2, 3 or 4 according to model).

Overhaul

5 Clean the exterior of the caliper and bracket with denatured alcohol or brake system cleaner. Have some clean rag ready to catch any spilled brake fluid. Clean off all traces of corrosion. On all except XT-R models clean off any hardened grease from the slider pins and from the boots in the caliper. Replace the rubber boots with new ones if they are damaged, deformed or deteriorated **(see illustration 2.11a)**. Make sure the slider pins are tight.

6 Make sure the bleed valve is tight. To remove the piston(s), cover it/them and the caliper with rag and apply compressed air gradually and progressively, starting with a fairly low pressure, to the fluid inlet in the caliper and allow the piston(s) to ease out of the bore(s) **(see illustration)**. On models with two pistons first mark the piston heads with a felt marker so that they can be returned to their original bores on installation. If one is being pushed out before the other, you may need to block that one so more pressure is applied to the sticking one, but do not use your fingers. Always make sure the caliper is covered, with the piston(s) pointing down onto the bench so they cannot fly out and hit something.

7 If a piston is stuck in its bore due to corrosion, find a suitable bolt to block the fluid inlet banjo bolt bore and thread it in, then unscrew the bleed valve and apply the air to this in the same way – the narrower bore will allow more air pressure to be applied to the piston as less can escape. Do not try to remove a piston by levering it out or by using pliers or other grips. If the piston has completely seized you may have to replace the caliper with a new one.

8 Remove the dust seal(s) and the piston seal(s) from the piston bore(s) using a soft wooden or plastic tool to avoid scratching the

3.8 Remove the seals and discard them

3.11a Lubricate the new piston seal with brake fluid . . .

3.11b . . . then fit it into its groove . . .

3.12 . . . followed by the new dust seal

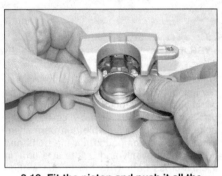

3.13 Fit the piston and push it all the way in

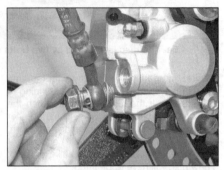

3.17 Always use new sealing washers and align the hose as noted on removal

bores **(see illustration)**. Discard the seals as new ones must be fitted.

9 Clean the piston(s) and bore(s) with new DOT 4 brake fluid. If compressed air is available, blow it through the fluid galleries in the caliper to ensure they are clear (make sure it is filtered and unlubricated).

Caution: Do not, under any circumstances, use a petroleum-based solvent to clean brake parts.

10 Inspect the caliper bore and piston for signs of corrosion, nicks and burrs and loss of plating. If surface defects are present, the pistons and/or the caliper assembly must be replaced with new ones.

11 Lubricate the new piston seal(s) with new brake fluid and fit it/them into the inner (large) groove(s) in the caliper bore(s) **(see illustrations)**.

12 Lubricate the new dust seal(s) with new brake fluid and fit it/them into the outer groove(s) in the caliper bore(s) **(see illustration)**.

13 Lubricate the piston(s) with new brake

fluid and fit it/them, closed-end first, into the caliper bore(s), taking care not to displace the seals **(see illustration)**. Using your thumbs, push the piston(s) squarely all the way in.

14 On all except XT-R models apply a smear of silicone-based grease to the boots and slider pins.

Installation

15 If removed, install the brake pads (see Section 2, Step 5-on, as required).

16 Slide the caliper onto the brake disc, making sure the pads locate correctly on each side **(see illustration 2.14c or 2.16c)**. Install the caliper mounting bolts and tighten them to the torque setting specified at the beginning of the Chapter.

17 If detached, connect the brake hose to the caliper, using new sealing washers on each side of the banjo fitting **(see illustration)**. Locate the hose elbow between or against the lug(s) on the caliper, where present. Tighten the banjo bolt to the specified torque setting.

18 On YBR models fit the brake hose guide if displaced **(see illustration 2.2a)**.

19 Top up the hydraulic reservoir with DOT 4 brake fluid (see *Pre-ride checks*) and bleed the system as described in Section 11. Check that there are no fluid leaks and test the operation of the brake before riding the motorcycle.

4 Front brake disc

Inspection

1 Inspect the surface of the disc for score marks and other damage. Light scratches are normal after use and won't affect brake operation, but deep grooves and heavy score marks will reduce braking efficiency and accelerate pad wear. If a disc is badly grooved it must be replaced with a new one.

2 The disc must not be machined or allowed to wear down to a thickness less than the service limit as listed in this Chapter's Specifications. The minimum thickness may also be stamped on the disc. Check the thickness of the disc in the middle of the pad contact area using a micrometer **(see illustration)** – do not measure across the rim of the disc with a ruler. Replace the disc with a new one if necessary.

3 To check if the disc is warped, position the bike on an auxiliary stand with the front wheel raised off the ground. Mount a dial gauge to the fork leg, with the gauge plunger touching the surface of the disc about 10 mm from the outer edge **(see illustration)**. Rotate the wheel and watch the gauge

4.2 Measure the thickness of the disc

4.3 Checking disc runout with a dial gauge

4.5a The disc is secured by five bolts on YBR models

4.5b The disc is secured by six bolts on XT models

needle, comparing the reading with the limit listed in the Specifications at the beginning of this Chapter. If the runout is greater than the service limit, check the wheel bearings for play (see Chapter 1). If the bearings are worn, install new ones (see Section 17) and repeat this check. If the disc runout is still excessive, a new disc will have to be fitted.

Removal

4 Remove the wheel (see Section 15).
Caution: Don't lay the wheel down and allow it to rest on the disc – the disc could become warped. Set the wheel on wood blocks so the wheel rim supports the weight of the wheel.
5 If you are not replacing the disc with a new one, mark the relationship of the disc to the wheel, so it can be installed in the same position. Unscrew the disc bolts, loosening them evenly and a little at a time in a criss-cross pattern to avoid distorting the disc, then remove the disc **(see illustrations)**.

Installation

6 Before installing the disc, make sure there is no dirt or corrosion where it seats on the hub. If the disc does not sit flat when it is bolted down, it will appear to be warped when checked or when the front brake is used.
7 Fit the disc onto the wheel with its marked side facing out, aligning the previously applied

matchmarks (if you're reinstalling the original disc), and making sure the arrow points in the direction of normal rotation.
8 Clean the threads of the disc mounting bolts, then apply a suitable non-permanent thread locking compound. Fit the bolts and tighten them evenly and a little at a time in a criss-cross pattern to the torque setting specified at the beginning of this Chapter. Clean the disc using acetone or brake system cleaner. If a new disc has been fitted, remove any protective coating from its working surfaces and fit new brake pads.
9 Install the front wheel (see Section 15).
10 Check the operation of the brake before riding the motorcycle.

5 Front brake master cylinder

> ⚠ **Warning: If the brake master cylinder is in need of an overhaul all old brake fluid should be flushed from the system. Overhaul of the brake master cylinder must be done in a spotlessly clean work area to avoid contamination and possible failure of the brake hydraulic system components. Do not, under any circumstances, use petroleum-based solvents to clean brake**

parts. Use new DOT 4 brake fluid, dedicated brake cleaner or denatured alcohol only, as described. To prevent damage from spilled brake fluid, always cover paintwork when working on the braking system.

Removal

Note: *If the master cylinder is being overhauled (usually due to sticking or poor action, or fluid leaks) read through the entire procedure first and make sure that you have obtained all the new parts required, including some new DOT 4 brake fluid.*
1 If the master cylinder is being overhauled, follow Step 2 onwards. If the master cylinder is just being displaced, follow this Step only: unscrew the master cylinder clamp bolts and remove the back of the clamp, noting how it fits, then position the master cylinder assembly clear of the handlebar **(see illustration)**. Ensure no strain is placed on the hydraulic hose. Keep the reservoir upright to prevent air entering the system.
2 Remove the brake lever (see Chapter 5). Remove the mirror (see Chapter 7).
3 On YBR models press the clip up on the underside of the brake light switch and draw the switch out of its housing **(see illustration)**. On XT models pull the rubber boot off the brake light switch and disconnect the wiring connectors, and if required unscrew and remove the switch **(see illustration)**.

5.1 Unscrew the bolts (arrowed) and remove the master cylinder and its clamp

5.3a Release the clip and withdraw the switch

5.3b Disconnect the brake light switch wires (arrowed)

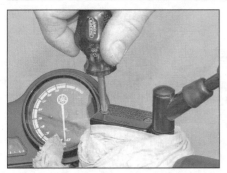

5.4 Slacken the cover screws

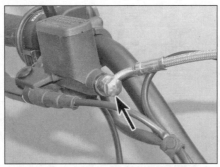

5.5 Brake hose banjo bolt (arrowed) – XT models

5.7 Lift out the master cylinder baffle plate

5.8 Remove the boot

5.9a Release the circlip . . .

5.9b . . . then draw out the piston assembly and the spring

4 Slacken the reservoir cover screws **(see illustration)**.
5 Unscrew the brake hose banjo bolt and detach the banjo union, noting its alignment with the master cylinder **(see illustration)**. Wrap plastic foodwrap around the banjo union and secure the hose in an upright position to minimise fluid loss. Discard the sealing washers as new ones must be fitted on reassembly.
6 Unscrew the master cylinder clamp bolts and remove the back of the clamp, noting how it fits, then lift the master cylinder and reservoir away from the handlebar **(see illustration 5.1)**.
7 Remove the reservoir cover, diaphragm plate (where fitted), and diaphragm. Drain the brake fluid from the master cylinder and reservoir into a suitable container. On 2010-on YBR125 ED models, note the location of the baffle plate in the bottom of the reservoir and lift it out carefully **(see illustration)**. Wipe any remaining fluid out of the reservoir with a clean rag.

Overhaul

8 Carefully remove the rubber boot from the master cylinder **(see illustration)**.
9 Depress the piston and use circlip pliers to remove the circlip, then slide out the piston assembly and the spring, noting how they fit **(see illustrations)**. If they are difficult to remove, apply low pressure compressed air to the brake fluid outlet. Lay the parts out in

the proper order to prevent confusion during reassembly.
10 Clean the master cylinder bore with new DOT 4 brake fluid. If compressed air is available, blow it through the fluid galleries to ensure they are clear (make sure the air is filtered and unlubricated).
Caution: Do not, under any circumstances, use a petroleum-based solvent to clean brake parts.
11 Check the master cylinder bore for corrosion, scratches, nicks and score marks.

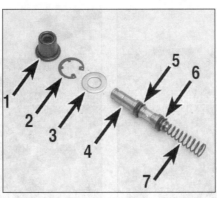

5.12 Master cylinder components – YBR models

1 Rubber boot   5 Seal
2 Circlip   6 Cup
3 Washer   7 Spring
4 Piston

If damage or wear is evident, the master cylinder must be replaced with a new one. If the master cylinder is in poor condition, then the caliper should be checked as well.
12 All the necessary parts are included in the master cylinder rebuild kit. Use all of the new parts, regardless of the apparent condition of the old ones. Lay out the new parts in their correct order according to those removed **(see illustration)**.
13 Smear the piston, cup and seal and the master cylinder bore with new brake fluid. Slide the piston and spring assembly into the master cylinder **(see illustration 5.9b)**. Push the piston in, making sure the lips on the cup and seal do not turn inside out **(see illustration)**. Fit the washer and circlip over

5.13a Push the piston into the bore

5.13b Fit the washer . . .

5.13c . . . and the circlip . . .

5.13d . . . pushing it down into its groove

5.14a Fit the new boot . . .

5.14b . . . making sure it locates correctly

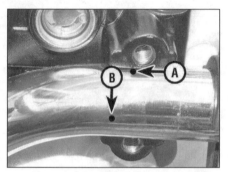

5.16a On YBR models align the master cylinder mating surface with the mark (A) and the side with the mark (B) . . .

the end of the piston (see illustrations). Push the circlip into its groove, making sure it locates correctly (see illustration).

14 Smear some silicone grease onto the lips and inside of the rubber boot. Fit the rubber boot onto the piston so its outer end lips locate in the groove and press the boot into place in the end of the cylinder (see illustrations).

15 Inspect the reservoir diaphragm and fit a new one if it is damaged or deteriorated.

Installation

16 Attach the master cylinder to the handlebar, aligning the clamp joint with the punch mark(s), then fit the back of the clamp, on YBR models with its UP mark facing up (see illustrations). Tighten the upper bolt first, then the lower bolt.

17 Connect the brake hose to the master cylinder, using new sealing washers on each side of the banjo fitting (see illustration). Align the hose as noted on removal and tighten the banjo bolt to the torque setting specified at the beginning of the Chapter.

18 On YBR models align the brake light switch tab with its hole and push the switch in until it clicks into place (see illustration 5.3a). On XT models, thread the switch

into its housing if removed, and connect the wiring connectors and fit the rubber boot (see illustration 5.3b).

19 Install the brake lever (see Chapter 5). Install the mirror (see Chapter 7).

20 On 2010-on YBR models, press the baffle plate firmly into the bottom of the reservoir (see illustration 5.7).

21 Fill the fluid reservoir with new DOT 4 brake fluid (see Pre-ride) checks). Refer to Section 11 and bleed the air from the system.

22 Check the operation of the brake before riding the motorcycle.

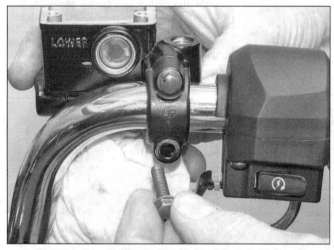

5.16b . . . then fit the clamp with the UP mark facing up

5.17 Always use new sealing washers

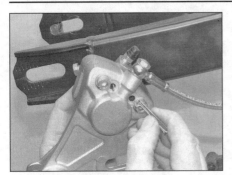

6.2a Withdraw the pins . . .

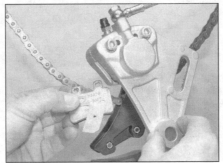

6.2b . . . and remove the pads and shims

6.7 Push the piston into the caliper using one of the methods described

6 Rear brake pads – XT models

⚠️ **Warning: The dust created by the brake system may contain asbestos, which is harmful to your health. Never blow it out with compressed air and don't inhale any of it. An approved filtering mask should be worn when working on the brakes.**

Note: *Do not operate the brake pedal while the pads are out of the caliper.*

1 Remove the rear wheel (see Section 16).

2 Withdraw the pad pins and remove the pads, noting how they fit **(see illustrations)**.

3 Inspect the surface of each pad for contamination and check that the friction material has not worn beyond its service limit (see Chapter 1, Section 8). If either pad is worn down to, or beyond, the service limit wear indicator, is fouled with oil or grease, or heavily scored or damaged, fit a new set of pads. If required measure the thickness of the friction material to determine the extent of wear – the service limit is 1 mm. **Note:** *It is not possible to degrease the friction material; if the pads are contaminated in any way they must be replaced with new ones.*

4 If the pads are in good condition clean them carefully, using a fine wire brush which is completely free of oil and grease to remove all traces of road dirt and corrosion. Using a pointed instrument, dig out any embedded particles of foreign matter. If required, spray

with a dedicated brake cleaner to remove any dust.

5 Check the condition of the brake disc (see Section 8).

6 Remove all traces of corrosion from the pad pins and check them for wear and damage, replacing them with new ones if necessary.

7 Clean around the exposed section of the piston to remove any dirt or debris that could cause the seals to be damaged. If new pads are being fitted, now push the piston all the way back into the caliper to create room for them **(see illustration)**; if the old pads are still serviceable push the piston in a little way. To push the piston back use finger pressure or a piece of wood as leverage, or place the old pads back in the caliper and use a metal bar or a screwdriver inserted between them, or use grips and a piece of wood, with rag or card to protect the caliper body. Alternatively obtain a proper piston-pushing tool from a good tool supplier **(see illustration 2.9b)**. If there is too much brake fluid in the reservoir It may be necessary to remove the master cylinder reservoir cover, plate and diaphragm and siphon some out (see *Pre-ride) checks*. If the piston is difficult to push back, remove the bleed valve cap, then attach a length of clear hose to the bleed valve and place the open end in a suitable container, then open the valve and try again (see Section 11). Take great care not to draw any air into the system. If in doubt, bleed the brake afterwards.

8 If the piston appears seized, apply the brake lever and check whether it moves at all. If it moves out but can't be pushed back in the

chances are there is some hidden corrosion stopping it. If it doesn't move at all, or to fully clean and inspect the piston, overhaul the caliper (see Section 7).

9 Fit the shim onto the back of each pad with the arrow pointing in the normal direction of disc rotation **(see illustration 6.2b)**. Lightly smear the shim with copper-based grease. Also smear the pad pins. Make sure the pad spring is correctly fitted in the caliper.

10 Slide the pads into the caliper so that the friction material of each pad faces the other **(see illustration)**. Use a spanner as shown to hold the pads in place and insert the pad pins **(see illustrations)**.

11 Install the rear wheel (see Section 16).

12 Operate the brake pedal until the pads contact with the disc. Check the level of fluid in the hydraulic reservoir and top-up if necessary (see *Pre-ride checks*).

13 Check the operation of the rear brake before riding the motorcycle.

7 Rear brake caliper – XT models

⚠️ **Warning: If the caliper is in need of an overhaul all old brake fluid should be flushed from the system. Also, the dust created by the brake system may contain asbestos, which is harmful to your health. Never blow it out with compressed air and do not inhale any of it. An approved filtering mask should**

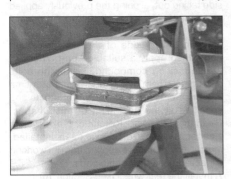

6.10a Fit the pads into the caliper . . .

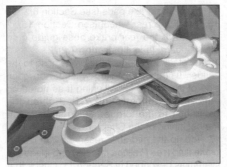

6.10b . . . then locate and hold a spanner as shown . . .

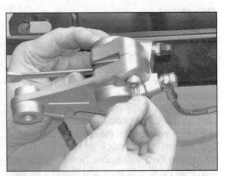

6.10c . . . to make it easier to fit the pad pins

7.1 Brake hose banjo bolt (arrowed) – note its alignment

7.2 Undo the bolt (arrowed) to free the hose

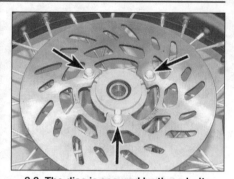

8.3 The disc is secured by three bolts (arrowed)

be worn when working on the brakes. Overhaul of the brake caliper must be done in a spotlessly clean work area to avoid contamination and possible failure of the brake hydraulic system components. Do not, under any circumstances, use petroleum-based solvents to clean brake parts. Use new DOT 4 brake fluid, dedicated brake cleaner or denatured alcohol only, as described. To prevent damage from spilled brake fluid, always cover paintwork when working on the braking system.

Removal

Note: If the caliper is being overhauled (usually due to a sticking piston or fluid leaks) read through the entire procedure first and make sure that you have obtained all the new parts required, including some new DOT 4 brake fluid.
Note: Do not operate the brake pedal while the caliper is off the disc.

1 If the caliper is being completely removed or overhauled, unscrew the brake hose banjo bolt and detach the banjo union, noting its alignment with the caliper **(see illustration).** Wrap plastic foodwrap around the banjo union and secure the hose in an upright position to minimise fluid loss. Discard the sealing washers as new ones must be fitted on reassembly.
2 If required, unscrew the bolt securing the brake hose guide to the swingarm **(see illustration).**
3 Remove the rear wheel (see Section 16).
4 If the caliper is being overhauled, remove the brake pads (see Section 6).

Overhaul

5 Clean the exterior of the caliper with denatured alcohol or brake system cleaner. Have some clean rag ready to catch any spilled brake fluid.
6 Cover the caliper body with rag and apply compressed air gradually and progressively, starting with a fairly low pressure, to the fluid inlet on the caliper body and allow the piston to ease out of its bore **(see illustration 3.6).**
7 If the piston is stuck in its bore due to corrosion, find a suitable bolt to block the fluid inlet banjo bolt bore and thread it in, then unscrew the bleed valve and apply the air to this in the same way – the narrower bore

will allow more air pressure to be applied to the piston as less can escape. Do not try to remove a piston by levering it out or by using pliers or other grips. If the piston has completely seized you may have to replace the caliper with a new one.
8 Remove the dust seal and the piston seal from the piston bore using a soft wooden or plastic tool to avoid scratching the bore **(see illustration 3.8).** Discard the seals as new ones must be fitted.
9 Clean the piston and bore with new DOT 4 brake fluid. If compressed air is available, blow it through the fluid galleries in the caliper to ensure they are clear (make sure it is filtered and unlubricated).
Caution: Do not, under any circumstances, use a petroleum-based solvent to clean brake parts.
10 Inspect the caliper bore and piston for signs of corrosion, nicks and burrs and loss of plating. If surface defects are present, the piston and/or the caliper must be replaced with new ones.
11 Lubricate the new piston seal with brake fluid and fit it into the inner (large) groove in the bore **(see illustrations 3.11a and b).**
12 Lubricate the new dust seal with silicone grease and fit it into the outer groove in the bore **(see illustration 3.12).**
13 Lubricate the piston with brake fluid and fit it, closed-end first, into the caliper bore, taking care not to displace the seals. Using your thumbs, push the piston squarely all the way in **(see illustration 6.7).**

Installation

14 Install the brake pads (see Section 6).
15 Install the rear wheel (see Section 16). If detached fit the rear brake hose guide onto the swingarm **(see illustration 7.2).**
16 If detached, connect the brake hose to the caliper, using new sealing washers on each side of the fitting, and aligning it as noted on removal **(see illustration 7.1).** Tighten the banjo bolt to the torque setting specified at the beginning of the Chapter.
17 Top up the hydraulic reservoir with DOT 4 brake fluid (see *Pre-ride checks*) and bleed the system as described in Section 11. Check that there are no fluid leaks and test the operation of the brake before riding the motorcycle.

8 Rear brake disc – XT models

Inspection

1 Refer to Section 4 of this Chapter, noting that the dial gauge should be attached to the swingarm.

Removal

2 Remove the wheel (see Section 16).
Caution: Don't lay the wheel down and allow it to rest on the disc or sprocket – they could become warped. Set the wheel on wood blocks so the wheel rim supports the weight of the wheel.
3 If you are not replacing the disc with a new one, mark the relationship of the disc to the wheel so it can be installed in the same position. Unscrew the disc retaining bolts, loosening them evenly and a little at a time in a criss-cross pattern to avoid distorting the disc, then remove the disc **(see illustration).** Note the dust seal that sits under the disc.

Installation

4 Before installing the disc, make sure there is no dirt or corrosion where it seats on the hub. If the disc does not sit flat when it is bolted down, it will appear to be warped when checked or when the rear brake is used. Make sure the dust seal is correctly in place.
5 Install the disc on the wheel with its marked side facing out, aligning the previously applied matchmarks (if you're reinstalling the original disc).
6 Clean the threads of the disc mounting bolts, then apply a suitable non-permanent thread locking compound. Install the bolts and tighten them evenly and a little at a time in a criss-cross pattern to the torque setting specified at the beginning of this Chapter. Clean the disc using acetone or brake system cleaner. If a new disc has been installed, remove any protective coating from its working surfaces and fit new brake pads.
7 Install the rear wheel (see Section 16).
8 Check the operation of the brake before riding the motorcycle.

9.1 Release the clip (arrowed) and withdraw the pin

9.2a Undo the screw and displace the reservoir . . .

9.2b . . . then remove the cap, plate and diaphragm and drain the reservoir

9 Rear brake master cylinder – XT models

⚠️ **Warning: If the brake master cylinder is in need of an overhaul all old brake fluid should be flushed from the system. Master cylinder overhaul must be done in a spotlessly clean work area to avoid contamination and possible failure of the brake hydraulic system components. Do not, under any circumstances, use petroleum-based solvents to clean brake parts. Use new DOT 4 brake fluid, dedicated brake cleaner or denatured alcohol only, as described. To prevent damage from spilled brake fluid, always cover paintwork when working on the braking system.**

Removal

Note: *If the master cylinder is being overhauled (usually due to sticking or poor action, or fluid leaks) read through the entire procedure first and make sure that you have obtained all the new parts required, including some new DOT 4 brake fluid.*

1 Release and remove the pivot pin securing the brake pedal to the master cylinder pushrod and detach the pushrod from the pedal **(see illustrations)**.

2 Counter-hold the nut on the back and undo the screw securing the fluid reservoir to the frame, then undo the reservoir cap and remove the diaphragm plate and diaphragm **(see illustrations)**. Pour the brake fluid into a suitable container. Wipe any remaining fluid out of the reservoir with a clean rag.

3 Pull the rubber boot up off the brake light switch and disconnect the wiring connectors **(see illustration)**. Unscrew the switch and detach the banjo union, noting its alignment with the master cylinder. Once disconnected, wrap plastic foodwrap around the banjo union and secure the hose in an upright position to minimise fluid loss. Discard the sealing washers as new ones must be fitted on reassembly.

4 Undo the bolts securing the master cylinder and remove the bushes, the shield, the master cylinder along with the reservoir, and the mounting plate from behind **(see illustration)**.

Overhaul

5 Release the clip securing the reservoir hose to the union on the master cylinder and detach the hose, being prepared to catch any residual fluid. Inspect the hose for cracks or splits and replace it with a new one if necessary.

6 Dislodge the rubber dust boot from the base of the master cylinder and from around the pushrod, noting how it locates. Push the pushrod in and, using circlip pliers, remove the circlip from its groove in the master cylinder and slide out the pushrod assembly, the piston assembly and the spring, noting how they fit. Lay the parts out in order as you remove them to prevent confusion during reassembly.

7 Slacken the locknut holding the clevis on the bottom of the pushrod. Note how far the clevis is threaded up the pushrod, then thread it off, followed by the locknut. Remove the rubber boot and the circlip.

8 Clean the master cylinder bore with brake fluid. If compressed air is available, blow it through the fluid galleries to ensure they are clear (make sure the air is filtered and unlubricated).

Caution: Do not, under any circumstances, use a petroleum-based solvent to clean brake parts.

9 Check the master cylinder bore for corrosion, scratches, nicks and score marks. If damage or wear is evident, the master cylinder must be replaced with a new one. If the master cylinder is in poor condition, then the caliper should be checked as well.

10 All the necessary parts are included in the

master cylinder rebuild kit. Use all of the new parts, regardless of the apparent condition of the old ones. Lay out the new parts in their correct order according to those removed.

11 Smear the piston, cup and seal and the master cylinder bore with new brake fluid. Slide the piston and spring assembly into the master cylinder. Make sure the lips on the cup and seal do not turn inside out.

12 Smear some silicone grease onto the lips and inside of the rubber boot and onto the rounded end of the pushrod. Make sure the washer is on the pushrod, then fit the new circlip and rubber boot onto the pushrod, then thread the locknut and clevis on. Set the position of the clevis as noted on removal and tighten the locknut securely against it.

13 Push the piston in using the pushrod and locate the circlip in the groove.

14 Press the rubber boot into place in the end of the cylinder.

15 Connect the hose to the union on the master cylinder and secure it with the clip. Check that the hose is secured with a clip at the reservoir end as well. If the clips have weakened, use new ones.

Installation

16 Locate the master cylinder along with its mounting plate and shield, then fit the bolts with their bushes and tighten them **(see illustration 9.4)**.

17 Align the clevis with the brake pedal, then insert the pivot pin and clip it around the pushrod **(see illustration 9.1)**.

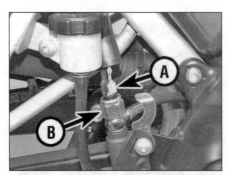

9.3 Disconnect the wiring connectors (A) then unscrew the switch (B)

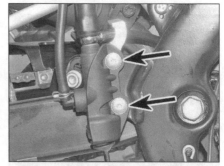

9.4 Unscrew the bolts (arrowed) and remove the master cylinder and reservoir assembly

18 Connect the brake hose to the master cylinder, using new sealing washers on each side of the banjo fitting, and aligning it as noted on removal **(see illustration 9.3)**. Fit the brake light switch and tighten it. Connect the wiring and fit the rubber boot.

19 Fill the fluid reservoir with new DOT 4 brake fluid (see *Pre-ride checks*). Refer to Section 11 and bleed the air from the system.

20 Fit the fluid reservoir onto its mount and tighten the bolt **(see illustration 9.2a)**.

21 Check the operation of the brake carefully before riding the motorcycle.

10 Brake hoses and fittings

Inspection

1 Brake hose condition should be checked regularly and the hoses replaced with new ones at the specified interval (see Chapter 1).

2 Twist and flex the hoses while looking for cracks, bulges and seeping hydraulic fluid. Check extra carefully around the areas where the hoses connect with the banjo fittings, as these are common areas for hose failure.

3 Inspect the banjo fittings connected to the brake hoses. If the fittings are rusted, scratched or cracked, fit new hoses.

Removal and installation

4 The brake hoses have banjo fittings on

each end – note that the rear master cylinder on XT models uses the brake light switch to secure the hose rather than a banjo bolt, so you must lift the rubber boot off the switch and disconnect the wiring connectors before unscrewing it. Cover the surrounding area with plenty of rags and unscrew the banjo bolt (or the switch) at each end of the hose, noting the alignment of the fitting with the master cylinder or brake caliper **(see illustrations 3.2a and b, 5.5, 7.1 and 9.3)**. Free the hose from any clips or guides and remove it, noting its routing. Discard the sealing washers. **Note:** *Do not operate the brake lever or pedal while a brake hose is disconnected.*

5 Position the new hose, making sure it isn't twisted or otherwise strained, and ensure that it is correctly routed through any clips or guides and is clear of all moving components. Make sure the elbow locates correctly.

6 Check that the fittings align correctly, then install the banjo bolts/brake light switch, using new sealing washers on both sides of the fittings **(see illustrations 3.17 and 5.17)**. Tighten the banjo bolts to the torque setting specified at the beginning of this Chapter – no torque setting is given for the brake light switch.

7 Flush the old brake fluid from the system, refill with new DOT 4 brake fluid (see *Pre-ride checks*) and bleed the air from the system (see Section 11).

8 Check the operation of the brakes before riding the motorcycle.

11 Brake system bleeding and fluid change

Note: *If bleeding the system using the conventional method does not work sufficiently well, you could try a commercially available vacuum-type brake bleeding tool, following the manufacturers instructions for using the tool.*

Bleeding

1 Bleeding the brakes is simply the process of removing air from the brake fluid reservoir, the hose and the brake caliper. Bleeding is necessary whenever a brake system hydraulic connection is loosened, after a component or hose is replaced with a new one, or when the master cylinder or caliper is overhauled. Leaks in the system may also allow air to enter, but leaking brake fluid will reveal their presence and warn you of the need for repair.

2 To bleed the brakes, you will need some new DOT 4 brake fluid, a length of clear flexible hose, a small container partially filled with clean brake fluid, some rags, a spanner to fit the brake caliper bleed valve, and possibly help from an assistant. Bleeding kits that include the hose, a one-way valve and a container are available relatively cheaply from a good auto store, and simplify the task as you don't need an assistant.

3 Cover painted components to prevent damage in the event that brake fluid is spilled.

4 Refer to 'Pre-ride checks' and remove the reservoir cover, diaphragm plate (where fitted) and diaphragm and slowly pump the brake lever (front brake) or pedal (rear brake) a few times, until no air bubbles can be seen floating up from the holes in the bottom of the reservoir. This bleeds the air from the master cylinder end of the line. Temporarily refit the reservoir cover.

5 Pull the dust cap off the bleed valve **(see illustrations)**. If using a ring spanner fit it onto the valve **(see illustration)**. Attach one end of the hose to the bleed valve and, if not using a kit, submerge the other end in the clean brake fluid in the container **(see illustration)**.

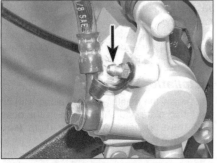

11.5a Front brake caliper bleed valve (arrowed) – YBR models

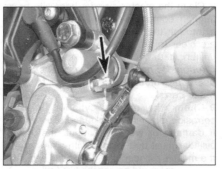

11.5b Front brake caliper bleed valve (arrowed) – XT models

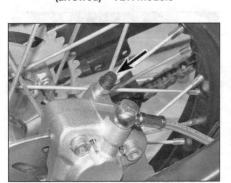

11.5c Rear brake caliper bleed valve (arrowed) – XT models

11.5d Fit the ring spanner before connecting the hose

11.5e One of several commercially available one-man bleeding kits

HAYNES HiNT *To avoid damaging the bleed valve during the procedure, loosen it and then tighten it temporarily with a ring spanner before attaching the hose. With the hose attached, the valve can then be opened and closed either with an open-ended spanner, or by leaving the ring spanner located on the valve and fitting the hose above it (see illustration 11.5d).*

6 Check the fluid level in the reservoir. Do not allow the fluid level to drop below the lower mark during the procedure.

7 Carefully pump the brake lever or pedal three or four times and hold it in (front) or down (rear) while opening the bleed valve. When the valve is opened, brake fluid will flow out of the caliper into the clear tubing, and the lever will move toward the handlebar, or the pedal will move down. If there is air in the system there will be air bubbles in the brake fluid coming out of the caliper.

8 Tighten the bleed valve, then release the brake lever or pedal gradually. Repeat the process until no air bubbles are visible in the brake fluid leaving the caliper, and the lever or pedal is firm when applied, topping the reservoir up when necessary. On completion, disconnect the hose, then tighten the bleed valve to the torque setting specified at the beginning of this Chapter and install the dust cap.

HAYNES HiNT *If it is not possible to produce a firm feel to the lever or pedal, the fluid may still be aerated. Let the brake fluid in the system stabilise for a few hours and then repeat the procedure when the tiny bubbles in the system have settled out.*

9 Top-up the reservoir, then install the diaphragm, diaphragm plate (where fitted), and cover (see *Pre-ride checks*). Wipe any spilled brake fluid. Check the entire system for fluid leaks.

10 Check the operation of the brakes before riding the motorcycle.

Fluid change

11 Changing the brake fluid is a similar process to bleeding the brakes and requires the same materials plus a suitable tool (such as a syringe) for siphoning the fluid out of the reservoir. Also ensure that the container is large enough to take all the old fluid when it is flushed out of the system.

12 Follow Steps 3 and 5, then remove the reservoir cap, diaphragm plate (where fitted) and diaphragm and siphon the old fluid out of the reservoir. Wipe the reservoir clean. Fill the reservoir with new brake fluid, then carefully pump the brake lever or pedal three or four times and hold it in (front) or down (rear) while

opening the caliper bleed valve. When the valve is opened, brake fluid will flow out of the caliper into the clear tubing, and the lever will move toward the handlebar, or the pedal will move down.

13 Tighten the bleed valve, then release the brake lever or pedal gradually. Keep the reservoir topped-up with new fluid to above the LOWER level at all times or air may enter the system and greatly increase the length of the task. Repeat the process until new fluid can be seen emerging from the caliper bleed valve.

HAYNES HiNT *Old brake fluid is invariably much darker in colour than new fluid, making it easy to see when all old fluid has been expelled from the system.*

14 Disconnect the hose, then tighten the bleed valve to the specified torque setting and install the dust cap.

15 Top-up the reservoir, then install the diaphragm, diaphragm plate (where fitted), and cover (see *Pre-ride checks*). Wipe up any spilled brake fluid. Check the entire system for fluid leaks.

16 Check the operation of the brakes before riding the motorcycle.

Draining the system for overhaul

17 Draining the brake fluid is again a similar process to bleeding the brakes. Follow the procedure described above for changing the fluid, but quite simply do not put any new fluid into the reservoir – the system fills itself with air instead. An alternative is to use a commercially available vacuum-type brake bleeding tool – follow the manufacturer's instructions.

12 Rear drum brake – YBR models

⚠️ **Warning: The dust created by the brake system may contain asbestos, which is harmful to your health. Never blow it out with**

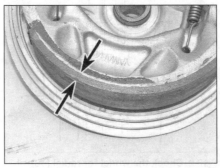

12.2 Check the amount of friction material on the shoe (arrowed)

12.1 Lift the brake plate out

compressed air and don't inhale any of it. An approved filtering mask should be worn when working on the brakes.

Check

1 Remove the rear wheel (see Section 16). Lift the brake plate out of the drum **(see illustration)**.

2 Measure the thickness of material remaining at the cam end (the thinnest point) of the shoe **(see illustration)**. The wear limit is 2 mm.

3 Inspect the surface of the friction material on each shoe for contamination. If either shoe is fouled with oil or grease, or heavily scored or damaged by dirt and debris, both shoes must be replaced as a set. Note that it is not possible to degrease the friction material; if the shoes are contaminated in any way they must be replaced.

4 If the shoes are in good condition clean them carefully, using a fine wire brush which is completely free of oil and grease, some sandpaper, to remove all traces of road dirt and corrosion. Using a pointed instrument, dig out any embedded particles of foreign matter. If the material appears glazed, roughen up the surface using course sandpaper, bearing in mind the *Warning* above.

5 Check the condition of the brake shoe springs and replace them if they appear weak or are obviously deformed or damaged. On 2005 and 2006 models both springs are the same. On 2007-on models the springs are different – the longer spring fits next to the cam with its upper end hooked under the shoe **(see illustration)**.

6 Clean the brake drum lining using brake

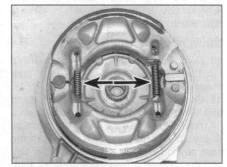

12.5 Check the springs (arrowed) and note which way round they fit

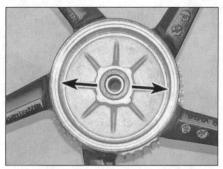

12.6 Measure the ID of the drum (arrowed)

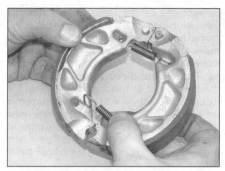

12.13a Fit the shoes together and join them with the springs

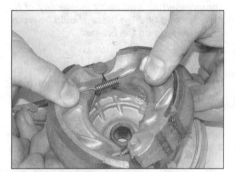

12.13b Locate the rounded ends around the post . . .

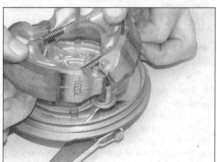

12.13c . . . and the flat ends on each side of the cam and fold them onto the plate

cleaner or a rag soaked in solvent. Examine the surface of the brake drum lining for scoring and excessive wear. While light scratches are expected, any heavy scoring or cracks will impair braking and there is no satisfactory way of removing them – the wheel should be replaced with a new one. Measure the internal diameter of the drum and replace the wheel with a new one if it has worn below the service limit specified at the beginning of the Chapter **(see illustration)**.

7 Check that the brake cam operates smoothly and to its full limits of travel by operating the lever arm. Clean off all traces of old and hardened grease from the cam and pivot post – remove the shoes to do this. If the bearing surfaces of the cam are worn or damaged it should be replaced with a new one.

8 Make sure the brake actuating rod is straight and the pivot bush in the arm is clean and greased. Clean off any corrosion if necessary.

9 Make sure the brake torque arm nuts are tight and secured by split pins.

Shoe replacement

10 Remove the wheel (see Section 16). Lift the brake plate out of the drum **(see illustration 12.1)**.

11 Grasp the outer edge of each shoe and fold them upwards and inwards to form a 'V', noting that they are under the pressure of the springs, then remove them from the plate noting how they locate around the cam and the pivot post **(see illustration 12.13b)**. Remove the springs from the shoes – see Step 5.

12 Check the shoes and the drum as outlined above.

13 Apply some copper grease to the bearing surfaces on the cam and pivot post. Fit the springs onto the shoes as in Step 5 **(see illustration)**. Position the shoes so that the rounded end of each shoe fits around the pivot post and the flat end against the flats on the cam **(see illustrations)**. Fold the shoes flat onto the plate making sure the shoes sit

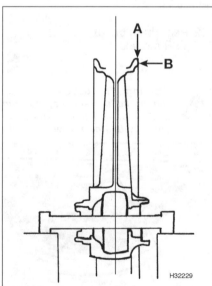

13.2 Check the wheel for radial (out-of-round) runout (A) and axial (side-to-side) runout (B)

correctly on each side of the pivot and the cam and the springs remain in place **(see illustration 12.5)**. Operate the lever arm to check that the cam and shoes work correctly.

14 Fit the brake plate into the drum **(see illustration 12.1)**. Install the wheel (see Section 16). Check the operation of the brake before riding the motorcycle.

13 Wheel inspection and repair

1 In order to carry out a proper inspection of the wheels, it is necessary to support the bike upright so that the wheel being inspected is raised off the ground. Position the motorcycle on an auxiliary stand. Clean the wheels thoroughly to remove mud and dirt that may interfere with the inspection procedure or mask defects. Make a general check of the wheels (see Chapter 1) and tyres (see *Pre-ride checks*).

2 Attach a dial gauge to the fork or the swingarm and position its tip against the side of the wheel rim. Spin the wheel slowly and check the axial (side-to-side) runout of the rim **(see illustration)**.

3 In order to accurately check radial (out of round) runout with the dial gauge, remove the wheel from the machine, and the tyre from the wheel. With the axle clamped in a vice and the dial gauge positioned on the top of the rim, the wheel can be rotated to check the runout **(see illustration 13.2)**.

4 An easier, though slightly less accurate, method is to attach a stiff wire pointer to the fork or the swingarm and position the end a fraction of an inch from the wheel rim where the wheel and tyre join. If the wheel is true, the distance from the pointer to the rim will be constant as the wheel is rotated. **Note:** *If wheel runout is excessive, check the wheel bearings very carefully before renewing the wheel.*

14 Wheel alignment check

1 Misalignment of the wheels due to a bent frame or forks can cause strange and possibly serious handling problems. If the frame or forks are at fault, repair by a frame specialist or renewal are the only options.

2 To check wheel alignment you will need an assistant, a length of string or a perfectly straight piece of wood and a ruler. A plumb bob or spirit level for checking that the wheels are vertical will also be required.

3 In order to make a proper check of the wheels it is necessary to support the bike in an upright position, using an auxiliary stand. First ensure that the chain adjuster markings coincide on each side of the swingarm (see Chapter 1, Section 1). Next, measure the

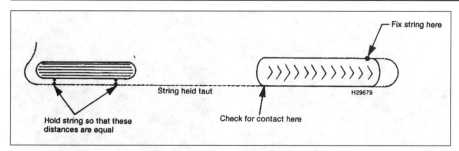

14.5 Wheel alignment check using string

width of both tyres at their widest points. Subtract the smaller measurement from the larger measurement, then divide the difference by two. The result is the amount of offset that should exist between the front and rear tyres on both sides of the machine.

4 If a string is used, have your assistant hold one end of it about halfway between the floor and the rear axle, with the string touching the back edge of the rear tyre sidewall.

5 Run the other end of the string forward and pull it tight so that it is roughly parallel to the floor (see illustration). Slowly bring the string into contact with the front edge of the rear tyre sidewall, then turn the front wheel until it is parallel with the string. Measure the distance from the front tyre sidewall to the string.

6 Repeat the procedure on the other side of the motorcycle. The distance from the front tyre sidewall to the string should be equal on both sides.

7 As previously mentioned, a perfectly straight length of wood or metal bar may be substituted for the string (see illustration).

8 If the distance between the string and tyre is greater on one side, or if the rear wheel appears to be out of alignment, have your machine checked by a Yamaha dealer or frame specialist.

9 If the front-to-back alignment is correct, the wheels still may be out of alignment vertically.

10 Using a plumb bob or spirit level, check the rear wheel to make sure it is vertical. To do this, hold the string of the plumb bob against the tyre upper sidewall and allow the weight to settle just off the floor. If the string touches both the upper and lower tyre sidewalls and is perfectly straight, the wheel is vertical. If it is not, adjust the stand until it is.

11 Once the rear wheel is vertical, check the front wheel in the same manner. If both wheels are not perfectly vertical, the frame and/or major suspension components are bent.

15 Front wheel

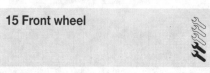

YBR models

Removal

1 Position the motorcycle on its centrestand or an auxiliary stand with a support under the engine so that the front wheel is off the ground. Always make sure the motorcycle is properly supported.

2 Displace the front brake caliper (see Section 3). Support the caliper with a cable-tie or a bungee cord so that no strain is placed on the hydraulic hose. There is no need to disconnect the hose from the caliper. **Note:** *Do not operate the front brake lever with the caliper removed.*

3 Unscrew the knurled ring securing the speedometer cable in the drive housing and draw the cable out (see illustration). Alternatively leave the cable connected and displace the drive housing from the wheel as it is removed.

4 Remove the cap from each end of the axle (see illustration). Unscrew the nut and remove the washer from the right-hand end (see illustration).

5 Take the weight of the wheel, then withdraw the axle from the left-hand side, bringing the washer with it (see illustration). Carefully lower the wheel and draw it forwards.

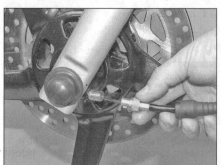

15.3 Detach the speedo cable

15.4a Remove the axle caps . . .

14.7 Wheel alignment check using a straight-edge

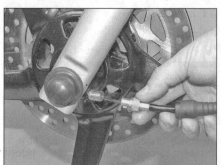

15.4b . . . then unscrew the nut and remove the washer

15.5 Withdraw the axle and remove the wheel

15.6a Remove the spacer and seal . . .

15.6b . . . and the drive housing

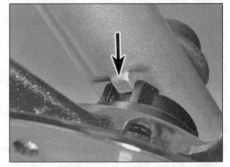

15.12 Locate the lug (arrowed) between
the raised tabs

6 Remove the spacer and dust seal from the right-hand side of the wheel and the speedometer drive housing from the left-hand side, noting how it fits **(see illustrations)**. Clean all dirt and old grease off the spacer, dust seal, drive housing, axle and bearing seal.

7 Check the axle is straight by rolling it on a flat surface such as a piece of plate glass (first remove any corrosion using wire wool or a suitable alternative). If the equipment is available, place the axle in V-blocks and measure the runout using a dial gauge. If the axle is bent, replace it with a new one.

8 Check the condition of the wheel bearings (see Section 17).

Caution: Don't lay the wheel down and allow it to rest on the disc – it could become warped. Set the wheel on wood blocks so the disc doesn't support the weight of the wheel.

Installation

9 Smear some grease to the inside of the wheel spacer and to the outside where it fits into the dust seal. Fit the spacer into the dust seal, then fit them into the right-hand side of the wheel **(see illustration 15.6a)**.

10 Smear grease into the speedometer drive housing. Fit the drive housing onto the left-hand side, locating the tabs in the cut-outs **(see illustration 15.6b)**.

11 Manoeuvre the wheel into position between the forks, making sure the brake disc is on the right-hand side. Apply a thin coat of grease to the axle, then slide the washer on with its raised tabs facing the axle head.

12 Lift the wheel into place, making sure the

spacer and speedometer drive housing remain in position, and that the lug on the bottom of the left-hand fork locates between the raised tabs on the top of the speedometer drive housing **(see illustration)**. Slide the axle in from the left-hand side **(see illustration 15.5)**.

13 Fit the washer onto the right-hand end of the axle with its raised tabs facing out, then fit the axle nut and tighten it to the torque setting specified at the beginning of the Chapter **(see illustration 15.4b)**. Counter-hold the axle head if necessary.

14 Fit the speedometer cable into the drive housing, aligning the tab with the slot, and tighten the knurled ring **(see illustration 15.3)**. Fit the axle caps **(see illustration 15.4a)**.

15 Install the brake caliper (see Section 3).

16 Apply the front brake lever a few times to bring the pads back into contact with the disc.

17 Check for correct operation of the front brake before riding the motorcycle.

XT models

Removal

18 Position the motorcycle on an auxiliary stand so that the front wheel is off the ground. Always make sure the motorcycle is properly supported. If a support is being placed under the engine, remove the sump guard (see Chapter 7).

19 Displace the front brake caliper (see Section 3). Support the caliper with a cable-tie or a bungee cord so that no strain is placed on the hydraulic hose. There is no need to disconnect the hose from the caliper. **Note:**

Do not operate the front brake lever with the caliper removed.

20 Undo the screw securing the speed sensor and withdraw the sensor **(see illustration)**.

21 Slacken the axle clamp bolt on the bottom of the right-hand fork **(see illustration)**. Unscrew the axle, then take the weight of the wheel and withdraw the axle from the right-hand side **(see illustration)**. Carefully lower the wheel and draw it forwards.

22 Remove the dust seal from the right-hand side of the wheel and the spacer from the left **(see illustrations 15.27a and b)**. Clean all dirt and old grease off the dust seal, spacer and axle.

23 Check the axle is straight by rolling it on a flat surface such as a piece of plate glass (first remove any corrosion using wire wool or a suitable alternative). If the equipment is available, place the axle in V-blocks and measure the runout using a dial gauge. If the axle is bent replace it with a new one.

24 Check the condition of the wheel bearings (see Section 17).

Caution: Don't lay the wheel down and allow it to rest on the disc – it could become warped. Set the wheel on wood blocks so the disc doesn't support the weight of the wheel.

Installation

25 Smear some grease onto the inside and each end of the spacer and inside the dust seal.

26 Manoeuvre the wheel into position between the forks, making sure the brake disc is on the left-hand side. Apply a thin coat of grease to the axle.

15.20 Undo the screw (arrowed) and
withdraw the sensor

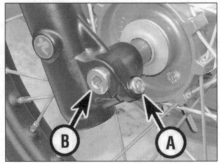

15.21a Slacken the clamp bolt (A), then
unscrew the axle (B)

15.21b Withdraw the axle and remove the
wheel

27 Slide the axle through the right-hand fork and fit the dust seal **(see illustration)**. Lift the wheel into place and slide the axle most of the way through, fitting the spacer onto the left-hand end, with its wider end against the wheel, as it comes through **(see illustration)**. Thread the axle into the left-hand fork and tighten it to the torque setting specified at the beginning of the Chapter **(see illustration)**.

28 Install the brake caliper (see Section 3). Apply the front brake a few times to bring the pads back into contact with the disc.

29 Lower the bike so the wheel is on the ground, then hold the front brake on and push down on the handlebars to compress the forks several times to align the right-hand fork on the axle. Tighten the axle clamp bolt to the specified torque **(see illustration 15.21a)**.

30 Clean the tip of the speed sensor, then fit it into the bracket and tighten its screw.

31 Check for correct operation of the front brake before riding the motorcycle.

32 Install the sump guard if removed (see Chapter 7).

16 Rear wheel

YBR models

Removal

1 Position the motorcycle on its centrestand where fitted, or on an auxiliary stand so that the rear wheel is off the ground. Always make sure the motorcycle is properly supported.

15.27a Fit the dust seal . . .

15.27c Tighten the axle to the specified torque

Create some slack in the chain (see Chapter 1, Section 1).

2 Unscrew the rear brake adjuster nut then draw the rod out of the arm **(see illustrations)**. Remove the spring from the rod and the pivot bush from the arm for safekeeping **(see illustration)**.

15.27b . . . and the spacer

15.30 Fit the speed sensor into the bracket

3 Remove the split pin from the brake torque arm bolt, then unscrew the nut and withdraw the bolt **(see illustration)**.

4 Unscrew the axle nut **(see illustration)**.

5 Take the weight of the wheel, then withdraw the axle from the left-hand side and lower the wheel to the ground **(see illustration)**. If the

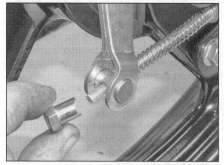

16.2a Unscrew the nut . . .

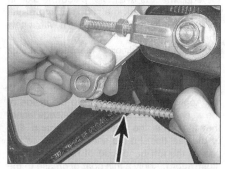

16.2b . . . and draw the rod out. Remove the spring (arrowed) . . .

16.2c . . . and the pivot bush for safekeeping

16.3 Remove the split pin (arrowed), then unscrew the nut and withdraw the bolt

16.4 Unscrew the axle nut

16.5 Withdraw the axle and lower the wheel

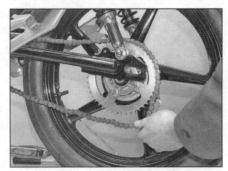

16.6 Remove the chain adjusters . . .

16.7 . . . then disengage the chain and draw the wheel out the back

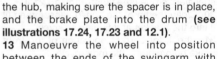

16.11 Fit the short spacer into the left-hand side

16.14a Fit the long spacer . . .

16.14b . . . and the chain adjuster as you slide the axle through

axle is difficult to withdraw, drive it through with a drift, making sure you don't damage the threads.

6 Remove the chain adjuster from each end of the swingarm **(see illustration)**. Retrieve the spacer from the right-hand side of the wheel which will have dropped out **(see illustration 16.14a)**.

7 Disengage the chain from the sprocket and draw the wheel back out of the swingarm **(see illustration)**. Remove the spacer from the left-hand side of the wheel **(see illustration 16.11)**. Keep the wheel upright – if you need to lay it down, first lift the brake plate out of the drum and the sprocket coupling out of the hub, then lay the wheel on wooden blocks **(see illustrations 12.1 and 17.23)**.

8 Clean all old grease of the spacers, axle and the seal in the sprocket coupling.

9 Check the axle is straight by rolling it on a flat surface such as a piece of plate glass (if the axle is corroded, first remove any corrosion with wire wool or a suitable alternative). If the equipment is available, place the axle in V-blocks and check the runout using a dial gauge. If the axle is bent, replace it with a new one.

10 Check the condition of the wheel bearings (see Section 17).

Installation

11 Apply a smear of grease to the inside of the wheel spacers, and also to the ends where they fit against the wheel and swingarm, and to the seal lips. Fit the short spacer into the seal in the left-hand side of the wheel **(see illustration)**. Apply a thin coat of grease to the axle.

12 If removed fit the sprocket coupling into the hub, making sure the spacer is in place, and the brake plate into the drum **(see illustrations 17.24, 17.23 and 12.1)**.

13 Manoeuvre the wheel into position between the ends of the swingarm with the sprocket to the left. Engage the drive chain with the sprocket **(see illustration 16.7)**. Slide the left-hand chain adjuster onto the end of the swingarm **(see illustration 16.6)**.

14 Lift the wheel into position and slide the axle in from the left, making sure it passes through the left-hand chain adjuster and the spacer **(see illustration 16.5)**. As you slide the axle through the brake plate fit the long spacer between it and the swingarm, then fit the right-hand chain adjuster between the spacer and the swingarm, and slide the axle through them **(see illustrations)**. Check that everything is correctly aligned, then fit the axle nut but leave it loose **(see illustration 16.4)**.

15 Check and adjust the drive chain slack (see Chapter 1). On completion tighten the axle nut to the torque setting specified at the beginning of the Chapter.

16 Align the torque arm with the brake plate then fit the bolt and tighten the nut to the torque setting specified at the beginning of the Chapter **(see illustration)**. Fit a new split pin through the hole in the end of the bolt and bend its ends round the bolt **(see illustration)**.

17 Fit the brake rod pivot bush into the arm. Fit the spring onto the rod. Fit the rod into the bush and thread the nut onto the rod. Refer to Chapter 1, Section 8 and set the correct amount of brake pedal freeplay. Check the operation of the rear brake carefully before riding the bike.

XT models

Removal

18 Position the motorcycle on an auxiliary stand so that the rear wheel is off the ground. Always make sure the motorcycle is properly supported. Create some slack in the chain (see Chapter 1, Section 1). Undo the screws securing the chain guide to the swingarm,

16.16a Align the arm with the plate and insert the bolt from the inside

16.16b Use a new split pin and bend the ends round as shown

16.18a Undo the screws (arrowed) . . .

16.18b . . . take care not to lose the captive nuts

16.19a Unscrew the nut and remove the washer . . .

noting the captive nuts in the back (see illustrations).

19 Unscrew the axle nut and remove the washer and the adjuster plate, noting how it fits (see illustrations).

20 Take the weight of the wheel, then withdraw the axle from the right-hand side, bringing the adjuster plate with it, and lower the wheel to the ground (see illustration). If the axle is difficult to withdraw, drive it through with a drift, making sure you don't damage the threads.

21 Disengage the chain from the sprocket (see illustration). Displace the rear brake caliper from the swingarm, noting how it locates, and rest it on some rag on the swingarm (see illustration). Draw the wheel back out of the swingarm. Retrieve the spacer from the left-hand side of the wheel which will have dropped out (see illustration 16.28b).

22 Free the brake hose from its guide on the inside of the swingarm, then cover the caliper in rag and rest it on a block of wood or tie it to the swingarm. **Note:** *Do not operate the brake pedal while the caliper is off the disc.*

Caution: Do not lay the wheel down and allow it to rest on the disc or the sprocket. Keep it upright, or set the wheel on wood blocks so the disc or the sprocket doesn't support the weight of the wheel. Do not

16.19b . . . and adjuster plate

operate the brake pedal with the wheel removed.

23 Clean all old grease off the spacer, caliper bracket and axle.

24 Check the axle is straight by rolling it on a flat surface such as a piece of plate glass (if the axle is corroded, first remove any corrosion with wire wool or a suitable alternative). If the equipment is available, place the axle in V-blocks and check the runout using a dial gauge. If the axle is bent, replace it with a new one.

25 Check the condition of the wheel bearings (see Section 17).

16.20 Withdraw the axle and lower the wheel

Installation

26 Apply a smear of grease to the inside of the wheel spacer and the axle bore in the caliper bracket, and also to the ends where they fit against the wheel and swingarm. Apply a thin coat of grease to the axle, then fit the right-hand chain adjuster plate on with the raised sections towards the axle head.

27 Manoeuvre the wheel into position between the ends of the swingarm with the sprocket to the left. Feed the brake hose into its guide on the inside of the swingarm and locate the caliper bracket on its guide (see

16.21a Disengage the chain . . .

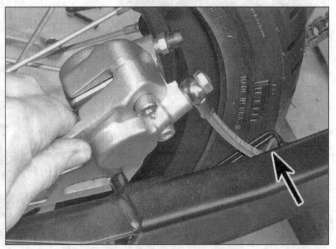

16.21b . . . and displace the caliper, noting how it locates. Note the hose in the guide (arrowed)

16.28a Make sure the disc sits between the pads

16.28b Fit the spacer as you slide the axle through

illustration 16.21b). Engage the drive chain with the sprocket (see illustration 16.21a).
28 Lift the wheel into position, making sure the disc locates between the brake pads and the caliper bracket locates in the middle of the dust seal over the wheel bearing (see illustration), and slide the axle in from the right (see illustration 16.20). As you slide the axle through fit the spacer between the wheel and the swingarm on the left-hand side, with the narrow end of the spacer facing out (see illustration). Check that everything is correctly aligned, then fit the left-hand adjuster block, washer and axle nut, but leave the nut loose (see illustrations 16.19b and a). Make sure both chain adjuster blocks have their open side facing back.
29 Check and adjust the drive chain slack (see Chapter 1). On completion tighten the axle nut to the torque setting specified at the beginning of the Chapter. Fit the chain guide onto the swingarm, making sure the captive

nuts are in place (see illustrations 16.18b and a).
30 Operate the brake pedal several times to bring the pads into contact with the disc. Check the operation of the rear brake carefully before riding the bike.

17 Wheel bearings

Caution: Don't lay the wheel down and allow it to rest on the disc or the sprocket – they could become warped. Set the wheel on wood blocks so the wheel rim supports the weight of the wheel, or keep the wheel upright. Don't operate the brake lever/ pedal with the wheel removed.
Note: Always renew the wheel bearings in

sets, never individually. Avoid using a high pressure cleaner on the wheel bearing area.

Front wheel bearings

1 Remove the wheel (see Section 15).
2 On YBR models lever out the bearing seal from the right-hand side of the hub using a flat-bladed screwdriver or a seal hook (see illustration). Take care not to damage the hub. Discard the seal as a new one must be fitted on reassembly.
3 Inspect the bearings – check that the inner race turns smoothly, quietly and freely and that the outer race is a tight fit in the hub.
Note: Yamaha recommends that the bearings are not removed unless they are going to be replaced with new ones.
4 If the bearings are worn, remove them using a metal rod (preferably a brass punch) inserted through the centre of the opposite bearing and locating it on the inner race, pushing the bearing spacer aside to expose it (see illustration). Curve the end of the drift to obtain better purchase if necessary. Strike the drift with a hammer, working evenly around the bearing, to drive it from the hub (see illustration). Remove the spacer which fits between the bearings. If the bearings are difficult to remove as described, use a puller with slide-hammer attachment (see Step 16).
5 Turn the wheel over and remove the other bearing using the same procedure.
6 Thoroughly clean the hub area of the wheel with a suitable solvent and inspect the bearing seats for scoring and wear. If the seats are damaged, consult a Yamaha dealer before reassembling the wheel.
7 Install new bearings using a drawbolt arrangement or a bearing driver or suitable socket (see illustration). Ensure that the drawbolt washer or driver (as applicable) bears only on the outer race and does not contact the bearing housing walls.
8 Install the bearings with the marked or sealed side facing outwards. Ensure the bearing is fitted squarely and all the way onto its seat.
9 Turn the wheel over then install the bearing spacer and the other new bearing.
10 On YBR models press the new seal into the hub and level it with the rim of the hub (see illustration). Smear the seal lips with grease.

17.2 Lever out the bearing seal

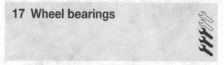

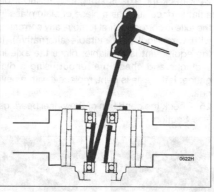

17.4a Locate the drift as shown . . .

17.4b . . . and drive the bearing out

17.7 Using a socket to drive the bearing in

17.10 Press the new seal into place

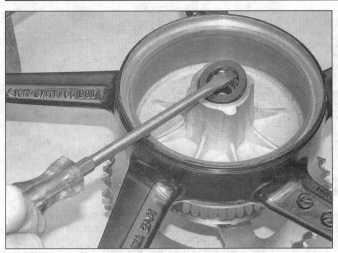

17.13 Lever out the bearing seal

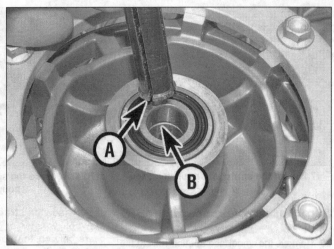

17.16a Locate the knife edges (A) under the lower edge of the bearing (B) and tighten the tool so they expand into the groove . . .

11 Clean the brake disc using acetone or brake system cleaner, then install the wheel (see Section 15).

Rear wheel bearings

12 Remove the wheel (see Section 16).

13 On YBR models lift the brake plate out of the drum and the sprocket coupling out of the hub, noting the spacer inside it **(see illustrations 12.1 and 17.23 and 24)**. Lever out the bearing seal from the right-hand side of the hub using a flat-bladed screwdriver or a seal hook **(see illustration)**. Take care not to damage the hub. Discard the seal as a new one should be fitted on reassembly.

14 Inspect the bearings in both sides of the hub – check that the inner race turns smoothly, quietly and freely and that the outer race is a tight fit in the hub. **Note:** *Yamaha recommends that the bearings are not removed unless they are going to be renewed.*

15 If the bearings are worn, on XT models remove the brake disc (see Section 8). Remove the dust seal, noting how it locates.

16 Remove the bearings using an internal expanding puller with slide-hammer attachment, which can be obtained commercially **(see illustrations)**. Remove the spacer which fits between the bearings.

17 Turn the wheel over and remove the remaining bearing using the same procedure.

17.16b . . . and pull the bearing out (arrowed)

18 Thoroughly clean the hub area of the wheel with a suitable solvent and inspect the bearing seats for scoring and wear. If the seats are damaged, consult a Yamaha dealer before reassembling the wheel.

19 Install new bearings using a drawbolt arrangement or a bearing driver or suitable socket **(see illustration)**. Ensure that the drawbolt washer or driver (as applicable) bears only on the outer race and does not contact the bearing housing walls.

20 Install the bearings with the marked or sealed side facing outwards. Ensure the bearing is fitted squarely and all the way onto its seat.

17.19 Using a socket to drive the bearing in

21 Turn the wheel over then install the bearing spacer and the other new bearing.

22 On YBR models press the new seal into the hub and level it with the rim **(see illustrations)**. Smear the seal lips with grease. Check the sprocket coupling/rubber dampers (see Section 21). Check the condition of the hub O-ring and clean it or replace it with a new one if necessary **(see illustration)**. Smear the O-ring with oil. Fit the sprocket coupling into the wheel, making sure the spacer is fitted **(see illustrations 17.24 and 17.23)**. Fit the brake plate into the drum **(see illustration 12.1)**. Install the wheel (see Section 16).

17.22a Press the seal into place . . .

17.22b . . . and set it flush as shown

17.22c Fit a new O-ring if necessary

17.23 Lift the sprocket coupling off the wheel

17.24 Remove the spacer from inside the coupling

17.25 Lever out the bearing seal

Sprocket coupling bearing (YBR models)

23 Remove the wheel (see Section 16). Lift the brake plate out of the drum **(see illustration 12.1)**. Lift the sprocket coupling out of the hub **(see illustration)**.

24 Remove the spacer from inside the coupling **(see illustration)**.

25 Lever out the bearing seal on the outside of the coupling using a flat-bladed screwdriver or a seal hook **(see illustration)**. Take care not to damage the rim of the coupling. Discard the seal as a new one should be fitted on reassembly.

26 Inspect the bearing – check that the inner races turn smoothly, quietly and freely, and that the outer race is a tight fit in the coupling. **Note:** *Yamaha recommends that the bearing is not removed unless it is going to be replaced with a new one.*

27 Support the coupling on blocks of wood, sprocket side down, and drive the bearing out from the inside using a bearing driver or socket **(see illustration)**.

28 Thoroughly clean the bearing seat with a suitable solvent and inspect it for scoring and wear. If the seat is damaged, consult a Yamaha dealer before reassembling the wheel.

29 Install the new bearing using a drawbolt arrangement or a bearing driver or suitable

socket **(see illustration)**. Ensure that the drawbolt washer or driver (as applicable) bears only on the outer race and does not contact the bearing housing walls. Install the bearing with the marked or sealed side facing outwards. Ensure the bearing is fitted squarely and all the way onto its seat.

30 Press the new seal into the coupling and level it with the rim **(see illustrations 17.22a and b)**. Smear the seal lips with grease.

31 Fit the spacer **(see illustration 17.24)**.

32 Check the sprocket coupling/rubber dampers (see Section 21). Check the condition of the hub O-ring and clean it or replace it with a new one if necessary **(see illustration 17.22c)**. Smear the O-ring with oil. Fit the sprocket coupling into the wheel **(see illustration 17.23)**. Fit the brake plate into the drum **(see illustration 12.1)**. Install the wheel (see Section 16).

18 Tyres

General information

1 The wheels fitted to all XT models and 2005/06 YBR models are designed to take tubed tyres. All later YBR models, including

the Custom, use tubeless tyres. Tyre sizes are given in the Specifications at the beginning of this Chapter.

2 Refer to the *Pre-ride checks* listed at the beginning of this manual for tyre maintenance.

Fitting new tyres

3 When selecting new tyres, refer to the tyre information in the Owner's Handbook. Ensure that front and rear tyre types are compatible, the correct size and correct speed rating; if necessary seek advice from a Yamaha dealer or tyre fitting specialist **(see illustration)**.

4 It is recommended that tyres are fitted by a motorcycle tyre specialist rather than attempted in the home workshop. The specialist will be able to balance the wheels after tyre fitting.

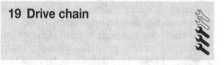

19 Drive chain

Cleaning

1 Refer to Chapter 1, Section 1, for details of routine cleaning with the chain installed on the sprockets.

2 If the chain is extremely dirty remove it from the motorcycle and soak it in paraffin

17.27 Drive the bearing out from the inside

17.29 Using a socket to drive the bearings in

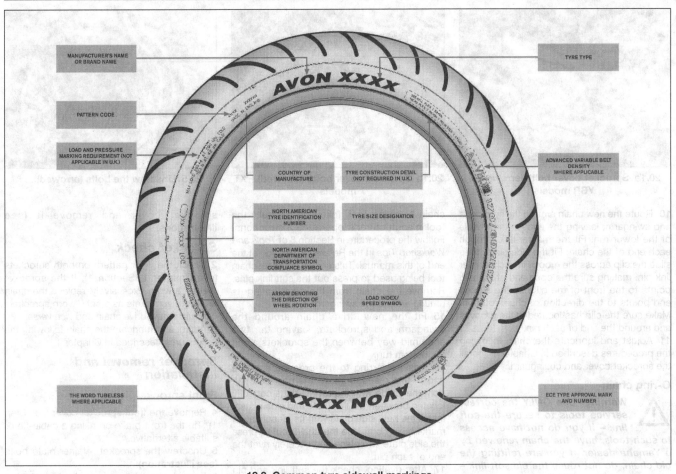

MANUFACTURER'S NAME OR BRAND NAME

PATTERN CODE

LOAD AND PRESSURE MARKING REQUIREMENT (NOT APPLICABLE IN U.K.)

COUNTRY OF MANUFACTURE

NORTH AMERICAN TYRE IDENTIFICATION NUMBER

NORTH AMERICAN DEPARTMENT OF TRANSPORTATION COMPLIANCE SYMBOL

ARROW DENOTING THE DIRECTION OF WHEEL ROTATION

THE WORD TUBELESS WHERE APPLICABLE

TYRE TYPE

ADVANCED VARIABLE BELT DENSITY WHERE APPLICABLE

TYRE CONSTRUCTION DETAIL (NOT REQUIRED IN U.K.)

TYRE SIZE DESIGNATION

LOAD INDEX/ SPEED SYMBOL

ECE TYPE APPROVAL MARK AND NUMBER

18.3 Common tyre sidewall markings

(kerosene) for approximately five or six minutes, then clean it using a soft brush.
Caution: Don't use gasoline (petrol), solvent or other cleaning fluids which might damage its internal sealing properties. Don't use high-pressure water. Remove the chain, wipe it off, then blow dry it with compressed air immediately. The entire process shouldn't take longer than ten minutes – if it does, the O-rings in the chain rollers could be damaged.

Removal and installation

3 Remove the chainguard **(see illustrations)**.

4 Remove the bolts securing the front sprocket cover and remove it **(see illustration 20.1a or b)**.
5 Fully slacken the drive chain as described in Chapter 1.
6 Inspect the chain closely to determine its type, i.e. standard chain or O-ring chain; those fitted as original equipment, along with their lengths, are given in the Specifications at the beginning of this Chapter. Rotate the rear wheel to locate, either the master clip link (standard chain) or soft link (O-ring chain). Proceed as described below according to the type fitted:

Standard chain

7 The clip-type master (split) link is identifiable by the open ended clip securing one of the outer side plates.
8 Support the motorcycle so that the rear wheel is off the ground. Tie the front brake on. Locate the master link in a suitable position to work on by rotating the back wheel.
9 Release the clip from the master link **(see illustration)**. Remove the side plate. Withdraw the master link from the inside. Remove the chain from the bike, noting its routing around the swingarm.

19.3a Chainguard screws (arrowed) – YBR models

19.3b Chainguard screws (arrowed) – XT models

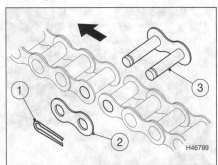

19.9 Clip (1), side plate (2), clip-type master link (3)

20.1a Sprocket cover bolts (arrowed) – YBR models

20.1b Sprocket cover bolts (arrowed) – XT models

20.5 Unscrew the bolts (arrowed) . . .

10 Route the new chain around the sprockets and swingarm, leaving the ends in the middle of the lower run. Fit the master link through each end of the chain. Fit the side plate, then slide the clip across the groove in each master link pin, making sure the open end of the clip points to the front of the bike so the closed end points to the direction of chain rotation. Make sure the clip has located in the grooves and around the end of each pin.

11 Adjust and lubricate the chain following the procedures described in Chapter 1. Install the sprocket cover and chainguard.

O-ring chain

⚠️ *Warning: Use ONLY the correct service tools to secure the soft link – if you do not have access to such tools, have the chain renewed by a Yamaha dealer. If you are refitting the old chain, do not reuse the old soft link – obtain a new one.*

12 The soft link is identifiable by the side plate's markings (and usually its different colour), as well as by the staked ends of the link's two pins which look as if they have been deeply centre-punched, instead of peened over as with all the other pins. A special drive chain cutting/staking tool (Yamaha part No. 90890-01286, or one of several commercially-available tools) is needed to unstake the link and stake the new one in place.

13 Support the motorcycle so that the rear wheel is off the ground. Tie the front brake on. Locate the soft link in a suitable position to work on by rotating the back wheel.

14 Split the chain at the soft link using the

chain breaking tool, following carefully the tool manufacturer's operating instructions. Follow the procedure in Section 8 of *Tools and Workshop Tips* in the Reference Section at the end of this manual. This shows a typical chain tool being used to press out the soft link pins. Remove the chain from the bike, noting its routing around the swingarm.

15 Fit the new drive chain around the swingarm and sprockets, leaving the two ends mid-way between the sprockets along the bottom run.

16 Again referring to the procedure at the end of this manual, install the new soft link from the inside with the four O-rings correctly located between the link plate and side plates. Install the new side plate with its identification marks facing out. Use the chain tool to press the side plate into place and securely rivet the end of each pin.

17 After riveting, check the soft link and pin ends for any signs of cracking. If there is any evidence of cracking, the soft link, O-rings and side plate must be renewed. Check that the soft link pivots freely.

18 Adjust and lubricate the chain following the procedures described in Chapter 1. Install the sprocket cover and chainguard.

20 Sprockets

Front sprocket cover

1 Unscrew the bolts securing the front

sprocket cover and remove it (see illustrations).

Sprocket check

2 Check the wear pattern on both sprockets (see Chapter 1, Section 1). If the sprocket teeth are worn excessively, replace the chain and both sprockets as a set – worn sprockets can ruin a new drive chain and *vice versa*.

3 Adjust and lubricate the chain following the procedures described in Chapter 1.

Sprocket removal and installation

Front sprocket

4 Remove the front sprocket cover (see Step 1). Tie the front brake on using a cable-tie or suitable alternative.

5 Unscrew the sprocket retainer plate bolts (see illustration).

6 Fully slacken the drive chain as described in Chapter 1. If the rear sprocket is being removed as well, remove the rear wheel now to create full slack (see Section 16). Otherwise disengage the chain from the rear sprocket if required to provide more slack.

7 Turn the sprocket retainer plate to unlock it from the splines then slide it off the shaft (see illustration). Slide the chain and sprocket off the input shaft then slip the sprocket out of the chain (see illustrations).

8 Engage the new sprocket with the chain, making sure the marked side is facing out, and slide it on the shaft (see illustration). Fit the retainer plate, then turn it in the groove so it is locked in the splines (see illustration 20.7a).

20.7a . . . and remove the retainer plate as described

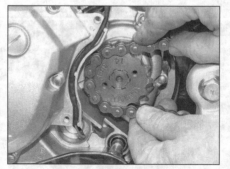

20.7b Draw the sprocket off the shaft and disengage the chain

20.8 Fit the sprocket into the chain and onto the shaft

20.13 Bend back the tabs (arrowed), then unscrew the bolts

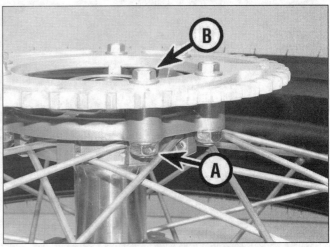

20.14 Hold the nuts (A) while unscrewing the bolts (B)

9 If the rear wheel was removed, change the sprocket now and install the wheel (see Section 16). If the chain was merely disengaged, fit it back onto the rear sprocket. Take up the slack in the chain.

10 Install the retainer plate bolts and tighten them to the torque setting specified at the beginning of the Chapter (see illustration 20.5).

11 Fit the sprocket cover (see Step 1). Adjust and lubricate the chain following the procedures described in Chapter 1.

Rear sprocket

12 Remove the rear wheel (see Section 16).

13 On YBR models lift the brake plate out of the drum but leave the sprocket coupling in the hub (see illustration 12.1). Lay the wheel on blocks with the sprocket facing up. Bend the retainer plate tabs away from the bolt heads (see illustration). Unscrew the bolts and remove the retainer plates. Remove the sprocket. Lift the sprocket coupling out of the hub (see illustration 17.23), turn it over and retrieve the captive nuts and spacer (see illustration 17.24).

14 On XT models hold the nuts and unscrew the bolts securing the sprocket to the hub (see illustration). Remove the sprocket.

15 Check the condition of the sprocket bolts and nuts and replace them all with new ones if any are damaged.

16 On YBR models fit the sprocket onto the hub with the stamped mark facing out. Fit the retainer plates, then fit the bolts through the coupling, turn the coupling over, fit the nuts into the back of the coupling so they become captive, and finger-tighten the bolts. Fit the spacer, then fit the coupling back into the hub (see illustrations 17.24 and 17.23). Tighten the bolts evenly and in a criss-cross sequence to the torque setting specified at the beginning of the Chapter. Bend the retainer plate tabs up against the bolt heads (see illustration 20.13).

17 On XT models fit the sprocket on to the hub with the stamped mark facing out. Apply some threadlock to the threads of the nuts. Fit the bolts through and thread the nuts on finger-tight (see illustration 20.14). Counter-hold the nuts and tighten the bolts evenly and in a criss-cross sequence to the torque setting specified at the beginning of the Chapter.

18 Install the rear wheel (see Section 16).

21 Rear sprocket coupling/ rubber dampers – YBR models

1 Remove the rear wheel (see Section 16). Grasp the sprocket and feel for play between the sprocket coupling and the wheel hub by attempting to twist the sprocket in each direction. Any play indicates worn rubber damper segments.

2 Lift the sprocket coupling out of the hub leaving the rubber dampers in position (see illustration 17.23). Note the spacer inside the coupling and remove it if it is likely to drop out (see illustration 17.24). Check the coupling for cracks or any obvious signs of damage.

3 Lift the rubber damper segments from the wheel and check them for cracks, hardening and general deterioration (see illustration). Renew them as a set if necessary.

4 Check the condition of the hub O-ring – if it is damaged, deformed or deteriorated replace it with a new one and smear it with oil (see illustration 17.22c). Otherwise clean it and smear it with oil.

5 Checking and replacement procedures for the sprocket coupling bearing are in Section 17.

6 Installation is the reverse of removal. Make sure the spacer is still correctly installed in the coupling, or install it if it was removed (see illustration 17.24).

7 Install the rear wheel (see Section 16).

21.3 Check the rubber dampers as described

Chapter 7
Bodywork

Contents

Degrees of difficulty

Easy, suitable for novice with little experience	**Fairly easy,** suitable for beginner with some experience	**Fairly difficult,** suitable for competent DIY mechanic	**Difficult,** suitable for experienced DIY mechanic	**Very difficult,** suitable for expert DIY or professional

Specifications

Torque settings

Luggage rack bolts
   YBR-ED models .... 30 Nm
   YBR Custom models .... 23 Nm

1 General information

This Chapter covers the procedures necessary to remove and install the bodywork. Since many service and repair operations on these motorcycles require the removal of the body panels, the procedures are grouped here and referred to from other Chapters.

In the case of damage to the bodywork, it is usually necessary to remove the broken component and replace it with a new (or used) one. The material that the body panels are composed of doesn't lend itself to conventional repair techniques. Note that there are however some companies that specialize in 'plastic welding' and there are a number of DIY bodywork repair kits now available for motorcycles.

When attempting to remove any body panel, first study it closely, noting any fasteners and associated fittings, to be sure of returning everything to its correct place on installation. Once the evident fasteners have been removed, try to withdraw the panel as described but DO NOT FORCE IT – if it will not release, check that all fasteners have been removed and try again.

When installing a body panel, first study it closely, noting any fasteners and associated fittings removed with it, to be sure of returning everything to its correct place. Check that all fasteners are in good condition, including the rubber mounts; replace any faulty fasteners with new ones before the panel is reassembled. Check also that all mounting brackets are straight and repair them or replace them with new ones if necessary before attempting to install the panel.

Tighten the fasteners securely, but be careful not to overtighten any of them or the panel may break (not always immediately) due to the uneven stress.

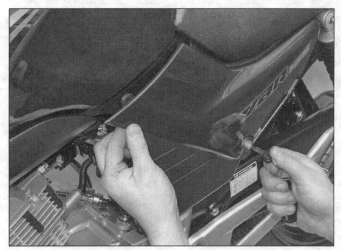

2.1a Unlock the panel using the ignition key . . .

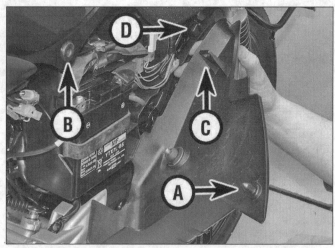

2.1b . . . then free the peg (A) from the grommet (B), and the bracket (C) from the lug (D)

2 YBR models

Side covers

1 To remove the left-hand cover insert the ignition key in the lock in the centre of the panel and turn it clockwise **(see illustration)**. Carefully pull the front away to free the peg from the grommet, then draw the cover forwards and down to free the slotted bracket from the rubber lug **(see illustration)**.

2 To remove the right-hand cover unscrew the bolt at the bottom **(see illustration)**. Carefully pull the front away to free the peg from the grommet, then draw the cover forwards and down to free the slotted bracket from the rubber lug **(see illustration 2.1b)**.

3 Installation is the reverse of removal. Make sure the rubber caps are fitted to the rear mounting lugs. Make sure the caps and grommets are in good condition. Make sure

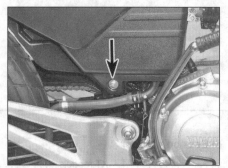

2.2 Unscrew the bolt (arrowed)

2.5 Unscrew the seat mounting bolts on both sides

the slot at the back locates correctly over the rubber lug **(see illustration 2.1b)**. When fitting the left-hand cover turn the key anti-clockwise to lock it.

Seat

4 Remove the side covers (see above).

5 Unscrew the bolt on each side **(see illustration)**.

6 On 2005 to 2009 ED models and all Custom models, lift the front of the seat and draw it forwards **(see illustration)**. Installation is the reverse of removal. Make sure the hook at the back locates correctly **(see illustration)**.

7 On 2010-on ED models, draw the seat backwards to release the securing hooks on the underside **(see illustration)**. Installation is the reverse of removal.

2.6a Draw the seat forwards . . .

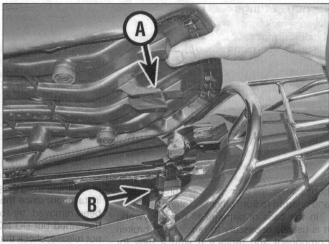

2.6b . . . noting how the hook (A) locates under the bracket (B)

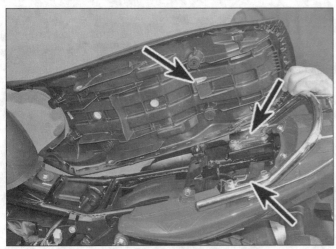

2.7 Draw the seat backwards to release the securing hooks (arrowed) – 2010-on ED models

2.8a Unscrew the bolt

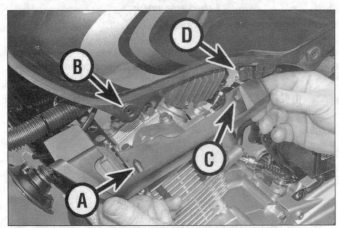

2.8b Free the peg (A) from the grommet (B), and the bracket (C) from the lug (D)

2.9a Support bracket bolt

Air ducts and fuel tank side panels

2005 to 2009 ED model air ducts

8 Unscrew the bolt on the underside **(see illustration)** – if removing both ducts you only need to do this to remove the first – bring the bracket joining them along with the second. Carefully pull the top away to free the peg from the grommet, then draw the duct forwards to free the slotted bracket from the rubber lug **(see illustration)**.

2010-on ED model side panels

9 Remove one or both side covers as appropriate (see Steps 1 and 2). Unscrew the bolt on the support bracket, then undo the front panel mounting bolt and rear mounting screw **(see illustrations)**.

2.9b Front panel mounting bolt

2.9c Rear panel mounting screw

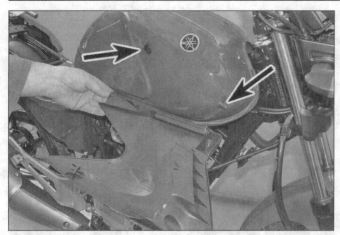

2.10a Location of the side panel mounting lugs

2.10b Support bracket mounting grommet (arrowed)

10 Draw the side panel forwards to free it from the mounting lugs on the tank **(see illustration)**. If required, draw the water drain funnel hose out of the guide on the support bracket and remove the bracket from its mounting grommet **(see illustration)**.

11 Installation is the reverse of removal.

Custom models

12 Remove the fuel tank (see Chapter 3B). Remove the fuel tank rubber support **(see illustration)**.

13 Unscrew the two bolts, then release the clip on the top and remove the duct **(see illustrations)**.

14 Installation is the reverse of removal.

Luggage rack
ED models

15 Remove the seat.

16 On 2005 to 2009 models, unscrew the three mounting bolts and remove the rack **(see illustration)**.

2.12 Remove the rubber support (arrowed)

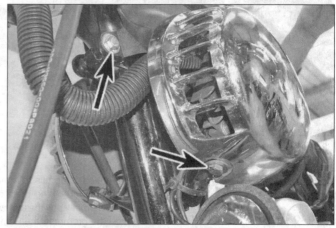

2.13a Unscrew the bolts (arrowed) . . .

2.13b . . . then release the clip (arrowed) and remove the duct

2.16 Unscrew the bolts (arrowed)

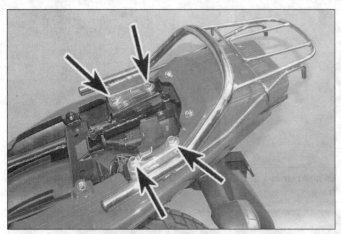

2.17a Unscrew the mounting bolts (arrowed) . . .

2.17b . . . and remove the seat hooks

17 On 2010-on models, unscrew the four mounting bolts and remove the seat hooks, noting how they fit **(see illustrations)**. Lift off the rack.

18 Installation is the reverse of removal. Tighten the bolts to the torque setting specified at the beginning of the Chapter.

Custom models

19 Remove the seat. Disconnect the rear turn signal wiring connectors. Unscrew the turn signal carrier bolts and remove the turn signal carrier assembly **(see illustration)**.

20 Unscrew the four bolts and remove the rack.

21 Installation is the reverse of removal. Tighten the bolts to the torque setting specified at the beginning of the Chapter.

Seat cowling (ED models)

22 Remove the seat and the luggage rack.

23 On 2005 to 2009 models, unscrew the four bolts and remove the cowling **(see illustration)**. If required separate the side sections of the cowling from the tail section.

24 On 2010-on models, undo the screws on both sides of the cowling lower edge **(see illustration)**. Undo the screws on the upper edge of the cowling assembly **(see illustration)**. Carefully ease the side sections of the cowling apart and ease the upper centre section up to release the tabs securing it to the side sections **(see illustration)**. Release the pegs on the inside of the side sections from the grommets on the frame and tail light unit **(see illustration)**.

25 Installation is the reverse of removal.

Mirrors

26 Unscrew the mirror using the hex at the base of the stem – the right-hand mirror has a left-hand thread, so turn it clockwise to

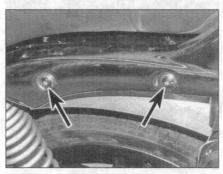

2.19 Unscrew the bolts (arrowed) and remove the carrier

2.23 Unscrew the bolts (arrowed) and remove the cowling

2.24a Screws secure lower edge of cowling

2.24b Screws secure upper edge of cowling

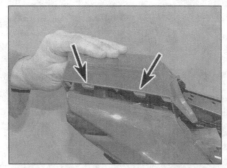

2.24c Remove the centre section noting the location of the tabs (arrowed)

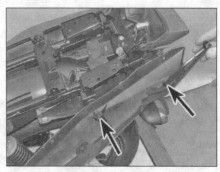

2.24d Pegs (arrowed) locate in grommets

2.26 Unscrew the mirror

2.29 Unscrew the bolts and remove the guide

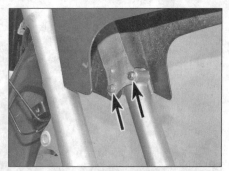

2.30a Unscrew the bolts (arrowed) . . .

2.30b . . . and remove the mudguard

2.32 Remove the headlight beam adjuster bolt

2.33 Note the plastic washers on the mounting screws

unscrew it, and anti-clockwise to thread it in **(see illustration)**, and the left-hand mirror has a right-hand thread, so turn it anti-clockwise to unscrew it, and clockwise to thread it in.

27 Installation is the reverse of removal – make sure the mirror is tight enough to stop it from unscrewing when the bike is moving.

Front mudguard

28 Remove the front wheel (see Chapter 6).
29 Unscrew the two bolts on the inside of the right-hand fork and remove the brake hose guide bracket **(see illustration)**.
30 Unscrew the two bolts on the inside of the left-hand fork and draw the mudguard forwards **(see illustrations)**.
31 Installation is the reverse of removal.

Fairing and windshield – 2014-on ED models

32 Note the position of the headlight beam adjuster bracket on the underside of the headlight unit, then unscrew the adjuster bolt **(see illustration)**.
33 Undo the left and right-hand screws securing the fairing assembly, noting the location of the plastic washers **(see illustration)**.
34 Ease the sides of the fairing apart and lift the assembly off the mounting bracket. Disconnect the sidelight and headlight wiring connectors and remove the fairing assembly **(see illustration)**.
35 If required, remove the headlight unit (see Chapter 8).
36 To remove the windshield, first remove the headlight unit. Taking great care not to damage the heads of the screws securing the windshield, unscrew the nuts on the inside of

the fairing and remove the steel and rubber washers **(see illustration)**.
37 Before installation, ensure the plastic and rubber washers are in good condition and renew them if necessary.
38 Installation is the reverse of removal. Check the operation of the headlight and sidelight. Check the headlight aim (see Chapter 8).

3 XT models

Seat

1 Unscrew the bolt on each side **(see illustration)**.

2.34 Lift off the fairing assembly

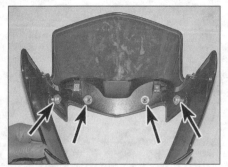

2.36 Undo the nuts (arrowed) on the plastic screws

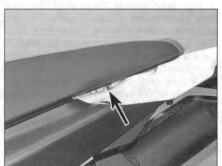

3.1 Unscrew the bolt (arrowed) on each side . . .

3.2 . . . then remove the seat, noting how it locates

3.3 Make sure the hooks (arrowed) locate correctly

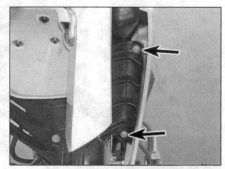

3.5 Undo the screws (arrowed)

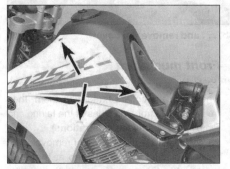

3.6 Undo the screws (arrowed) and remove the panel

3.7a Remove the filler cap . . .

3.7b . . . to release the top panel

2 Lift the back of the seat and draw it backwards **(see illustration)**.

3 Installation is the reverse of removal. Make sure the three hooks at the front locate correctly **(see illustration)**.

Fuel tank panels

4 Remove the seat.

5 Undo the two screws securing the outer edge of the air duct to the inside of the panel at the front **(see illustration)**.

6 Undo the four screws, noting which fits where and the collars fitted with them, and remove the panel **(see illustration)**.

7 If required remove the fuel tank filler cap and lift the top panel off **(see illustrations)**. Refit the filler cap.

8 Installation is the reverse of removal – the long collar fits with the top screw, and the next longest screw goes in the side.

Air duct

9 Undo the two screws securing the outer edge of the air duct to the inside of each fuel tank panel **(see illustration 3.5)**.

10 Undo the two centre screws and remove the duct **(see illustration)**.

11 Installation is the reverse of removal.

Side covers

12 Remove the seat.

13 Undo the two screws and remove the collars **(see illustration)**. Pull the bottom edge away to free the cut-out from the peg, then

3.10 Undo the screws (arrowed) and remove the duct

draw the cover forwards, again to free the cut-out from the peg **(see illustration)**.

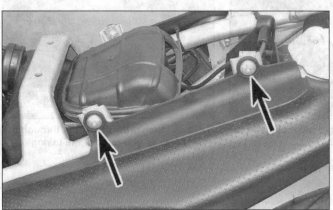

3.13a Undo the screws (arrowed) . . .

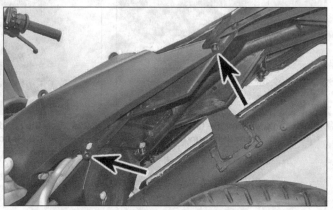

3.13b . . . then release the cut-outs from around the pegs (arrowed)

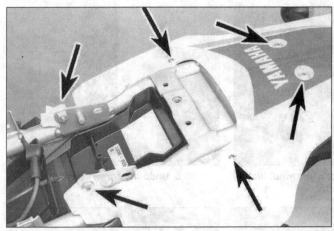

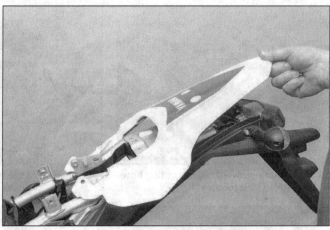

3.16a Undo the screws (arrowed) . . .

3.16b . . . and remove the cover

14 Installation is the reverse of removal.

Tail cover

15 Remove the seat.
16 Undo the six screws, and remove the collars with the front and rear screws (see illustration). Lift the cover off (see illustration).
17 Installation is the reverse of removal.

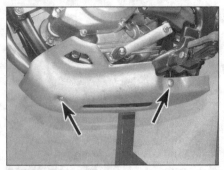

3.18 Undo the bolt at the front and the bolt at the back on each side (arrowed)

Sump guard

18 Unscrew the three bolts and remove the guard (see illustration).
19 Installation is the reverse of removal.

Mirrors

20 Unscrew the mirror using the hex at the base of the stem.
21 Installation is the reverse of removal.

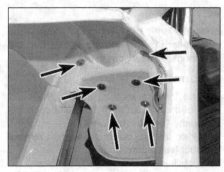

3.22a Undo the screws (arrowed) . . .

Front mudguard

22 Undo the six screws, noting which fits where and the collars fitted with them, then free each side from the sides of the fairing and remove the guard (see illustrations).
23 Installation is the reverse of removal – the two unpolished Torx screws go at the front, the two black hex screws go in the middle, and the two stainless hex screws go at the back.

Fairing

24 Remove the mudguard.
25 Remove the turn signal assemblies (see Chapter 8).
26 Carefully pull each side away to free the headlight pivot posts from their holders in the fairing, then remove the fairing, taking care not to snag the turn signal wiring as you draw it through (see illustrations).
27 Installation is the reverse of removal.

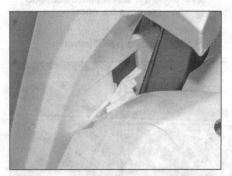

3.22b . . . then free the tab on each side from the fairing

3.26a Free the headlight pivot posts from their holders . . .

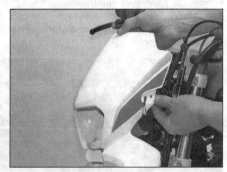

3.26b . . . then draw the wiring through the holes as you remove the fairing

Chapter 8
Electrical system

Contents

Degrees of difficulty

Easy, suitable for novice with little experience 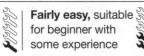	**Fairly easy,** suitable for beginner with some experience	**Fairly difficult,** suitable for competent DIY mechanic	**Difficult,** suitable for experienced DIY mechanic	**Very difficult,** suitable for expert DIY or professional

Specifications

Battery

Capacity and type
2005 and 2006 YBR models	12V 5Ah, Yuasa YB5L-B
2007 to 2009 YBR125 ED models, all Custom and XT models	12V 6Ah, GS GTX7L-BS MF
2010-on YBR125 ED models	12V 6Ah, YTX7L-BS

Voltage
Fully-charged	above 12.8V
Uncharged	below 12.7V

Charging rate
2005 and 2006 YBR models	0.5A for 5 to 10 hrs
2007-on YBR models and all XT models	0.6A for 5 to 10 hrs

Bulbs

Headlight	35/35W
Sidelight	5W
Brake/tail light	21/5W
Licence plate light (XT models)	5W
Turn signal lights	10W

Instrument lights
YBR models	1.7W
XT models	LED

Warning lights
2005 to 2009 YBR125 ED and all Custom models	3W
2010-on YBR125 ED models	2W
XT models	LED

Charging system

Stator coil resistance
2005 and 2006 YBR models.	0.64 to 0.96 ohms
2007-on YBR models	0.45 to 0.67 ohms

2005 to 2007 XT models
Charge coil resistance	0.65 to 0.95 ohms
Lighting coil resistance.	0.48 to 0.72 ohms
2008-on XT models	0.64 to 0.96 ohms

Regulated voltage output
2005 and 2006 YBR models.	13.7 to 14.7V
2007-on YBR models.	14.1 to 14.9V
2005 to 2007 XT models	13.0 to 14.0V
2008-on XT models	13.7 to 14.7V
Current leakage	0.1 mA (max)

Fuse

YBR models	15A
2005 to 2007 XT models	10A
2008-on XT models	15A

Fuel level sensor (YBR models)

Resistance – FULL position	4 to 10 ohms
Resistance – EMPTY position	90 to 100 ohms

Starter motor

YBR models
Brush length
Standard.	10 mm
Service limit (min)	3.5 mm

Commutator diameter
Standard.	22.0 mm
Service limit (min)	21.0 mm
Mica undercut (depth)	1.5 mm

XT models
Brush length
Standard.	12.5 mm
Service limit (min)	3.5 mm

Commutator diameter
Standard.	17.6 mm
Service limit (min)	16.6 mm
Mica undercut (depth)	1.5 mm

Starter relay

Coil resistance
YBR models	3.6 to 4.4 ohms
XT models.	90 to 100 ohms

Torque settings

Alternator rotor nut.	70 Nm
Fuel level sensor bolts (2005 and 2006 YBR models)	4 Nm

1 General information

All models have a 12 volt electrical system charged by an alternator with separate regulator/rectifier. XT models have separate charging and lighting coils.

The regulator maintains the charging system output within the specified range to prevent overcharging, and the rectifier converts the ac (alternating current) output of the alternator to dc (direct current) to power the lights and other components and to charge the battery. The alternator rotor is mounted on the left-hand end of the crankshaft.

The starter motor is mounted on the front of the crankcase. The starting system includes the motor, the battery, the relay and the various wires and switches. Some of the switches are part of a starter safety interlock system – see Chapter 1 for further information and checks on the system.

Note: *Keep in mind that electrical parts, once purchased, often cannot be returned. To avoid unnecessary expense, make very sure the faulty component has been positively identified before buying a replacement part.*

2 Electrical system fault finding

1 A typical electrical circuit consists of an electrical component, the switches, relays, etc, related to that component and the wiring and connectors that link the component to the battery and the frame.

2 Before tackling any troublesome electrical circuit, first study the wiring diagram thoroughly to get a complete picture of what makes up that individual circuit. Trouble

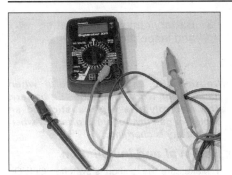

2.4a A digital multimeter can be used for all electrical tests

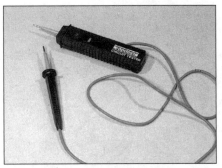

2.4b A battery-powered continuity tester

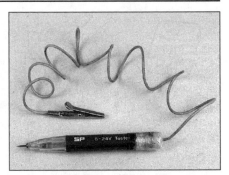

2.4c A simple test light is useful for voltage tests

spots, for instance, can often be narrowed down by noting if other components related to that circuit are operating properly or not. If several components or circuits fail at one time, chances are the fault lies either in the fuse or in the common earth (ground) connection, as several circuits are often routed through the same fuse and earth (ground) connections.

3 Electrical problems often stem from simple causes, such as loose or corroded connections or a blown fuse. Prior to any electrical fault finding, always visually check the condition of the fuse, wires and connections in the problem circuit. Intermittent failures can be especially frustrating, since you can't always duplicate the failure when it's convenient to test. In such situations, a good practice is to clean all connections in the affected circuit, whether or not they appear to be good – where possible use a dedicated electrical cleaning spray along with sandpaper, wire wool or other abrasive material to remove corrosion, and a dedicated electrical protection spray to prevent further problems. All of the connections and wires should also be wiggled to check for looseness which can cause intermittent failure.

4 If you don't have a multimeter it is highly advisable to obtain one – they are not expensive and will enable a full range of electrical tests to be made. Go for a modern digital one with LCD display as they are easier to use. A continuity tester and/or test light are useful for certain electrical checks as an alternative, though are limited in their usefulness compared to a multimeter **(see illustrations)**.

Continuity checks

5 The term continuity describes the uninterrupted flow of electricity through an electrical circuit. Continuity can be checked with a multimeter set either to its continuity function (a beep is emitted when continuity is found), or to the resistance (ohms / Ω) function, or with a dedicated continuity tester. Both instruments are powered by an internal battery, therefore the checks are made with the ignition OFF. As a safety precaution, always disconnect the battery negative (-) lead before making continuity checks, particularly if ignition switch checks are being made.

6 If using a multimeter, select the continuity

function if it has one, or the resistance (ohms) function. Touch the meter probes together and check that a beep is emitted or the meter reads zero, which indicates continuity. If there is no continuity there will be no beep or the meter will show infinite resistance. After using the meter, always switch it OFF to conserve its battery.

7 A continuity tester can be used in the same way – its light should come on or it should beep to indicate continuity in the switch ON position, but should be off or silent in the OFF position.

8 Note that the polarity of the test probes doesn't matter for continuity checks, although care should be taken to follow specific test procedures if a diode or solid-state component is being checked.

Switch continuity checks

9 If a switch is at fault, trace its wiring to the wiring connectors. Separate the connectors and inspect them for security and condition. A build-up of dirt or corrosion here will most likely be the cause of the problem – clean up and apply a water dispersant such as WD40, or alternatively use a dedicated contact cleaner and protection spray.

10 If using a multimeter, select the continuity function if it has one, or the resistance (ohms) function, and connect its probes to the terminals in the connector **(see illustration)**.

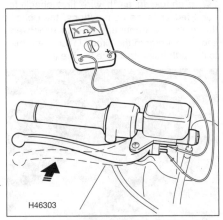

2.10 Continuity should be indicated across switch terminals when the lever is operated

Simple ON/OFF type switches, such as brake light switches, only have two wires whereas combination switches, like the handlebar switches, have many wires. Study the wiring diagram to ensure that you are connecting to the correct pair of wires. Continuity should be indicated with the switch ON and no continuity with it OFF.

Wiring continuity checks

11 Many electrical faults are caused by damaged wiring, often due to incorrect routing or chaffing on frame components. Loose, wet or corroded wire connectors can also be the cause of electrical problems.

12 A continuity check can be made on a single length of wire by disconnecting it at each end and connecting the meter or continuity tester probes to each end of the wire **(see illustration)**. Continuity (low or no resistance – 0 ohms) should be indicated if the wire is good. If no continuity (high resistance) is shown, suspect a broken wire.

13 To check for continuity to earth in any earth wire connect one probe of your meter or tester to the earth wire terminal in the connector and the other to the frame, engine, or battery earth (-) terminal. Continuity (low or no resistance – 0 ohms) should be indicated if the wire is good. If no continuity (high resistance) is shown, suspect a broken wire or corroded or loose earth point (see below).

Voltage checks

14 A voltage check can determine whether power is reaching a component. Use a

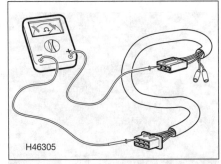

2.12 Wiring continuity check. Connect the meter probes across each end of the same wire

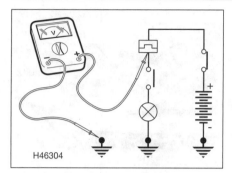

2.15 Voltage check. Connect the meter positive probe to the component and the negative probe to earth

multimeter set to the dc voltage scale, or a test light. The test light is the cheaper component, but the meter has the advantage of being able to give a voltage reading.

15 Connect the meter or test light in parallel, i.e. across the load **(see illustration)**.

16 First identify the relevant wiring circuit by referring to the wiring diagram at the end of this manual. If other electrical components share the same power supply (i.e. are fed from the same fuse), take note whether they are working correctly – this is useful information in deciding where to start checking the circuit.

17 If using a meter, check first that the meter leads are plugged into the correct terminals on the meter (red to positive (+), black to negative (-). Set the meter to the dc volts function, where necessary at a range suitable for the battery voltage – 0 to 20 vdc. Connect the meter red probe (+) to the power supply wire and the black probe to a good metal earth (ground) on the motorcycle's frame or directly to the battery negative terminal. Battery voltage should be shown on the meter with the ignition switch, and if necessary any other relevant switch, ON.

18 If using a test light, connect its positive (+) probe to the power supply terminal and its negative (-) probe to a good earth (ground) on the motorcycle's frame. With the switch, and if necessary any other relevant switch, ON, the test light should illuminate.

19 If no voltage is indicated, work back towards the fuse continuing to check for voltage. When you reach a point where there

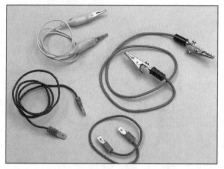

2.23 A selection of insulated jumper wires

is voltage, you know the problem lies between that point and your last check point.

Earth (ground) checks

20 Earth connections are made either directly to the engine or frame (such as the neutral switch which only has a positive feed) or by a separate wire into the earth circuit of the wiring harness. Alternatively a short earth wire is sometimes run from the component directly to the motorcycle's frame.

21 Corrosion is a common cause of a poor earth connection, as is a loose earth terminal fastener.

22 If total or multiple component failure is experienced, check the security of the main earth lead from the negative (-) terminal of the battery, the earth lead bolted to the engine, and the main earth point(s) on the frame. If corroded, dismantle the connection and clean all surfaces back to bare metal. Remake the connection and prevent further corrosion from forming by smearing battery terminal grease over the connection.

23 To check the earth of a component, use an insulated jumper wire to temporarily bypass its earth connection **(see illustration)** – connect one end of the jumper wire to the earth terminal or metal body of the component and the other end to the motorcycle's frame. If the circuit works with the jumper wire installed, the earth circuit is faulty.

24 To check an earth wire first check for corroded or loose connections, then check the wiring for continuity (Step 13) between each connector in the circuit in turn, and then to its earth point, to locate the break.

3 Battery removal, installation and inspection

Caution: Be extremely careful when handling or working around the battery. The electrolyte is very caustic and an explosive gas (hydrogen) is given off when the battery is charging.

Removal and installation

1 Make sure the ignition is switched OFF. On YBR models remove the left-hand side cover (see Chapter 7). On XT models remove the seat (see Chapter 7).

2 Unscrew the negative (–) terminal bolt first and disconnect the lead from the battery **(see illustration)**. Lift up the insulating cover to access the positive (+) terminal, then unscrew the bolt and disconnect the lead.

3 On YBR models release the battery strap and draw the battery out **(see illustrations)**.

4 On XT models lift the battery from the bike.

5 On installation, clean the battery terminals and lead ends with a wire brush, fine sandpaper or steel wool. Reconnect the leads, connecting the positive (+) terminal first.

> **HAYNES HINT** *Battery corrosion can be kept to a minimum by applying a layer of battery terminal grease or petroleum jelly (Vaseline) to the terminals after the leads have been connected. DO NOT use a mineral based grease.*

6 Install the side cover or seat (see Chapter 7).

Inspection and maintenance

Note: A standard type battery is fitted to 2005 and 2006 YBR models, and a maintenance free (MF) battery is fitted to all other models. It is possible however that the standard battery on 2005 and 2006 YBR models has been replaced with a maintenance free (MF) battery at some point. It is also possible that models fitted with an MF battery have had a standard battery fitted. The batteries are easy to distinguish – standard ones have removable caps across

3.2 Disconnect the negative lead first, then disconnect the positive lead (arrowed)

3.3a Release the strap . . .

3.3b . . . and remove the battery

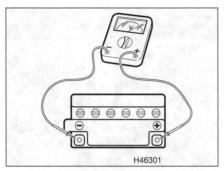

3.16 Checking battery voltage – connect the meter as shown

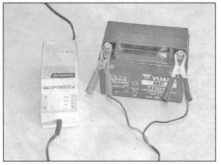

4.1 Battery connected to a charger

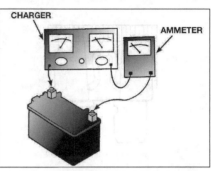

4.2 If the charger doesn't have ammeter built in, connect one in series as shown. DO NOT connect the ammeter between the battery terminals or it will be ruined

the top and electrolyte level lines (marked UPPER and LOWER or MAX and MIN), while MF batteries do not, and are usually marked MF on the front. Identify the type of battery fitted on your bike before proceeding.

Standard battery

7 Check the battery terminals and leads are tight and free of corrosion. If corrosion is evident, clean the terminals as described in Step 5, then protect them from further corrosion (see *Haynes Hint*).

8 Keep the battery case clean to prevent current leakage, which can discharge the battery over a period of time (especially when it sits unused). Wash the outside of the case with a solution of baking soda and water. Rinse the battery thoroughly, then dry it.

9 Look for cracks in the case and replace the battery with a new one if any are found. If acid has been spilled on the frame or battery box, neutralise it with a baking soda and water solution, dry it thoroughly, then touch up any damaged paint.

10 If the motorcycle sits unused for long periods of time, disconnect the cables from the battery terminals, negative (–) terminal first. Refer to Section 4 and charge the battery once every month to six weeks.

11 Battery terminal voltage can be measured as described in Step 16. Battery condition can be determined by measuring the specific gravity of the electrolyte using a battery hydrometer. Remove each cell cap and draw some electrolyte into the hydrometer and note the reading. Return the electrolyte to the cell and install the cap. The specific gravity should be 1.280. If less than this the battery needs charging.

Maintenance-free battery

12 Check the battery terminals and leads are tight and free of corrosion. If corrosion is evident, clean the terminals as described in Step 5, then protect them from further corrosion (see *Haynes Hint*).

13 Keep the battery case clean to prevent current leakage, which can discharge the battery over a period of time (especially when it sits unused). Wash the outside of the case with a solution of baking soda and water. Rinse the battery thoroughly, then dry it.

14 Look for cracks in the case and replace

the battery with a new one if any are found. If acid has been spilled on the frame or battery box, neutralise it with a baking soda and water solution, dry it thoroughly, then touch up any damaged paint.

15 If the motorcycle sits unused for long periods of time, disconnect the cables from the battery terminals, negative (–) terminal first. Refer to Section 4 and charge the battery once every month to six weeks.

16 Check the condition of the battery by measuring the voltage present at the battery terminals. Connect the voltmeter positive (+) probe to the battery positive (+) terminal, and the negative (–) probe to the battery negative (–) terminal **(see illustration)**. When fully-charged there should be 12.8 to 13.2 volts present. If the voltage falls much below this remove the battery (see above), and recharge it as described below in Section 4.

4 Battery charging

Caution: Be extremely careful when handling or working around the battery. The electrolyte is very caustic and an explosive gas (hydrogen) is given off when the battery is charging.

1 Remove the battery (see Section 3). Connect the charger to the battery, making sure that the positive (+) lead on the charger is connected to the positive (+) terminal on the battery, and the negative (–) lead is connected to the negative (–) terminal **(see illustration)**.

2 Yamaha recommend that the battery is charged at the rate specified at the beginning of the Chapter. Exceeding this figure can cause the battery to overheat, buckling the plates and rendering it useless. Few owners will have access to an expensive current controlled charger, so if a normal domestic charger is used check that after a possible initial peak, the charge rate falls to a safe level **(see illustration)**. If the battery becomes hot during charging **stop**. Further charging will cause damage. You are advised to use one of the bike-specific chargers (as shown in illustration 4.1) which are designed for the maintenance and recovery

of motorcycle batteries, in particular catering for the requirements of heavily discharged MF batteries. They are not too expensive, and are a worthwhile investment, especially if the bike is not used over winter. Follow the manufacturer's instructions.

3 If the recharged battery discharges rapidly if left disconnected it is likely that an internal short caused by physical damage or sulphation has occurred. A new battery will be required. A sound item will tend to lose its charge at about 1% per day.

4 Install the battery (see Section 3).

5 If the motorcycle sits unused for long periods of time, charge the battery once every month to six weeks and leave it disconnected.

5 Fuse

1 The electrical system is protected by a single fuse. On YBR models and 2008-on XT models the fuse is integral with the starter relay, which is located behind the left-hand side cover. On 2005 to 2007 XT models the fuse is in a holder located under the seat next to the battery.

2 Remove the side cover or seat, according to model (see Chapter 7).

3 On YBR models and 2008-on XT models disconnect the starter relay wiring connector **(see illustration)**.

5.3 Disconnect the relay wiring connector to access the fuse (arrowed)

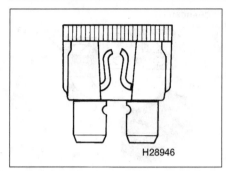

5.5 A blown fuse can be identified by a break in its element

5.6 Spare fuse (arrowed)

6.3 Headlight relay (arrowed) – YBR models

4 On 2005 to 2007 XT models unclip the lid of the fuse holder.

5 The fuse can be removed and checked visually. If you can't pull the fuse out with your fingertips, use a pair of suitable pliers. A blown fuse is easily identified by a break in the element **(see illustration)**. The fuse is clearly marked with its rating and must only be replaced by a fuse of the correct rating.

6 On YBR models and 2008-on XT models a spare fuse is housed in the back of the relay holder **(see illustration)**. If the spare fuse is used, always replace it with a new one so that a spare is carried on the bike at all times.

 Warning: Never put in a fuse of a higher rating or bridge the terminals with any other substitute, however temporary it may be. Serious damage may be done to the circuit, or a fire may start.

7 If the new fuse blows immediately check the wiring circuit very carefully for evidence of a short-circuit. Look for bare wires and chafed, melted or burned insulation.

8 Occasionally a fuse will blow or cause an open-circuit for no obvious reason. Corrosion of the fuse ends and fusebox terminals may occur and cause poor fuse contact. If this happens, remove the corrosion with a wire brush or emery paper, then spray the fuse end and terminals with electrical contact cleaner.

6 Lighting system check

1 If a light fails, first check the bulb (see relevant Section), the bulb terminals in the holder, and the wiring connector(s). If none of the lights work, check battery voltage – low voltage indicates either a faulty battery or a defective charging system. Refer to Section 3 for battery checks and Section 28 for charging system tests. If there is a problem with more than one circuit at the same time, or with all circuits, it is likely to be a fault relating to a multi-function component, such as the fuse or the ignition switch. When checking for a blown filament in a bulb, it is advisable to back up a visual check with a continuity test of the filament as it is not always apparent that

a bulb has blown. When testing for continuity, remember that on single terminal bulbs it is the metal body of the bulb that is the earth (ground).

YBR models

Headlight

2 All models have a twin filament bulb, one for high beam and one for low beam. If either or both beams fail to work, first check the bulb (see Section 7). If it is good, the problem lies in the wiring or connectors, the headlight relay, or the dimmer switch. Refer to Section 19 for the switch testing procedures, and also to the wiring diagrams at the end of this Chapter.

3 To check the relay remove the left-hand side panel (see Chapter 7), then displace the relay from its mount and disconnect the wiring connector **(see illustration)**. Set a multimeter to the ohms x 1 scale and connect it across the relay's blue/black and adjacent brown wire terminals. There should be no continuity (infinite resistance). Using a fully-charged 12 volt battery and two insulated jumper wires, connect the positive (+) terminal of the battery to the other brown wire terminal on 2005 and 2006 models or the yellow wire terminal on 2007-on models, and the negative (–) terminal to the white/black wire terminal. At this point the relay should be heard to click and the meter read 0 ohms (continuity). If this is the case the relay is good. If the relay does not click when battery voltage is applied and indicates no continuity (infinite resistance) across its terminals, it is faulty and must be replaced with a new one.

4 If the relay is good, check for battery voltage at each brown wire terminal on 2005 and 2006 models or at the brown and yellow wire terminals on 2007-on models in the wiring connector with the ignition ON. If there is no voltage check the wiring between the connector and the ignition switch. If the voltage is good check the wiring between the relay and the dimmer switch, and then from the switch to the headlight for continuity, referring to the wiring diagrams at the end of the Chapter. Also make sure that all the terminals and connectors are clean and secure. Repair or renew the wiring or connectors as necessary.

5 If the LO beam does not work, and the

bulb is good, check for battery voltage at the green wire terminal on the headlight wiring connector with the ignition ON. If the HI beam does not work, and the bulb is good, check for battery voltage at the yellow wire terminal on the headlight wiring connector with the ignition ON. If voltage is present, check for continuity to earth (ground) in the black wire from the wiring connector. Repair or renew the wiring or connectors as necessary.

Sidelight

6 If the sidelight fails to work, first check the bulb (Section 7). If it is good, disconnect the sidelight wiring connector(s), and check for battery voltage at the blue wire terminal on the loom side of the connector with the ignition switch ON. If voltage is present, check for continuity to earth (ground) in the black wire from the wiring connector. If no voltage is indicated, check the wiring and connectors in sidelight circuit, referring to the wiring diagrams at the end of this Chapter.

Tail light

7 If the tail light fails to work, first check the bulb (Section 9). If it is good, remove the seat (see Chapter 7), disconnect the tail light wiring connector, and check for battery voltage at the blue wire terminal on the loom side of the connector with the ignition switch ON. If voltage is present, check for continuity to earth (ground) in the black wire from the wiring connector. If no voltage is indicated, check the wiring and connectors in the tail light circuit, referring to the wiring diagrams at the end of this Chapter.

Brake light

8 If the brake light fails to work, first check the bulb (Section 9). If it is good remove the seat (see Chapter 7), disconnect the tail light wiring connector, and check for battery voltage at the yellow wire terminal on the loom side of the connector, first with the front brake lever pulled in, then with the rear brake pedal pressed down. If voltage is present with one brake on but not the other, then the switch or its wiring is faulty. If voltage is present in both cases, check for continuity to earth (ground) in the black wire from the wiring connector. If no voltage is indicated, check the wiring and connectors between the brake light and the switches, then check the switches themselves. Refer to Section 14 for the switch testing procedures, and also to the wiring diagrams at the end of this Chapter.

Turn signals

9 See Section 11.

2005 to 2007 XT models

10 If all lights fail to work check the lighting coil as follows: trace the wiring from the top of the alternator cover on the left-hand side of the engine and disconnect it at the connector. Set a multimeter to the ohms x 1 scale and connect it across the yellow and black wire terminals in the alternator side of the connector. The resistance should be as specified at the beginning of the Chapter under the charging system specifications. If not, it is faulty and the alternator stator must be replaced with a new one.

Headlight

11 All models have a twin filament bulb, one for high beam and one for low beam. If either or both beams fail to work, first check the bulb (see Section 7). If it is good, the problem lies in the wiring or connectors, the lighting coil (Step 10), or the dimmer switch. Refer to Section 19 for the switch testing procedures, and also to the wiring diagrams at the end of this Chapter.

12 If the lighting coil is good check the pink wire between the alternator wiring connector and the dimmer switch, and then the blue/white and white/black wires from the switch to the headlight for continuity, referring to the wiring diagrams at the end of the Chapter. Also make sure that all the terminals and connectors are clean and secure. Repair or renew the wiring or connectors as necessary.

13 If the LO beam does not work, and the bulb is good, check for battery voltage at the blue/white wire terminal on the headlight wiring connector with the ignition ON. If the HI beam does not work, and the bulb is good, check for battery voltage at the white/black wire terminal on the headlight wiring connector with the engine running. If voltage is present, check for continuity to earth (ground) in the black wire from the wiring connector with the engine stopped. Repair or renew the wiring or connectors as necessary.

Sidelight

14 If the sidelight fails to work, first check the bulb (Section 7). If it is good, disconnect the sidelight wiring connector, and check for battery voltage at the pink wire terminal on the loom side of the connector with the engine running. If voltage is present, check for continuity to earth (ground) in the black wire from the wiring connector with the engine stopped. If no voltage is indicated, check the wiring and connectors in sidelight circuit.

Tail light and licence plate light

15 If either bulb fails to work, first check the bulb (Section 9). If it is good, remove the tail cover (see Chapter 7), disconnect the wiring

connector with the pink wire, and check for battery voltage at the connector with the engine running. If voltage is present, check for continuity to earth (ground) in the black wire from the wiring connector with the engine stopped. If no voltage is indicated, check the wiring and connectors in the tail light circuit, referring to the wiring diagrams at the end of this Chapter.

Brake light

16 If the brake light fails to work, first check the bulb (Section 9). If it is good remove the tail cover (see Chapter 7), disconnect the wiring connector with the red wire, and check for battery voltage at the connector, first with the front brake lever pulled in, then with the rear brake pedal pressed down. If voltage is present with one brake on but not the other, then the switch or its wiring is faulty. If voltage is present in both cases, check for continuity to earth (ground) in the black wire from the wiring connector. If no voltage is indicated, check the wiring and connectors between the brake light and the switches, then check the switches themselves. Refer to Section 14 for the switch testing procedures, and also to the wiring diagrams at the end of this Chapter.

Turn signals

17 See Section 11.

2008-on XT models

Headlight

18 All models have a twin filament bulb, one for high beam and one for low beam. If either or both beams fail to work, first check the bulb (see Section 7). If it is good, the problem lies in the wiring or connectors, the headlight relay, or the dimmer switch. Refer to Section 19 for the switch testing procedures, and also to the wiring diagrams at the end of this Chapter.

19 To check the relay remove the right-hand side panel (see Chapter 7), then displace the relay from its mount and disconnect the wiring connector **(see illustration)**. Set a multimeter to the ohms x 1 scale and connect it across the relay's red and adjacent blue wire terminals. There should be no continuity (infinite resistance). Using a fully-charged 12 volt battery and two insulated jumper wires, connect the positive (+) terminal of the battery to the other blue wire terminal, and the negative (–) terminal to the white/black wire terminal. At this point the relay should be heard to click and the meter read 0 ohms (continuity). If this is the case the relay is good. If the relay does not click when battery voltage is applied and indicates no continuity (infinite resistance) across its terminals, it is faulty and must be replaced with a new one.

20 If the relay is good, check for battery voltage at each blue wire terminal in the wiring connector with the ignition ON. If there is no voltage check the wiring between the connector and the ignition switch. If the voltage is good check the wiring between the relay and the dimmer switch, and

6.19 Headlight relay (arrowed) – later XT models

then from the switch to the headlight for continuity, referring to the wiring diagrams at the end of the Chapter. Also make sure that all the terminals and connectors are clean and secure. Repair or renew the wiring or connectors as necessary.

21 If the LO beam does not work, and the bulb is good, check for battery voltage at the light blue/white wire terminal on the headlight wiring connector with the ignition ON. If the HI beam does not work, and the bulb is good, check for battery voltage at the white/black wire terminal on the headlight wiring connector with the ignition ON. If voltage is present, check for continuity to earth (ground) in the black wire from the wiring connector. Repair or renew the wiring or connectors as necessary.

Sidelight

22 If the sidelight fails to work, first check the bulb (Section 7). If it is good, disconnect the sidelight wiring connector, and check for battery voltage at the blue wire terminal on the loom side of the connector with the ignition switch ON. If voltage is present, check for continuity to earth (ground) in the black wire from the wiring connector. If no voltage is indicated, check the wiring and connectors in sidelight circuit, referring to the wiring diagrams at the end of this Chapter.

Tail light and licence plate light

23 If either bulb fails to work, first check the bulb (Section 9). If it is good, remove the tail cover (see Chapter 7), disconnect the wiring connector with the blue wire, and check for battery voltage at the connector with the ignition switch ON. If voltage is present, check for continuity to earth (ground) in the black wire. If no voltage is indicated, check the wiring and connectors in the tail light circuit, referring to the wiring diagrams at the end of this Chapter.

Brake light

24 If the brake light fails to work, first check the bulb (Section 9). If it is good remove the tail cover (see Chapter 7), disconnect the wiring connector with the red wire, and check for battery voltage at the connector, first with the front brake lever pulled in, then with the rear brake pedal pressed down. If voltage is present with one brake on but not the other, then the switch or its wiring is

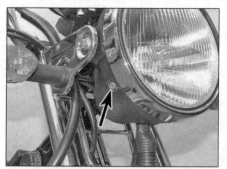

7.1a Undo the screw (arrowed) on each side . . .

7.1b . . . and release the headlight beam unit

7.1c Disconnect the wiring connectors (arrowed) and remove the beam unit

faulty. If voltage is present in both cases, check for continuity to earth (ground) in the black wire. If no voltage is indicated, check the wiring and connectors between the brake light and the switches, then check the switches themselves. Refer to Section 14 for the switch testing procedures, and also to the wiring diagrams at the end of this Chapter.

Turn signals

25 See Section 11.

7 Headlight bulb and sidelight bulb

YBR models

Headlight – 2005 to 2009 ED and all Custom models

1 Undo the screws securing the beam unit and draw it out of the shell **(see illustrations)**.

If required disconnect the headlight and sidelight wiring connectors and remove the beam unit to a bench **(see illustrations)**.

2 Pull the rubber cover off the bulbholder **(see illustration)**. Twist the bulbholder anti-clockwise and withdraw it **(see illustration)**.

3 Carefully push the bulb in and turn it anti-clockwise to release it from the holder **(see illustration)**.

4 Line up the pins on the new bulb with the slots in the holder, then push the bulb in and turn it clockwise. Fit the bulbholder into the beam unit and turn it clockwise to lock it. Fit the rubber cover.

5 If disconnected connect the headlight and sidelight wiring connectors **(see illustration 7.1c)**. Fit the beam unit into the shell, locating the hook section of the rim at the top behind the tab in the shell, and secure it with the screws **(see illustration)**.

6 Check the operation of the headlight.

Headlight – 2010 to 2013 ED models

Note: *The headlight bulb is of the quartz-halogen type. Do not touch the bulb glass as skin acids will shorten the bulb's service life. If the bulb is accidentally touched, it should be wiped carefully when cold with a rag soaked in methylated spirit and dried before fitting.*

7 Undo the screws securing the beam unit and draw it out of the shell **(see illustrations 7.1a and b)**. Pull the sidelight bulbholder out of the beam unit and disconnect the headlight wiring connector **(see illustration)**.

8 Pull the rubber cover off the bulbholder **(see illustration)**. Twist the bulbholder anti-clockwise and remove it, then lift out the bulb noting how it fits, bearing in mind the information in the **Note** above **(see illustrations)**.

9 Line up the metal body of the new bulb with the slots in the back of the beam unit, then fit the bulbholder and turn it clockwise to lock it. Install the rubber cover.

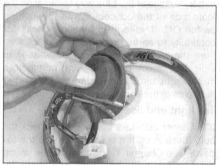

7.2a Remove the dust cover

7.2b Release the bulbholder . . .

7.3 . . . and remove the bulb

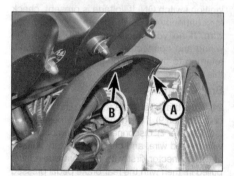

7.5 Locate the hook (A) behind the tab (B)

7.7 Disconnect the headlight wiring connector

7.8a Pull off the rubber cover . . .

10 Connect the headlight wiring connector and install the sidelight bulbholder. Fit the beam unit into the shell, locating the hook section of the rim at the top behind the tab in the shell, and secure it with the screws **(see illustration 7.5)**.

11 Check the operation of the headlight.

Sidelight

12 Undo the screws securing the beam unit and draw it out of the shell **(see illustrations 7.1a and b)**. If required disconnect the headlight and sidelight wiring connectors and remove the beam unit to a bench **(see illustration 7.1c or 7.7)**.

13 Carefully pull the bulbholder out of the beam unit, then pull the bulb out of the holder **(see illustrations)**.

14 Fit the new bulb in the bulbholder, then fit the holder into the beam unit.

15 If disconnected connect the headlight and sidelight wiring connectors **(see illustration 7.1c or 7.7)**. Fit the beam unit into the shell, locating the hook section of the rim at the top behind the tab in the shell, and secure it with the screws **(see illustration 7.5)**.

16 Check the operation of the sidelight.

Headlight – 2014-on models

Note: *The headlight bulb is of the quartz-halogen type. Do not touch the bulb glass as skin acids will shorten the bulb's service life. If the bulb is accidentally touched, it should be wiped carefully when cold with a rag soaked in methylated spirit and dried before fitting.*

17 Follow the procedure in Chapter 7 to remove the fairing assembly and disconnect the sidelight and headlight wiring connectors **(see illustration)**.

18 Pull the rubber cover off the back of the headlight unit, noting how it fits **(see illustration)**. Release the bulb retaining clip and withdraw the bulb **(see illustrations)**.

19 Line up the metal body of the new bulb with the slots in the back of the bulbholder, bearing in mind the information in the **Note** above, then secure the bulb with the retaining clip. Install the rubber cover.

20 Connect the headlight and sidelight wiring connectors, then install the fairing assembly.

21 Check the operation of the headlight.

Sidelight

22 Follow the procedure in Chapter 7 to

7.8b . . . release the bulbholder . . .

7.13a **Release the sidelight bulbholder . . .**

7.8c . . . and remove the bulb

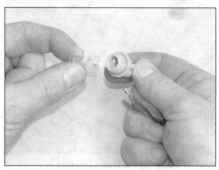

7.13b **. . . and pull the bulb out**

remove the fairing assembly and disconnect the sidelight and headlight wiring connectors **(see illustration 7.17)**.

23 Carefully pull the bulbholder out of the headlight unit, then pull the bulb out of the holder **(see illustration)**.

24 Fit the new bulb in the bulbholder, then fit the bulbholder.

25 Connect the headlight and sidelight wiring connectors, then install the fairing assembly.

26 Check the operation of the sidelight.

7.17 **Disconnect the wiring connectors**

7.18a **Remove the rubber cover**

7.18b **Release the wire clip . . .**

7.18c **. . . and withdraw the headlight bulb**

7.23 **Pull out the sidelight bulbholder**

7.28 Disconnect the wiring connector

7.29a On XT models remove the dust cover . . .

7.29b . . . release the clip . . .

7.29c . . . and remove the headlight bulb

7.35a Release the bulbholder . . .

7.35b . . . and pull the sidelight bulb out

XT models

Headlight

Note: *The headlight bulb is of the quartz-halogen type. Do not touch the bulb glass as skin acids will shorten the bulb's service life. If the bulb is accidentally touched, it should be wiped carefully when cold with a rag* soaked in methylated spirit and dried before fitting.

27 Remove the fairing (see Chapter 7).
28 Disconnect the headlight wiring connector **(see illustration)** – if required carefully pull the sidelight bulbholder out and remove the headlight to a bench **(see illustration 7.25a)**.
29 Pull the rubber cover off **(see illustration)**.

Release the bulb retaining clip and withdraw the bulb, bearing in mind the information in the **Note** above **(see illustrations)**.
30 Fit the new bulb and secure it with the retaining clip. Fit the rubber cover.

> **HAYNES HiNT** *Always use a paper towel or dry cloth when handling the new bulb to prevent injury if the bulb should break and to increase bulb life.*

31 Connect the headlight wiring connector, and if removed fit the sidelight bulbholder.
32 Check the operation of the headlight.
33 Install the fairing (see Chapter 7).

Sidelight

34 Remove the fairing (see Chapter 7).
35 Carefully pull the sidelight bulbholder out, then carefully pull the bulb out of the holder **(see illustrations)**.
36 Fit the new bulb, then fit the holder into the headlight.
37 Check the operation of the sidelight.
38 Install the fairing (see Chapter 7).

8 Headlight

Removal

YBR – 2005 to 2013 models

1 Undo the screws securing the beam unit and draw it out of the shell **(see illustrations 7.1a and b)**. Disconnect the headlight and sidelight wiring connectors **(see illustration 7.1c or 7.7)**.
2 If required release the wiring guides and disconnect all the wiring connectors, then feed the wiring out the back of the shell – note what routes where **(see illustration)**. Unscrew the nuts and withdraw the bolts securing the shell to the brackets and remove the shell **(see illustration)**. Note the collars in the grommets.

YBR – 2014-on models

3 Follow the procedure in Chapter 7 to remove the fairing assembly **(see illustration 7.17)**.
4 If required, undo the screws securing the headlight beam adjuster bracket and remove the bracket **(see illustration)**.

8.2a Disconnect, release and draw out all the wiring . . .

8.2b . . . then unscrew the nut (arrowed) and withdraw the bolt on each side

8.4 Screws (arrowed) secure headlight beam adjuster bracket

8.5 Screws secure headlight unit in the fairing

8.10 Location of the headlight beam adjuster bolt – 2014-on

8.11 On XT models turn the screw (arrowed) to adjust the height of the beam

9.1a On YBR models undo the screws (arrowed) . . .

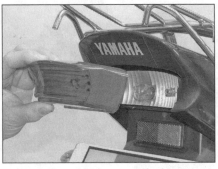

9.1b . . . and remove the lens

9.2 Release the bulb from the tail light

5 Undo the screws securing the headlight unit in the fairing and separate the components (see illustration). Note the location of the U-clips for the headlight unit screws and renew any that are loose or damaged.

XT models

6 Remove the fairing (see Chapter 7).
7 Disconnect the headlight wiring connector and carefully pull the sidelight bulbholder out (see illustrations 7.13 and 7.20a).

Installation

8 Installation is the reverse of removal. Make sure all the wiring is correctly routed, connected and secured. Check the operation of the headlight and sidelight. Check the headlight aim.

Headlight aim

Note: *An improperly adjusted headlight may cause problems for oncoming traffic or provide poor, unsafe illumination of the road ahead. Before adjusting the headlight aim, be sure to consult with local traffic laws and regulations.*

9 The headlight beam can adjusted vertically. Before making any adjustment, check that the tyre pressures are correct. Make any adjustments to the headlight aim with the machine on level ground, with the fuel tank half full and with an assistant sitting in the normal riding position.
10 On YBR models adjustment is made by pivoting the complete headlight up or down. On 2005 to 2013 models, loosen the left and right hand mounting bolts and pivot the headlight to the desired position, then tighten

the bolts. On 2014-on models, first loosen the fairing assembly mounting screws. Loosen the beam adjuster bolt on the underside of the assembly, pivot the headlight to the desired position and tighten the adjuster bolt (see illustration). Tighten the mounting screws.
11 On XT models adjustment is made by turning the adjuster screw under the headlight (see illustration).

9 Brake/tail light bulb and licence plate bulb

Brake/tail light bulb

YBR models

1 Undo the screws and remove the lens (see illustrations).
2 Carefully push the bulb in and turn it anti-clockwise to release it from the holder (see illustration).
3 Line up the pins on the new bulb with the slots in the holder, then push the bulb in and turn it clockwise, making sure it locates correctly.
4 Fit the lens – take care not to overtighten the screws as it is easy to strip the threads or crack the lens.

XT models

5 Remove the tail cover (see Chapter 7).
6 Undo the screws and remove the lens, noting the rubber seal (see illustrations).
7 Carefully push the bulb in and turn it anti-

9.6a On XT models undo the screws (arrowed) . . .

9.6b . . . and remove the lens

9.7 Release the bulb from the tail light

9.9 Make sure the seal is correctly seated

9.11 Undo the screw and detach the housing

9.12a Undo the screws (arrowed) . . .

9.12b . . . detach the bulbholder . . .

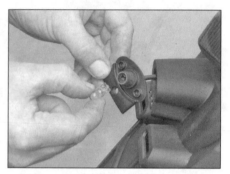

9.12c . . . and remove the licence plate bulb

clockwise to release it from the holder **(see illustration)**.

8 Line up the pins on the new bulb with the slots in the holder, then push the bulb in and turn it clockwise, making sure it locates correctly.

9 Fit the lens – make sure the rubber seal is correctly in place, and take care not to overtighten the screws as it is easy to strip the threads or crack the lens **(see illustration)**.

10 Install the tail cover (see Chapter 7).

Licence plate light bulb (XT models only)

11 Counter-hold the nut on the inner side of the mudguard and undo the screw to release the housing **(see illustration)**.

12 Undo the two screws and remove the bulbholder **(see illustrations)**. Carefully pull the bulb out of its socket and replace it with a new one **(see illustration)**.

13 Fit the bulbholder into the housing then fit the housing onto the mudguard.

10 Tail light

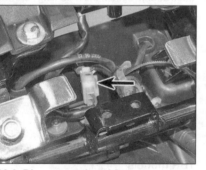

10.2 Disconnect the wiring connector (arrowed) . . .

10.3 . . . then unscrew the nuts (arrowed) and remove the tail light

YBR models

2005 to 2009 ED and all Custom models

1 Remove the seat (see Chapter 8).

2 Disconnect the wiring connector **(see illustration)**.

3 Unscrew the nuts and draw the tail light out **(see illustration)**.

4 Installation is the reverse of removal. Check the operation of the tail and brake lights.

2010-on ED models

5 Remove the side covers, seat and seat cowling (see Chapter 7).

6 Lift the rubber cover and disconnect the wiring connector **(see illustrations)**.

7 Unhook the sides of the unit from the

10.6a Lift the rubber cover . . .

10.6b . . . to access the wiring connector

frame bracket and draw the tail light out **(see illustration)**.

8 Installation is the reverse of removal. Check the operation of the tail and brake lights.

XT models

9 Remove the tail cover (see Chapter 7). Disconnect the wiring connectors **(see illustration)**.

10 Undo the screws and remove the tail light, detaching the lens if required, noting the rubber seal **(see illustration 9.6a)**.

11 Installation is the reverse of removal. Check the operation of the tail and brake lights.

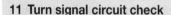

11 Turn signal circuit check

1 Most turn signal problems are the result of a burned out bulb or corroded socket. This is especially true when the turn signals function on one side (although possibly too quickly), but fail to work on the other side. If this is the case, first check the bulbs, the sockets and the wiring connectors. If all the turn signals fail to work, check the relay (see below). If it is good, the problem lies in the wiring or connectors, or the switch. Refer to Section 19 for the switch testing procedures, and also to the wiring diagrams at the end of this Chapter.

2 To check the relay remove the left-hand side cover (see Chapter 7). Disconnect the relay wiring connector **(see illustrations)**.

3 Check for battery voltage at the brown (YBR

12.1a Removing the lens on YBR-ED models

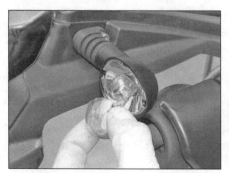

12.2 Remove the orange bulb cover

10.7 Lift off the tail light unit

11.2a Turn signal relay (arrowed) – YBR models

models) or blue (XT models) wire terminal on the loom side of the connector with the ignition ON. If no voltage is present, check the wiring from the relay to the ignition (main) switch for continuity.

12.1b Removing the lens on XT models

12.3 Release the bulb and replace it with a new one

10.9 Disconnect the wiring connectors (arrowed)

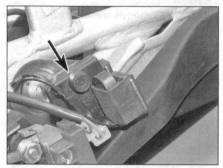

11.2b Turn signal relay (arrowed) – XT models

4 If voltage was present, short between the brown and brown/white (YBR models) or blue and brown (XT models) wire terminals on the connector using a jumper wire. Turn the ignition ON and operate the turn signal switch, first in one direction, then the other. If the turn signal lights come on in each direction (they won't flash), the relay is confirmed faulty.

5 If none of the lights come on, check the brown/white (YBR models) or brown (XT models) wire for continuity to the left-hand switch housing, and repair or renew the wiring or connectors as required.

6 If all is good so far, or if some of the lights work but not all, check the wiring for the lights concerned between the left-hand switch housing and the turn signals themselves. Repair or renew the wiring or connectors as necessary.

12 Turn signal bulbs
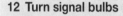

1 Undo the screw securing the lens and detach it from the housing, noting how it fits **(see illustrations)**.

2 On XT models remove the coloured bulb cover **(see illustration)**.

3 Push the bulb into the holder and twist it anti-clockwise to remove it **(see illustration)**. Check the socket terminals for corrosion and clean them if necessary.

4 Line up the pins of the new bulb with the slots in the socket, then push the bulb in and turn it clockwise until it locks into place.

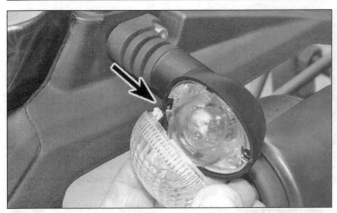

12.5 On XT models make sure the tab (arrowed) locates in the cut-out

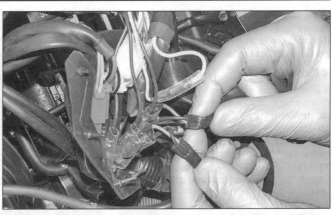

13.1 Locate the turn signal wiring connectors inside the boot – 2014-on

5 Fit the lens onto the housing, making sure it locates correctly, and install the screw **(see illustration)**. Do not over-tighten the screw as it is easy to strip the threads or crack the lens.

13 Turn signal assemblies

YBR models

1 On 2005 to 2013 models, to access the front turn signal wiring connectors, undo the screws securing the beam unit and draw it out of the shell **(see illustrations 7.1a and b)**. Trace the wiring from the turn signals and disconnect it at the connectors **(see illustration 8.2a)**. On 2014-on models, to access the front turn signal wiring connectors, first remove the fairing assembly (see Chapter 7). The wiring is located inside a protective boot – unclip the boot, identify and disconnect the turn signal connectors **(see illustration)**.

2 To access the rear turn signal wiring connectors remove the seat (see Chapter 7). Trace the wiring from the turn signal and disconnect it at the connectors **(see illustration)**.

3 Release the retainer plate securing the stem to the inside of the headlight bracket or rear mudguard **(see illustration)**. Carefully release the stem and remove the turn signal, taking care as you draw the wiring through **(see illustration)**.

4 Installation is the reverse of removal. Make

sure the stem and its retainer plate locate correctly. Check the operation of the turn signals.

XT models

5 Remove the screw securing the lens and detach it from the housing, noting how it fits **(see illustration 12.1b)**.

6 Release the bulbholder from the housing, noting how it locates, and disconnect the wiring connectors **(see illustrations)**.

7 Draw the housing off the stem, taking care not to snag the wiring **(see illustration)**.

8 Unscrew the bolt securing the stem and draw the wiring out, taking care not to snag it **(see illustrations)**.

9 Installation is the reverse of removal. Make sure the housing and the bulbholder

13.2 Rear turn signal wiring connectors (arrowed) on YBR models

13.3a On YBR models release the retainer . . .

13.3b . . . then detach the stem and draw the wiring through

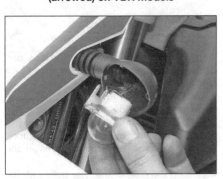

13.6a Detach the bulbholder . . .

13.6b . . . and disconnect the wiring connectors

13.7 On XT models detach the housing from the stem . . .

13.8a ... then unscrew the bolt (arrowed) and remove the stem ...

13.8b ... drawing the wiring out

13.9 Locate the tabs on the inner end of the housing in the groove around the end of the stem

locate correctly **(see illustration)**. Check the operation of the turn signals.

14 Brake light switches

Circuit check

1 Before checking the switches, and if not already done, check the brake light circuit (see Section 6).

Front brake lever switch

2 The switch is mounted in the brake master cylinder.

3 On 2005 to 2013 YBR models, undo the screws securing the headlight beam unit and draw it out of the shell **(see illustrations 7.1a and b)**. Trace the wiring from the switch and disconnect it at the connector **(see illustration 8.2a)**. On 2014-on YBR models, to access the front brake light switch wiring connector, first remove the fairing assembly

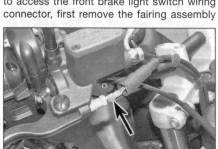

14.4 Disconnect the wiring connectors (arrowed)

14.8 Lift the boot and disconnect the wiring connectors (arrowed) – XT models

(see Chapter 7). The wiring is located inside a protective boot – unclip the boot, identify and disconnect the brake light switch connector.

4 On XT models pull the boot off the switch and disconnect the wiring connectors **(see illustration)**.

5 Using a continuity tester, connect the probes to the terminals on the switch side of the connector on YBR models, and to the terminals on the switch on XT models. With the brake lever at rest, there should be no continuity. With the lever applied, there should be continuity. If the switch does not behave as described, replace it with a new one (see below).

6 If the switch is good, check for voltage at the brown wire terminal on the loom side of the connector on YBR models and the blue wire connector on XT models, with the ignition switch ON – there should be battery voltage. If there's no voltage present, check the wiring between the connector and the ignition switch (see the wiring diagrams at the end of this Chapter). If voltage is present, check the yellow

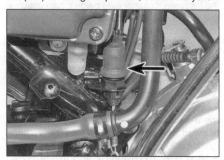

14.7 Rear brake light switch (arrowed) – YBR models

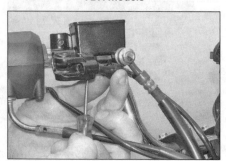

14.12 Release the clip and withdraw the switch

wire on YBR models and red wire on XT models for continuity to the brake light wiring connector, referring to the relevant wiring diagram. Repair or renew the wiring as necessary.

Rear brake pedal switch

7 On YBR models the rear brake light switch is behind the right-hand side cover. Remove the cover (see Chapter 7), then trace the wiring from the switch and disconnect it at the connector(s) **(see illustration)**.

8 On XT models the switch is hydraulic and is threaded into the top of the master cylinder. Pull the boot off the switch and disconnect the wiring connectors **(see illustration)**.

9 Using a continuity tester, connect the probes to the terminals on the switch side of the wiring connector(s) on YBR models and to the terminals on the switch on XT models. With the brake pedal at rest, there should be no continuity. With the pedal applied, there should be continuity. If the switch does not behave as described, replace it with a new one, although check first that switch is adjusted correctly (see Step 11).

10 If the switch is good, check for voltage at the brown wire terminal on the loom side of the connector on YBR models and the blue wire connector on XT models, with the ignition switch ON – there should be battery voltage. If there's no voltage present, check the wiring between the connector and the ignition switch (see the wiring diagrams at the end of this Chapter). If voltage is present, check the yellow wire on YBR models and red wire on XT models for continuity to the brake light wiring connector, referring to the relevant wiring diagram. Repair or renew the wiring as necessary.

Switch replacement

Front brake lever switch

11 The switch is mounted in the brake master cylinder.

12 On YBR models, refer to Step 3 then trace the wiring from the switch and disconnect it at the connector. Feed the wiring back to the switch, noting its routing and releasing it from any ties. Press the switch retaining clip up from the underside using a small screwdriver and draw the switch out of its housing **(see illustration)**.

13 On XT models pull the boot off the switch and disconnect the wiring connectors **(see illustration 14.4)**. Unscrew the switch from its housing.

14.17 Unhook the spring (arrowed)

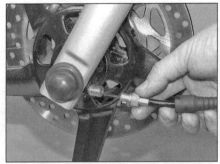

15.4 Check the speedometer cable at each end

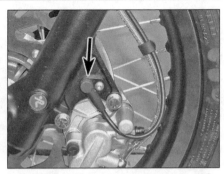

15.5 Check the speed sensor (arrowed)

14 Installation is the reverse of removal. On YBR models make sure the clip on the switch is correctly located in its hole.

Rear brake pedal switch – YBR models

15 On YBR models the rear brake light switch is behind the right-hand side cover (see illustration 14.7).
16 Remove the cover (see Chapter 7), then trace the wiring from the switch and disconnect it at the connector(s). Feed the wiring down to the switch, noting its routing and releasing it from any ties.
17 Unhook the switch spring from the pedal (see illustration).
18 Thread the switch out of its adjustment nut, then remove the nut from the mounting.
19 Installation is the reverse of removal. Make sure the brake light is activated just before the rear brake pedal takes effect. If adjustment is necessary, hold the switch body and turn the adjustment nut as required until the brake light is activated correctly – if the brake light comes on too late or not at all, turn the ring clockwise (when looked at from the top) so the switch threads up the nut. If the brake light comes on too soon or is permanently on, turn the ring anti-clockwise so the switch threads down the nut.

Rear brake pedal switch – XT models

20 The switch is hydraulic and is threaded into the top of the master cylinder.
21 Pull the boot off the switch and disconnect the wiring connectors (see illustration 14.8).
22 Unscrew the switch and detach the banjo union, noting its alignment with the master cylinder. Once disconnected, wrap plastic foodwrap around the banjo union and secure

the hose in an upright position to minimise fluid loss. Discard the sealing washers as new ones must be fitted on reassembly.
23 Connect the brake hose to the master cylinder, using new sealing washers on each side of the banjo fitting, and aligning it as noted on removal. Fit the brake light switch and tighten it. Connect the wiring and fit the rubber boot.
24 Refer to Chapter 6 and bleed the rear brake.

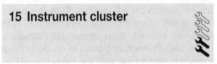

15 Instrument cluster

Check

1 There are no test details for the individual instruments.
2 If there is a problem with the instrument cluster, first check the wiring connector(s) is/are secure and that all wires and terminals are securely connected – refer below for access. On YBR models you will also need to remove the instrument cluster (see below), then unscrew the rear cover nuts and remove the cover and lift the bracket off, to access the connectors on the back of the individual instruments. Make sure the power supply to the cluster is good by checking for battery voltage at the brown wire terminal in the loom side of the wiring connector on YBR models, and at the blue wire terminal on XT models, with the ignition ON. On XT models there should also be battery voltage at the blue/red wire terminal at all times (i.e. with the ignition off).
3 Next refer to Section 2 and to the Wiring Diagrams at the end of the Chapter and check

the wiring and connectors in the relevant circuit. Also check the other components relevant to the circuit, e.g. neutral switch, dimmer switch, turn signals, fuel level sensor.
4 If there is a problem with the speedometer on YBR models first check the cable is securely connected at each end (see illustration and 15.6). Next detach the cable and make sure the inner cable is not broken – if it is, replace the cable with a new one.
5 If there is a problem with the speedometer on XT models first check the sensor is securely mounted in the bottom of the left-hand fork, and that the sensor head is not broken or covered in dirt (see illustration). Next check the sensor wire between the sensor and the instrument cluster.

Removal and installation
YBR models

6 Unscrew the knurled ring and detach the speedometer cable (see illustration).
7 On 2005 to 2013 models, undo the screws securing the beam unit and draw it out of the shell (see illustrations 7.1a and b). Trace the wiring from the instrument cluster and disconnect it at the connectors (see illustration 8.2a). Release the wiring from any guides.
8 On 2014-on models, first remove the fairing assembly (see Chapter 7). Unclip the protective boot, then trace the wiring from the instrument cluster and disconnect it at the connectors (see illustration 13.1).
9 Unscrew the two bolts, then lift the instrument cluster off the bracket (see illustration). On 2005 to 2013 models, draw the wiring out the back of the headlight shell (see illustration).

15.6 On YBR models unscrew the ring and detach the cable

15.9a Unscrew the bolts (arrowed) . . .

15.9b . . . then remove the cluster, drawing the wiring out

15.11 On XT model disconnect the wiring connector (arrowed) . . .

15.12a . . . then hold the nuts (arrowed) . . .

15.12b . . . and unscrew the bolts (arrowed)

10 Installation is the reverse of removal.

XT models

11 Remove the fairing (see Chapter 7). Disconnect the instrument cluster wiring connector **(see illustration)**.

12 Counter hold the nuts on the underside of the top yoke, noting how they secure the headlight bracket, and unscrew the two bolts on the top, then lift the instrument cluster off the top yoke **(see illustrations)**.

---

16 Instrument and warning light bulbs

YBR models

1 Remove the instrument cluster (Section 15).

2 On 2005 to 2009 ED and all Custom models, access to the bulbs varies. If necessary unscrew the rear cover nuts and remove the washers, then remove the cover and lift the bracket off **(see illustrations)**.

3 On 2010-on ED models, undo the screws and lift off the cover **(see illustrations)**. If

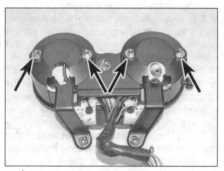

16.2a Undo the nuts (arrowed) . . .

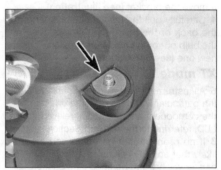

16.2b . . . noting how the shaped washers fit (arrowed) . . .

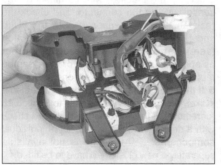

16.2c . . . and remove the cover . . .

16.2d . . . and the bracket

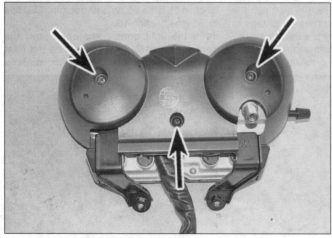

16.3a Undo the screws (arrowed) . . .

16.3b . . . and remove the cover

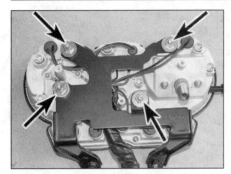

16.3c Nuts (arrowed) secure mounting bracket

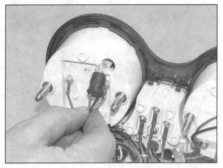

16.4a Carefully pull the bulbholder out . . .

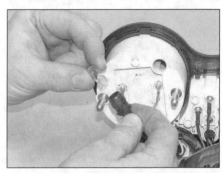

16.4b . . . then remove the bulb

necessary unscrew the bracket nuts and remove the bracket (see illustration).

4 Carefully pull the relevant bulbholder out of the back of the instrument cluster, then pull the bulb out of the holder and replace it with a new one (see illustrations).

XT models

5 All instrument and warning lights are LEDs. If a particular light fails to come on first check the component and the circuit relevant to that LED, referring to the relevant Section.

6 If no problem can be found and it seems likely that an LED has failed a new instrument cluster will have to be fitted (see Section 15).

17 Fuel level sensor

⚠️ **Warning: Petrol (gasoline) is extremely flammable, so take extra precautions when you work on any part of the fuel system. Don't smoke or allow open flames or bare light bulbs near the work area, and don't work in a garage where a natural gas-type appliance is present. If you spill any fuel on your skin, rinse it off immediately with soap and water. When you perform any kind of work on the fuel system, wear safety glasses and have a fire extinguisher suitable for a class B type fire (flammable liquids) on hand.**

YBR models

Check

1 The circuit consists of the level sensor

mounted in the fuel tank and the gauge mounted in the instrument cluster.

2 If the gauge does not work as it should first check the wiring between the sensor connector and the instrument cluster for continuity, referring to Section 15 for access to the instrument cluster wiring, Section 2 for continuity testing details, and to the end of the Chapter for the wiring diagrams. If the wiring is good check the power supply to the cluster (Section 15, Step 2).

3 If the wiring is good, remove the level sensor from the tank (see below). Check that no fuel has entered the float due to a leak, and check that the arm moves up and down smoothly.

4 Connect the probes of an ohmmeter to the green (+) and black (-) wire terminals on the sensor side of the connector and check the resistance of the sensor in both the FULL and EMPTY positions for each connection (see illustrations). If the readings are not as specified at the beginning of the Chapter, replace the sensor with a new one.

5 If the sensor and all the wiring is good then it is likely the gauge is faulty – refer to Section 15 for removal of the instrument cluster, and check with a dealer as to the availability of individual components. If the gauge is not available separately a new cluster will have to be fitted.

Replacement

6 Remove the fuel tank (see Chapter 3A or 3B).

7 Make sure the cap is secure, then turn the tank over and lay it on a cushion of rags to protect it and soak up any fuel that may leak.

8 On 2005 and 2006 models unscrew the bolts securing the sensor and carefully manoeuvre

it out of the tank, taking care not to snag the float arm, and noting which way it fits. Discard the seal as a new one must be used. Fit a new seal onto the tank. Fit the sensor into the tank. Tighten the bolts evenly and a little at a time in a criss-cross pattern to the torque setting specified at the beginning of the Chapter.

9 On 2007-on models the sensor is part of the fuel pump assembly – refer to Chapter 3B.

10 Install the tank (see Chapter 3A or 3B), and check carefully for leaks around the sensor before using the bike.

XT models

Check

11 The circuit consists of the sensor in the fuel tank, and the warning light in the instrument cluster. The warning light comes on when the amount of fuel drops to 2 litres.

12 If the warning light does not work, remove the left-hand fuel tank panel (see Chapter 7). Disconnect the sensor wiring connector (see illustration).

13 Short between the terminals in the loom side of the connector using an auxiliary piece of wire, with the ignition ON – the warning light should come on. If it doesn't check the wiring connector for a loose wire or corroded or broken terminal, then check the grey wire between the sensor and the instrument cluster and the black wire to earth for continuity (see Section 2). If the wiring is all good the LED has failed (see Section 16).

14 If the light does come on remove the sensor (Step 15). First make sure the float moves smoothly and freely on its rod (see

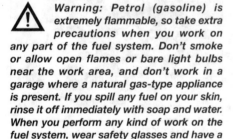

17.4a On YBR models check the resistance with the float in the full position . . .

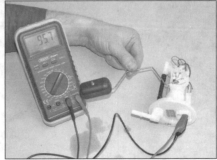

17.4b . . . and the empty position

17.12 Disconnect the wiring connector (arrowed) – XT models

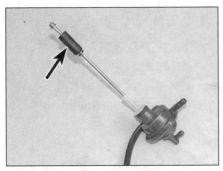

17.14 Check the sensor float (arrowed) as described – XT models

illustration). Next connect the probes of a continuity tester to the terminals in the sensor connector. With the sensor float at the top of its rod there should be no continuity. With it at the bottom there should be continuity. If not replace the sensor with a new one.

Replacement

15 The sensor is part of the fuel tap assembly – refer to Chapter 3A.

18 Ignition switch

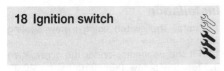

 Warning: To prevent the risk of short circuits, disconnect the battery negative (–) lead before making any ignition (main) switch checks.

Check

1 On 2005 to 2013 YBR models, undo the screws securing the beam unit and draw it out of the shell **(see illustrations 7.1a and b)**. On 2014-on YBR models, first remove the fairing assembly (see Chapter 7), then unclip the wiring boot to access the wiring.
2 On XT models remove the fairing (see Chapter 7).
3 Trace the wiring from the ignition switch and disconnect it at the connector.
4 Using an ohmmeter or a continuity tester, check the continuity of the connector terminal pairs (see the wiring diagrams at the end of this Chapter). Continuity should exist between the terminals connected by a solid line on the diagram when the switch is in the indicated position.
5 If the switch fails the test, check for continuity in the wiring between the connector and the switch, and check the terminals on the switch. If necessary replace the switch with a new one.
6 If the switch is good, check for battery voltage at the red wire terminal on YBR models or the blue/red wire terminal on XT models, on the loom side of the connector. If there is none, check for continuity in the wire to the starter relay (Section 25), and check the fuse (Section 5).

Removal

7 Remove the instrument cluster (see Section 15).
8 Trace the wiring from the ignition switch

18.10 Ignition switch bolts (arrowed) – XT models

and disconnect it at the connector. Feed the wiring back to the switch, freeing it from any clips and ties and noting its routing.
9 On YBR models remove the top yoke (see Chapter 1, Section 16, and follow the relevant steps). The switch is secured by shear-head bolts, which have to be drifted round until loose using a punch.
10 On XT models undo the security Torx screws, for which a special Torx bit is needed, and remove the switch from the top yoke **(see illustration)**.

Installation

11 Installation is the reverse of removal. On YBR models fit new bolts and tighten them until their heads shear off. Make sure the wiring connector is correctly routed and securely connected.

19 Handlebar switches

Check

1 Generally speaking, the switches are reliable and trouble-free. Most troubles, when they do occur, are caused by dirty or corroded contacts, but wear and breakage of internal parts is a possibility that should not be overlooked. If breakage does occur, the entire switch and related wiring harness will have to be replaced with a new one, as individual parts are not available.
2 The switches can be checked for continuity using an ohmmeter or a continuity test light. Disconnect the battery negative (–) cable,

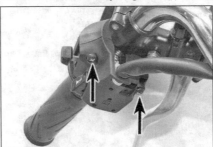

19.12a Left-hand switch housing screws (arrowed) – YBR models

which will prevent the possibility of a short circuit, before making the checks.
3 On 2005 to 2013 YBR models, undo the screws securing the beam unit and draw it out of the shell **(see illustrations 7.1a and b)**. On 2014-on YBR models, first remove the fairing assembly (see Chapter 7), then unclip the wiring boot to access the wiring **(see illustration 13.1)**.
4 On XT models remove the fairing (see Chapter 7).
5 Trace the wiring from the relevant switch and disconnect it at the connector(s).
6 Check for continuity between the terminals of the switch connector with the switch in the various positions (i.e. switch off – no continuity, switch on – continuity) – see the wiring diagrams at the end of this Chapter. Continuity should exist between the terminals connected by a solid line on the diagram when the switch is in the indicated position.
7 If the continuity check indicates a problem exists, displace the switch housing and spray the switch contacts with electrical contact cleaner (there is no need to remove the switch completely). If they are accessible, the contacts can be scraped clean with a knife or polished with crocus cloth. If switch components are damaged or broken, it will be obvious when the switch is disassembled.

Removal

8 On 2005 to 2013 YBR models, undo the screws securing the beam unit and draw it out of the shell **(see illustrations 7.1a and b)**. On 2014-on YBR models, first remove the fairing assembly (see Chapter 7), then unclip the wiring boot to access the wiring **(see illustration 13.1)**.
9 On XT models remove the fairing (see Chapter 7).
10 Trace the wiring from the relevant switch and disconnect it at the connector(s). Feed the wiring back to the switch, freeing it from any clips and ties and noting its routing.
11 To remove the right-hand switch on YBR models, refer to Chapter 3A or 3B for removal of the throttle cable from the switch (there is no need to detach it from the carburettor or throttle body), which involves detaching the switch housing from the handlebars.
12 To remove the left-hand switch on YBR models, and to remove either switch on XT models, undo the switch housing screws and free it from the handlebar by separating the halves **(see illustrations)** – on XT models

19.12b Left-hand switch housing screws (arrowed) – XT models

19.12c Right-hand switch housing screws (arrowed) – XT models . . .

19.12d . . . slacken the throttle housing screws (arrowed) and twist the housing round to access the front screw

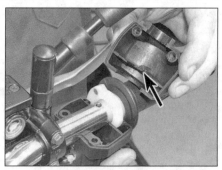

19.13 Locate the pin (arrowed) in the handlebar hole

slacken the throttle housing screws slightly and pivot the housing round slightly for access to the front screw on the right-hand housing **(see illustrations)**.

Installation

13 Installation is the reverse of removal. Make sure the locating pin in the switch housing locates in the hole in the handlebar **(see illustration)**. Refer to Chapter 3A or 3B for installation of the throttle cable and right-hand switch housing on YBR models.

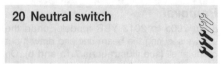

20 Neutral switch

1 The neutral switch is part of the starter safety circuit (see Chapter 1).

Check

2 Before checking the electrical circuit, check the neutral warning light in the instrument cluster (Section 16).
3 The switch is located in the left-hand side of the transmission casing below the front sprocket cover. Slacken the wire terminal screw and detach the wire **(see illustration)**.
4 Make sure the transmission is in neutral. With the connector disconnected and the ignition switch ON, the neutral light should be out. If not, the wire between the connector and instrument cluster must be earthed (grounded) at some point.

5 Check for continuity between the switch terminal and the crankcase. With the transmission in neutral, there should be continuity. With the transmission in gear, there should be no continuity. If the tests prove otherwise, then remove the switch (see below) and check whether the plunger is bent or damaged, or just stuck. Replace the switch with a new one if necessary.
6 If the continuity tests prove the switch is good, check for voltage at the wire terminal with the ignition on. If there's no voltage present, check the wire between the switch and the instrument cluster (see the wiring diagrams at the end of this Chapter).
7 If the switch is good, check the other components (sidestand switch, clutch switch and diodes) and their wiring and connectors in the starter circuit as described in the relevant sections of this Chapter. If all components are good, check the wiring between the various components (see the wiring diagrams at the end of this Chapter). Repair or renew the wiring as required.

Removal

8 The switch is located in the left-hand side of the transmission casing below the front sprocket cover. Stand the bike upright – if it is on the sidestand you will have to drain some oil before removing the switch (see Chapter 1).
9 Undo the wire terminal screw and detach the wire **(see illustration 20.3)**.
10 Clean the area around the switch. Unscrew

and remove the switch. Discard the sealing washer,
11 Check the contact plunger on the inner end of the switch for wear and damage, and make sure it moves smoothly against the pressure of its spring. Make sure the wiring connector end of the switch is not damaged. Replace the switch with a new one if necessary.

Installation

12 Install the switch using a new sealing washer.
13 Fit the connector under the screw then tighten the screw **(see illustration 20.3)**. Check the operation of the switch.

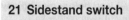

21 Sidestand switch

1 The sidestand switch is part of the starter safety circuit (see Chapter 1). It is not fitted on 2005 and 2006 YBR models.

Check

2 On YBR models the switch is mounted on the stand bracket **(see illustration)**. Remove the left-hand side cover to access the wiring connector (see Chapter 7).
3 On XT models the sidestand switch is mounted on the frame above the stand **(see illustration)**. Remove the seat to access the wiring connector (see Chapter 7).
4 Trace the wiring from the switch and

20.3 Slacken the screw (arrowed) and detach the neutral wire

21.2 Sidestand switch (arrowed) – YBR models

21.3 Sidestand switch (arrowed) – XT models

21.4a Sidestand switch wiring connector (arrowed) – YBR models

21.4b Sidestand switch wiring connector (arrowed) – XT models

21.5 Make sure the plunger works properly

disconnect it at the connector **(see illustrations)**.

5 Check the operation of the switch using an ohmmeter or continuity test light. Connect the meter between the terminals on the switch side of the connector. With the sidestand up there should be continuity (zero resistance) between the terminals, and with the stand down there should be no continuity (infinite resistance). Make sure the switch plunger is clean and not stuck, and that it moves freely and smoothly in and out of the switch under spring pressure **(see illustration)**.

6 If the switch does not perform as expected, it is faulty and must be replaced with a new one. If the switch is good, check the other components (clutch switch, neutral switch and diodes) and their wiring and connectors in the starter circuit as described in the relevant sections of this Chapter. If all components are good, check the wiring between the various components (see the wiring diagrams at the end of this Chapter). Repair or renew the wiring as required.

Replacement

7 On YBR models the switch is mounted on the stand bracket **(see illustration 21.2)**. Remove the left-hand side cover to access the wiring connector (see Chapter 7).
8 On XT models the sidestand switch is mounted on the frame above the stand **(see illustration 21.3)**. Remove the seat to access the wiring connector (see Chapter 7).
9 Trace the wiring from the switch and disconnect it at the connector **(see**

illustration 21.4a or b). Feed the wiring back to the switch, freeing it from any clips and ties and noting its routing.
10 Make sure the sidestand is retracted. Undo the screws and remove the switch **(see illustration 21.2 or 21.3)**.
11 Fit the new switch and tighten the screws.
12 Feed the wiring up to its connector, making sure it is correctly routed and secured by any clips and ties.
13 Reconnect the wiring connector and check the operation of the switch.
14 Install the side cover or seat (see Chapter 7).

22 Clutch switch

1 The clutch switch is part of the starter safety circuit (see Chapter 1).

Check

2 On 2005 to 2013 YBR models, undo the screws securing the beam unit and draw it out of the shell **(see illustrations 7.1a and b)**. On 2014-on YBR models, first remove the fairing assembly (see Chapter 7), then unclip the wiring boot to access the wiring **(see illustration 13.1)**. Trace the wiring from the switch and disconnect it at the connector.
3 On XT models pull the boot off the switch and disconnect the wiring connectors **(see illustration)**.
4 Connect the probes of an ohmmeter or a continuity tester to the terminals on the switch

side of the connector on YBR models, and to the terminals on the switch on XT models. With the clutch lever pulled in, continuity should be indicated. With the clutch lever out, no continuity (infinite resistance) should be indicated. If the results are not as stated remove the switch (see below) and check the plunger for damage. Replace the switch with a new one if necessary.
5 If the switch is good, check the other components (sidestand switch, neutral switch and diodes) and their wiring and connectors in the starter circuit as described in the relevant sections of this Chapter. If all components are good, check the wiring between the various components (see the wiring diagrams at the end of this Chapter).

Replacement

6 The clutch switch is mounted in the clutch lever bracket.
7 On YBR models, refer to Step 2 then trace the wiring from the switch and disconnect it at the connector. Feed the wiring back to the switch, noting its routing and releasing it from any ties. Press the switch retaining clip up from the underside using a small screwdriver and draw the switch out of its housing **(see illustration)**.
8 On XT models pull the boot off the switch and disconnect the wiring connectors **(see illustration 22.3)**. Unscrew the switch from its housing **(see illustration)**.
9 Installation is the reverse of removal. On YBR models make sure the clip on the switch is correctly located in its hole.

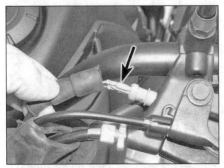

22.3 Clutch switch wiring connectors (arrowed) – XT models

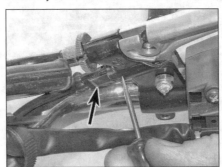

22.7 Release the clip and withdraw the switch – YBR models

22.8 Unscrew and remove the switch – XT models

23 Diodes

1 The diode(s) for the starter safety circuit are housed in a block or blocks which plug into the wiring loom, and on YBR models are wrapped in insulating tape. 2005 and 2006 YBR models have one diode in the main loom near the ignition coil, and 2007-on models have three diodes **(see illustration)** – remove the fuel tank for access (see Chapter 3A or 3B). XT models have three diodes within one unit that plugs into the loom behind the right-hand side cover **(see illustration)** – remove the cover for access (see Chapter 7).

2 Remove the diode from the loom.

3 Test the diode(s) using an ohmmeter or continuity tester.

4 On YBR models connect the meter probes between the two wire terminals on the diode block. Now reverse the probes. The diode should show no continuity in one direction and no continuity in the other. If it doesn't behave as stated, replace the diode block with a new one. On 2007-on YBR models refer to the wiring diagram at the end of this chapter to identify which one of the three diodes you need to test.

5 On XT models connect the positive (+) probe to the red/black. Pink/black or yellow (according to which diode is being tested) wire terminal on the diode block and the negative (–) probe to the yellow/green wire terminal. The diode should show continuity.

23.1a Diode blocks (arrowed) – 2007-on YBR models

Now reverse the probes. The diode should show no continuity. If it doesn't behave as stated, replace the diode block with a new one.

6 If the diode block is good, push it back into its socket, then check the other components in the starter circuit as described in the relevant sections of this Chapter. If all components are good, check the wiring between the various components (see the wiring diagrams at the end of this Chapter).

24 Horn

Check

1 The horn is mounted on the front of the frame on YBR models and between the

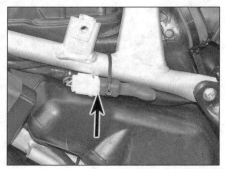

23.1b Diode block (arrowed) – XT models

top and bottom yokes on XT models **(see illustrations)**. Turn the handlebars as required for best access.

2 Disconnect the wiring connectors from the horn. Check them for loose wires. Using two jumper wires, apply voltage from a fully-charged 12V battery directly to the terminals on the horn. If the horn doesn't sound, replace it with a new one.

3 If the horn works check for voltage at the brown (YBR models) or orange (XT models) wire connector with the ignition ON, and on XT models with the horn button pressed. If voltage is present, on YBR models check the pink wire for continuity to earth with the horn button pushed, and on XT models check the black wire for continuity straight to earth.

4 If no voltage was present, check the brown (YBR models) or orange (XT models) wire for continuity between the horn and the ignition switch on YBR models and the horn button on XT models (see the wiring diagrams at the end of this Chapter).

5 If all the wiring and connectors are good, check the ignition switch on YBR models (see Section 18) or the horn button contacts in the switch housing on XT models (see Section 19).

Replacement

6 The horn is mounted on the front of the frame on YBR models and between the top and bottom yokes on XT models **(see illustrations 24.1a and b or 24.1c)**. Turn the handlebars as required for best access.

7 Disconnect the wiring connectors from the horn. Unscrew the bolt and remove the horn.

8 Install the horn, connect the wiring, and check that it works.

25 Starter relay

Check

1 If the starter circuit is faulty, first check the fuse (see Section 5).

2 The starter relay is located behind the left-hand side cover **(see illustrations)** – remove the cover for access (see Chapter 7).

3 Lift the rubber terminal cover and unscrew

24.1a Horn wiring connectors (arrowed) . . .

24.1b . . . and mounting bolt (arrowed) – YBR models

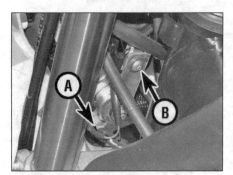

24.1c Horn wiring connectors (A) and mounting bolt (B) – XT models

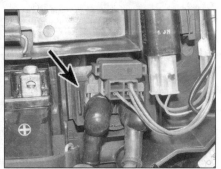

25.2a Starter relay (arrowed) – YBR models

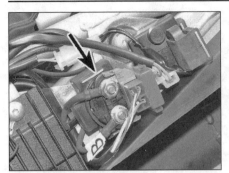

25.2b Starter relay (arrowed) – XT models

25.3 Unscrew the nut (arrowed) and detach the lead

25.4 Measure the resistance between the coil terminals (arrowed)

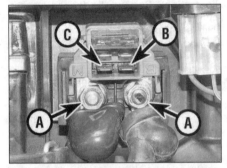

25.5 Connect the tester to the terminals (A), the battery + to (B) and the battery – to (C)

25.11a Disconnect the wiring connector . . .

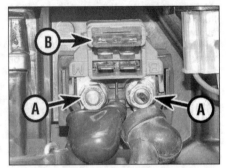

25.11b . . . then unscrew the nuts (A) and detach the leads, and if required remove the fuse (B)

the nut (marked M) securing the starter motor lead **(see illustration)**; position the lead away from the relay terminal. With the ignition switch ON, the engine kill switch in the RUN position, and the transmission in neutral, press the starter switch. The relay should be heard to click.

4 If the relay doesn't click, switch off the ignition and remove the relay as described below; test it as follows. First check the resistance of the coil by connecting an ohmmeter across the two wire terminals next to the B and M **(see illustration)** – it should be as specified at the beginning of the chapter.

5 Now connect the tester across the relay's starter motor and battery lead terminals (marked B and M) **(see illustration)**. There should be no continuity. Using a fully-charged 12 volt battery and two insulated jumper wires, connect the positive (+) terminal of the battery to the wiring connector terminal on the relay next to the B, and the negative (–) terminal to the terminal next to the M. At this point the relay should be heard to click and the multimeter read 0 ohms (continuity). If this is the case the relay is proved good. If the relay does not click when battery voltage is applied and indicates no continuity (infinite resistance) across its terminals, it is faulty and must be replaced with a new one.

6 If the relay is good, check the main lead from the battery to the relay, and the lead from the relay to the starter motor – check that the terminals and connectors at each end are tight and corrosion-free.

7 Next check the wiring from the switch housing to the relay wiring connector, referring to Section 2 and to the wiring Diagrams at the end of the chapter, and then check the switches (see Section 19).

8 If all appears good check the neutral switch, clutch switch, sidestand switch (except early YBR) and diodes as described in the relevant sections of this Chapter. If all components are good, check the wiring between the various components (see the wiring diagrams at the end of this Chapter).

Replacement

9 The starter relay is located behind the left-hand side cover **(see illustration 25.2a or b)** – remove the cover for access (see Chapter 7).

10 Disconnect the battery terminals, remembering to disconnect the negative (–) terminal first (see Section 3).

11 Disconnect the relay wiring connector **(see illustration)**. Lift the insulating cover and unscrew the nuts securing the starter motor and battery leads to the relay and detach the leads **(see illustration)**. Remove the relay from its rubber sleeve. If the relay is being replaced with a new one, remove the fuse (except on 2005 to 2007 XT models which have a separate fuse holder).

12 Installation is the reverse of removal. Make sure the terminal bolts are securely tightened. Do not forget to fit the main fuse into the relay, where applicable. Connect the negative (–) lead last when reconnecting the battery.

26 Starter motor removal and installation

Removal

1 Disconnect the battery negative (–) lead (see Section 3). The starter motor is mounted on the front of the engine.

2 Peel back the rubber terminal cover on the starter motor. Undo the screw securing the starter lead to the motor and detach the lead – if the terminal is corroded spray it with some penetrating fluid and leave it for a while before attempting to undo it **(see illustration)**.

3 Unscrew the two bolts securing the

26.2 Pull back the terminal cover then undo the screw and detach the lead

26.3a Unscrew the two bolts . . .

26.3b . . . and remove the starter motor

26.5 Fit a new O-ring and lubricate it

starter motor to the crankcase **(see illustration)**. Slide the starter motor out and remove it **(see illustration)**.

4 Remove the O-ring on the end of the starter motor and discard it as a new one must be used **(see illustration 26.5)**.

Installation

5 Fit a new O-ring onto the end of the starter motor, making sure it is seated in its groove **(see illustration)**. Apply a smear of engine oil to the O-ring.

6 Manoeuvre the motor into position and slide it into the crankcase **(see illustration 26.3b)**. Ensure that the starter motor teeth mesh correctly with those of the starter idle/reduction gear. Install the mounting bolts and tighten them **(see illustration 26.3a)**.

7 Connect the starter lead to the motor and secure it with the screw **(see illustration 26.2)**. Fit the rubber cover over the terminal.

8 Connect the battery negative (–) lead.

---

27 Starter motor overhaul

Check

1 Remove the starter motor (see Section 26). Cover the body in some rag and clamp the motor in a soft-jawed vice – do not over-tighten it.

2 Using a fully-charged 12 volt battery and

two insulated jumper wires, connect the positive (+) terminal of the battery to the protruding terminal on the starter motor, and the negative (–) terminal to one of the motor's mounting lugs. At this point the starter motor should spin. If this is the case the motor is proved good, though it is worth overhauling it if you suspect it of not working properly under load. If the motor does not spin, disassemble it for inspection.

Disassembly

3 Remove the starter motor (see Section 26).

4 Note any alignment marks between the main housing and the front and rear covers, or make your own if they aren't clear **(see illustration)**.

5 Unscrew the two long bolts, noting the washers where fitted, and the O-rings, then remove the front cover from the motor **(see**

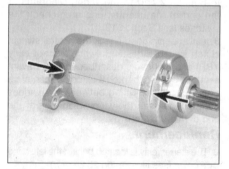

27.4 Note the alignment marks between the housing and the covers (arrowed)

illustration). Remove the tabbed washer, either from the cover or the shaft, and the shim **(see illustration)**.

6 Draw the main housing off the armature **(see illustration)** – it is held in by the attraction of the magnets.

7 Withdraw the armature from the rear cover **(see illustration)**.

8 At this stage check for continuity between the terminal and its brush – there should be continuity (zero resistance). Check for continuity between the terminal bolt and the cover – there should be no continuity (infinite resistance). Also check for continuity between the other brush and the rear cover – there should be continuity (zero resistance). If there is no continuity when there should be or *vice versa*, identify the faulty component and replace it with a new one.

9 Slide the brushes out of their housings

27.5a Unscrew and remove the two bolts (arrowed) . . .

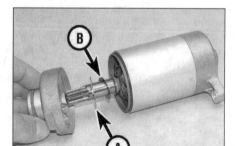

27.5b . . . then remove the front cover, the tabbed washer (A) and shim (B)

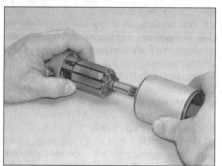

27.6 Draw the housing off the armature

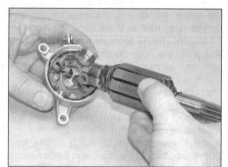

27.7 Draw the armature out of the rear cover

27.9 Slide the brushes out and remove the springs (arrowed)

27.10 Undo the screws (arrowed) and remove the brushplate

27.11 Measure the length of each brush

27.12a Check the bars for wear and damage . . .

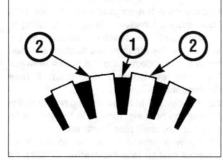

27.12b . . . and make sure the Mica (1) is the correct depth below the bars (2)

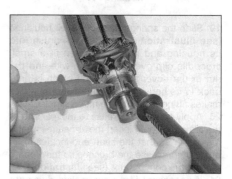

27.13a There should be continuity between the bars . . .

and remove the springs for safekeeping **(see illustration)**.

10 If required undo the two screws securing the brushplate, noting how one secures a brush, and remove the washers **(see illustration)**. Lift the brushplate out of the cover.

Inspection

11 The parts of the starter motor that are most likely to require attention are the brushes. Measure the length of each brush and compare the results to the length listed in this Chapter's Specifications **(see illustration)**. If either of the brushes are worn beyond the service limit, fit a new set (Step 10) – you will have to unsolder the positive brush from the terminal, and solder the new one on. If the brushes are not worn excessively, nor cracked, chipped, or otherwise damaged, they may be reused. Check the brush springs for distortion and

fatigue. Check the brushplate for damage.
12 Inspect the commutator bars on the armature for scoring, scratches and discoloration **(see illustrations)**. The commutator can be cleaned and polished with crocus cloth, but do not use sandpaper or emery paper. After cleaning, wipe away any residue with a cloth soaked in electrical system cleaner or denatured alcohol. Make sure the insulating Mica is 1.5 mm below the depth of each commutator bar.
13 Using an ohmmeter or a continuity test light, check for continuity between the commutator bars **(see illustration)**. Continuity should exist between each bar and all of the others. Also, check for continuity between the commutator bars and the armature shaft **(see illustration)**. There should be no continuity (infinite resistance) between the commutator and the shaft. If the checks indicate otherwise, the armature is faulty.

14 Check the front end of the armature shaft for worn, cracked, chipped and broken teeth. If any are found inspect the starter clutch and gears (see Chapter 2, Section 14).
15 Inspect the front and rear covers for signs of cracks or wear. Check the oil seal and the needle bearing in the front cover and the bush in the rear cover for wear and damage **(see illustrations)**.
16 Inspect the magnets in the main housing and the housing itself for cracks.
17 Inspect the housing sealing rings and long bolt O-rings for signs of damage, deformation and deterioration and replace them with new ones if necessary.

Reassembly

18 If removed fit the brushplate into the rear cover, making sure it locates correctly, then fit the washers and the screws, not forgetting to secure the brush **(see illustration 27.10)**.

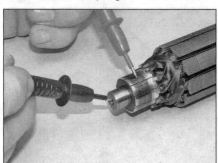

27.13b . . . and no continuity between the bars and the shaft

27.15a Check the bearing and seal in the front cover . . .

27.15b . . . and the bush (arrowed) in the rear cover

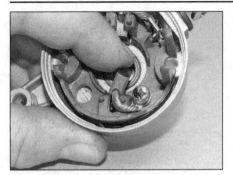

27.19a Push each brush into its housing . . .

27.19b . . . then fit crocodile clips to keep them retracted

27.20 Fit the armature into the rear cover making sure the brushes locate correctly

19 Slide the springs back into their housings **(see illustration 27.9)**. Fit each brush into its housing and push it in, then fit a small crocodile clip over each brush wire and the rim of the cover so that each brush is held back in its housing **(see illustrations)** – this makes fitting the armature much simpler.

20 Apply a smear of grease to the rear end of the armature shaft. Insert the armature into the rear cover so that the shaft end locates in its bush, then release the brushes so they locate against the commutator **(see illustration)**.

21 If necessary fit a new sealing ring onto the rear of the main housing. Grasp both the armature and the rear cover in one hand and hold them together – this will prevent the armature being drawn out by the magnets in the housing. Note however that you should take care not to let the housing be drawn

forcibly onto the armature or you will trap your fingers. Carefully allow the housing to be drawn onto the armature, making sure the end where the magnets are further recessed faces the rear cover, and the marks between the cover and housing align (Step 4) **(see illustrations)**.

22 If necessary fit a new sealing ring onto the front of the housing, then slide the shim onto the armature shaft **(see illustration)**.

23 Apply a smear of grease to the front cover oil seal lip **(see illustration 27.15a)**. Fit the tabbed washer into the cover so that its tabs locate in the cut-outs **(see illustration)**. Slide the front cover into position, aligning the marks **(see illustration 27.4)**.

24 Check the marks made on removal are correctly aligned then fit the long bolts, not forgetting the O-rings (using new

ones if necessary) and tighten them **(see illustration)**.

25 Install the starter motor (see Section 26).

28 Charging system testing

1 If the performance of the charging system is suspect, the system as a whole should be checked first, followed by testing of the individual components. **Note:** *Before beginning the checks, make sure the battery is fully charged and that all system connections are clean and tight.*

2 Checking the output of the charging system and the performance of the various components within the charging system requires the use of a multimeter (with voltage, current, and resistance functions). If a multimeter is not available, the job of checking the charging system should be left to a Yamaha dealer.

3 When making the checks, follow the procedures carefully to prevent incorrect connections or short circuits resulting in irreparable damage to electrical system components.

Leakage test

Caution: Always connect an ammeter in series, never in parallel with the battery, otherwise it will be damaged. Do not turn the ignition ON or operate the starter motor when the ammeter is connected – a sudden surge in current will blow the meter's fuse.

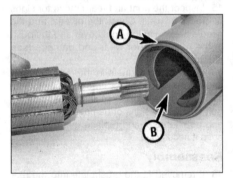

27.21a Make sure the sealing ring (A) is in place and the housing is the correct way round (B) . . .

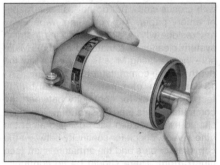

27.21b . . . then carefully allow the magnets to draw the housing over the shaft

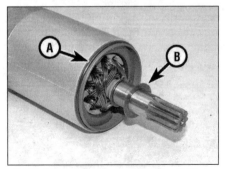

27.22 Make sure the sealing ring (A) is in place then fit the shim (B)

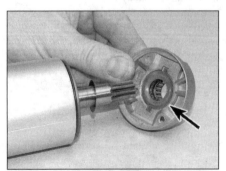

27.23 Fit the washer (arrowed), locating the tabs in the cut-outs

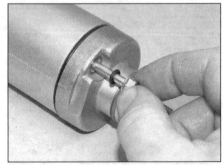

27.24 Fit the long bolts with their O-rings

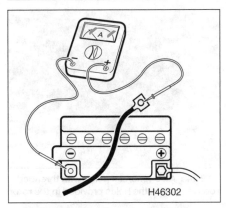

28.5 Checking the charging system leakage rate - connect the meter as shown

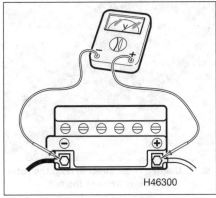

28.9 Checking regulated voltage output – connect the meter as shown

4 Ensure the ignition is OFF, then disconnect the battery negative (-) lead (see Section 3).
5 Set the multimeter to the Amps function and connect its negative (-) probe to the battery negative (-) terminal, and positive (+) probe to the disconnected negative (-) lead **(see illustration)**. Always set the meter to a high amps range initially and then bring it down to the mA (milli Amps) range; if there is a high current flow in the circuit it may blow the meter's fuse.
6 Battery current leakage should not exceed the maximum limit (see Specifications). If a higher leakage rate is shown there is a short circuit in the wiring, although if an after-market immobiliser or alarm is fitted, its current draw should be taken into account. Disconnect the meter and reconnect the battery negative (-) lead.
7 If leakage is indicated, refer to *Wiring Diagrams* at the end of this Chapter to systematically disconnect individual electrical components and repeat the test until the source is identified.

Regulated output test

8 On YBR models remove the left-hand side cover (see Chapter 7). On XT models remove the seat (see Chapter 7). Start the engine and warm it up.
9 To check the regulated (DC) voltage output, allow the engine to idle. Connect a multimeter set to the 0-20 volts DC scale across the terminals of the battery with the positive (+) meter probe to battery positive (+) terminal and the negative (-) meter probe to battery negative (-) terminal **(see illustration)**.
10 Slowly increase the engine speed to 5000 rpm and note the reading obtained. Compare the result with the Specification at the beginning of this Chapter. If the regulated voltage output is outside the specification, check the alternator and the regulator (see Sections 29 and 30).

 Clues to a faulty regulator are constantly blowing bulbs, with brightness varying considerably with engine speed, and battery overheating.

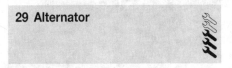

29 Alternator

Check

1 On YBR models remove the left-hand side cover (see Chapter 7).
2 Trace the wiring from the alternator on the left-hand side of the engine and disconnect it at the 4-pin connector on 2005 to 2007 XT models, and at the 3-pin connector on all other models **(see illustrations)**. Check the connector terminals for corrosion and security.
3 Using a multimeter set to the ohms x 1 (ohmmeter) scale measure the resistance

of the stator's charging coil(s) as described according to model, as follows:
4 On 2005 and 2006 YBR models, and on 2008-on XT models, measure between the two white wire terminals on the alternator side of the connector, then check for continuity between each terminal and ground (earth).
5 On 2007-on YBR models measure between each pair of white wire terminals on the alternator side of the connector, taking a total of three readings, then check for continuity between each terminal and ground (earth).
6 On 2005 to 2007 XT models, measure between the white and black wire terminals on the alternator side of the connector, then check for continuity between each terminal and ground (earth).
7 If the coil windings are in good condition the reading(s) should be within the range shown in the Specifications at the start of this Chapter, and there should be no continuity (infinite resistance) between the terminals and ground (earth). If not, the alternator stator coil assembly is at fault and should be replaced with a new one. **Note:** *Before condemning the stator coils, check the fault is not due to damaged wiring between the connector and the coils.*

Removal

8 On YBR models remove the left-hand side cover (see Chapter 7).
9 Remove the front sprocket cover **(see illustrations)**.
10 Drain the engine oil (see Chapter 1).
11 Trace the wiring from the alternator on the

29.2a Alternator wiring connector (arrowed) – 2007-on YBR models

29.2b Alternator wiring connector (arrowed) – 2008-on XT models

29.9a Sprocket cover bolts (arrowed) – YBR models

29.9b Sprocket cover bolts (arrowed) – XT models

29.12 Unscrew the bolts (arrowed) and remove the cover

29.13 Using a rotor strap to hold the rotor while unscrewing the nut

29.14a A commercial puller with threaded rods located in the holes provided in the rotor

29.14b Remove the Woodruff key (A) if loose, and slide the thrust washer (B) off

29.15a Unscrew the stator bolts (arrowed) . . .

29.15b . . . the CKP sensor bolts (A), wiring clamp screw (B) and free the grommet (C)

left-hand side of the engine and disconnect it at the connectors **(see illustration 29.2a or b)**. Also slacken the neutral switch wire terminal screw and detach the wire **(see illustration 20.3)**.

12 Working in a criss-cross pattern, evenly slacken the alternator cover bolts **(see illustration)**. Draw the cover off the engine, noting that it will be restrained by the force of the rotor magnets, and be prepared to catch any residual oil. Remove and discard the gasket **(see illustration 29.20a)**. Remove the dowels from either the cover or the crankcase if loose.

13 To remove the rotor nut it is necessary to stop the rotor from turning. The best way is to use a commercially available rotor strap, taking care to avoid the raised triggers for the crankshaft position sensor on the outside of the rotor **(see illustration)**. Alternatively, try

placing the transmission in gear and having an assistant sit on the seat and apply the rear brake hard whilst you unscrew the nut and remove the washer.

14 To remove the rotor from the crankshaft taper it is necessary to use a rotor puller (Yamaha part No.90890-01362 on 2005 and 2006 YBR models and all XT models, or 90890-01468 on 2007-on YBR models, or its commercially available equivalent). Fit the puller onto the rotor, then tighten the bolt in its centre until the rotor is displaced from the shaft **(see illustration)**. If the starter driven gear does not come away with it, slide it off the end of the crankshaft. Remove the Woodruff key from its slot in the crankcase if it is loose, and the thrust washer **(see illustration)**. If required detach the starter clutch from the rotor (see Chapter 2).

15 To remove the stator from the cover,

unscrew its bolts and the bolts securing the crankshaft position sensor and the screw securing the wiring clamp, then remove the assembly, noting how the clamp and the rubber wiring grommet fit **(see illustrations)**.

Installation

16 Fit the stator, wiring clamp and CKP sensor into the cover, aligning the rubber wiring grommet with the groove, and tighten the clamp screw before locating the sensor **(see illustration 29.15b)**. Apply a suitable thread locking compound to the stator and sensor bolts, and tighten them. Apply a suitable sealant to the wiring grommet, then press it into the cut-out in the cover.

17 Slide on the thrust washer **(see illustration)**. Clean the tapered end of the crankshaft and the corresponding mating surface on the inside of the rotor with a suitable solvent **(see illustration)**. Smear some clean oil onto the inner un-tapered section of the crankshaft that the starter driven gear runs on. Fit the Woodruff key into its slot in the crankshaft if removed **(see illustration 29.14b)**.

18 If removed fit the starter clutch onto the rotor, and fit the driven gear into the clutch (see Chapter 2). Make sure that no metal objects have attached themselves to the magnet on the inside of the rotor. Slide the rotor onto the shaft, making sure the cutout on the inside of the rotor is aligned with and

29.17a Slide the thrust washer onto the shaft

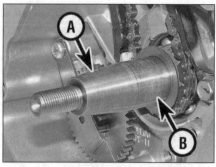

29.17b Clean the tapered section (A) and lubricate the inner section (B)

fits over the Woodruff key **(see illustration)**. Make sure the Woodruff key does not become dislodged when installing the rotor.

19 Fit the nut with its washer and tighten it to the torque setting specified at the beginning of the Chapter, using the method employed on removal to prevent the rotor from turning **(see illustrations)**.

20 Fit the dowels into the crankcase if removed, then locate a new gasket onto the dowels **(see illustration)**. Smear a suitable sealant onto the wiring grommet. Install the alternator cover, noting that the rotor magnets will forcibly draw the cover/stator on, making sure it locates onto the dowels **(see illustration)**. Tighten the cover bolts evenly in a criss-cross sequence **(see illustration 29.12)**.

21 Reconnect the wiring at the connectors, not forgetting the neutral switch wire and routing it in the groove in the cover **(see illustration 29.2a or b)**.

22 Replenish the engine oil (see Chapter 1 and *Pre-ride checks*). Install the sprocket cover and on YBR models the side cover.

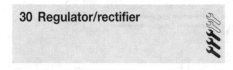

30 Regulator/rectifier

Check

1 No test details are given for the regulator/rectifier. If having checked the charging system as in Section 28 and there is obviously a problem, and the alternator stator and the wiring is all good, the regulator/rectifier unit is probably faulty. Take it to a Yamaha dealer for confirmation of its condition before replacing it with a new one.

Removal and installation

2 On YBR-ED models remove the fuel tank (see Chapter 3A or 3B). On YBR Custom models remove the left-hand air duct (see Chapter 7). On XT models remove the left-hand side cover (see Chapter 7).

29.18 Slide the rotor onto the shaft, aligning the cut-out with the Woodruff key

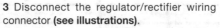

29.19b ... and tighten the nut to the specified torque

3 Disconnect the regulator/rectifier wiring connector **(see illustrations)**.

4 Unscrew the two bolts securing the regulator/rectifier, on XT models noting the earth wire secured by one bolt, and remove it.

5 Fit the new unit and tighten its bolts, not forgetting the earth wire on XT models. Connect the wiring connector.

6 On YBR-ED models install the fuel tank (see Chapter 3A or 3B). On Custom YBR models install the left-hand air duct (see Chapter 7). On XT models install the left-hand side cover (see Chapter 7).

29.19a Fit the nut and washer . . .

29.20a Make sure the dowels (arrowed) are in place, then fit the new gasket

29.20b Fit the cover onto the dowels

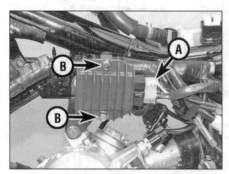

30.3a Regulator/rectifier wiring connector (A) and mounting bolts (B) – YBR-ED models

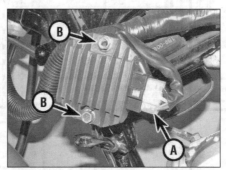

30.3b Regulator/rectifier wiring connector (A) and mounting bolts (B) – YBR Custom models

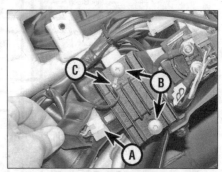

30.3c Regulator/rectifier wiring connector (A), mounting bolts (B) and earth wire (C) – XT models

YBR125-ED 2005 and 2006

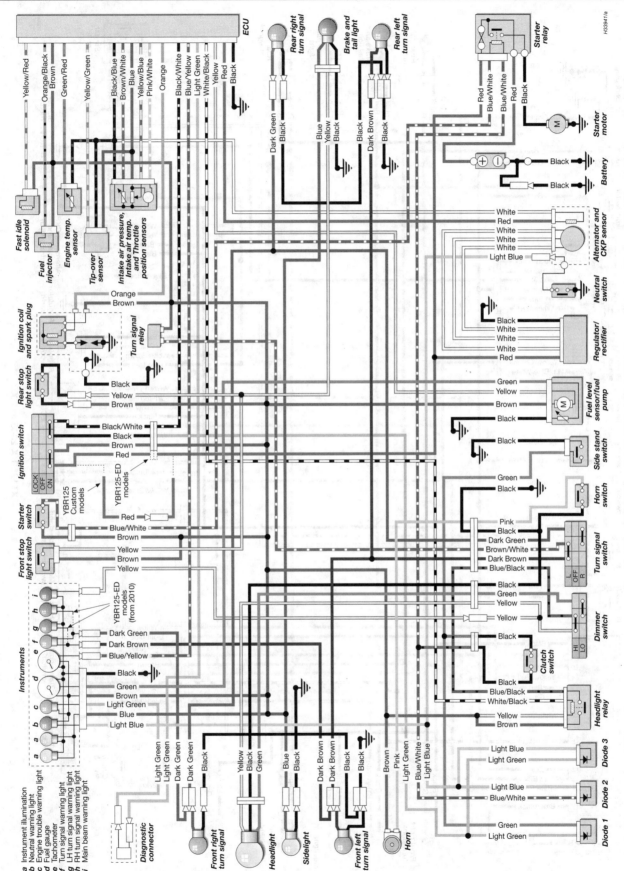

YBR125-ED 2007 on and YBR125 Custom 2008 on

H33941/8

XT125R/X 2005 to 2007

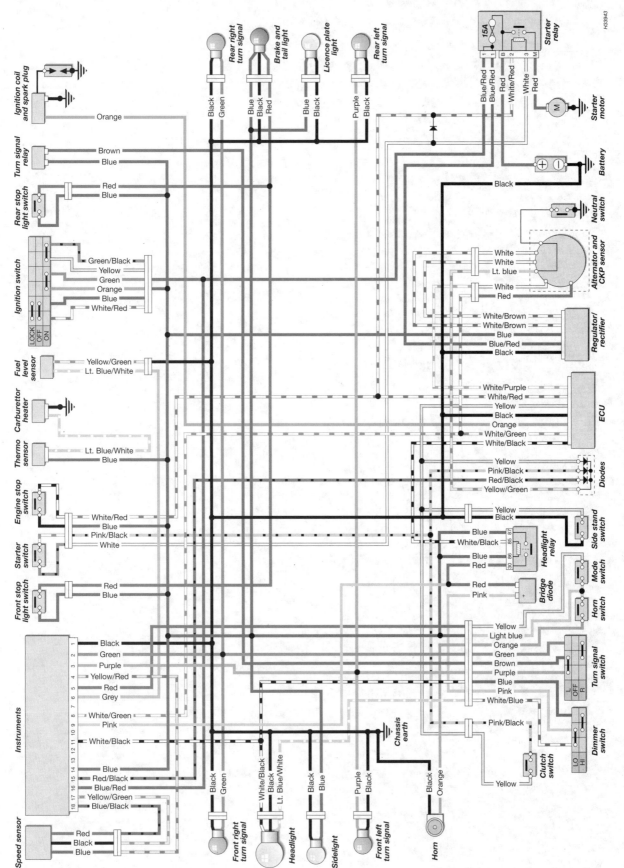

XT125R/X 2008

Notes

Buying tools

A toolkit is a fundamental requirement for servicing and repairing a motorcycle. Although there will be an initial expense in building up enough tools for servicing, this will soon be offset by the savings made by doing the job yourself. As experience and confidence grow, additional tools can be added to enable the repair and overhaul of the motorcycle. Many of the specialist tools are expensive and not often used so it may be preferable to hire them, or for a group of friends or motorcycle club to join in the purchase.

As a rule, it is better to buy more expensive, good quality tools. Cheaper tools are likely to wear out faster and need to be renewed more often, nullifying the original saving.

> **Warning: To avoid the risk of a poor quality tool breaking in use, causing injury or damage to the component being worked on, always aim to purchase tools which meet the relevant national safety standards.**

The following lists of tools do not represent the manufacturer's service tools, but serve as a guide to help the owner decide which tools are needed for this level of work. In addition, items such as an electric drill, hacksaw, files, soldering iron and a workbench equipped with a vice, may be needed. Although not classed as tools, a selection of bolts, screws, nuts, washers and pieces of tubing always come in useful.

For more information about tools, refer to the Haynes *Motorcycle Workshop Practice Techbook* (Bk. No. 3470).

Manufacturer's service tools

Inevitably certain tasks require the use of a service tool. Where possible an alternative tool or method of approach is recommended, but sometimes there is no option if personal injury or damage to the component is to be avoided. Where required, service tools are referred to in the relevant procedure.

Service tools can usually only be purchased from a motorcycle dealer and are identified by a part number. Some of the commonly-used tools, such as rotor pullers, are available in aftermarket form from mail-order motorcycle tool and accessory suppliers.

Maintenance and minor repair tools

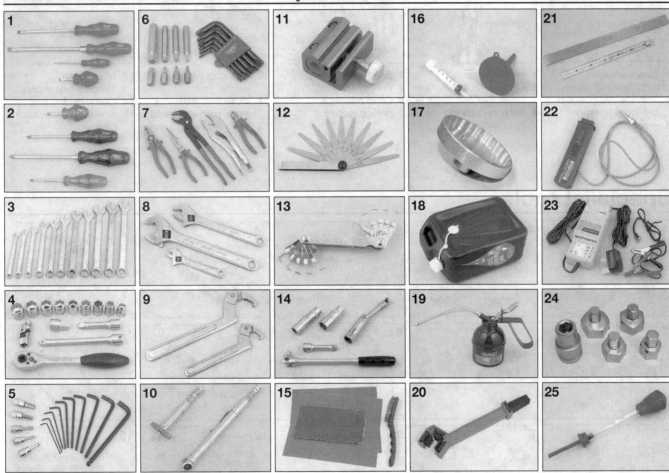

1 Set of flat-bladed screwdrivers	**6** Set of Torx keys or bits
2 Set of Phillips head screwdrivers	**7** Pliers, cutters and self-locking grips (Mole grips)
3 Combination open-end and ring spanners	**8** Adjustable spanners
4 Socket set (3/8 inch or 1/2 inch drive)	**9** C-spanners
5 Set of Allen keys or bits	**10** Tread depth gauge and tyre pressure gauge

11 Cable oiler clamp	**16** Calibrated syringe, measuring vessel and funnel
12 Feeler gauges	**17** Oil filter adapter
13 Spark plug gap measuring tool	**18** Oil drainer can or tray
14 Spark plug spanner or deep plug sockets	**19** Pump type oil can
15 Wire brush and emery paper	**20** Chain cleaning brush

21 Straight-edge and steel rule
22 Continuity tester
23 Battery charger
24 Wheel axle hex-bit set
25 Anti-freeze tester (for liquid-cooled engines)

Repair and overhaul tools

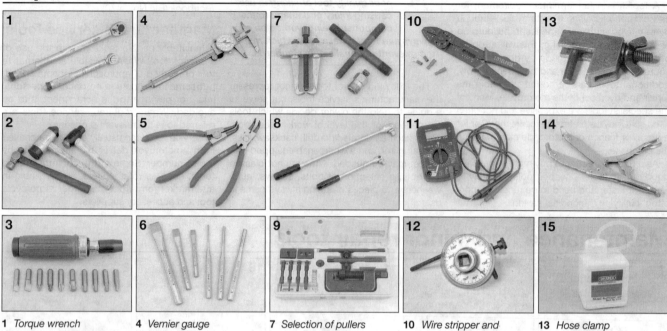

1 Torque wrench
   (small and mid-ranges)
2 Conventional, plastic or
   soft-faced hammers
3 Impact driver set
4 Vernier gauge
5 Circlip pliers (internal and
   external, or combination)
6 Set of cold chisels
   and punches
7 Selection of pullers
8 Breaker bars
9 Chain breaking/
   riveting tool set
10 Wire stripper and
   crimper tool
11 Multimeter (measures
   amps, volts and ohms)
12 Angle-tightening gauge
13 Hose clamp
   (wingnut type shown)
14 Clutch holding tool
15 One-man brake/clutch
   bleeder kit

Specialist tools

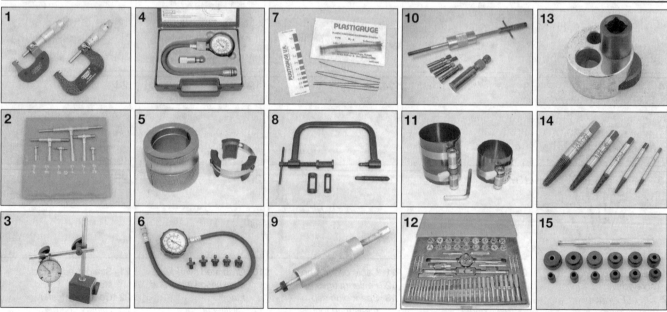

1 Micrometers
   (external type)
2 Telescoping gauges
3 Dial gauge
4 Cylinder
   compression gauge
5 Fork seal driver
6 Oil pressure gauge
7 Plastigauge kit
8 Valve spring compressor
   (4-stroke engines)
9 Piston pin drawbolt tool
10 Slide-hammer and knife-
   edged bearing extractors
11 Piston ring clamps
12 Tap and die set
13 Stud extractor
14 Screw extractor set
15 Bearing driver set

1 Workshop equipment and facilities

The workbench

● Work is made much easier by raising the bike up on a ramp - components are much more accessible if raised to waist level. The hydraulic or pneumatic types seen in the dealer's workshop are a sound investment if you undertake a lot of repairs or overhauls **(see illustration 1.1)**.

1.1 Hydraulic motorcycle ramp

● If raised off ground level, the bike must be supported on the ramp to avoid it falling. Most ramps incorporate a front wheel locating clamp which can be adjusted to suit different diameter wheels. When tightening the clamp, take care not to mark the wheel rim or damage the tyre - use wood blocks on each side to prevent this.
● Secure the bike to the ramp using tie-downs **(see illustration 1.2)**. If the bike has only a sidestand, and hence leans at a dangerous angle when raised, support the bike on an auxiliary stand.

1.2 Tie-downs are used around the passenger footrests to secure the bike

● Auxiliary (paddock) stands are widely available from mail order companies or motorcycle dealers and attach either to the wheel axle or swingarm pivot **(see illustration 1.3)**. If the motorcycle has a centrestand, you can support it under the crankcase to prevent it toppling whilst either wheel is removed **(see illustration 1.4)**.

1.3 This auxiliary stand attaches to the swingarm pivot

1.4 Always use a block of wood between the engine and jack head when supporting the engine in this way

Fumes and fire

● Refer to the Safety first! page at the beginning of the manual for full details. Make sure your workshop is equipped with a fire extinguisher suitable for fuel-related fires (Class B fire - flammable liquids) - it is not sufficient to have a water-filled extinguisher.
● Always ensure adequate ventilation is available. Unless an exhaust gas extraction system is available for use, ensure that the engine is run outside of the workshop.
● If working on the fuel system, make sure the workshop is ventilated to avoid a build-up of fumes. This applies equally to fume build-up when charging a battery. Do not smoke or allow anyone else to smoke in the workshop.

Fluids

● If you need to drain fuel from the tank, store it in an approved container marked as suitable for the storage of petrol (gasoline) **(see illustration 1.5)**. Do not store fuel in glass jars or bottles.

1.5 Use an approved can only for storing petrol (gasoline)

● Use proprietary engine degreasers or solvents which have a high flash-point, such as paraffin (kerosene), for cleaning off oil, grease and dirt - never use petrol (gasoline) for cleaning. Wear rubber gloves when handling solvent and engine degreaser. The fumes from certain solvents can be dangerous - always work in a well-ventilated area.

Dust, eye and hand protection

● Protect your lungs from inhalation of dust particles by wearing a filtering mask over the nose and mouth. Many frictional materials still contain asbestos which is dangerous to your health. Protect your eyes from spouts of liquid and sprung components by wearing a pair of protective goggles **(see illustration 1.6)**.

1.6 A fire extinguisher, goggles, mask and protective gloves should be at hand in the workshop

● Protect your hands from contact with solvents, fuel and oils by wearing rubber gloves. Alternatively apply a barrier cream to your hands before starting work. If handling hot components or fluids, wear suitable gloves to protect your hands from scalding and burns.

What to do with old fluids

● Old cleaning solvent, fuel, coolant and oils should not be poured down domestic drains or onto the ground. Package the fluid up in old oil containers, label it accordingly, and take it to a garage or disposal facility. Contact your local authority for location of such sites or ring the oil care hotline.

OIL CARE FOLLOW THE CODE

Note: It is antisocial and illegal to dump oil down the drain. To find the location of your local oil recycling bank in the UK, call 03708 506 506 or visit www.oilbankline.org.uk

In the USA, note that any oil supplier must accept used oil for recycling.

2 Fasteners -
screws, bolts and nuts

Fastener types and applications

Bolts and screws

● Fastener head types are either of hexagonal, Torx or splined design, with internal and external versions of each type **(see illustrations 2.1 and 2.2)**; splined head fasteners are not in common use on motorcycles. The conventional slotted or Phillips head design is used for certain screws. Bolt or screw length is always measured from the underside of the head to the end of the item **(see illustration 2.11)**.

2.1 Internal hexagon/Allen (A), Torx (B) and splined (C) fasteners, with corresponding bits

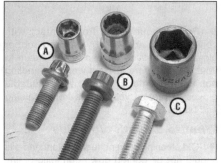

2.2 External Torx (A), splined (B) and hexagon (C) fasteners, with corresponding sockets

● Certain fasteners on the motorcycle have a tensile marking on their heads, the higher the marking the stronger the fastener. High tensile fasteners generally carry a 10 or higher marking. Never replace a high tensile fastener with one of a lower tensile strength.

Washers **(see illustration 2.3)**

● Plain washers are used between a fastener head and a component to prevent damage to the component or to spread the load when torque is applied. Plain washers can also be used as spacers or shims in certain assemblies. Copper or aluminium plain washers are often used as sealing washers on drain plugs.

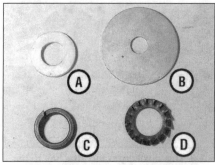

2.3 Plain washer (A), penny washer (B), spring washer (C) and serrated washer (D)

● The split-ring spring washer works by applying axial tension between the fastener head and component. If flattened, it is fatigued and must be renewed. If a plain (flat) washer is used on the fastener, position the spring washer between the fastener and the plain washer.

● Serrated star type washers dig into the fastener and component faces, preventing loosening. They are often used on electrical earth (ground) connections to the frame.

● Cone type washers (sometimes called Belleville) are conical and when tightened apply axial tension between the fastener head and component. They must be installed with the dished side against the component and often carry an OUTSIDE marking on their outer face. If flattened, they are fatigued and must be renewed.

● Tab washers are used to lock plain nuts or bolts on a shaft. A portion of the tab washer is bent up hard against one flat of the nut or bolt to prevent it loosening. Due to the tab washer being deformed in use, a new tab washer should be used every time it is disturbed.

● Wave washers are used to take up endfloat on a shaft. They provide light springing and prevent excessive side-to-side play of a component. Can be found on rocker arm shafts.

Nuts and split pins

● Conventional plain nuts are usually six-sided **(see illustration 2.4)**. They are sized by thread diameter and pitch. High tensile nuts carry a number on one end to denote their tensile strength.

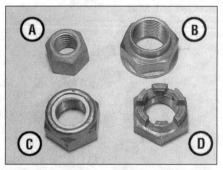

2.4 Plain nut (A), shouldered locknut (B), nylon insert nut (C) and castellated nut (D)

● Self-locking nuts either have a nylon insert, or two spring metal tabs, or a shoulder which is staked into a groove in the shaft - their advantage over conventional plain nuts is a resistance to loosening due to vibration. The nylon insert type can be used a number of times, but must be renewed when the friction of the nylon insert is reduced, ie when the nut spins freely on the shaft. The spring tab type can be reused unless the tabs are damaged. The shouldered type must be renewed every time it is disturbed.

● Split pins (cotter pins) are used to lock a castellated nut to a shaft or to prevent slackening of a plain nut. Common applications are wheel axles and brake torque arms. Because the split pin arms are deformed to lock around the nut a new split pin must always be used on installation - always fit the correct size split pin which will fit snugly in the shaft hole. Make sure the split pin arms are correctly located around the nut **(see illustrations 2.5 and 2.6)**.

2.5 Bend split pin (cotter pin) arms as shown (arrows) to secure a castellated nut

2.6 Bend split pin (cotter pin) arms as shown to secure a plain nut

Caution: If the castellated nut slots do not align with the shaft hole after tightening to the torque setting, tighten the nut until the next slot aligns with the hole - never slacken the nut to align its slot.

● R-pins (shaped like the letter R), or slip pins as they are sometimes called, are sprung and can be reused if they are otherwise in good condition. Always install R-pins with their closed end facing forwards **(see illustration 2.7)**.

2.7 Correct fitting of R-pin. Arrow indicates forward direction

Circlips (see illustration 2.8)

● Circlips (sometimes called snap-rings) are used to retain components on a shaft or in a housing and have corresponding external or internal ears to permit removal. Parallel-sided (machined) circlips can be installed either way round in their groove, whereas stamped circlips (which have a chamfered edge on one face) must be installed with the chamfer facing away from the direction of thrust load **(see illustration 2.9)**.

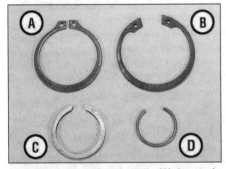

2.8 External stamped circlip (A), internal stamped circlip (B), machined circlip (C) and wire circlip (D)

● Always use circlip pliers to remove and install circlips; expand or compress them just enough to remove them. After installation, rotate the circlip in its groove to ensure it is securely seated. If installing a circlip on a splined shaft, always align its opening with a shaft channel to ensure the circlip ends are well supported and unlikely to catch **(see illustration 2.10)**.

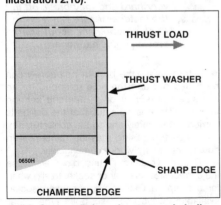

2.9 Correct fitting of a stamped circlip

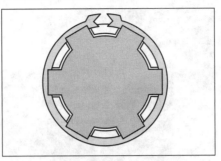

2.10 Align circlip opening with shaft channel

● Circlips can wear due to the thrust of components and become loose in their grooves, with the subsequent danger of becoming dislodged in operation. For this reason, renewal is advised every time a circlip is disturbed.

● Wire circlips are commonly used as piston pin retaining clips. If a removal tang is provided, long-nosed pliers can be used to dislodge them, otherwise careful use of a small flat-bladed screwdriver is necessary. Wire circlips should be renewed every time they are disturbed.

Thread diameter and pitch

● Diameter of a male thread (screw, bolt or stud) is the outside diameter of the threaded portion **(see illustration 2.11)**. Most motorcycle manufacturers use the ISO (International Standards Organisation) metric system expressed in millimetres, eg M6 refers to a 6 mm diameter thread. Sizing is the same for nuts, except that the thread diameter is measured across the valleys of the nut.

● Pitch is the distance between the peaks of the thread **(see illustration 2.11)**. It is expressed in millimetres, thus a common bolt size may be expressed as 6.0 x 1.0 mm (6 mm thread diameter and 1 mm pitch). Generally pitch increases in proportion to thread diameter, although there are always exceptions.

● Thread diameter and pitch are related for conventional fastener applications and the accompanying table can be used as a guide. Additionally, the AF (Across Flats), spanner or socket size dimension of the bolt or nut **(see illustration 2.11)** is linked to thread and pitch specification. Thread pitch can be measured with a thread gauge **(see illustration 2.12)**.

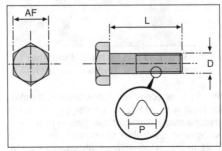

2.11 Fastener length (L), thread diameter (D), thread pitch (P) and head size (AF)

2.12 Using a thread gauge to measure pitch

AF size	Thread diameter x pitch (mm)
8 mm	M5 x 0.8
8 mm	M6 x 1.0
10 mm	M6 x 1.0
12 mm	M8 x 1.25
14 mm	M10 x 1.25
17 mm	M12 x 1.25

● The threads of most fasteners are of the right-hand type, ie they are turned clockwise to tighten and anti-clockwise to loosen. The reverse situation applies to left-hand thread fasteners, which are turned anti-clockwise to tighten and clockwise to loosen. Left-hand threads are used where rotation of a component might loosen a conventional right-hand thread fastener.

Seized fasteners

● Corrosion of external fasteners due to water or reaction between two dissimilar metals can occur over a period of time. It will build up sooner in wet conditions or in countries where salt is used on the roads during the winter. If a fastener is severely corroded it is likely that normal methods of removal will fail and result in its head being ruined. When you attempt removal, the fastener thread should be heard to crack free and unscrew easily - if it doesn't, stop there before damaging something.

● A smart tap on the head of the fastener will often succeed in breaking free corrosion which has occurred in the threads **(see illustration 2.13)**.

● An aerosol penetrating fluid (such as WD-40) applied the night beforehand may work its way down into the thread and ease removal. Depending on the location, you may be able to make up a Plasticine well around the fastener head and fill it with penetrating fluid.

2.13 A sharp tap on the head of a fastener will often break free a corroded thread

● If you are working on an engine internal component, corrosion will most likely not be a problem due to the well lubricated environment. However, components can be very tight and an impact driver is a useful tool in freeing them **(see illustration 2.14)**.

2.14 Using an impact driver to free a fastener

● Where corrosion has occurred between dissimilar metals (eg steel and aluminium alloy), the application of heat to the fastener head will create a disproportionate expansion rate between the two metals and break the seizure caused by the corrosion. Whether heat can be applied depends on the location of the fastener - any surrounding components likely to be damaged must first be removed **(see illustration 2.15)**. Heat can be applied using a paint stripper heat gun or clothes iron, or by immersing the component in boiling water - wear protective gloves to prevent scalding or burns to the hands.

2.15 Using heat to free a seized fastener

● As a last resort, it is possible to use a hammer and cold chisel to work the fastener head unscrewed **(see illustration 2.16)**. This will damage the fastener, but more importantly extreme care must be taken not to damage the surrounding component.

Caution: Remember that the component being secured is generally of more value than the bolt, nut or screw - when the fastener is freed, do not unscrew it with force, instead work the fastener back and forth when resistance is felt to prevent thread damage.

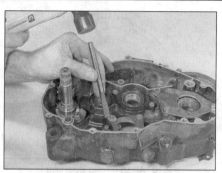

2.16 Using a hammer and chisel to free a seized fastener

Broken fasteners and damaged heads

● If the shank of a broken bolt or screw is accessible you can grip it with self-locking grips. The knurled wheel type stud extractor tool or self-gripping stud puller tool is particularly useful for removing the long studs which screw into the cylinder mouth surface of the crankcase or bolts and screws from which the head has broken off **(see illustration 2.17)**. Studs can also be removed by locking two nuts together on the threaded end of the stud and using a spanner on the lower nut **(see illustration 2.18)**.

2.17 Using a stud extractor tool to remove a broken crankcase stud

2.18 Two nuts can be locked together to unscrew a stud from a component

● A bolt or screw which has broken off below or level with the casing must be extracted using a screw extractor set. Centre punch the fastener to centralise the drill bit, then drill a hole in the fastener **(see illustration 2.19)**. Select a drill bit which is approximately half to three-quarters the diameter of the fastener

2.19 When using a screw extractor, first drill a hole in the fastener . . .

and drill to a depth which will accommodate the extractor. Use the largest size extractor possible, but avoid leaving too small a wall thickness otherwise the extractor will merely force the fastener walls outwards wedging it in the casing thread.

● If a spiral type extractor is used, thread it anti-clockwise into the fastener. As it is screwed in, it will grip the fastener and unscrew it from the casing **(see illustration 2.20)**.

2.20 . . . then thread the extractor anti-clockwise into the fastener

● If a taper type extractor is used, tap it into the fastener so that it is firmly wedged in place. Unscrew the extractor (anti-clockwise) to draw the fastener out.

 Warning: Stud extractors are very hard and may break off in the fastener if care is not taken - ask an engineer about spark erosion if this happens.

● Alternatively, the broken bolt/screw can be drilled out and the hole retapped for an oversize bolt/screw or a diamond-section thread insert. It is essential that the drilling is carried out squarely and to the correct depth, otherwise the casing may be ruined - if in doubt, entrust the work to an engineer.

● Bolts and nuts with rounded corners cause the correct size spanner or socket to slip when force is applied. Of the types of spanner/socket available always use a six-point type rather than an eight or twelve-point type - better grip

2.21 Comparison of surface drive ring spanner (left) with 12-point type (right)

is obtained. Surface drive spanners grip the middle of the hex flats, rather than the corners, and are thus good in cases of damaged heads **(see illustration 2.21)**.

● Slotted-head or Phillips-head screws are often damaged by the use of the wrong size screwdriver. Allen-head and Torx-head screws are much less likely to sustain damage. If enough of the screw head is exposed you can use a hacksaw to cut a slot in its head and then use a conventional flat-bladed screwdriver to remove it. Alternatively use a hammer and cold chisel to tap the head of the fastener around to slacken it. Always replace damaged fasteners with new ones, preferably Torx or Allen-head type.

HAYNES
HiNT

A dab of valve grinding compound between the screw head and screwdriver tip will often give a good grip.

Thread repair

● Threads (particularly those in aluminium alloy components) can be damaged by overtightening, being assembled with dirt in the threads, or from a component working loose and vibrating. Eventually the thread will fail completely, and it will be impossible to tighten the fastener.

● If a thread is damaged or clogged with old locking compound it can be renovated with a thread repair tool (thread chaser) **(see illustrations 2.22 and 2.23)**; special thread

2.22 A thread repair tool being used to correct an internal thread

2.23 A thread repair tool being used to correct an external thread

chasers are available for spark plug hole threads. The tool will not cut a new thread, but clean and true the original thread. Make sure that you use the correct diameter and pitch tool. Similarly, external threads can be cleaned up with a die or a thread restorer file **(see illustration 2.24)**.

2.24 Using a thread restorer file

● It is possible to drill out the old thread and retap the component to the next thread size. This will work where there is enough surrounding material and a new bolt or screw can be obtained. Sometimes, however, this is not possible - such as where the bolt/screw passes through another component which must also be suitably modified, also in cases where a spark plug or oil drain plug cannot be obtained in a larger diameter thread size.

● The diamond-section thread insert (often known by its popular trade name of Heli-Coil) is a simple and effective method of renewing the thread and retaining the original size. A kit can be purchased which contains the tap, insert and installing tool **(see illustration 2.25)**. Drill out the damaged thread with the size drill specified **(see illustration 2.26)**. Carefully retap the thread **(see illustration 2.27)**. Install the

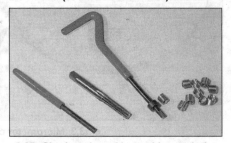

2.25 Obtain a thread insert kit to suit the thread diameter and pitch required

2.26 To install a thread insert, first drill out the original thread . . .

2.27 . . . tap a new thread . . .

2.28 . . . fit insert on the installing tool . . .

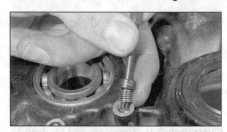

2.29 . . . and thread into the component . . .

2.30 . . . break off the tang when complete

insert on the installing tool and thread it slowly into place using a light downward pressure **(see illustrations 2.28 and 2.29)**. When positioned between a 1/4 and 1/2 turn below the surface withdraw the installing tool and use the break-off tool to press down on the tang, breaking it off **(see illustration 2.30)**.

● There are epoxy thread repair kits on the market which can rebuild stripped internal threads, although this repair should not be used on high load-bearing components.

Thread locking and sealing compounds

● Locking compounds are used in locations where the fastener is prone to loosening due to vibration or on important safety-related items which might cause loss of control of the motorcycle if they fail. It is also used where important fasteners cannot be secured by other means such as lockwashers or split pins.

● Before applying locking compound, make sure that the threads (internal and external) are clean and dry with all old compound removed. Select a compound to suit the component being secured - a non-permanent general locking and sealing type is suitable for most applications, but a high strength type is needed for permanent fixing of studs in castings. Apply a drop or two of the compound to the first few threads of the fastener, then thread it into place and tighten to the specified torque. Do not apply excessive thread locking compound otherwise the thread may be damaged on subsequent removal.

● Certain fasteners are impregnated with a dry film type coating of locking compound on their threads. Always renew this type of fastener if disturbed.

● Anti-seize compounds, such as copper-based greases, can be applied to protect threads from seizure due to extreme heat and corrosion. A common instance is spark plug threads and exhaust system fasteners.

---

3   Measuring tools and gauges

Feeler gauges

● Feeler gauges (or blades) are used for measuring small gaps and clearances **(see illustration 3.1)**. They can also be used to measure endfloat (sideplay) of a component on a shaft where access is not possible with a dial gauge.

● Feeler gauge sets should be treated with care and not bent or damaged. They are etched with their size on one face. Keep them clean and very lightly oiled to prevent corrosion build-up.

3.1 Feeler gauges are used for measuring small gaps and clearances - thickness is marked on one face of gauge

● When measuring a clearance, select a gauge which is a light sliding fit between the two components. You may need to use two gauges together to measure the clearance accurately.

Micrometers

● A micrometer is a precision tool capable of measuring to 0.01 or 0.001 of a millimetre. It should always be stored in its case and not in the general toolbox. It must be kept clean and never dropped, otherwise its frame or measuring anvils could be distorted resulting in inaccurate readings.

● External micrometers are used for measuring outside diameters of components and have many more applications than internal micrometers. Micrometers are available in different size ranges, eg 0 to 25 mm, 25 to 50 mm, and upwards in 25 mm steps; some large micrometers have interchangeable anvils to allow a range of measurements to be taken. Generally the largest precision measurement you are likely to take on a motorcycle is the piston diameter.

● Internal micrometers (or bore micrometers) are used for measuring inside diameters, such as valve guides and cylinder bores. Telescoping gauges and small hole gauges are used in conjunction with an external micrometer, whereas the more expensive internal micrometers have their own measuring device.

External micrometer

Note: *The conventional analogue type instrument is described. Although much easier to read, digital micrometers are considerably more expensive.*

● Always check the calibration of the micrometer before use. With the anvils closed (0 to 25 mm type) or set over a test gauge

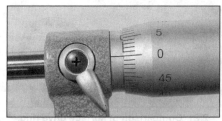

3.2 Check micrometer calibration before use

(for the larger types) the scale should read zero **(see illustration 3.2)**; make sure that the anvils (and test piece) are clean first. Any discrepancy can be adjusted by referring to the instructions supplied with the tool. Remember that the micrometer is a precision measuring tool - don't force the anvils closed, use the ratchet (4) on the end of the micrometer to close it. In this way, a measured force is always applied.

● To use, first make sure that the item being measured is clean. Place the anvil of the micrometer (1) against the item and use the thimble (2) to bring the spindle (3) lightly into contact with the other side of the item **(see illustration 3.3)**. Don't tighten the thimble down because this will damage the micrometer - instead use the ratchet (4) on the end of the micrometer. The ratchet mechanism applies a measured force preventing damage to the instrument.

● The micrometer is read by referring to the linear scale on the sleeve and the annular scale on the thimble. Read off the sleeve first to obtain the base measurement, then add the fine measurement from the thimble to obtain the overall reading. The linear scale on the sleeve represents the measuring range of the micrometer (eg 0 to 25 mm). The annular scale

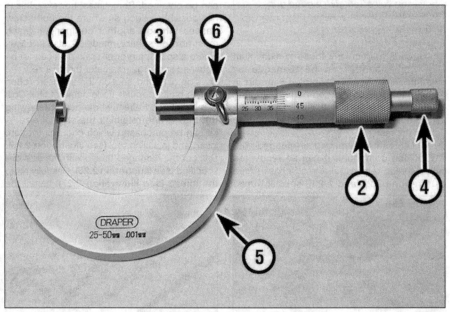

3.3 Micrometer component parts

1 Anvil	3 Spindle	5 Frame
2 Thimble	4 Ratchet	6 Locking lever

on the thimble will be in graduations of 0.01 mm (or as marked on the frame) - one full revolution of the thimble will move 0.5 mm on the linear scale. Take the reading where the datum line on the sleeve intersects the thimble's scale. Always position the eye directly above the scale otherwise an inaccurate reading will result.

In the example shown the item measures 2.95 mm **(see illustration 3.4)**:

Linear scale	2.00 mm
Linear scale	0.50 mm
Annular scale	0.45 mm
Total figure	2.95 mm

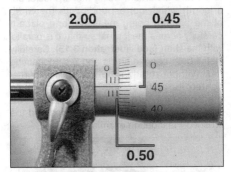

3.4 Micrometer reading of 2.95 mm

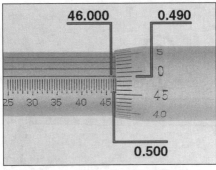

3.5 Micrometer reading of 46.99 mm on linear and annular scales . . .

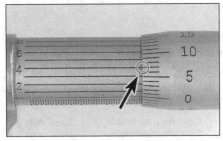

3.6 . . . and 0.004 mm on vernier scale

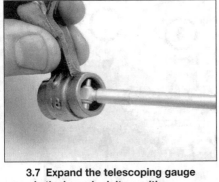

3.7 Expand the telescoping gauge in the bore, lock its position . . .

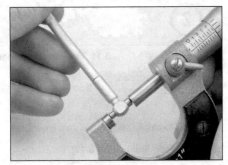

3.8 . . . then measure the gauge with a micrometer

3.9 Expand the small hole gauge in the bore, lock its position . . .

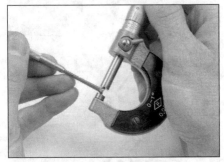

3.10 . . . then measure the gauge with a micrometer

Most micrometers have a locking lever (6) on the frame to hold the setting in place, allowing the item to be removed from the micrometer.

● Some micrometers have a vernier scale on their sleeve, providing an even finer measurement to be taken, in 0.001 increments of a millimetre. Take the sleeve and thimble measurement as described above, then check which graduation on the vernier scale aligns with that of the annular scale on the thimble **Note:** *The eye must be perpendicular to the scale when taking the vernier reading - if necessary rotate the body of the micrometer to ensure this.* Multiply the vernier scale figure by 0.001 and add it to the base and fine measurement figures.

In the example shown the item measures 46.994 mm **(see illustrations 3.5 and 3.6)**:

Linear scale (base)	46.000 mm
Linear scale (base)	00.500 mm
Annular scale (fine)	00.490 mm
Vernier scale	00.004 mm
Total figure	46.994 mm

Internal micrometer

● Internal micrometers are available for measuring bore diameters, but are expensive and unlikely to be available for home use. It is suggested that a set of telescoping gauges and small hole gauges, both of which must be used with an external micrometer, will suffice for taking internal measurements on a motorcycle.

● Telescoping gauges can be used to measure internal diameters of components. Select a gauge with the correct size range, make sure its ends are clean and insert it into the bore. Expand the gauge, then lock its position and withdraw it from the bore **(see illustration 3.7)**. Measure across the gauge ends with a micrometer **(see illustration 3.8)**.

● Very small diameter bores (such as valve guides) are measured with a small hole gauge. Once adjusted to a slip-fit inside the component, its position is locked and the gauge withdrawn for measurement with a micrometer **(see illustrations 3.9 and 3.10)**.

Vernier caliper

Note: *The conventional linear and dial gauge type instruments are described. Digital types are easier to read, but are far more expensive.*

● The vernier caliper does not provide the precision of a micrometer, but is versatile in being able to measure internal and external diameters. Some types also incorporate a depth gauge. It is ideal for measuring clutch plate friction material and spring free lengths.

● To use the conventional linear scale vernier, slacken off the vernier clamp screws (1) and set its jaws over (2), or inside (3), the item to be measured **(see illustration 3.11)**. Slide the jaw into contact, using the thumbwheel (4) for fine movement of the sliding scale (5) then tighten the clamp screws (1). Read off the main scale (6) where the zero on the sliding scale (5) intersects it, taking the whole number to the left of the zero; this provides the base measurement. View along the sliding scale and select the division which lines up exactly with any of the divisions on the main scale, noting that the divisions usually represents 0.02 of a millimetre. Add this fine measurement to the base measurement to obtain the total reading.

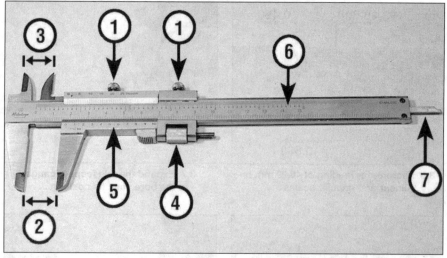

3.11 Vernier component parts (linear gauge)

1 Clamp screws	3 Internal jaws	5 Sliding scale	7 Depth gauge
2 External jaws	4 Thumbwheel	6 Main scale	

In the example shown the item measures 55.92 mm **(see illustration 3.12)**:

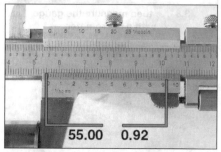

3.12 Vernier gauge reading of 55.92 mm

Base measurement	55.00 mm
Fine measurement	00.92 mm
Total figure	**55.92 mm**

● Some vernier calipers are equipped with a dial gauge for fine measurement. Before use, check that the jaws are clean, then close them fully and check that the dial gauge reads zero. If necessary adjust the gauge ring accordingly. Slacken the vernier clamp screw (1) and set its jaws over (2), or inside (3), the item to be measured **(see illustration 3.13)**. Slide the jaws into contact, using the thumbwheel (4) for fine movement. Read off the main scale (5) where the edge of the sliding scale (6) intersects it, taking the whole number to the left of the zero; this provides the base measurement. Read off the needle position on the dial gauge (7) scale to provide the fine measurement; each division represents 0.05 of a millimetre. Add this fine measurement to the base measurement to obtain the total reading.

In the example shown the item measures 55.95 mm **(see illustration 3.14)**:

Base measurement	55.00 mm
Fine measurement	00.95 mm
Total figure	**55.95 mm**

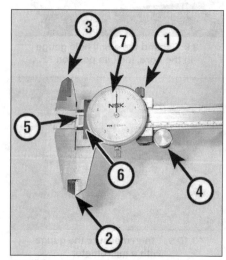

3.13 Vernier component parts (dial gauge)

1 Clamp screw	5 Main scale
2 External jaws	6 Sliding scale
3 Internal jaws	7 Dial gauge
4 Thumbwheel	

3.14 Vernier gauge reading of 55.95 mm

Plastigauge

● Plastigauge is a plastic material which can be compressed between two surfaces to measure the oil clearance between them. The width of the compressed Plastigauge is measured against a calibrated scale to determine the clearance.

● Common uses of Plastigauge are for measuring the clearance between crankshaft journal and main bearing inserts, between crankshaft journal and big-end bearing inserts, and between camshaft and bearing surfaces. The following example describes big-end oil clearance measurement.

● Handle the Plastigauge material carefully to prevent distortion. Using a sharp knife, cut a length which corresponds with the width of the bearing being measured and place it carefully across the journal so that it is parallel with the shaft **(see illustration 3.15)**. Carefully install both bearing shells and the connecting rod. Without rotating the rod on the journal tighten its bolts or nuts (as applicable) to the specified torque. The connecting rod and bearings are then disassembled and the crushed Plastigauge examined.

3.15 Plastigauge placed across shaft journal

● Using the scale provided in the Plastigauge kit, measure the width of the material to determine the oil clearance **(see illustration 3.16)**. Always remove all traces of Plastigauge after use using your fingernails.

Caution: Arriving at the correct clearance demands that the assembly is torqued correctly, according to the settings and sequence (where applicable) provided by the motorcycle manufacturer.

3.16 Measuring the width of the crushed Plastigauge

Dial gauge or DTI (Dial Test Indicator)

● A dial gauge can be used to accurately measure small amounts of movement. Typical uses are measuring shaft runout or shaft endfloat (sideplay) and setting piston position for ignition timing on two-strokes. A dial gauge set usually comes with a range of different probes and adapters and mounting equipment.

● The gauge needle must point to zero when at rest. Rotate the ring around its periphery to zero the gauge.

● Check that the gauge is capable of reading the extent of movement in the work. Most gauges have a small dial set in the face which records whole millimetres of movement as well as the fine scale around the face periphery which is calibrated in 0.01 mm divisions. Read off the small dial first to obtain the base measurement, then add the measurement from the fine scale to obtain the total reading.

In the example shown the gauge reads 1.48 mm (see illustration 3.17):

Base measurement	1.00 mm
Fine measurement	0.48 mm
Total figure	1.48 mm

3.17 Dial gauge reading of 1.48 mm

● If measuring shaft runout, the shaft must be supported in vee-blocks and the gauge mounted on a stand perpendicular to the shaft. Rest the tip of the gauge against the centre of the shaft and rotate the shaft slowly whilst watching the gauge reading (see illustration 3.18). Take several measurements along the length of the shaft and record the

3.18 Using a dial gauge to measure shaft runout

maximum gauge reading as the amount of runout in the shaft. **Note:** *The reading obtained will be total runout at that point - some manufacturers specify that the runout figure is halved to compare with their specified runout limit.*

● Endfloat (sideplay) measurement requires that the gauge is mounted securely to the surrounding component with its probe touching the end of the shaft. Using hand pressure, push and pull on the shaft noting the maximum endfloat recorded on the gauge (see illustration 3.19).

3.19 Using a dial gauge to measure shaft endfloat

● A dial gauge with suitable adapters can be used to determine piston position BTDC on two-stroke engines for the purposes of ignition timing. The gauge, adapter and suitable length probe are installed in the place of the spark plug and the gauge zeroed at TDC. If the piston position is specified as 1.14 mm BTDC, rotate the engine back to 2.00 mm BTDC, then slowly forwards to 1.14 mm BTDC.

Cylinder compression gauges

● A compression gauge is used for measuring cylinder compression. Either the rubber-cone type or the threaded adapter type can be used. The latter is preferred to ensure a perfect seal against the cylinder head. A 0 to 300 psi (0 to 20 Bar) type gauge (for petrol/gasoline engines) will be suitable for motorcycles.

● The spark plug is removed and the gauge either held hard against the cylinder head (cone type) or the gauge adapter screwed into the cylinder head (threaded type) (see illustration 3.20). Cylinder compression is measured with the engine turning over, but not running. The

3.20 Using a rubber-cone type cylinder compression gauge

gauge will hold the reading until manually released.

Oil pressure gauge

● An oil pressure gauge is used for measuring engine oil pressure. Most gauges come with a set of adapters to fit the thread of the take-off point (see illustration 3.21). If the take-off point specified by the motorcycle manufacturer is an external oil pipe union, make sure that the specified replacement union is used to prevent oil starvation.

3.21 Oil pressure gauge and take-off point adapter (arrow)

● Oil pressure is measured with the engine running (at a specific rpm) and often the manufacturer will specify pressure limits for a cold and hot engine.

Straight-edge and surface plate

● If checking the gasket face of a component for warpage, place a steel rule or precision straight-edge across the gasket face and measure any gap between the straight-edge and component with feeler gauges (see illustration 3.22). Check diagonally across the component and between mounting holes (see illustration 3.23).

3.22 Use a straight-edge and feeler gauges to check for warpage

3.23 Check for warpage in these directions

● Checking individual components for warpage, such as clutch plain (metal) plates, requires a perfectly flat plate or piece or plate glass and feeler gauges.

4 Torque and leverage

What is torque?

● Torque describes the twisting force about a shaft. The amount of torque applied is determined by the distance from the centre of the shaft to the end of the lever and the amount of force being applied to the end of the lever; distance multiplied by force equals torque.

● The manufacturer applies a measured torque to a bolt or nut to ensure that it will not slacken in use and to hold two components securely together without movement in the joint. The actual torque setting depends on the thread size, bolt or nut material and the composition of the components being held.

● Too little torque may cause the fastener to loosen due to vibration, whereas too much torque will distort the joint faces of the component or cause the fastener to shear off. Always stick to the specified torque setting.

Using a torque wrench

● Check the calibration of the torque wrench and make sure it has a suitable range for the job. Torque wrenches are available in Nm (Newton-metres), kgf m (kilograms-force metre), lbf ft (pounds-feet), lbf in (inch-pounds). Do not confuse lbf ft with lbf in.

● Adjust the tool to the desired torque on the scale (see illustration 4.1). If your torque wrench is not calibrated in the units specified, carefully convert the figure (see Conversion Factors). A manufacturer sometimes gives a torque setting as a range (8 to 10 Nm) rather than a single figure - in this case set the tool midway between the two settings. The same torque may be expressed as 9 Nm ± 1 Nm. Some torque wrenches have a method of locking the setting so that it isn't inadvertently altered during use.

4.1 Set the torque wrench index mark to the setting required, in this case 12 Nm

● Install the bolts/nuts in their correct location and secure them lightly. Their threads must be clean and free of any old locking compound. Unless specified the threads and flange should be dry - oiled threads are necessary in certain circumstances and the manufacturer will take this into account in the specified torque figure. Similarly, the manufacturer may also specify the application of thread-locking compound.

● Tighten the fasteners in the specified sequence until the torque wrench clicks, indicating that the torque setting has been reached. Apply the torque again to double-check the setting. Where different thread diameter fasteners secure the component, as a rule tighten the larger diameter ones first.

● When the torque wrench has been finished with, release the lock (where applicable) and fully back off its setting to zero - do not leave the torque wrench tensioned. Also, do not use a torque wrench for slackening a fastener.

Angle-tightening

● Manufacturers often specify a figure in degrees for final tightening of a fastener. This usually follows tightening to a specific torque setting.

● A degree disc can be set and attached to the socket (see illustration 4.2) or a protractor can be used to mark the angle of movement on the bolt/nut head and the surrounding casting (see illustration 4.3).

4.2 Angle tightening can be accomplished with a torque-angle gauge ...

4.3 ... or by marking the angle on the surrounding component

Loosening sequences

● Where more than one bolt/nut secures a component, loosen each fastener evenly a little at a time. In this way, not all the stress of the joint is held by one fastener and the components are not likely to distort.

● If a tightening sequence is provided, work in the REVERSE of this, but if not, work from the outside in, in a criss-cross sequence (see illustration 4.4).

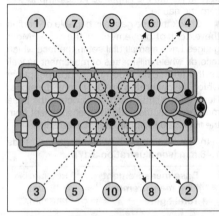

4.4 When slackening, work from the outside inwards

Tightening sequences

● If a component is held by more than one fastener it is important that the retaining bolts/nuts are tightened evenly to prevent uneven stress build-up and distortion of sealing faces. This is especially important on high-compression joints such as the cylinder head.

● A sequence is usually provided by the manufacturer, either in a diagram or actually marked in the casting. If not, always start in the centre and work outwards in a criss-cross pattern (see illustration 4.5). Start off by securing all bolts/nuts finger-tight, then set the torque wrench and tighten each fastener by a small amount in sequence until the final torque is reached. By following this practice,

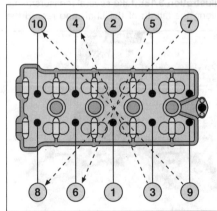

4.5 When tightening, work from the inside outwards

the joint will be held evenly and will not be distorted. Important joints, such as the cylinder head and big-end fasteners often have two- or three-stage torque settings.

Applying leverage

● Use tools at the correct angle. Position a socket wrench or spanner on the bolt/nut so that you pull it towards you when loosening. If this can't be done, push the spanner without curling your fingers around it **(see illustration 4.6)** - the spanner may slip or the fastener loosen suddenly, resulting in your fingers being crushed against a component.

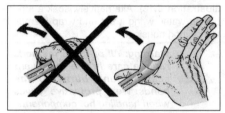

4.6 If you can't pull on the spanner to loosen a fastener, push with your hand open

● Additional leverage is gained by extending the length of the lever. The best way to do this is to use a breaker bar instead of the regular length tool, or to slip a length of tubing over the end of the spanner or socket wrench.
● If additional leverage will not work, the fastener head is either damaged or firmly corroded in place (see Fasteners).

5 Bearings

Bearing removal and installation

Drivers and sockets

● Before removing a bearing, always inspect the casing to see which way it must be driven out - some casings will have retaining plates or a cast step. Also check for any identifying markings on the bearing and if installed to a certain depth, measure this at this stage. Some roller bearings are sealed on one side - take note of the original fitted position.
● Bearings can be driven out of a casing using a bearing driver tool (with the correct size head) or a socket of the correct diameter. Select the driver head or socket so that it contacts the outer race of the bearing, not the balls/rollers or inner race. Always support the casing around the bearing housing with wood blocks, otherwise there is a risk of fracture. The bearing is driven out with a few blows on the driver or socket from a heavy mallet. Unless access is severely restricted (as with wheel bearings), a pin-punch is not recommended unless it is moved around the bearing to keep it square in its housing.

● The same equipment can be used to install bearings. Make sure the bearing housing is supported on wood blocks and line up the bearing in its housing. Fit the bearing as noted on removal - generally they are installed with their marked side facing outwards. Tap the bearing squarely into its housing using a driver or socket which bears only on the bearing's outer race - contact with the bearing balls/rollers or inner race will destroy it **(see illustrations 5.1 and 5.2)**.
● Check that the bearing inner race and balls/rollers rotate freely.

5.1 Using a bearing driver against the bearing's outer race

5.2 Using a large socket against the bearing's outer race

Pullers and slide-hammers

● Where a bearing is pressed on a shaft a puller will be required to extract it **(see illustration 5.3)**. Make sure that the puller clamp or legs fit securely behind the bearing and are unlikely to slip out. If pulling a bearing

5.3 This bearing puller clamps behind the bearing and pressure is applied to the shaft end to draw the bearing off

off a gear shaft for example, you may have to locate the puller behind a gear pinion if there is no access to the race and draw the gear pinion off the shaft as well **(see illustration 5.4)**.

> **Caution: Ensure that the puller's centre bolt locates securely against the end of the shaft and will not slip when pressure is applied. Also ensure that puller does not damage the shaft end.**

5.4 Where no access is available to the rear of the bearing, it is sometimes possible to draw off the adjacent component

● Operate the puller so that its centre bolt exerts pressure on the shaft end and draws the bearing off the shaft.
● When installing the bearing on the shaft, tap only on the bearing's inner race - contact with the balls/rollers or outer race with destroy the bearing. Use a socket or length of tubing as a drift which fits over the shaft end **(see illustration 5.5)**.

5.5 When installing a bearing on a shaft use a piece of tubing which bears only on the bearing's inner race

● Where a bearing locates in a blind hole in a casing, it cannot be driven or pulled out as described above. A slide-hammer with knife-edged bearing puller attachment will be required. The puller attachment passes through the bearing and when tightened expands to fit firmly behind the bearing **(see illustration 5.6)**. By operating the slide-hammer part of the tool the bearing is jarred out of its housing **(see illustration 5.7)**.
● It is possible, if the bearing is of reasonable weight, for it to drop out of its housing if the casing is heated as described opposite.

5.6 Expand the bearing puller so that it locks behind the bearing . . .

5.7 . . . attach the slide hammer to the bearing puller

If this method is attempted, first prepare a work surface which will enable the casing to be tapped face down to help dislodge the bearing - a wood surface is ideal since it will not damage the casing's gasket surface. Wearing protective gloves, tap the heated casing several times against the work surface to dislodge the bearing under its own weight **(see illustration 5.8)**.

5.8 Tapping a casing face down on wood blocks can often dislodge a bearing

● Bearings can be installed in blind holes using the driver or socket method described above.

Drawbolts

● Where a bearing or bush is set in the eye of a component, such as a suspension linkage arm or connecting rod small-end, removal by drift may damage the component. Furthermore, a rubber bushing in a shock absorber eye cannot successfully be driven out of position. If access is available to a engineering press, the task is straightforward. If not, a drawbolt can be fabricated to extract the bearing or bush.

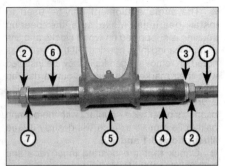

5.9 Drawbolt component parts assembled on a suspension arm

1 Bolt or length of threaded bar
2 Nuts
3 Washer (external diameter greater than tubing internal diameter)
4 Tubing (internal diameter sufficient to accommodate bearing)
5 Suspension arm with bearing
6 Tubing (external diameter slightly smaller than bearing)
7 Washer (external diameter slightly smaller than bearing)

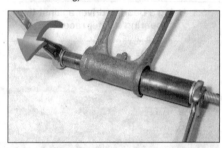

5.10 Drawing the bearing out of the suspension arm

● To extract the bearing/bush you will need a long bolt with nut (or piece of threaded bar with two nuts), a piece of tubing which has an internal diameter larger than the bearing/ bush, another piece of tubing which has an external diameter slightly smaller than the bearing/bush, and a selection of washers **(see illustrations 5.9 and 5.10)**. Note that the pieces of tubing must be of the same length, or longer, than the bearing/bush.
● The same kit (without the pieces of tubing) can be used to draw the new bearing/bush back into place **(see illustration 5.11)**.

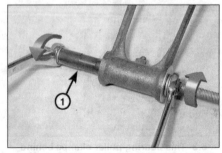

5.11 Installing a new bearing (1) in the suspension arm

Temperature change

● If the bearing's outer race is a tight fit in the casing, the aluminium casing can be heated to release its grip on the bearing. Aluminium will expand at a greater rate than the steel bearing outer race. There are several ways to do this, but avoid any localised extreme heat (such as a blow torch) - aluminium alloy has a low melting point.
● Approved methods of heating a casing are using a domestic oven (heated to 100°C) or immersing the casing in boiling water **(see illustration 5.12)**. Low temperature range localised heat sources such as a paint stripper heat gun or clothes iron can also be used **(see illustration 5.13)**. Alternatively, soak a rag in boiling water, wring it out and wrap it around the bearing housing.

> ⚠ **Warning: All of these methods require care in use to prevent scalding and burns to the hands. Wear protective gloves when handling hot components.**

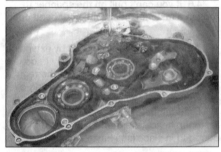

5.12 A casing can be immersed in a sink of boiling water to aid bearing removal

5.13 Using a localised heat source to aid bearing removal

● If heating the whole casing note that plastic components, such as the neutral switch, may suffer - remove them beforehand.
● After heating, remove the bearing as described above. You may find that the expansion is sufficient for the bearing to fall out of the casing under its own weight or with a light tap on the driver or socket.
● If necessary, the casing can be heated to aid bearing installation, and this is sometimes the recommended procedure if the motorcycle manufacturer has designed the housing and bearing fit with this intention.

Installation of bearings can be eased by placing them in a freezer the night before installation. The steel bearing will contract slightly, allowing easy insertion in its housing. This is often useful when installing steering head outer races in the frame.

Bearing types and markings

Plain shell bearings, ball bearings, needle roller bearings and tapered roller bearings will all be found on motorcycles (see illustrations 5.14 and 5.15). The ball and roller types are usually caged between an inner and outer race, but uncaged variations may be found.

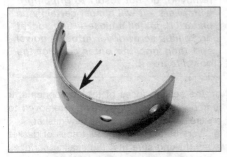

5.14 Shell bearings are either plain or grooved. They are usually identified by colour code (arrow)

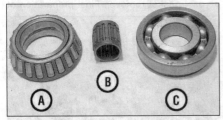

5.15 Tapered roller bearing (A), needle roller bearing (B) and ball journal bearing (C)

Shell bearings (often called inserts) are usually found at the crankshaft main and connecting rod big-end where they are good at coping with high loads. They are made of a phosphor-bronze material and are impregnated with self-lubricating properties.

Ball bearings and needle roller bearings consist of a steel inner and outer race with the balls or rollers between the races. They require constant lubrication by oil or grease and are good at coping with axial loads. Taper roller bearings consist of rollers set in a tapered cage set on the inner race; the outer race is separate. They are good at coping with axial loads and prevent movement along the shaft - a typical application is in the steering head.

Bearing manufacturers produce bearings to ISO size standards and stamp one face of the bearing to indicate its internal and external diameter, load capacity and type (see illustration 5.16).

Metal bushes are usually of phosphor-bronze material. Rubber bushes are used in suspension mounting eyes. Fibre bushes have also been used in suspension pivots.

5.16 Typical bearing marking

Bearing fault finding

If a bearing outer race has spun in its housing, the housing material will be damaged. You can use a bearing locking compound to bond the outer race in place if damage is not too severe.

Shell bearings will fail due to damage of their working surface, as a result of lack of lubrication, corrosion or abrasive particles in the oil (see illustration 5.17). Small particles of dirt in the oil may embed in the bearing material whereas larger particles will score the bearing and shaft journal. If a number of short journeys are made, insufficient heat will be generated to drive off condensation which has built up on the bearings.

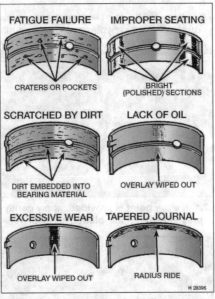

5.17 Typical bearing failures

Ball and roller bearings will fail due to lack of lubrication or damage to the balls or rollers. Tapered-roller bearings can be damaged by overloading them. Unless the bearing is sealed on both sides, wash it in paraffin (kerosene) to remove all old grease then allow it to dry. Make a visual inspection looking to dented balls or rollers, damaged cages and worn or pitted races (see illustration 5.18).

A ball bearing can be checked for wear by listening to it when spun. Apply a film of light oil to the bearing and hold it close to the ear - hold the outer race with one hand and spin the

5.18 Example of ball journal bearing with damaged balls and cages

5.19 Hold outer race and listen to inner race when spun

inner race with the other hand (see illustration 5.19). The bearing should be almost silent when spun; if it grates or rattles it is worn.

6 Oil seals

Oil seal removal and installation

Oil seals should be renewed every time a component is dismantled. This is because the seal lips will become set to the sealing surface and will not necessarily reseal.

Oil seals can be prised out of position using a large flat-bladed screwdriver (see illustration 6.1). In the case of crankcase seals, check first that the seal is not lipped on the inside, preventing its removal with the crankcases joined.

6.1 Prise out oil seals with a large flat-bladed screwdriver

New seals are usually installed with their marked face (containing the seal reference code) outwards and the spring side towards the fluid being retained. In certain cases, such as a two-stroke engine crankshaft seal, a double lipped seal may be used due to there being fluid or gas on each side of the joint.

● Use a bearing driver or socket which bears only on the outer hard edge of the seal to install it in the casing - tapping on the inner edge will damage the sealing lip.

Oil seal types and markings

● Oil seals are usually of the single-lipped type. Double-lipped seals are found where a liquid or gas is on both sides of the joint.

● Oil seals can harden and lose their sealing ability if the motorcycle has been in storage for a long period - renewal is the only solution.

● Oil seal manufacturers also conform to the ISO markings for seal size - these are moulded into the outer face of the seal **(see illustration 6.2)**.

6.2 These oil seal markings indicate inside diameter, outside diameter and seal thickness

7 Gaskets and sealants

Types of gasket and sealant

● Gaskets are used to seal the mating surfaces between components and keep lubricants, fluids, vacuum or pressure contained within the assembly. Aluminium gaskets are sometimes found at the cylinder joints, but most gaskets are paper-based. If the mating surfaces of the components being joined are undamaged the gasket can be installed dry, although a dab of sealant or grease will be useful to hold it in place during assembly.

● RTV (Room Temperature Vulcanising) silicone rubber sealants cure when exposed to moisture in the atmosphere. These sealants are good at filling pits or irregular gasket faces, but will tend to be forced out of the joint under very high torque. They can be used to replace a paper gasket, but first make sure that the width of the paper gasket is not essential to the shimming of internal components. RTV sealants should not be used on components containing petrol (gasoline).

● Non-hardening, semi-hardening and hard setting liquid gasket compounds can be used with a gasket or between a metal-to-metal joint. Select the sealant to suit the application: universal non-hardening sealant can be used on virtually all joints; semi-hardening on joint faces which are rough or damaged; hard setting sealant on joints which require a permanent bond and are subjected to high temperature and pressure. **Note:** Check first if the paper gasket has a bead of sealant

impregnated in its surface before applying additional sealant.

● When choosing a sealant, make sure it is suitable for the application, particularly if being applied in a high-temperature area or in the vicinity of fuel. Certain manufacturers produce sealants in either clear, silver or black colours to match the finish of the engine. This has a particular application on motorcycles where much of the engine is exposed.

● Do not over-apply sealant. That which is squeezed out on the outside of the joint can be wiped off, whereas an excess of sealant on the inside can break off and clog oilways.

Breaking a sealed joint

● Age, heat, pressure and the use of hard setting sealant can cause two components to stick together so tightly that they are difficult to separate using finger pressure alone. Do not resort to using levers unless there is a pry point provided for this purpose **(see illustration 7.1)** or else the gasket surfaces will be damaged.

● Use a soft-faced hammer **(see illustration 7.2)** or a wood block and conventional hammer to strike the component near the mating surface. Avoid hammering against cast extremities since they may break off. If this method fails, try using a wood wedge between the two components.

Caution: If the joint will not separate, double-check that you have removed all the fasteners.

7.1 If a pry point is provided, apply gently pressure with a flat-bladed screwdriver

7.2 Tap around the joint with a soft-faced mallet if necessary - don't strike cooling fins

Removal of old gasket and sealant

● Paper gaskets will most likely come away complete, leaving only a few traces stuck

HAYNES HiNT

Most components have one or two hollow locating dowels between the two gasket faces. If a dowel cannot be removed, do not resort to gripping it with pliers - it will almost certainly be distorted. Install a close-fitting socket or Phillips screwdriver into the dowel and then grip the outer edge of the dowel to free it.

on the sealing faces of the components. It is imperative that all traces are removed to ensure correct sealing of the new gasket.

● Very carefully scrape all traces of gasket away making sure that the sealing surfaces are not gouged or scored by the scraper **(see illustrations 7.3, 7.4 and 7.5)**. Stubborn deposits can be removed by spraying with an aerosol gasket remover. Final preparation of

7.3 Paper gaskets can be scraped off with a gasket scraper tool . . .

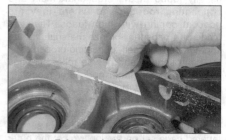

7.4 . . . a knife blade . . .

7.5 . . . or a household scraper

7.6 Fine abrasive paper is wrapped around a flat file to clean up the gasket face

7.7 A kitchen scourer can be used on stubborn deposits

the gasket surface can be made with very fine abrasive paper or a plastic kitchen scourer **(see illustrations 7.6 and 7.7)**.

● Old sealant can be scraped or peeled off components, depending on the type originally used. Note that gasket removal compounds are available to avoid scraping the components clean; make sure the gasket remover suits the type of sealant used.

8 Chains

Breaking and joining final drive chains

● Drive chains for all but small bikes are continuous and do not have a clip-type connecting link. The chain must be broken using a chain breaker tool and the new chain securely riveted together using a new soft rivet-type link. Never use a clip-type connecting link instead of a rivet-type link, except in an emergency. Various chain breaking and riveting tools are available, either as separate tools or combined as illustrated in the accompanying photographs - read the instructions supplied with the tool carefully.

> ⚠ **Warning: The need to rivet the new link pins correctly cannot be overstressed - loss of control of the motorcycle is very likely to result if the chain breaks in use.**

● Rotate the chain and look for the soft link. The soft link pins look like they have been

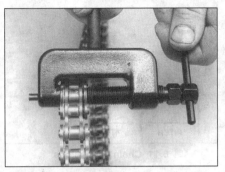

8.1 Tighten the chain breaker to push the pin out of the link . . .

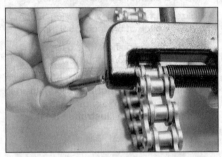

8.2 . . . withdraw the pin, remove the tool . . .

8.3 . . . and separate the chain link

deeply centre-punched instead of peened over like all the other pins **(see illustration 8.9)** and its sideplate may be a different colour. Position the soft link midway between the sprockets and assemble the chain breaker tool over one of the soft link pins **(see illustration 8.1)**. Operate the tool to push the pin out through the chain **(see illustration 8.2)**. On an O-ring chain, remove the O-rings **(see illustration 8.3)**. Carry out the same procedure on the other soft link pin.

> **Caution: Certain soft link pins (particularly on the larger chains) may require their ends to be filed or ground off before they can be pressed out using the tool.**

● Check that you have the correct size and strength (standard or heavy duty) new soft link - do not reuse the old link. Look for the size marking on the chain sideplates **(see illustration 8.10)**.

● Position the chain ends so that they are engaged over the rear sprocket. On an O-ring

8.4 Insert the new soft link, with O-rings, through the chain ends . . .

8.5 . . . install the O-rings over the pin ends . . .

8.6 . . . followed by the sideplate

chain, install a new O-ring over each pin of the link and insert the link through the two chain ends **(see illustration 8.4)**. Install a new O-ring over the end of each pin, followed by the sideplate (with the chain manufacturer's marking facing outwards) **(see illustrations 8.5 and 8.6)**. On an unsealed chain, insert the link through the two chain ends, then install the sideplate with the chain manufacturer's marking facing outwards.

● Note that it may not be possible to install the sideplate using finger pressure alone. If using a joining tool, assemble it so that the plates of the tool clamp the link and press the sideplate over the pins **(see illustration 8.7)**. Otherwise, use two small sockets placed over

8.7 Push the sideplate into position using a clamp

8.8 Assemble the chain riveting tool over one pin at a time and tighten it fully

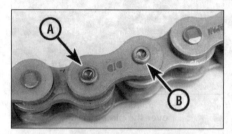

8.9 Pin end correctly riveted (A), pin end unriveted (B)

the rivet ends and two pieces of the wood between a G-clamp. Operate the clamp to press the sideplate over the pins.

● Assemble the joining tool over one pin (following the maker's instructions) and tighten the tool down to spread the pin end securely **(see illustrations 8.8 and 8.9)**. Do the same on the other pin.

 Warning: Check that the pin ends are secure and that there is no danger of the sideplate coming loose. If the pin ends are cracked the soft link must be renewed.

Final drive chain sizing

● Chains are sized using a three digit number, followed by a suffix to denote the chain type **(see illustration 8.10)**. Chain type is either standard or heavy duty (thicker sideplates), and also unsealed or O-ring/X-ring type.

● The first digit of the number relates to the pitch of the chain, ie the distance from the centre of one pin to the centre of the next pin **(see illustration 8.11)**. Pitch is expressed in eighths of an inch, as follows:

8.10 Typical chain size and type marking

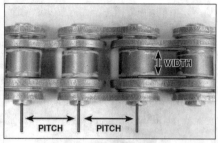

8.11 Chain dimensions

Sizes commencing with a 4 (eg 428) have a pitch of 1/2 inch (12.7 mm)

Sizes commencing with a 5 (eg 520) have a pitch of 5/8 inch (15.9 mm)

Sizes commencing with a 6 (eg 630) have a pitch of 3/4 inch (19.1 mm)

● The second and third digits of the chain size relate to the width of the rollers, again in imperial units, eg the 525 shown has 5/16 inch (7.94 mm) rollers **(see illustration 8.11)**.

9 Hoses

Clamping to prevent flow

● Small-bore flexible hoses can be clamped to prevent fluid flow whilst a component is worked on. Whichever method is used, ensure that the hose material is not permanently distorted or damaged by the clamp.

a) A brake hose clamp available from auto accessory shops **(see illustration 9.1)**.
b) A wingnut type hose clamp **(see illustration 9.2)**.

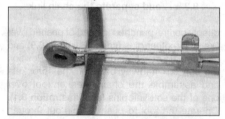

9.1 Hoses can be clamped with an automotive brake hose clamp . . .

9.2 . . . a wingnut type hose clamp . . .

c) Two sockets placed each side of the hose and held with straight-jawed self-locking grips **(see illustration 9.3)**.
d) Thick card each side of the hose held between straight-jawed self-locking grips **(see illustration 9.4)**.

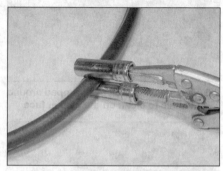

9.3 . . . two sockets and a pair of self-locking grips . . .

9.4 . . . or thick card and self-locking grips

Freeing and fitting hoses

● Always make sure the hose clamp is moved well clear of the hose end. Grip the hose with your hand and rotate it whilst pulling it off the union. If the hose has hardened due to age and will not move, slit it with a sharp knife and peel its ends off the union **(see illustration 9.5)**.

● Resist the temptation to use grease or soap on the unions to aid installation; although it helps the hose slip over the union it will equally aid the escape of fluid from the joint. It is preferable to soften the hose ends in hot water and wet the inside surface of the hose with water or a fluid which will evaporate.

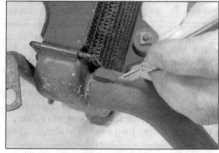

9.5 Cutting a coolant hose free with a sharp knife

Length (distance)

Inches (in)	x 25.4	= Millimetres (mm)	x 0.0394	= Inches (in)	
Feet (ft)	x 0.305	= Metres (m)	x 3.281	= Feet (ft)	
Miles	x 1.609	= Kilometres (km)	x 0.621	= Miles	

Volume (capacity)

Cubic inches (cu in; in³)	x 16.387	= Cubic centimetres (cc; cm³)	x 0.061	= Cubic inches (cu in; in³)	
Imperial pints (Imp pt)	x 0.568	= Litres (l)	x 1.76	= Imperial pints (Imp pt)	
Imperial quarts (Imp qt)	x 1.137	= Litres (l)	x 0.88	= Imperial quarts (Imp qt)	
Imperial quarts (Imp qt)	x 1.201	= US quarts (US qt)	x 0.833	= Imperial quarts (Imp qt)	
US quarts (US qt)	x 0.946	= Litres (l)	x 1.057	= US quarts (US qt)	
Imperial gallons (Imp gal)	x 4.546	= Litres (l)	x 0.22	= Imperial gallons (Imp gal)	
Imperial gallons (Imp gal)	x 1.201	= US gallons (US gal)	x 0.833	= Imperial gallons (Imp gal)	
US gallons (US gal)	x 3.785	= Litres (l)	x 0.264	= US gallons (US gal)	

Mass (weight)

Ounces (oz)	x 28.35	= Grams (g)	x 0.035	= Ounces (oz)	
Pounds (lb)	x 0.454	= Kilograms (kg)	x 2.205	= Pounds (lb)	

Force

Ounces-force (ozf; oz)	x 0.278	= Newtons (N)	x 3.6	= Ounces-force (ozf; oz)	
Pounds-force (lbf; lb)	x 4.448	= Newtons (N)	x 0.225	= Pounds-force (lbf; lb)	
Newtons (N)	x 0.1	= Kilograms-force (kgf; kg)	x 9.81	= Newtons (N)	

Pressure

Pounds-force per square inch (psi; lbf/in²; lb/in²)	x 0.070	= Kilograms-force per square centimetre (kgf/cm²; kg/cm²)	x 14.223	= Pounds-force per square inch (psi; lbf/in²; lb/in²)
Pounds-force per square inch (psi; lbf/in²; lb/in²)	x 0.068	= Atmospheres (atm)	x 14.696	= Pounds-force per square inch (psi; lbf/in²; lb/in²)
Pounds-force per square inch (psi; lbf/in²; lb/in²)	x 0.069	= Bars	x 14.5	= Pounds-force per square inch (psi; lbf/in²; lb/in²)
Pounds-force per square inch (psi; lbf/in²; lb/in²)	x 6.895	= Kilopascals (kPa)	x 0.145	= Pounds-force per square inch (psi; lbf/in²; lb/in²)
Kilopascals (kPa)	x 0.01	= Kilograms-force per square centimetre (kgf/cm²; kg/cm²)	x 98.1	= Kilopascals (kPa)
Millibar (mbar)	x 100	= Pascals (Pa)	x 0.01	= Millibar (mbar)
Millibar (mbar)	x 0.0145	= Pounds-force per square inch (psi; lbf/in²; lb/in²)	x 68.947	= Millibar (mbar)
Millibar (mbar)	x 0.75	= Millimetres of mercury (mmHg)	x 1.333	= Millibar (mbar)
Millibar (mbar)	x 0.401	= Inches of water (inH₂O)	x 2.491	= Millibar (mbar)
Millimetres of mercury (mmHg)	x 0.535	= Inches of water (inH₂O)	x 1.868	= Millimetres of mercury (mmHg)
Inches of water (inH₂O)	x 0.036	= Pounds-force per square inch (psi; lbf/in²; lb/in²)	x 27.68	= Inches of water (inH₂O)

Torque (moment of force)

Pounds-force inches (lbf in; lb in)	x 1.152	= Kilograms-force centimetre (kgf cm; kg cm)	x 0.868	= Pounds-force inches (lbf in; lb in)
Pounds-force inches (lbf in; lb in)	x 0.113	= Newton metres (Nm)	x 8.85	= Pounds-force inches (lbf in; lb in)
Pounds-force inches (lbf in; lb in)	x 0.083	= Pounds-force feet (lbf ft; lb ft)	x 12	= Pounds-force inches (lbf in; lb in)
Pounds-force feet (lbf ft; lb ft)	x 0.138	= Kilograms-force metres (kgf m; kg m)	x 7.233	= Pounds-force feet (lbf ft; lb ft)
Pounds-force feet (lbf ft; lb ft)	x 1.356	= Newton metres (Nm)	x 0.738	= Pounds-force feet (lbf ft; lb ft)
Newton metres (Nm)	x 0.102	= Kilograms-force metres (kgf m; kg m)	x 9.804	= Newton metres (Nm)

Power

Horsepower (hp)	x 745.7	= Watts (W)	x 0.0013	= Horsepower (hp)

Velocity (speed)

Miles per hour (miles/hr; mph)	x 1.609	= Kilometres per hour (km/hr; kph)	x 0.621	= Miles per hour (miles/hr; mph)

Fuel consumption*

Miles per gallon (mpg)	x 0.354	= Kilometres per litre (km/l)	x 2.825	= Miles per gallon (mpg)

Temperature

Degrees Fahrenheit = (°C x 1.8) + 32   Degrees Celsius (Degrees Centigrade; °C) = (°F - 32) x 0.56

It is common practice to convert from miles per gallon (mpg) to litres/100 kilometres (l/100km), where mpg x l/100 km = 282

This Section provides an easy reference-guide to the more common faults that are likely to afflict your machine. Obviously, the opportunities are almost limitless for faults to occur as a result of obscure failures, and to try and cover all eventualities would require a book. Indeed, a number have been written on the subject.

Successful troubleshooting is not a mysterious 'black art' but the application of a bit of knowledge combined with a systematic and logical approach to the problem. Approach any troubleshooting by first accurately identifying the symptom and then checking through the list of possible causes, starting with the simplest or most obvious and progressing in stages to the most complex.

Take nothing for granted, but above all apply liberal quantities of common sense.

The main symptom of a fault is given in the text as a major heading below which are listed the various systems or areas which may contain the fault. Details of each possible cause for a fault and the remedial action to be taken are given, in brief, in the paragraphs below each heading. Further information should be sought in the relevant Chapter.

1 Engine doesn't start or is difficult to start

☐ Starter motor doesn't rotate
☐ Starter motor rotates but engine does not turn over
☐ No fuel flow
☐ Engine flooded
☐ No spark or weak spark
☐ Compression low
☐ Stalls after starting
☐ Rough idle

2 Poor running at low speed

☐ Spark weak
☐ Fuel/air mixture incorrect
☐ Compression low
☐ Poor acceleration

3 Poor running or no power at high speed

☐ Firing incorrect
☐ Fuel/air mixture incorrect
☐ Compression low
☐ Knocking or pinking
☐ Miscellaneous causes

4 Overheating

☐ Firing incorrect
☐ Fuel/air mixture incorrect
☐ Compression too high
☐ Engine load excessive
☐ Lubrication inadequate
☐ Miscellaneous causes

5 Clutch problems

☐ Clutch slipping
☐ Clutch not disengaging completely

6 Gearchange problems

☐ Doesn't go into gear, or lever doesn't return
☐ Jumps out of gear
☐ Overselects

7 Abnormal engine noise

☐ Knocking or pinking
☐ Piston slap or rattling
☐ Valve noise
☐ Other noise

8 Abnormal driveline noise

☐ Clutch noise
☐ Transmission noise
☐ Final drive noise

9 Abnormal frame and suspension noise

☐ Front end noise
☐ Shock absorber noise
☐ Brake noise

10 Excessive exhaust smoke

☐ White smoke
☐ Black smoke
☐ Brown smoke

11 Poor handling or stability

☐ Handlebar hard to turn
☐ Handlebar shakes or vibrates excessively
☐ Handlebar pulls to one side
☐ Poor shock absorbing qualities

12 Braking problems

☐ Brakes are spongy or don't hold
☐ Brake lever or pedal pulsates
☐ Brakes drag

13 Electrical problems

☐ Battery dead or weak
☐ Battery overcharged

1 Engine doesn't start or is difficult to start

Starter motor doesn't rotate

☐ Fuse blown. Check fuse (Chapter 8).
☐ Battery voltage low. Check and recharge battery (Chapter 8).
☐ Starter motor defective. Make sure the wiring to the starter is secure. Make sure the starter relay clicks when the start button is pushed. If the relay clicks, then the fault is probably in the wiring or motor.
☐ Starter relay faulty. Check it according to the procedure in Chapter 8.
☐ Starter button not contacting. The contacts could be wet, corroded or dirty. Disassemble and clean the switch (Chapter 8).
☐ Wiring open or shorted. Check all wiring connections and harnesses to make sure that they are dry, tight and not corroded. Also check for broken or frayed wires that can cause a short to ground (earth) (see wiring diagram, Chapter 8).
☐ Ignition switch defective. Check the switch according to the procedure in Chapter 8. Replace the switch with a new one if it is defective.
☐ Faulty neutral/sidestand/clutch switch(es) or diodes. Check the wiring to each switch and the switch itself, and check the diodes, according to the procedures in Chapter 8.

Starter motor rotates but engine does not turn over

☐ Starter clutch defective. Inspect and repair or replace (Chapter 2).
☐ Damaged idle/reduction or starter gears. Inspect and replace the damaged parts (Chapter 2).

No fuel flow

☐ No fuel in tank.
☐ Fuel tap vacuum hose broken or disconnected (XT models).
☐ Tank cap air vent obstructed. Usually caused by dirt or water. Remove it and clean the cap vent hole.
☐ Fuel tap strainer clogged (2005 and 2006 YBR models). Remove the tap and clean the strainer (Chapter 1).
☐ Fuel pump strainer clogged (2007-on YBR models). Remove the pump and clean the strainer (Chapter 3B).
☐ Fuel pump failure or fuel injection system fault (2007-on YBR models) (Chapter 3B).
☐ Fuel hose clogged. Detach the fuel hose and carefully blow through it.

Engine flooded (carburettor engines)

☐ Float height too high. Check as described in Chapter 4.
☐ Inlet needle valve worn or stuck open. A piece of dirt, rust or other debris can cause the inlet needle to seat improperly, causing excess fuel to be admitted to the float bowl. In this case, the float chamber should be cleaned and the needle and seat inspected. If the needle and seat are worn, then the leaking will persist and the parts should be replaced with new ones (Chapter 3A).
☐ Starting technique incorrect. Under normal circumstances (e.g., if all the carburettor functions are sound) the machine should start with little or no throttle. When the engine is cold, the choke should be operated and the engine started without opening the throttle. When the engine is at operating temperature, only a very slight amount of throttle should be necessary. If the engine is flooded, hold the throttle fully open while cranking the engine. This will allow additional air to reach the cylinder.

No spark or weak spark

☐ Ignition switch OFF. Engine stop switch OFF (XT only).
☐ Battery voltage low. Check and recharge battery as necessary (Chapter 8).
☐ Spark plug dirty, defective or worn out. Locate reason for fouled plug using spark plug condition chart and follow the plug maintenance procedures in Chapter 1.
☐ Spark plug cap or lead faulty. Check condition. Replace either or both components if cracks or deterioration are evident.
☐ Spark plug cap not making good contact. Make sure that the plug cap fits snugly over the plug end.
☐ ECU defective. Check the unit, referring to Chapter 4 for details.
☐ Crankshaft position sensor defective. Check the unit, referring to Chapter 4 for details.
☐ Ignition coil defective. Check the coil, referring to Chapter 4.
☐ Ignition switch shorted. This is usually caused by water, corrosion, damage or excessive wear. If cleaning with electrical contact cleaner does not help, replace the switch (Chapter 8).
☐ Wiring shorted or broken. Make sure that all wiring connections are clean, dry and tight. Look for chafed and broken wires (Chapters 4 and 8).

Compression low

☐ Spark plug loose. Remove the plug and inspect the threads. Reinstall and tighten to the specified torque (Chapter 1).
☐ Cylinder head not sufficiently tightened down. If the cylinder head is suspected of being loose, then there's a chance that the gasket or head is damaged if the problem has persisted for any length of time. The cylinder head bolts should be tightened to the proper torque in the correct sequence (Chapter 2).
☐ Improper valve clearance. This means that the valve is not closing completely and compression pressure is leaking past the valve. Check and adjust the valve clearances (Chapter 1).
☐ Cylinder and/or piston worn. Excessive wear will cause compression pressure to leak past the rings. This is usually accompanied by worn rings as well. A top-end overhaul is necessary (Chapter 2).
☐ Piston rings worn, weak, broken, or sticking. Broken or sticking piston rings usually indicate a lubrication or carburetion problem that causes excess carbon deposits or seizures to form on the pistons and rings. Top-end overhaul is necessary (Chapter 2).
☐ Piston ring-to-groove clearance excessive. This is caused by excessive wear of the piston ring lands. Piston replacement is necessary (Chapter 2).
☐ Cylinder head gasket damaged. If the head is allowed to become loose, or if excessive carbon build-up on the piston crown and combustion chamber causes extremely high compression, the head gasket may leak. Retorquing the head is not always sufficient to restore the seal, so gasket replacement is necessary (Chapter 2).
☐ Cylinder head warped. This is caused by overheating or improperly tightened head bolts. Machine shop resurfacing or head replacement is necessary (Chapter 2).
☐ Valve spring broken or weak. Caused by component failure or wear; the spring on each valve must be replaced (Chapter 2).
☐ Valve not seating properly. This is caused by a bent valve (from over-revving or improper valve adjustment), burned valve or seat (improper carburetion) or an accumulation of carbon deposits on the seat (from carburetion or lubrication problems). The valves must be cleaned and/or replaced and the seats serviced if possible (Chapter 2).

1 Engine doesn't start or is difficult to start (continued)

Stalls after starting

☐ Ignition malfunction. See Chapter 4.
☐ Carburettor malfunction. See Chapter 3A. Check the choke action.
☐ Fuel contaminated. The fuel can be contaminated with either dirt or water, or can change chemically if the machine is allowed to sit for several months or more. Drain the tank and clean the carburettor or throttle body (Chapter 3A or 3B).
☐ Intake air leak. Check the carburettor or throttle body connection with the cylinder head (Chapter 3A or 3B).
☐ Engine idle speed incorrect. Turn throttle stop screw until the engine idles at the specified rpm (Chapter 1).
☐ Fault fast idle solenoid on fuel injection models (Chapter 3B).

Rough idle

☐ Ignition malfunction. See Chapter 4.
☐ Idle speed incorrect. See Chapter 1.
☐ Carburettor malfunction or fuel injection system fault. See Chapter 3A or 3B.
☐ Fuel contaminated. The fuel can be contaminated with either dirt or water, or can change chemically if the machine is allowed to sit for several months or more. Drain the tank and clean the carburettor or throttle body (Chapter 3A or 3B).
☐ Intake air leak. Check the carburettor or throttle body connection with the cylinder head (Chapter 3A or 3B).
☐ Air filter clogged. Service or replace air filter element (Chapter 1).
☐ Air induction system fault. Check the system (Chapters 1 and 3A or 3B).
☐ Fuel injection system fault. See Chapter 3B.

2 Poor running at low speed

Spark weak

☐ Battery voltage low. Check and recharge battery (Chapter 8).
☐ Spark plug fouled, defective or worn out. Refer to Chapter 1 for spark plug maintenance.
☐ Spark plug cap or lead defective. Refer to Chapters 1 and 4 for details on the ignition system.
☐ Spark plug cap not making contact.
☐ Incorrect spark plug. Wrong type, heat range or cap configuration. Check and install correct plug listed in Chapter 1.
☐ ECU defective. See Chapter 4.
☐ Crankshaft position sensor defective. See Chapter 4.
☐ Ignition coil defective. See Chapter 4.

Fuel/air mixture incorrect (carburettor models)

☐ Pilot screw out of adjustment (Chapter 3A).
☐ Pilot jet or air passage clogged. Remove and overhaul the carburettor (Chapter 3A).
☐ Air bleed holes clogged. Remove carburettor and blow out all passages (Chapter 3A).
☐ Air filter clogged, poorly sealed or missing (Chapter 1).
☐ Air filter housing poorly sealed. Look for cracks, holes or loose clamps and replace or repair defective parts.
☐ Fuel level too high or too low. Check the fuel level and float height (Chapter 3A).
☐ Fuel tank air vent obstructed. Make sure that the air vent passage in the filler cap is open.
☐ Carburettor intake duct loose. Check for cracks, breaks, tears or loose clamps.

Compression low

☐ Spark plug loose. Remove the plug and inspect the threads. Reinstall and tighten to the specified torque (Chapter 1).
☐ Cylinder head not sufficiently tightened down. If the cylinder head is suspected of being loose, then there's a chance that the gasket and head are damaged if the problem has persisted for any length of time. The cylinder head bolts should be tightened to the proper torque in the correct sequence (Chapter 2).
☐ Improper valve clearance. This means that the valve is not closing completely and compression pressure is leaking past the valve. Check and adjust the valve clearances (Chapter 1).

☐ Cylinder and/or piston worn. Excessive wear will cause compression pressure to leak past the rings. This is usually accompanied by worn rings as well. A top-end overhaul is necessary (Chapter 2).
☐ Piston rings worn, weak, broken, or sticking. Broken or sticking piston rings usually indicate a lubrication or carburetion problem that causes excess carbon deposits or seizures to form on the pistons and rings. Top-end overhaul is necessary (Chapter 2).
☐ Piston ring-to-groove clearance excessive. This is caused by excessive wear of the piston ring lands. Piston replacement is necessary (Chapter 2).
☐ Cylinder head gasket damaged. If the head is allowed to become loose, or if excessive carbon build-up on the piston crown and combustion chamber causes extremely high compression, the head gasket may leak. Retorquing the head is not always sufficient to restore the seal, so gasket replacement is necessary (Chapter 2).
☐ Cylinder head warped. This is caused by overheating or improperly tightened head bolts. Machine shop resurfacing or head replacement is necessary (Chapter 2).
☐ Valve spring broken or weak. Caused by component failure or wear; the spring on both valves must be replaced (Chapter 2).
☐ Valve not seating properly. This is caused by a bent valve (from over-revving or improper valve adjustment), burned valve or seat (improper carburetion) or an accumulation of carbon deposits on the seat (from carburetion, lubrication problems). The valves must be cleaned and/or replaced and the seats serviced if possible (Chapter 2).

Poor acceleration

☐ Carburettor leaking or dirty. Overhaul the carburettor (Chapter 3A).
☐ Timing not advancing. The crankshaft position sensor or the ECU may be defective. If so, they must be replaced with new ones, as they can't be repaired.
☐ Engine oil viscosity too high. Using a heavier oil than that recommended in Chapter 1 can damage the oil pump or lubrication system and cause drag on the engine.
☐ Brakes dragging. Usually caused by debris which has entered the brake piston seals (disc brake), sticking brake operating mechanism (drum brake) or from a warped disc or bent axle. Repair as necessary (Chapter 6).

3 Poor running or no power at high speed

Firing incorrect

☐ Air filter restricted. Clean or replace filter (Chapter 1).
☐ Spark plug fouled, defective or worn out. See Chapter 1 for spark plug maintenance.
☐ Spark plug cap or lead wiring defective. See Chapters 1 and 4 for details of the ignition system.
☐ Spark plug cap not in good contact.
☐ Incorrect spark plug. Wrong type, heat range or cap configuration. Check and install correct plug listed in Chapter 1.
☐ ECU defective. See Chapter 4.
☐ Ignition coil defective. See Chapter 4.
☐ Fuel injection system fault. See Chapter 3B.

Fuel/air mixture incorrect (carburettor models)

☐ Main jet clogged. Dirt, water or other contaminants can clog the main jet. Clean the fuel tap strainer (YBR models), the float bowl area, and the jets and carburettor orifices (Chapter 3A).
☐ Main jet wrong size. The standard jetting is for sea level atmospheric pressure and oxygen content.
☐ Air bleed holes clogged. Remove and overhaul carburettor (Chapter 3A).
☐ Air filter clogged, poorly sealed, or missing (Chapter 1).
☐ Air filter housing poorly sealed. Look for cracks, holes or loose clamps, and replace or repair defective parts.
☐ Fuel level too high or too low. Check the fuel level and float height (Chapter 3A).
☐ Fuel tank air vent obstructed. Make sure the air vent passage in the filler cap is open.
☐ Carburettor intake duct loose. Check for cracks, breaks, tears or loose clamps.
☐ Fuel tap strainer clogged (YBR models). Remove the tap and clean it and the strainer (Chapter 1).
☐ Fuel hose clogged. Detach the fuel hose and carefully blow through it.

Compression low

☐ Spark plug loose. Remove the plug and inspect the threads. Reinstall and tighten to the specified torque (Chapter 1).
☐ Cylinder head not sufficiently tightened down. If the cylinder head is suspected of being loose, then there's a chance that the gasket and head are damaged if the problem has persisted for any length of time. The cylinder head bolts should be tightened to the proper torque in the correct sequence (Chapter 2).
☐ Improper valve clearance. This means that the valve is not closing completely and compression pressure is leaking past the valve. Check and adjust the valve clearances (Chapter 1).
☐ Cylinder and/or piston worn. Excessive wear will cause compression pressure to leak past the rings. This is usually accompanied by worn rings as well. A top-end overhaul is necessary (Chapter 2).
☐ Piston rings worn, weak, broken, or sticking. Broken or sticking piston rings usually indicate a lubrication or carburetion problem that causes excess carbon deposits or seizures to form on the pistons and rings. Top-end overhaul is necessary (Chapter 2).
☐ Piston ring-to-groove clearance excessive. This is caused by excessive wear of the piston ring lands. Piston replacement is necessary (Chapter 2).
☐ Cylinder head gasket damaged. If the head is allowed to become loose, or if excessive carbon build-up on the piston crown and combustion chamber causes extremely high compression, the head gasket may leak. Retorquing the head is not always sufficient to restore the seal, so gasket replacement is necessary (Chapter 2).
☐ Cylinder head warped. This is caused by overheating or improperly tightened head bolts. Machine shop resurfacing or head replacement is necessary (Chapter 2).
☐ Valve spring broken or weak. Caused by component failure or wear; the spring on each valve must be replaced (Chapter 2).
☐ Valve not seating properly. This is caused by a bent valve (from over-revving or improper valve adjustment), burned valve or seat (improper carburetion) or an accumulation of carbon deposits on the seat (from carburetion, lubrication problems). The valves must be cleaned and/or replaced and the seats serviced if possible (Chapter 2).

Knocking or pinking

☐ Carbon build-up in combustion chamber. Use of a fuel additive that will dissolve the adhesive bonding the carbon particles to the crown and chamber is the easiest way to remove the build-up. Otherwise, the cylinder head will have to be removed and decarbonised (Chapter 2).
☐ Incorrect or poor quality fuel. Old or improper grades of fuel can cause detonation. This causes the piston to rattle, thus the knocking or pinking sound. Drain old fuel and always use the recommended fuel grade.
☐ Spark plug heat range incorrect. Uncontrolled detonation indicates the plug heat range is too hot. The plug in effect becomes a glow plug, raising cylinder temperatures. Install the proper heat range plug (Chapter 1).
☐ Improper air/fuel mixture (carburettor models). This will cause the cylinder to run hot, which leads to detonation. Clogged jets or an air leak can cause this imbalance. See Chapter 3A.
☐ Fuel injection system fault. See Chapter 3B.

Miscellaneous causes

☐ Throttle valve doesn't open fully. Adjust the cable slack (Chapter 1).
☐ Clutch slipping. May be caused by loose or worn clutch components. Refer to Chapter 2 for clutch overhaul procedures.
☐ Engine oil viscosity too high. Using a heavier oil than the one recommended in Chapter 1 can damage the oil pump or lubrication system and cause drag on the engine.
☐ Brakes dragging. Usually caused by debris which has entered the brake piston seals (disc brake), sticking brake operating mechanism (drum brake), or from a warped disc or bent axle. Repair as necessary.

4 Overheating

Firing incorrect

- [ ] Spark plug fouled, defective or worn out. See Chapter 1 for spark plug maintenance.
- [ ] Incorrect spark plug.
- [ ] Faulty ignition coil (Chapter 4).

Fuel/air mixture incorrect (carburettor models)

- [ ] Main jet clogged. Dirt, water and other contaminants can clog the main jets. Clean the fuel tap filter (YBR models), the float bowl area and the jets and carburettor orifices (Chapter 3A).
- [ ] Main jet wrong size. The standard jetting is for sea level atmospheric pressure and oxygen content.
- [ ] Air filter clogged, poorly sealed or missing (Chapter 1).
- [ ] Air filter housing poorly sealed. Look for cracks, holes or loose clamps and replace or repair.
- [ ] Fuel level too low. Check fuel level and float height (Chapter 3A).
- [ ] Fuel tank air vent obstructed. Make sure that the air vent passage in the filler cap is open.
- [ ] Carburettor intake duct loose. Check for cracks, breaks, tears or loose clamps.

Compression too high

- [ ] Carbon build-up in combustion chamber. Use of a fuel additive that will dissolve the adhesive bonding the carbon particles to the piston crown and chamber is the easiest way to remove the build-up. Otherwise, the cylinder head will have to be removed and decarbonised (Chapter 2).
- [ ] Improperly machined head surface.

Engine load excessive

- [ ] Clutch slipping. Can be caused by damaged, loose or worn clutch components. Refer to Chapter 2 for overhaul procedures.
- [ ] Engine oil level too high. The addition of too much oil will cause pressurisation of the crankcase and inefficient engine operation. Check the level (Pre-ride checks).
- [ ] Engine oil viscosity too high. Using a heavier oil than the one recommended in Chapter 1 can damage the oil pump or lubrication system as well as cause drag on the engine.
- [ ] Brakes dragging. Usually caused by debris which has entered the brake piston seals (disc brake), sticking brake operating mechanism (drum brake), or from a warped disc or bent axle. Repair as necessary.

Lubrication inadequate

- [ ] Engine oil level too low. Friction caused by intermittent lack of lubrication or from oil that is overworked can cause overheating. The oil provides a definite cooling function in the engine. Check the oil level (Pre-ride checks).
- [ ] Poor quality engine oil or incorrect viscosity or type. Oil is rated not only according to viscosity but also according to type. Some oils are not rated high enough for use in this engine. Check the Specifications section and change to the correct oil (Chapter 1).

Miscellaneous causes

- [ ] Modification to exhaust system. Most aftermarket exhaust systems cause the engine to run leaner, this makes it run hotter. When installing an accessory exhaust system you may need to rejet the carburettor.

5 Clutch problems

Clutch slipping

- [ ] Cable freeplay insufficient. Check and adjust cable (Chapter 1).
- [ ] Friction plates worn or warped. Overhaul the clutch assembly (Chapter 2).
- [ ] Steel plates worn or warped (Chapter 2).
- [ ] Clutch spring(s) broken or weak. Old or heat-damaged (from slipping clutch) springs should be replaced with new ones (Chapter 2).
- [ ] Clutch release mechanism defective. Replace any defective parts (Chapter 2).
- [ ] Clutch centre or housing unevenly worn. This causes improper engagement of the plates. Replace the damaged or worn parts (Chapter 2).

Clutch not disengaging completely

- [ ] Cable freeplay excessive. Check and adjust cable (Chapter 1).
- [ ] Clutch plates warped or damaged. This will cause clutch drag, which in turn will cause the machine to creep. Overhaul the clutch assembly (Chapter 2).

- [ ] Clutch spring tension uneven. Usually caused by a sagged or broken spring. Check and replace the springs as a set (Chapter 2).
- [ ] Engine oil deteriorated. Old, thin, worn out oil will not provide proper lubrication for the discs, causing the clutch to drag. Change the oil and clean the strainer (Chapter 1).
- [ ] Engine oil viscosity too high. Using a heavier oil than recommended in Chapter 1 can cause the plates to stick together, putting a drag on the engine. Change to the correct weight oil (Chapter 1).
- [ ] Clutch housing seized on input shaft. Lack of lubrication, severe wear or damage can cause the housing to seize on the shaft. Overhaul of the clutch, and perhaps transmission, may be necessary to repair the damage (Chapter 2).
- [ ] Clutch release mechanism defective. Worn or damaged release mechanism parts can stick and fail to apply force to the pressure plate. Overhaul the clutch cover components (Chapter 2).
- [ ] Loose clutch centre nut. Causes drum and centre misalignment putting a drag on the engine. Engagement adjustment continually varies. Overhaul the clutch assembly (Chapter 2).

6 Gearchange problems

Doesn't go into gear or lever doesn't return

- ☐ Clutch not disengaging.
- ☐ Selector fork(s) bent or seized. Often caused by dropping the machine or from lack of lubrication. Overhaul the transmission (Chapter 2).
- ☐ Gear(s) stuck on shaft. Most often caused by a lack of lubrication or excessive wear in transmission bearings and bushes. Overhaul the transmission (Chapter 2).
- ☐ Selector drum binding. Caused by lubrication failure or excessive wear. Replace the drum and bearing (Chapter 2).
- ☐ Gearchange lever return spring weak or broken (Chapter 2).
- ☐ Gearchange lever broken. Splines stripped out of lever or shaft, caused by allowing the lever to get loose or from dropping the machine. Replace necessary parts (Chapter 2).
- ☐ Gearchange mechanism stopper arm broken or worn. Full

engagement and rotary movement of selector drum results. Replace the arm (Chapter 2).
- ☐ Stopper arm spring broken. Allows arm to float, causing sporadic selector operation. Replace spring (Chapter 2).

Jumps out of gear

- ☐ Selector fork(s) worn. Overhaul the transmission (Chapter 2).
- ☐ Gear groove(s) worn. Overhaul the transmission (Chapter 2).
- ☐ Gear dogs or dog slots worn or damaged. The gears should be inspected and replaced. No attempt should be made to service the worn parts.

Overselects

- ☐ Stopper arm spring weak or broken (Chapter 2).
- ☐ Gearchange shaft return spring post broken or distorted (Chapter 2).

7 Abnormal engine noise

Knocking or pinking

- ☐ Carbon build-up in combustion chamber. Use of a fuel additive that will dissolve the adhesive bonding the carbon particles to the piston crown and chamber is the easiest way to remove the build-up. Otherwise, the cylinder head will have to be removed and decarbonised (Chapter 2).
- ☐ Incorrect or poor quality fuel. Old or improper fuel can cause detonation. This causes the piston to rattle, thus the knocking or pinking sound. Drain the old fuel and always use the recommended grade fuel (Chapter 3A or 3B).
- ☐ Spark plug heat range incorrect. Uncontrolled detonation indicates that the plug heat range is too hot. The plug in effect becomes a glow plug, raising cylinder temperatures. Install the proper heat range plug (Chapter 1).
- ☐ Improper air/fuel mixture (carburettor models). This will cause the cylinder to run hot and lead to detonation. Clogged jets or an air leak can cause this imbalance. See Chapter 3A.
- ☐ Fuel injection system fault. See Chapter 3B.

Piston slap or rattling

- ☐ Cylinder-to-piston clearance excessive. Caused by improper assembly. Inspect and overhaul top-end parts (Chapter 2).
- ☐ Connecting rod bent. Caused by over-revving, trying to start a badly flooded engine or from ingesting a foreign object into the combustion chamber. Replace the damaged parts (Chapter 2).
- ☐ Piston pin or piston pin bore worn or seized from wear or lack of lubrication. Replace damaged parts (Chapter 2).
- ☐ Piston ring(s) worn, broken or sticking. Overhaul the top-end (Chapter 2).
- ☐ Piston seizure damage. Usually from lack of lubrication or

overheating. Replace the piston and bore the cylinder, as necessary (Chapter 2).
- ☐ Connecting rod upper or lower end clearance excessive. Caused by excessive wear or lack of lubrication. Replace worn parts.

Valve noise

- ☐ Incorrect valve clearances. Adjust the clearances by referring to Chapter 1.
- ☐ Valve spring broken or weak. Check and replace weak valve springs (Chapter 2).
- ☐ Camshaft or cylinder head worn or damaged. Lack of lubrication at high rpm is usually the cause of damage. Insufficient oil or failure to change the oil at the recommended intervals are the chief causes (Chapter 2).

Other noise

- ☐ Cylinder head gasket leaking.
- ☐ Exhaust pipe leaking at cylinder head connection. Caused by improper fit of pipe or loose exhaust flange. All exhaust fasteners should be tightened evenly and carefully. Failure to do this will lead to a leak.
- ☐ Crankshaft runout excessive. Caused by a bent crankshaft (from over-revving) or damage from an upper cylinder component failure. Can also be attributed to dropping the machine on either of the crankshaft ends.
- ☐ Engine mounting bolts loose. Tighten all engine mount bolts (Chapter 2).
- ☐ Crankshaft bearings worn (Chapter 2).
- ☐ Cam chain tensioner defective. Replace according to the procedure in Chapter 2.
- ☐ Cam chain, sprockets or guides worn (Chapter 2).

8 Abnormal driveline noise

Clutch noise

☐ Clutch housing/friction plate clearance excessive (Chapter 2).
☐ Loose or damaged clutch pressure plate and/or bolts (Chapter 2).

Transmission noise

☐ Bearings worn. Also includes the possibility that the shafts are worn. Overhaul the transmission (Chapter 2).
☐ Gears worn or chipped (Chapter 2).
☐ Metal chips jammed in gear teeth. Probably pieces from a broken clutch, gear or selector mechanism that were picked up by the gears. This will cause early bearing failure (Chapter 2).

☐ Engine oil level too low. Causes a howl from transmission. Also affects engine power and clutch operation (Pre-ride checks).

Final drive noise

☐ Chain not adjusted properly (Chapter 1).
☐ Engine sprocket or rear sprocket loose. Tighten fasteners (Chapter 6).
☐ Sprocket(s) worn. Replace sprocket(s) (Chapter 6).
☐ Rear sprocket warped. Replace (Chapter 6).
☐ Sprocket coupling worn (YBR models). Check coupling, dampers and bearing (Chapter 6).

9 Abnormal frame and suspension noise

Front end noise

☐ Low fluid level or improper viscosity oil in forks. This can sound like spurting and is usually accompanied by irregular fork action (Chapter 5).
☐ Spring weak or broken. Makes a clicking or scraping sound. Fork oil, when drained, will have a lot of metal particles in it (Chapter 5).
☐ Steering head bearings loose or damaged. Clicks when braking. Check and adjust or replace as necessary (Chapters 1 and 5).
☐ Fork clamp bolts loose. Make sure all fork clamp bolts are tight (Chapter 5).
☐ Fork tube bent. Good possibility if machine has been dropped. Replace tube with a new one (Chapter 5).
☐ Front axle nut loose. Tighten it to the specified torque (Chapter 6).

Shock absorber noise

☐ Fluid level incorrect. Indicates a leak caused by defective seal. Shock will be covered with oil. Replace shock (Chapter 5).
☐ Defective shock absorber with internal damage. This is in the body of the shock and can't be remedied. The shock must be replaced with a new one (Chapter 5).
☐ Bent or damaged shock body. Replace the shock with a new one (Chapter 5).

Brake noise

☐ Squeal caused by dust on brake pads. Usually found in combination with glazed pads. Clean using brake cleaning solvent (Chapter 6).
☐ Contamination of brake pads. Oil, brake fluid or dirt causing brake to chatter or squeal. Clean or replace pads (Chapter 6).
☐ Pads glazed. Caused by excessive heat from prolonged use or from contamination. Do not use sandpaper, emery cloth, carborundum cloth or any other abrasive to roughen the pad surfaces as abrasives will stay in the pad material and damage the disc. A very fine flat file can be used, but pad replacement is suggested as a cure (Chapter 6).
☐ Disc warped. Can cause a chattering, clicking or intermittent squeal. Usually accompanied by a pulsating lever and uneven braking. Replace the disc (Chapter 6).
☐ Loose or worn wheel bearings. Check and replace as needed (Chapter 6).

10 Excessive exhaust smoke

White smoke

☐ Piston oil ring worn. The ring may be broken or damaged, causing oil from the crankcase to be pulled past the piston into the combustion chamber. Replace the rings with new ones (Chapter 2).

☐ Cylinder worn, cracked, or scored. Caused by overheating or oil starvation. The cylinder will have to be rebored and a new piston and rings installed.

☐ Valve oil seal damaged or worn. Replace oil seals with new ones (Chapter 2).

☐ Valve guide worn. Perform a complete valve job (Chapter 2).

☐ Engine oil level too high, which causes the oil to be forced past the rings. Drain oil to the proper level (Chapter 1 and Pre-ride checks).

☐ Head gasket broken between oil return and cylinder. Causes oil to be pulled into the combustion chamber. Replace the head gasket and check the head for warpage (Chapter 2).

☐ Abnormal crankcase pressurisation, which forces oil past the rings. Clogged breather or hose usually the cause (Chapter 2).

Black smoke (carburettor models)

☐ Air filter clogged. Clean or replace the element (Chapter 1).

☐ Main jet too large or loose. Compare the jet size to the Specifications (Chapter 3A).

☐ Choke stuck, causing fuel to be pulled through choke circuit (Chapter 3A).

☐ Fuel level too high. Check and adjust the float height as necessary (Chapter 3A).

☐ Float needle valve held off needle seat. Clean the float bowls and fuel line and replace the needles and seats if necessary (Chapter 3A).

Brown smoke (carburettor models)

☐ Main jet too small or clogged. Lean condition caused by wrong size main jet or by a restricted orifice. Clean float bowl and jets and compare jet size to Specifications (Chapter 3A).

☐ Fuel flow insufficient. Fuel inlet needle valve stuck closed due to chemical reaction with old fuel. Fuel level incorrect. Restricted fuel line. Clean line and float bowl and adjust float height if necessary.

☐ Carburettor intake duct loose (Chapter 3A).

☐ Air filter poorly sealed or not installed (Chapter 1).

11 Poor handling or stability

Handlebar hard to turn

☐ Steering stem nut too tight (Chapter 5).

☐ Bearings damaged. Roughness can be felt as the bars are turned from side-to-side. Replace bearings and races (Chapter 5).

☐ Races dented or worn. Denting results from wear in only one position (e.g. straight-ahead), from a collision or hitting a pothole or from dropping the machine. Replace races and bearings (Chapter 5).

☐ Steering stem lubrication inadequate. Causes are grease getting hard from age or being washed out by high pressure washers. Disassemble steering head and repack bearings (Chapter 5).

☐ Steering stem bent. Caused by a collision, hitting a pothole or by dropping the machine. Replace damaged part. Don't try to straighten the steering stem (Chapter 5).

☐ Front tyre air pressure too low (Pre-ride checks).

Handlebar shakes or vibrates excessively

☐ Tyres worn or out of balance.

☐ Swingarm bearings worn. Replace worn bearings by referring to Chapter 5.

☐ Rim(s) warped or damaged. Inspect wheels for runout (Chapter 6).

☐ Wheel bearings worn. Worn front or rear wheel bearings can cause poor tracking. Worn front bearings will cause wobble (Chapter 6).

☐ Handlebar clamp bolts loose (Chapter 5).

☐ Steering stem or fork clamp bolts loose. Tighten them to the specified torque (Chapter 5).

☐ Engine mounting bolts loose. Will cause excessive vibration with increased engine rpm (Chapter 2).

Handlebar pulls to one side

☐ Frame bent. Definitely suspect this if the machine has been dropped. May or may not be accompanied by cracking near the bend. Replace the frame (Chapter 5).

☐ Wheel out of alignment. Caused by improper location of axle spacers (Chapter 6) or from bent steering stem or frame (Chapter 5).

☐ Swingarm bent or twisted. Caused by age (metal fatigue) or impact damage. Replace the swingarm (Chapter 5).

☐ Steering stem bent. Caused by impact damage or by dropping the motorcycle. Replace the steering stem (Chapter 5).

☐ Fork leg bent. Disassemble the forks and replace the damaged parts (Chapter 5).

☐ Fork oil level uneven. Check and add or drain as necessary (Chapter 5).

Poor shock absorbing qualities

☐ Too hard:
   a) Fork oil level excessive (Chapter 5).
   b) Fork oil viscosity too high. Use a lighter oil (see the Specifications in Chapter 5).
   c) Fork tube bent. Causes a harsh, sticking feeling (Chapter 5).
   d) Shock shaft or body bent or damaged (Chapter 5).
   e) Fork internal damage (Chapter 65.
   f) Shock internal damage.
   g) Tyre pressure too high (Pre-ride checks).

☐ Too soft:
   a) Fork or shock oil insufficient and/or leaking (Chapter 5).
   b) Fork oil level too low (Chapter 5).
   c) Fork oil viscosity too light (Chapter 5).
   d) Fork springs weak or broken (Chapter 5).
   e) Shock internal damage or leakage (Chapter 5).

12 Braking problems

Brakes are spongy or don't hold (disc brake)

☐ Air in brake line or brake fluid leak. Caused by inattention to master cylinder fluid level or by leakage. Locate problem and bleed brakes (Chapter 6).

☐ Pad or disc worn (Chapters 1 and 6).

☐ Contaminated pads. Caused by contamination with oil, grease, brake fluid, etc. Replace pads. Clean disc thoroughly with brake cleaner (Chapter 6).

☐ Brake fluid deteriorated. Fluid is old or contaminated. Drain system, replenish with new fluid and bleed the system (Chapter 6).

☐ Master cylinder internal parts worn or damaged causing fluid to bypass (Chapter 6).

☐ Master cylinder bore scratched by foreign material or broken spring. Repair or replace master cylinder (Chapter 6).

☐ Disc warped. Replace disc (Chapter 6).

Brake doesn't hold (drum brake)

☐ Brake incorrectly adjusted (Chapter 1).

☐ Brake shoes worn. Renew shoes (Chapter 6).

Brake lever or pedal pulsates (disc brake)

☐ Disc warped. Replace disc (Chapter 6).

☐ Wheel axle bent. Replace axle (Chapter 6).

☐ Brake caliper bolts loose (Chapter 6).

☐ Wheel warped or otherwise damaged (Chapter 6).

☐ Wheel bearings damaged or worn (Chapter 6).

Brake pedal pulsates (drum brake – YBR models)

☐ Brake drum out of round. Renew rear wheel or seek advice on having the drum skimmed (Chapter 6).

☐ Wheel bearings damaged or worn (Chapter 6).

Brakes drag (disc brake)

☐ Master cylinder piston seized. Caused by wear or damage to piston or cylinder bore (Chapter 6).

☐ Lever/pedal balky or stuck. Check pivot and lubricate (Chapter 5).

☐ Brake caliper piston seized in bore. Caused by wear or ingestion of dirt past deteriorated seal (Chapter 6).

☐ Brake caliper slider pins damaged or sticking, causing caliper to bind. Lube the slider pins (Chapter 6).

☐ Brake pad damaged. Pad material separated from backing plate. Usually caused by faulty manufacturing process or from contact with chemicals. Replace pads (Chapter 6).

☐ Pads improperly installed (Chapter 6).

☐ Rear brake pedal freeplay insufficient (Chapter 1).

Brakes drag (drum brake – YBR models)

☐ Brake pedal freeplay insufficient (Chapter 1).

☐ Brake shoe springs weak or broken (Chapter 6).

☐ Brake shoe operating cam sticking due to lack of lubrication (Chapter 6).

13 Electrical problems

Battery dead or weak

☐ Battery faulty or worn out. On MF batteries check the terminal voltage and renew battery if recharging doesn't work (Chapter 8). On conventional batteries, check the electrolyte level (Chapter 1), check specific gravity (Chapter 8) and renew if recharging doesn't work.

☐ Battery leads making poor contact (Chapter 8).

☐ Load excessive. Caused by addition of high wattage lights or other electrical accessories.

☐ Ignition switch defective. Switch either grounds (earths) internally or fails to shut off system. Replace the switch (Chapter 8).

☐ Regulator/rectifier defective (Chapter 8).

☐ Alternator stator coil open or shorted (Chapter 8).

☐ Wiring faulty. Wiring grounded (earthed) or connections loose in ignition, charging or lighting circuits (Chapter 8).

Battery overcharged

☐ Regulator/rectifier defective. Overcharging is noticed when battery gets excessively warm or boils over (Chapter 8).

☐ Battery defective. Replace battery with a new one (Chapter 8).

☐ Battery amperage too low, wrong type or size. Install manufacturer's specified amp-hour battery to handle charging load (Chapter 8).

Note: *References throughout this index are in the form - "Chapter number" • "Page number"*